lonely planet

Lonely Planet Publications
Melbourne | Oakland | London | Paris

Regis St. Louis

Rio de Janeiro

The Top Five

1 Samba Clubs
Experience the rebirth of Lapa's old dancehalls (p134)

2 Cristo Redentor
View the city from below this statue of the open-armed savior (p76)

3 Ipanema Beach
Bask on one of Rio's loveliest beaches (p58)

4 Carnaval
Dance for days on end at the world's largest party (p23)

5 Pão de Açúcar
Gaze over Rio from atop the city's most famous peak (p65)

Contents

Published by Lonely Planet Publications Pty Ltd
ABN 36 005 607 983

Australia Head Office, Locked Bag 1, Footscray,
Victoria 3011, ☎ 03 8379 8000, fax 03 8379 8111,
talk2us@lonelyplanet.com.au

USA 150 Linden St, Oakland, CA 94607,
☎ 510 893 8555, toll free 800 275 8555,
fax 510 893 8572, info@lonelyplanet.com

UK 72–82 Rosebery Ave, Clerkenwell, London,
EC1R 4RW, ☎ 020 7841 9000, fax 020 7841 9001,
go@lonelyplanet.co.uk

France 1 rue du Dahomey, 75011 Paris,
☎ 01 55 25 33 00, fax 01 55 25 33 01,
bip@lonelyplanet.fr, www.lonelyplanet.fr

The Authors

REGIS ST. LOUIS

Regis' longtime admiration of samba, bossa nova and Brazil's beautiful game *(futebol)* led to his deep involvement with the country – both as a traveler and as a writer. Rio is one of his great loves, and he has spent years immersing himself in the vibrant culture of the Cidade Maravilhosa (Marvelous City). He speaks Portuguese (the Carioca version), along with Spanish and Russian and has traveled widely. He covered both Rio and the Amazon region for LP's *South America on a Shoestring* and contributed to the updating of LP's *Brazil* guide.

CONTRIBUTING AUTHORS

RODOLFO KLAUTAU
Rodolfo is a resident of Abraão, where he runs Sudoeste SW Turismo, the first local tour operator on Ilha Grande. He contributed a piece about the rich history of the island (p186).

CASSANDRA LOOMIS
Cassandra is a New York–based fashion designer. She has traveled the world researching the relationship between textiles and indigenous cultures. She wrote about a Rio-based company that is making a positive contribution to the Amazon (p161).

CARMEN MICHAEL
Carmen is an Australian writer living and working in Rio. Her contributions on *malandros* (p49), samba (p135), *gafieiras* (p34) and life in Santa Teresa (p86) are the product of a nocturnal existence dedicated to the research of bohemia in Rio.

TOM PHILLIPS
British journalist Tom Phillips has spent two years in Rio and Belo Horizonte familiarizing himself with the intricacies of Brazilian popular culture. When not hammering away on his laptop, he works as a volunteer in the Rocinha community. Tom contributed pieces on Rio's largest favela (p54), hip-hop (p133) and soccer (p17), among other topics.

MARCOS SILVIANO DO PRADO
Born and raised in Ipanema, Marcos used 40 years of Carnaval experience to develop the Party Planner (p25). He operates a travel agency in Rio, helping thousands of international visitors yearly.

PHOTOGRAPHERS
RICARDO GOMES &
JOHN MAIER JR
For both Ricardo Gomes and John Maier Jr, there is no better city to live in than Rio de Janeiro. Both Ricardo and John work with photographs and video; they also have a production company, which covers news and feature stories from Latin America. Their work has appeared in the *New York Times*, *Time*, and *Spiegel*, and on the BBC, HBO and Discovery.

Introducing Rio de Janeiro

When Brazilians say *'Deus e Brasileiro'* (God is Brazilian), some of Rio's citizens probably think, *'Deus e Carioca'* (God is a Rio-dweller). The city has received more than its fair share of natural and cultural riches. Its setting is spectacular: 37 white-sand beaches fronting blue sea with lush green peaks rising up around them. On the streets, Rio's energy is blazing...

One typical Friday night reveals the city at her most vibrant: in Lapa, samba spills out of old colonial buildings as revelers dance in the streets, wandering among the bars and old music halls in search of the soul of samba. Just around the corner, a long stretch of antique shops double as jazz spots, with bossa nova–infused sounds filling warmly lit 19th-century mansions. A few kilometers away, in Rio's Southern Zone (Zona Sul), another scene is unfolding. The open-air bars and restaurants along the lake fill with music rising over the din of conversation. Stylish lounges lie just a few blocks south, and the DJs haven't arrived. They're still chattering with friends at old-school bars scattered throughout the tree-lined streets of Leblon.

In other parts of the city, galleries are opening their doors for art openings, orchestras are poised over their instruments and avant-garde films are flickering on art-house movie screens. Meanwhile, Fluminense fans are celebrating a hard-won football match at neighborhood bars and sidewalk cafés in Flamengo and Botafogo.

As night turns into day, and the first light of dawn illuminates Cristo Redentor (Christ the Redeemer) atop Corcovado, another brand of Carioca is taking over the streets. Early morning joggers and cyclists move swiftly along the shoreline against a backdrop of palm trees and crashing waves. Out in the water, a handful of surfers and swimmers are already there, greeting the morning rays as the sun rises from the sea. Other Cariocas have grander schemes involving the outdoors – some are packing gear for rock-climbing the face of Pão de Açúcar (Sugarloaf), while a few are already out on lush trails, absorbing

Essential Rio

- Catching the sunset while sipping *caipirinhas* (cane liquor cocktail) or *agua de coco* (coconut water) on **Ipanema Beach** (p58).
- Riding the *bonde* (tram) to the lovely hilltop neighborhood of **Santa Teresa** (p84).
- Feeling the beat at one of the many vibrant samba clubs in **Lapa** (p134).
- Heading to cobblestoned Rua do Lavradio and sifting through antique stores – which by night transform into **jazz clubs** (p132).
- Drinking, dancing and discovering the soul of the Northeast at Rio's weekend **Feira Nordestina** (p88).

the sights and sounds hidden in old Atlantic rain forest. A little later, a hang-glider cuts through the air over São Conrado as sun worshippers, football and volleyball players, and roaming vendors take to the sands of Barra, Ipanema and Leblon.

As the rest of the city awakes, Cariocas gather around newsstands to peruse the newspapers posted there. Celebrity spotting, trouble brewing in the favelas, corruption in high places – headlines carry the gossip into the neighborhood juice bars and

cafés throughout the city. By midday, the trendy boutiques of Leblon and Ipanema fill with shoppers while restaurants all over the city serve heaps of *feijoada* (black beans and pork stew), the traditional Saturday meal for Brazilians. *Caipirinhas* (*cachaça*-fueled cocktails) and *chope* (draft beer) flow in abundance (another Saturday tradition) as Cariocas hash out the previous night or scheme about the one ahead.

This portrait of the city would not be complete without considering the city's age (around 500 years old) and its place in history. Rio's landmarks downtown are a testament to its prominence. Hillside colonial churches, palaces from the Portuguese reign and splendid neoclassical buildings all lie scattered about the city's bustling downtown area. Not ones to watch history slowly crumble around them, Cariocas infuse these places with new energy: cultural centers, galleries, concert halls and theaters (of both the live and cinematic variety) all inhabit old spaces, which allows Rio to move forward without losing sight of the past.

Even at its most brazen, Rio clings to its traditions. The world's largest party is no exception. When Carnaval's bacchanalian spirit descends upon the city in late summer (February or March), the city transforms (as do many of her seven million inhabitants). Parties flare throughout Rio all night long for at least four days straight.

Like any city of its size, Rio has its problems. Crime, poverty and gang warfare are among Rio's worst concerns – and unfortunately, are given much play in the world media. All the same, the Cidade Maravilhosa (Marvelous City) has lost none of its luster, and Cariocas are full of pride for their city. New projects are growing at an exponential rate – plans are in the works to build a Guggenheim Museum, the Pan Am games are on their way in 2007 and Rio is even putting in its bid to host the 2012 Olympics. The city's coffers are full, the beaches are as beautiful as ever and the cultural renaissance is in full swing. More than ever Rio de Janeiro is on the verge of something big. Are you going to be there to see it?

REGIS' TOP RIO DAY

Start the morning in lovely Ipanema, grabbing freshly squeezed juice and famous *pão de queijo* (cheese-filled roll) at one of Ipanema's stand-up juice bars. Assuming it's not the weekend (when it gets too crowded), I head to the beach at **Posto 9** (p58) for a bit of sun, surf and people-watching. As lunchtime nears I head to Santa Teresa, taking the *bonde* (tram) from Lapa. I eat at **Bar do Mineiro** (p121), enjoying traditional Mineiran cuisine and a few *chopes*, which are best dealt with by a walk down the hill, visiting a few of the thrift shops and handicrafts stores. In Lapa I continue window shopping, visiting the antique stores and record and bookshops that recall a bygone era. By the time I reach Centro, I need a recharge, and I head to neoclassical **Confeitaria Colombo** (p113) for *bolo* (cake) and thick *cafezinho* (little coffee), which does the job nicely. I continue my stroll, heading to **Centro Cultural Banco do Brasil** (p80), which often hosts some of the city's best (and avant-garde leaning) exhibits. Once my eyes are watery with art and Portuguese descriptions, it's time to meet a few friends for dinner around the corner. We dine at **Cais do Oriente** (p120), its lovely tiled floors and colonial walls putting us in the mood for music. If it's a weeknight, we head to Lapa – **Democraticus** (p136) – where great samba can be heard. Heading back to Ipanema we stop for a nightcap at sceney **Bar d'Hotel** (p126). We meet a couple of acquaintances who drag us to **Melt** (p140), up the road in Leblon, where we soak up a few electronic tunes before calling it a night.

City Life

City Life

RIO TODAY

Vinícius de Moraes and Tom Jobim, Rio's founding fathers of bossa nova, might have been describing their native city when they composed the famous line, 'mais linda e cheia de graça' (most beautiful and full of grace). As it happens, the pair were talking about a particularly striking young garota (young woman) who walked by their bar stools every day en route to Ipanema Beach. Gracefulness, beauty and sensuality are never far from mind when taking in Rio's landscape – whether it's contemplating the sea at Posto 9 (nove; p58) in Ipanema, listening to a samba de roda at a sidewalk café or attending a football match at Maracanã (p88).

The city seethes sensuality, and as Jobim and Moraes pointed out, this is clearly personified by at least one – if not six million – of the city's inhabitants. In some circles (like those orbiting Leblon, Ipanema and Barra), this means working out and looking good. Others interpret this sensuality differently: creating a thing of beauty in the dance hall, onstage, perhaps even in the political arena. However this nebulous characteristic is interpreted, sensuality on some level becomes a manner of living. Cariocas have it in spades.

In Rio, your social connections play a big role in your professional (and often romantic) future. They also help you cope with the bureaucratic nature of getting things done. Kindness is both commonplace and expected, and even a casual introduction can lead to deeper friendships. This altruism comes in handy in a country noted for its bureaucracy and long lines. There's the official way of doing things, then there's the jeitinho (the little way around it), and some kindness – and a few friends – can go a long way. One need only have patience, something Brazilians seem to have no shortage of.

Rio's lovely tropical setting draws everything out into the streets – the juice bars and botecos (small open-air bar) are the place for discussing politics, and love happens on the streets (or beaches) just as war does. Betrayal, longing, anger, grief – charting the city's emotions is like watching a telenovela (TV soap opera), only the actors are a little more convincing. The intensity of the Carioca street scene is nearly as exhausting as the city's high temperatures.

Cariocas are social creatures. Around the newsstands in the mornings, the young and old, joggers and stroller-pushing moms, browse the front pages of O Globo, Jornal do Brasil and half-a-dozen other periodicals. The news becomes the day's gossip, which is as likely to be a source of conversation among strangers at the juice bar as it is among friends at their neighborhood coffee shop.

Rio's news often highlights the social failures of the state (such reportage didn't happen when the military was in power) and the violence in the favelas (shanty towns), though it also distracts Cariocas from these alarming issues with celebrity spottings. Footballers are a favorite topic on the streets, as is President Lula, one of the country's more closely watched celebrities.

Meeting Cariocas

One kiss on each cheek for ladies (start to the left – her right); a handshake between gents. The same holds true when bidding goodbye.

Hot Conversation Topics

- **Beaches** What's the choice new spot for the gatos (boys) and gatas (girls) of the Zona Sul?
- **Bikinis** What's the new look and which Brazilian actress started the trend?
- **Crime** When was the last time you got mugged?
- **Football** What's wrong with the damned national team (eg Olympics 2004)? And will Fluminense (or Vasco or Flamengo or Botafogo) ever get their shit together?
- **Restaurants** What's the fashion food of the month?

Other recurring topics in the news revolve around Rio's buoyant economy and mayor Cesar Maia's pet projects. Scoring the Pan Am games in 2007 was of course a big topic – though there's some concern as to whether the city can safely get athletes to the game, given the volatile eruptions happening in the favelas bordering the Linha Vermelha Hwy. The Guggenheim, which should be in the process of construction by the time you read this, is another popular topic. It will be Latin America's first branch of this museum – yet another indication that Rio is on the verge.

CITY CALENDAR

Rio's Carnaval is the world's biggest party, but Cariocas make plenty of other occasions for celebrating. Reveillon (New Year's Eve) is another citywide celebration, when Cariocas and visitors pack Copacabana Beach. Although both of these events occur in Brazil's summer (December through February), other *festas* (parties) occur throughout the year. Those looking to escape the crowds (and the humidity) might consider the low season from April to June and August to December (July is a school-holiday month throughout Brazil).

JANUARY & FEBRUARY

CARMEN MIRANDA ANNIVERSARY
☎ 2551 2597; Museu Carmen Miranda, facing Av Rui Barbosa 560, Flamengo
On February 9, the Carmen Miranda museum celebrates the birthday of the Brazilian entertainer with special exhibitions and a mini film festival that features the movies she starred in. If you're a fan, it's a kitschy good time.

CARNAVAL
Rio de Janeiro, everywhere
In February or March, the city puts on its famous no-holds-barred party. For information on how to spend a few nights without sleep, see p24.

DIA DE SÃO SEBASTIÃO
On January 20, the patron saint of the city is commemorated with a procession carrying the image of São Sebastião from Igreja de São Sebastião dos Capuchinos in Tijuca (Rua Haddock Lobo 266) to the **Catedral Metropolitana** (p86), where the image is blessed in a Mass celebrated by the Archbishop of Rio de Janeiro.

NOITES CARIOCAS
Marina de Glória, Glória
The Noites Cariocas (Carioca Nights) are open-air samba, Música Popular Brasileira (MPB) or

Top Five Quirky Events

- **Lighting of the Lagoa Christmas Tree** Catch live shows celebrating the onset of Christmas to the backdrop of the glowing tree, which glows brighter each year.
- **Rio International Film Festival** One of Latin America's largest film fests with screenings all over the city.
- **Carnaval** Hundreds of ways to rack up some sins before Lent arrives (see p24).
- **Festa de Iemanjá** Put on your whites, think positive thoughts and cast your petitions out to sea on this feast day of the well-known *orixá*.
- **Festas Juninas** Eat your way into a tizzy at this folkloric festival that takes place throughout the city.

electronic music shows staged at Marina de Glória or on the beaches of the Zona Sul. A large crowd gathers for dancing, drinking and celebrating the Carioca night. The shows usually start around midnight and continue to 5am.

SKOL RIO
Marina de Glória, Glória
During the first two weekends in February, the Marina de Glória hosts live DJs and samba bands, this time sponsored by the prominent beer manufacturer, Skol, whose product would get consumed in abundance here even without the name recognition.

VIVO OPEN-AIR
www.vivo.com.br in Portuguese; Jockey Club Brasileiro, Rua Jardim Botânico 1003, Gávea
Throughout three weekends toward the beginning of the year, Vivo sponsors open-air cinema at the Jockey Club in Jardim Botânico. Films range from avant-garde to classics, and afterward, DJs and bands often take the stage for concerts. This annual event usually begins the second week in January and runs through the first week in February.

Public Holidays

On national holidays, Brazilians take the day off and head to the beach, the park or a friend's place. Banks, offices and most stores remain closed for the day.

New Year's Day January 1.

Epiphany January 6.

Carnaval (Saturday to Tuesday prior to Ash Wednesday) February or March.

Tiradentes Day April 21.

Labor Day May 1.

Corpus Christi June (60 days after Easter).

Independence Day October 12.

All Souls' Day November 15.

Zumbi Day November 20.

Christmas Day December 25.

MARCH & APRIL
DIA DA FUNDAÇÃO DA CIDADE

On March 1, the city commemorates its founding by Estácio de Sá in 1565 with a Mass in the church of its patron saint, Igreja de São Sebastião dos Capuchinos.

DIA DO ÍNDIO

☎ 2286 8899; www.museudoindio.org.br; Rua das Palmeiras 55; ⏱ 9:30am-5:30pm Tue-Fri, 1-5pm Sat & Sun; admission US$2

April 4 is recognized in Brazil as Indian's day. Although this holiday is largely overlooked (much like the indigenous themselves), the **Museu do Índio** (p65) has special celebrations throughout the week. Exhibitions, dance and film presentations are staged daily.

SEXTA-FEIRA DA PAIXÃO

In March or April (depending when Easter falls), Good Friday is celebrated throughout the city. The most important ceremony re-enacts the Stations of the Cross under the **Arcos da Lapa** (p86), with more than 100 actors.

MAY & JUNE
FESTAS JUNINAS

Spanning the month of June, the feast days of various saints mark some of the most important folkloric festivals in Brazil. In Rio, celebrations are held in various public squares, with lots of food stands, music, fireworks and an occasional bonfire or two. The big feast days are June 13 (Dia de Santo Antônio), June 24 (São João) and June 29 (São Pedro).

JULY & AUGUST
FESTA DA SÃO PEDRO DO MAR

On July 3, the fishing fraternity pays homage to its patron saint in a maritime procession. Their decorated boats leave from the fishing community of Caju and sail to the statue of São Pedro in Urca.

FESTA DE NS DA GLÓRIA DO OUTEIRO

On August 15, a solemn Mass is held at the historic church overlooking Glória and the bay. From a church ablaze with decorated lights, a procession travels out into the streets of Glória to mark the Feast of the Assumption. This festa includes music and colorful stalls set up in the Praça NS da Glória. Festivities start at 8am and continue all day.

SEPTEMBER & OCTOBER
DIA DE INDEPENDÊNCIA DO BRASIL

On September 7, Independence Day is celebrated with a large military parade down Av Presidente Vargas. It starts at 8am at Candelária and goes down just past Praça XI.

FESTA DA PENHA

One of the largest religious and popular festivals in the city takes place every Sunday in October and the first Sunday in November. The lively celebrations commence in the northern suburb of Penha at Igreja NS da Penha de França, Largo da Penha 19.

RIO DE JANEIRO INTERNATIONAL FILM FESTIVAL

www.festivaldorio.com.br

This five-year-old festival is one of the biggest in Latin America. Over 200 films from all over

Open Studios

In May and November, Santa Teresa becomes the site of one of the city's most colorful arts events (Arte de Portas Abertas). The artists of the Bohemian neighborhood open their doors to visitors, creating a neighborhood-wide art gallery. But the art doesn't always stay hidden away. Installation artists have begun using the streets, the colonial buildings, the *bonde* (trams) as the backdrop to vibrant works. If you're in town, don't miss it (stop by the **Cama e Café** (p177) or the **Parque das Ruínas** (p86) for more information).

the world are shown at some 35 theaters in Rio. Often they hold open-air screenings on Copacabana Beach. The festival runs from the last week of September through the first week of October.

RIO JAZZ FESTIVAL
Though dates for this October music festival vary from year to year, the Rio Jazz Festival is an opportunity for Rio's beautiful people to come out together for three nights of great music. Local, national and international acts present a wide variety of music, playing jazz and its many relatives – samba-jazz, bossa nova, samba, MPB.

SAMBA SCHOOL REHEARSALS
Usually in September (though some begin as early as July or August), samba schools host open rehearsals once a week (usually on Friday or Saturday night). In spite of the name, these are less a dress rehearsal than just an excuse to dance (to samba, of course), celebrate and pass on the good vibe to the big show come Carnaval time. Anyone can come, and it's a mixed crowd of Cariocas and tourists, though it gets more and more crowded the closer it is to Carnaval.

NOVEMBER & DECEMBER
FESTA DE IEMANJÁ
Dwarfed by secular New Year's Eve celebrations, this Candomblé festival celebrates the feast day of Iemanjá, the goddess of the sea. Celebrants dress in white and place their petitions on small boats and send them out to sea. If their petitions return, their prayers will not be answered. Along with the petitions, celebrants place candles, perfumes and talcum powder to appease the blue-cloaked *orixá* (spirits or deities). Until recently, devotees gathered in Copacabana, Ipanema and Leblon, but owing to the popularity of Reveillon, and chaotic spillover, devotees are seeking more tranquil spots – Barra da Tijuca and Recreio dos Bandeirantes – to make their offerings.

LIGHTING OF THE LAGOA CHRISTMAS TREE
From the end of November to the first week of January, the Christmas tree glows brightly on the **Lagoa de Rodrigo de Freitas** (p61). To celebrate its lighting, the city often throws big concerts in Parque Brigadeiro Faria Lima – usually the first Saturday in December. Big Brazilian names like Milton Nascimento have performed in the past.

REVEILLON
Rio's biggest holiday after Carnaval takes place on Copacabana Beach, where some two million pack the sands to welcome the new year. A spectacular fireworks display lights up the sky as top bands perform in the area. The hardiest of revelers keep things going all night long, then watch the sun rise the next morning.

CULTURE
Rio is not called the Cidade Maravilhosa (Marvelous City) simply for its lovely beaches and lush mountains. The moniker might equally be extended to its *maravilhosa* inhabitants, whose interests and ethnic backgrounds diverge considerably.

IDENTITY
Jammed into an area of almost 1200 sq km, Rio de Janeiro is one of the most crowded cities in Brazil. Its population of more than 11 million inhabitants – six million in the city itself and five million in the surrounding areas – makes Rio the second largest city in Brazil, after São Paulo. Rio's population density is one of the highest in the world.

The racial composition of Rio's population reflects its past, a mix of Africans, Europeans and Indians who have intermarried freely since colonial times. The Portuguese gave the country its religion and language, while Indian culture helped shape the legends, dance, music and other aspects of modern Brazilian culture. The influence of African culture is also prominent as the early slaves brought with them their religion, music and cuisine, all of which profoundly influenced Brazilian identity. Rio's rich melting pot is also a product of many immigrants who began arriving in the late 19th century – Italians, Spaniards, Germans, Japanese, Russians and Lebanese among others.

To make things even more complex (at least for the purposes of trying to figure out what exactly a Carioca *is*), the legions of Brazilians from other parts of the country who've moved to Rio must be added to the picture. There are *caboclos*, descendents of the Indians, who come from Amazonia; and *gaúchos* from Rio Grande do Sul, who speak a Spanish-inflected Portuguese and can't quite shake the reputation for being rough-edged cowboys. Then there are Baianos, descendents of the first Africans in Brazil, who are stereotyped as being extroverted and celebratory. And let's not forget Paulistanos (who inhabit Rio's rival city, São Paolo), Mineiros (who come from the colonial towns of Minas Gerais – and speak rather slowly), and Sertanejos (denizens of the drought-stricken interior *sertão*).

Carioca Not Karaoke

Carioca was the name the Tupi Indians gave to the funny-looking Portuguese settlers shortly after they arrived. It comes from 'kara 'i oca,' which means the white house, in reference to the white masonry the newcomers used in their building. The name stuck, and today Carioca are Cariocas. You'll probably hear the word frequently while you're in town – a small indication that Rio's citizens are not shy about talking about themselves.

Out of this thick cultural and ethnic brew, a Carioca emerges – one who's been stereotyped in the West as spontaneous, friendly and prone to kicking footballs – when not dancing to samba. Meanwhile, Paulistanos and other Brazilians – but especially Paulistanos – unfairly paint Cariocas as materialistic and superficial (much as Angelinos get stereotyped by New Yorkers). All the same, elements of these personality traits exist in Cariocas, and certainly an open friendliness can't be too far off the mark if we have to tread in the realm of stereotypes. This was even documented by a team of social psychologists who rated Rio among the world's friendliest cities, after a six-year study of urban environments. Their findings were published in the *New Scientist* in 2003. (New York, incidentally, ranked toward the bottom.)

Of course, immigration, ancestry and regional characteristics are only one way of defining Cariocas. The other and far more obvious way is by class. It is income, more than anything that separates Rio's citizens. At least one in five Cariocas lives in a favela. Rio is one of the only places in the world where the rich live at sea level while the poor are packed atop scenic mountains overlooking the city.

Sometimes, the dividing line between favelas and luxury condominiums is nothing more than a highway.

In a city of have and have-nots, education is directly linked to class. Public primary and secondary schools are so bad that people with the means send their children to private school. Almost all university students attended private schools, and so very few poor children reach university, a circumstance that continually renews the poverty cycle. Many poor children must work to eat and never attend school. And for those who are able to go, there aren't enough schools, teachers or desks to go around.

The government of Leonel Brizola of Rio de Janeiro was one of the first to understand and act upon the connections between poverty, hunger and illiteracy, and set up food programs in schools. The kids came to school for the food and stayed for the lessons. Some schools had classes at night for those children who worked during the day.

Mass media has also been used in Brazil for education, with some success. Since 1972, TV and radio educational programs

Cristo Redentor (p76)

The Gods of Rio

Candomblé is the most orthodox of the religions brought from Africa by the Nago, Yoruba and Jeje peoples. Candomblé is an African word denoting a dance in honor of the gods, and is a general term for the religion; it's also called Macumba in Rio. The religion centers around the *orixás* (spirits or deities). Like the gods in Greek mythology, each *orixá* has a unique personality and history. Although *orixás* are divided into male and female types, there are some that can switch from one sex to the other, like Logunedé, son of two male gods, Ogun and Oxoss, or Oxumaré, who is male for six months of the year and female for the other six. (Candomblé, not surprisingly, is much more accepting of homosexuality and bisexuality than other religions.)

Candomblé followers believe that every person has a particular deity watching over them – from birth until death. A person's *orixá* can be identified when a *pai* or *mãe de santo* (male or female priest) makes successive throws with a handful of *búzios* (shells), in a divination ritual known as Jogo dos Búzios (Casting of Shells). The position of the shells is used to interpret one's luck, one's future and one's past relation with the gods.

To keep themselves strong and healthy, followers of Candomblé give food or other offerings to their respective *orixá*. The offering to the *orixá* depends on the *orixá*'s particular preferences. For example, to please Iemanjá, the goddess or queen of the sea, one should give perfumes, white and blue flowers, rice and fried fish. Oxalá, the greatest god, the god and owner of the sun, eats cooked white corn. Oxúm, god of fresh waters and waterfalls, is famous for his vanity. He should be honored with earrings, necklaces, mirrors, perfumes, champagne and honey. Whichever god is receiving the offering, Exú must first be appeased, as he serves as the messenger between the individual and the god. (Exú, incidentally, likes *cachaça* (cane spirit) and other alcoholic drinks, cigarettes and cigars, strong perfumes and meats.)

In Rio, followers of Afro-Brazilian cults turn out in huge numbers to attend a series of festivals at the year's end – especially those held during the night of December 31 and on New Year's Day, to pay homage to Iemanjá, the queen of the sea (p11).

have been on the air. These concentrate on primary *(primeiro grau)* and secondary *(segundo grau)* students, but not exclusively. In 1989 Universidade Aberta (Open University), a tertiary education program, was introduced. You'll often see the workbooks on newsstands.

While these measures are not enough – many primary school students still have only three hours of classes per day – they show that some programs are successful.

Another way of understanding the culture in Rio is by religion. Officially, Brazil is Catholic, claiming the largest Catholic population of any country in the world. But Catholicism is declining in popularity as more and more are heading to Protestantism and evangelical churches, like Bishop Edir Macedo's Universal Church of the Kingdom of God. As many as 30 million Brazilians now regard themselves to be evangelicals, and the Catholic Church itself estimates that 600,000 of its faithful convert annually. In Rio, this trend has waned since the rise of Padre Marcelinho, a charismatic young Catholic priest who attracts hundreds of thousands of followers to his Masses for the masses. In addition, Candomblé (above) is still very much alive. But whatever one's religion, Cariocas generally have a more flexible view of spirituality than others. Without much difficulty it's possible to find churchgoing Catholics who attend spiritualist gatherings or appeal for help at a *terreiro* (the house of an Afro-Brazilian religious group).

LIFESTYLE

Living in such a gorgeous place, Cariocas aren't known for spending a lot of time indoors. In fact, when it rains, it brings a deep wave of sadness over the city, and people are likely to cancel their appointments and stay at home feeling *saudades* (that uniquely Brazilian mix of longing and nostalgia) for some past flame. When the weather is nice, Cariocas are outside, which is where everything happens – playing, romancing, socializing. Open-air restaurants and bars are found all over town, and street parties can happen anywhere; open-air film screenings, concerts and theater are also commonplace. During the weekend, the beach often plays at least some role in the social calendar. Friends have their standby meeting spots; they drop by, meet up, make plans and go from there. Or those who shun the crowds use the beach as the backdrop for a jog, a swim, a bike ride or an outing with the dog, the spouse, the kids or all three.

Celebrity Spotting *Tom Phillips*

While in Rio, keep your eyes peeled for these famous Cariocas.

- **Chico Buarque** Sambista (samba composer), novelist, playwright and general god's gift to women. Often spotted power walking between Ipanema and his seafront Leblon penthouse. Look out for the entourage of beautiful women that normally floats around him.
- **Ronaldo** The buck-toothed Brazil and Real Madrid striker lives in Spain these days, but it's not unheard of to spot him on the beach in São Conrado. Look out for the footballer's near-invisible *sunga* (swimming trunks), a must-have on Rio's beaches.
- **Giselle Bündchen** Country bumpkin turned supermodel, recently spotted filming in Ipanema. Look out for admirer Leonardo DiCaprio (or her latest beau) and the nearby packs of paparazzi.
- **Humberto Costa** Brazilian Health Minister. Listen out for his spiky Northeastern accent as he sips Skol beer on Ipanema.

Although Cariocas are a laidback bunch, city life moves fast here, and no one likes to sit around. Even when they're on the beach Cariocas are active – playing *frescobal* (beach sport using racquets and a rubber ball), *futebol* (soccer), *voleibol* (volleyball), or waving down maté (tealike beverage) vendors as they pass by their lounge chairs. Leisure time means going to galleries, listening to music shows, power shopping, trying the new restaurant or bar up the street, or heading to a house party. Cariocas aren't likely to show up for the appointments on time, by the way.

Those who have cars head out of town every few weeks (or every weekend) to the lovely beaches west or east, or up to the cooler mountains to get a break from Rio's humidity.

Cariocas are labeled a body-conscious bunch, and there's much truth to that. How could they be otherwise when youth and beauty are unspoken mantras delivered via TV novelas, the newsstands, the beaches, and the streets? Tanning is de rigueur whether you're 16 or 60 (that pale, hollowed-eye look never caught on here). Working out, staying fit and looking young are one facet of the Carioca experience, one that often bleeds over into other aspects of city life. The socially minded are often seeking to put on the map the newest beach or the newest 'undiscovered' neighborhood. Trading the old for something better – the trade-up theory – also characterizes Cariocas' romantic outlook. Outsiders often characterize Cariocas as being flippant about adultery and cheating, but it's no more common here than it is in the West, though perhaps it's a bit more open.

Ipanema (p57)

Rio's Youth Tribes

Finding your clique is as much a part of growing up in Rio as it is anywhere else, and kids have plenty of options to choose from. Mauricinhos and Patricinhas are the slang names for the rich young men and women who consume every fashionable new product and behavior from abroad and deny their Brazilian cultural roots. Though Mauricio and Patricia are common names given to children of upper-middle-class families, nobody knows how they were chosen to stand for a particular style of living. You'll see plenty of them at the shopping malls, the trendy cafés, and even in the bars and lounges in Ipanema, Leblon and Barra da Tijuca.

In Santa Teresa you'll see the sons and daughters of artists and intellectuals who moved to the suburb in the early '70s. They wear their hair long, dress casually and dance to *forró* (traditional music from the Northeast) or reggae. Then there are the Vanguard Clubbers, technoheads who hit all the out-of-town raves. Cliquey surfer groups are found with their boards on Rio's wilder beaches, including Macumba and Prainha.

Pitbulls have shaved heads and chewed ears, and are strong jujitsu fighters that sensible people steer clear of when entering or leaving nightclubs. Their girlfriends are often referred to as Maria Tatame after the exercise mats in the practice dojos.

Anxious middle-class parents worry about their daughter being nicknamed Maria Fuzil (Rifle Mary) and visiting funk parties in the favelas, chasing boyfriends who are sometimes very young, armed drug dealers. These *baile* funks boast the wildest parties in the dark and dangerous side of town that so often fascinates youth.

FOOD

Rio de Janeiro's diverse attractions only begin with its beaches, mountains and forests. The city's numerous restaurants offer yet another version of its eclecticism. They lie in every part of the Cidade Maravilhosa – along its tree-lined streets, overlooking its beaches, hidden in old colonial buildings, atop skyscrapers or spilling onto its pedestrian-filled neighborhoods.

The vast numbers of immigrants ensures that every type of cuisine is well represented. Stroll about Centro and you will discover Lebanese, Spanish, German, French and Italian cuisines, all laboriously prepared according to tradition. Speaking of tradition, Japanese cuisine and sushi – the city's latest 'fashion' food – has divided restaurateurs into two schools: those who cling to tradition and those who push the boundaries (the recently opened Mexican-sushi combo is a case in point).

A flair for the new is no small part of Rio's dining scene. From the city that brought the world the *fio dental* (dental-floss bikini), the culinary arts are no less flashy. You are likely to encounter daring – and not always successful – combinations in Rio blending old with new (or new with newer).

Those who prefer tradition to flash should explore time-tested favorites of Brazil's many regional dishes. Diners can sample rich, shrimp-filled *moqueca* from Bahia or tender *carne seca* (jerked meat) covered in *farofa* (manioc flour), a staple in Minas Gerais. Daring palates can venture north into Amazonia, enjoying savory *tacacá* or creamy *cupuaçu* ice cream. Cowboys and the *gaúcho* south bring the city its *churrascarias*, Brazil's famous all-you-can-eateries where crisply dressed waiters bring piping-hot spits of fresh roasted meats to your table.

Cachaça, Caipirinhas and Chope

Cachaça, also known as *pinga* or *aguardente*, is a high-proof (40% or so) cane spirit produced and consumed throughout the country. *Cachaça* literally means booze. *Pinga* (which literally means drop) is considered more polite. The production of *cachaça* is as old as slavery in Brazil. The distilleries grew up with the sugar plantations, first to satisfy local consumption and then to export to Africa in exchange for slaves.

Caipirinha is the unofficial national drink and Cariocas are not unfamiliar with them. The ingredients are simple – *cachaça*, lime, sugar and crushed ice – but a well-made *caipirinha* is a work of art. Order one on the beach and watch them make it. *Caipirosca* and *caipivodcas* have vodka replacing the *cachaça*. *Batidas* are wonderful mixes of sugar, *cachaça* and assorted fruit juices.

Chope (pronounced *shoh*-pee) is a pale blond pilsner draft, lighter and far superior to canned or bottled beer. It's served ice cold in most bars, which is perhaps one reason why Cariocas are the largest consumers of *chope* in the country.

Feijoada

As distinctively Carioca as the **Pão de Açúcar** (p65) or **Cristo Redentor** (p76), the *feijoada completa* is a dish that constitutes an entire meal, often beginning with a *caipirinha* aperitif.

A properly prepared *feijoada* is made up of black beans slowly cooked with a great variety of meat – including dried tongue and pork offcuts – seasoned with salt, garlic, onion and oil. The stew is accompanied by white rice and finely shredded kale, then tossed with croutons, fried manioc flour and pieces of orange.

Feijoada has its origins in Portuguese cooking, which uses a large variety of meats and vegetables; fried manioc flour (inherited from the Indians) and kale are also Portuguese favorites. The African influence comes with the spice and the tradition of using pork offcuts, which were the only part of the pig given to slaves.

Traditionally, Cariocas eat *feijoada* for lunch on Saturday. (It's rarely served on other days.) For tips on good places to sample the signature dish, see the Eating chapter (p102).

Brazil's verdant natural setting produces no shortage of delicacies. Its 4000km-long coastline ensures an abundance of fresh fish, just as its tropical forests produce savory fruits of every shape and size. In the mornings, Cariocas stop by their neighborhood juice bars for a shot of fresh-squeezed vitamins. The best juice bars offer dozens of varieties, featuring flavors from all over the country. Many don't translate – since some of these fruits don't exist elsewhere – so you'll have to try for yourself.

Like elsewhere, setting is as much a part of the culinary experience as the food itself. (In Leblon some critics say the experience is *only* about ambience.) Rio has 100-year-old botecos (sometimes staffed by fussy waiters who don't seem much younger), bordello-esque cafés full of models and their admirers, no-nonsense lunch bars designed for powering through a meal in a hurry, and longstanding, character-filled eateries that open late into the night – or morning, rather – perfect for those who only eat filet mignon and pineapple sandwiches at 4am.

FASHION

Rio's fashion has a lot to do with the tropical climate and the belief in the body aesthetic: Cariocas have them, and they're going to use them.

Although the French invented the bikini in 1946, it's Brazilian designers – and the models promoting them – who reinvent them every season. The *fio dental* (dental floss bikini) emerged in the '80s, and is still an icon on beaches here. Exposed *bundas* (bottoms), at least for the women, are generally the style. Whether you're six or 60, fat or skinny, the rule on the beach is to wear as little as possible, while still covering up the essentials (topless bathing is not allowed in Rio, by the way) – this applies to men, to some extent. About 15% of men wear *Bermudas*, while the vast majority stick to *sungas*, hip-hugging skimpy briefs.

Off the beach, women show up the men quite a bit. Most men, according to one disgruntled Carioca woman, are seriously fashion challenged. A night out for most means putting on a clean T-shirt and jeans. This is perhaps a bit unfair, as men are beginning to catch on; a growing number of boutiques in Ipanema, Leblon and the *shoppings* (shopping malls) are dedicated to pushing men in the right direction.

A tan is the most common fashion accessory, and it's rare to find a Carioca that doesn't have at least some color to their skin, if not an outright deep, dark – somewhat dermatologically troubling – glow.

Facts about Flip-Flops

Cassandra Loomis

Havaianas are one of Brazil's leading exports. Every second, five pairs of the rubber sandals are born, adding up to some 2.2 billion pairs since the inception of the company (also called Havaianas) in 1962. In recent years, designers have tapped in to Havaianas' popularity and have accessorized them, selling them for up to US$100 in shops in Los Angeles, New York and Paris. In Rio you can find them in dozens of styles and colors from US$3.50 at pharmacies and clothing stores.

SPORT

Cariocas have a fairly one-track mind when it comes to sport. There's soccer, and then there's, well, what else? Auto-racing, as a matter of fact. Brazilian drivers have won more Formula One world championships than any other nationality, which probably won't surprise anyone who rents a car for the weekend. The greatest racer was three-time world-champion Ayrton Senna, who was almost canonized after his death.

Tennis is growing in popularity, after Gustavo 'Guga' Kuerten helped put Brazil on the map. Volleyball, basketball – even professional bull riding – has its Brazilian advocates, if not its stars. All of this means that kids growing up in Brazil can now watch something on the TV besides soccer. Which isn't to say that any of them have an interest in anything besides soccer.

Most people acknowledge that Brazilians play the world's most creative, artistic and thrilling style of soccer, and Brazil is the only country to have won five World Cups (1958, 1962, 1970, 1994 and 2002).

Futebol (soccer) games are an intense spectacle – as much for the crazed fans as is it is for either team out on the field. The rivalries are particularly intense when it involves two of Rio's club teams playing against each other. The major teams are Botafogo (black-and-white striped jerseys), Flamengo (red jerseys with black hoops), Fluminense (red, green and white stripes) and Vasco da Gama (white with a black sash). Nearly every Carioca supports a team, to which they are undyingly devoted. Professional club competitions are held year-round and the games can be played on any day of the week (though Saturday, Sunday and Wednesday are favorites). An excellent book on understanding Brazil's great sport – and its relationship to culture, religion and politics – is the recently published (2002) *Futebol* by Alex Bellos. For results, schedules and league tables visit www.netgol.com.

Football Crisis *Tom Phillips*

When Brazil's soccer players failed to qualify for the Olympics in 2004 one word echoed around the country. 'Nightmare!' screamed supporters, pundits and newspaper headlines alike. In Rio de Janeiro it's not just the Olympics they're worried about. Recent seasons have been among the most miserable in the recent history of Carioca soccer. In the Brazilian Championship (known locally as the Brasileirão), the highest placed Rio team was Flamengo in eighth position. Local rivals Vasco da Gama and Fluminense, after a lengthy flirtation with relegation, eventually rattled in 17th and 19th respectively. Perhaps the only positive note was the return to the top flight of Botafogo, relegated during an equally dismal championship the previous year. Attendances at Rio's Maracanã stadium have plummeted as fans stay away, disgusted at Rio's *jogadores* (footballers) and a hike in ticket prices.

One moment from last season captured perfectly the current crisis in the city's soccer. Appalled at the abysmal form of his team, one Fluminense supporter decided to hurl six chickens at World Cup '94 star Romário during a training session in Laranjeiras. The striker, feathers clearly ruffled, responded by pursuing his assailant into the stands, and attacking him. 'You're going to give me a bollocking in my own home?' he ranted. 'If you want to have a go at me go to the Maracanã, but don't do it here!'

The calamity was complete when police took steps to charge not just Romário – for assault – but also the supporter. One of the chickens had died en route to the pitch.

MEDIA

Until fairly recently, the media and political demagogues worked hand in hand. Shortly after radio arrived in Brazil in the 1930s, President Vargas initiated weekday transmissions of the Voice of Brazil, as a means of instilling government propaganda into the people. The rise of Brazil's great media mogul, Roberto Marinho, was largely assisted by his decision not to criticize the fascistic regimes of the military government from 1964 to 1985. Other newspapers simply foundered if anything remotely critical of the government was published.

Roberto was the son of Irineu Marinho, who began in Rio in the 1920s with the newspaper *O Globo*. It remained a modest enterprise until 1931 when it was passed to the oldest son, Roberto. *O Globo* began transmitting over the radio in 1944, and the TV network emerged in Rio in 1965, under a controversial agreement with the Time-Life Group.

Top Five Rio Media Musts

- *Cidade de Deus* (City of God) The beautifully shot, Academy Award–nominated film portrays life from inside a favela.
- *How to Be a Carioca* Priscilla Goslin captures the essence of Carioca-hood in her humorous book (it's easier to find in Rio's bookstores than outside the country).
- *Orfeu Negro* (Black Orpheus) The original version of this film is the best. It's dated and syrupy sweet, but the music helped launch the popularity of bossa nova (the Tom Jobim – Vinícius de Moraes soundtrack is tops); plus you'll see some excellent old shots of Rio in this classic.
- *São Paolo Confessions* Electronic music master Suba died shortly after mixing this album, but it gives a perspective on where music is headed in the future…to Brazil.
- *Tropicalia ou Panis et Circenses* This excellent album, which features songs by Gilberto Gil, Caetano Veloso, Gal Costa and Os Mutantes, was recorded by Gilberto Gil and Caetano Veloso, and was at the forefront of a musical and cultural revolution termed Tropicalismo.

By the time patriarch Roberto Marinho's three sons took over, O Globo was the world's fourth-largest TV network (behind NBC, CBS and ABC). The Organizações Globo also includes Brazil's major radio network (Radio Globo), the country's second-biggest publishing house (Editra Globo), and of course the leading Rio newspaper (*O Globo*). Currently, *O Globo* receives half of the total amount spent annually in Brazil on advertising.

LANGUAGE

Portuguese is the seventh most commonly spoken language in the world, with 190 million speakers worldwide (170 million of whom live in Brazil). Owing to Brazil's unique colonial history, it is the only Portuguese-speaking country in South America. Brazilian Portuguese differs from that spoken in Portugal, owing in part to New World influences. When Portuguese colonists first arrived in the 16th century, many of them brought their own dialectical variations with them. As the Portuguese came into contact with the Tupi tribes that lived along the Atlantic coast, they began adopting the Tupi language and it, along with Portuguese, became the unofficial languages of the colony. The Jesuits had a great deal to do with this. They translated prayers and songs into Tupi, and in so doing recorded and promoted the language. The situation lasted only as long as the Jesuits. Tupi was banned when the Jesuits were expelled in 1759, and Portuguese became the country's official language.

Portuguese was influenced by the Tupi, and later by the Bantu and Yoruba languages of African slaves who arrived in Brazil in the 19th century. At the same time, European Portuguese went through linguistic changes as it came in contact with the French (thanks in part to Napoleon Bonaparte, who invaded the country). Today, the differences between the two variations are about as pronounced as that between American English and British English.

Oi, Cara (Hey, Guy/Gal)

A few phrases and gestures can go a long way in Brazil. And learning a language – or getting your point across – is all about making an effort, of which Brazilians will be most appreciative. *Diria* (slang) is a big part of the Carioca dialect. Here's a few words and phrases to help you along.

babaca (bah-*bah*-kah) Jerk.

bunda (*boon*-duh) Bottom.

chocante (show-*kahn*-chee) Way cool.

eu gosto de você (*ey*-ooh go-shtoo jih vo-*say*) I like you.

falou (fah-*low*) Agreed, you're welcome.

fio dental (*fee*-ooh den-*towh*) Dental floss, aka bikini.

gata, gato (*gah*-tah, *gah*-too) Good-looking woman/man.

nossa! (*noh*-sah) Gosh, shit, you don't say.

ótimo (*ah*-tche-moo) Cool.

sunga (*soohn*-guh) Tiny Speedo-type swimshorts favored by Carioca men.

'ta legal (*ta* lee-*gowh*) That's cool.

tudo bem? (*too*-doo behm) Everything good?

valeu (vah-*lay*-ooh) Thanks.

vamu nessa (vah-moo-*neh*-suh) Let's go.

Although Portuguese shares many lexical similarities with its romance-language cousin Spanish, the two are quite different. Spanish speakers will be able to read many things in Portuguese, but will have great difficulty understanding it when spoken. Fortunately, Brazilians are quite patient, and they appreciate any effort to speak their language. Incidentally, English is not commonly studied in Brazil, except by the best educated.

ECONOMY & COSTS

As well as being the most popular tourist destination in Brazil, Rio is a thriving shipping, banking, cultural, publishing and administrative center. Within 500km of the city are more than 30% of Brazil's population, 60% of its industries and 40% of its agricultural production. Its port trades more than 30 million metric tons of goods each year. More than 80% of Brazil's visitors pass through the city's airports. Most of Brazil's main film and record companies are based in the city, as are O Globo and Manchete – the country's largest and most influential TV networks.

As far as visitors are considered, Brazil is cheaper now for foreign travelers than it's been in years. This isn't to say that it really is cheap. The prices in Rio are much higher than you'll find in Bahia or other regions of Brazil. But compared to metropolitan destinations in other parts of the world – Los Angeles or Sydney, for example – Rio compares well. If you're traveling with another person, and split the cost of a decent hotel room (US$60 and up), eat in restaurants and have a few drinks in bars every night, US$70 to US$100 would be a rough estimate for what you'll spend.

> ## How Much?
>
> Glass of chope (draft beer) US$1.25.
>
> Admission to the opera at the Teatro Municipal US$10.
>
> Metro ticket US$0.75.
>
> Pair of Havaianas US$3.50.
>
> Admission to samba club US$4.
>
> Agua de coco (coconut water) on the beach US$0.80.
>
> Dinner for two at Zazá Bistro Tropical US$24.
>
> Hang-gliding flight over São Conrado US$80.
>
> Admission to top of Corcovado or Pão de Açúcar US$12.
>
> Admission to Maracanã football match US$4.

Brazil is not among the kinder destinations for solo travelers. The cost of a single room in a hotel is not much less than for a double, and when you eat, you'll find most dishes in restaurants are priced for two people.

If you have more to spend, the quality of your vacation increases quite a bit more. For US$120 per person, a couple can get a good hotel room in Copacabana or Ipanema on or near the beach, eat at excellent restaurants, and still have some money left for shopping.

Keep in mind that during the December-to-February holiday season, lodging costs generally increase by around 25% to 30% (and sometimes more in popular resorts close to Rio).

GOVERNMENT & POLITICS

The state of Rio de Janeiro (one of Brazil's 24 states) has a governor, elected for a four-year term, and then there's the city council, which is headed by the mayor.

Rio politics is colorful, to say the least. A metal detector had to be installed at the entrance to Palácio Tiradentes (p82), where the state assembly meets, to stop politicians packing revolvers.

The excessive number of public servants is a huge burden on the state. It means that 60% of the budget is earmarked just for wages.

Corruption is rife. Some examples: one previous head of the legislative house was accused of tax evasion, of illicit enrichment and of buying 70 new cars for political allies. Also, nine deputies who controlled the Secretariat of Health are alleged to have devastated the state's hospitals through over billing and fictitious billing.

Fact or Fiction: Telenovelas Take on Politics *Tom Phillips*

There was outcry last year when a former hooker called Fernanda was killed by a *bala perdida* (stray bullet) in the chic Rio neighborhood of Leblon. Yet it was actually just a soap opera storyline. The bloodthirsty twist was part of a drive by media giant O Globo to promote a new disarmament bill. Confusingly, the producers of the *Mulheres Apaixonadas* (Women in Love) telenovela went on to film a real-life anti-gun demo in Copacabana and incorporate it into the program. Have you ever thought you were living inside a telenovela? In Rio, you really are.

The biggest breakdown over the last few years has been in the area of law and order. Corruption got so bad in the Polícia Civil and the Polícia Militar that the state was forced to ask the federal government to send the army into the favelas to fight drug traffickers.

At city level, government is, fortunately, a little better. The last few mayors have been committed to 'trimming the fat' in city spending, and this policy has been so successful that the city has the money to finance several large projects, including the ongoing Favela-Bairro project. For more information on this project, see p44.

ENVIRONMENT
THE LAND

Rio is blessed by nature. Its location between the mountains and the sea, bathed by the sun, has entranced visitors for centuries. Darwin called it 'more magnificent than anything any European has ever seen in his country of origin.'

It all started millions of years ago, when the movement of the earth pushed the rock crystal and granite, already disturbed by faults and fractures, into the sea. Low-lying areas were flooded and the high granite peaks became islands.

The plains and swamps on which the city is built were slowly created through many centuries of erosion from the peaks and the gradual accumulation of river and ocean sediment.

The mountains, their granite peaks worn by intense erosion and their slopes covered with Atlantic rain forest, form three ranges: the Rural da Pedra Branca massif, the Rural Marapicu-Gericinó massif and the Tijuca-Carioca massif.

The Tijuca-Carioca massif can be seen from almost everywhere in Rio and is responsible for the coastline, which alternates between bare granite escarpments and Atlantic beaches. Its most famous peaks are **Pão de Açúcar** (Sugarloaf; p65), the Morro do Leme, the Ponta do Arpoador, Morro Dona Marta, Corcovado and the Dois Irmãos at the end of Leblon Beach.

The sea has also played its part. The stretch of coast between Dois Irmãos and Arpoador was once a large spit, and **Lagoa Rodrigo de Freitas** (p61) was a bay. Between Arpoador and Morro do Leme the sea created the beautiful curved beach of Copacabana. Praia Vermelha, the smallest of Rio's Atlantic beaches, is the only one with yellow sand instead of white. Inside Baía de Guanabara (Guanabara Bay), river sediment and reclamation projects formed the present bay rim.

Historically, the most important river is the Rio Carioca, which begins near Corcovado and meets the sea between Flamengo and Glória. Today it's completely channeled, but to the Tamoio Indians it was a sacred river, capable of endowing women with beauty and poets and singers with good voices.

GREEN RIO

Baía de Guanabara, one of the symbols of Rio, is badly polluted and smelly, and its western sections are effectively dead. Rio's beaches are sometimes contaminated by sewage, depending on the direction of the ocean currents; this increases health risks, such as liver, intestinal and skin diseases. Even though treatment facilities are now being built, current measures are insufficient to create any major improvement in the water quality of the bay.

While Rio doesn't have the very worst air pollution problems in the world, road dust and emissions from industry, transport and rubbish incineration etc are enough to cause serious health problems, including premature mortality. The mountains that surround the city enclose the air pollution, aggravating the problem.

In spite of all this, Rio has made some modest advances in ecology in some parts of the city. Lagoa Rodrigo de Freitas is one example. Until recently, it was polluted. Now the city is reintroducing some wildlife – and the elegant egret has returned to its shores. Although Rio is nothing like it was when tropical rain forest covered its landscape, there is still a variety of wildlife in the city. In Campo de Santana, *agoutis* (rodents that look like large hamsters), peacocks, white-faced tree ducks, geese, egrets and curassows abound.

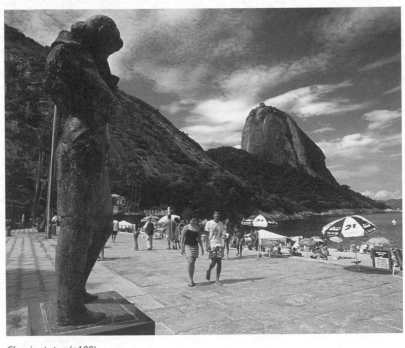

Chopin statue (p100)

The park near Leme has many plants and birds native to the Atlantic rain forest, such as saddle and bishop tanagers, thrushes and the East Brazilian house wren, which has a distinctive trill. Also, the nearby **Parque Nacional de Tijuca** (p56) contains many more rain forest species.

The **Jardim Botânico** (p61) has a huge variety of native and imported plant species, including the Vítoria Régia water lilies from the Amazon and impressive rows of royal palms, whose seeds originally came from France. The orchid greenhouse contains many beautiful native species. Watch for the brightly plumed hummingbirds, known in Brazil as *beija-flores* (literally, flower-kissers).

Micos (small monkeys) and macaws can be seen in surprising places in the city, including Pista Cláudio Coutinho in Urca and Parque Lage on the back side of Corcovado.

URBAN PLANNING & DEVELOPMENT

Rio suffers from the same urban sprawl affecting many other cities. Today Rio occupies around 1200 sq km, with 8400 people packed in each square kilometer, which makes it one of the world's 25 most populous cities.

Favelas contribute to much of this urban density. The number of people living in them grows at an annual rate (7.5%) about three times that of the overall population growth (2.5%). For the most part, the government has largely ignored the favelas (their poor sanitation, lack of schools, police and other public services), but in the last few years, the city has begun addressing (albeit reluctantly) the needs of Rio's 500 favelas, where an estimated 1.8 million Cariocas (or one-third of the population) live.

The Favela-Bairro project instituted in the mid '90s was designed to bring basic infrastructure and municipal and social services to the favelas. At the Inter-American Development Bank's Washington headquarters in October 2003, Rio Mayor Cesar Maia pledged US$1 billion for the project's lifespan. The city claims to have benefited 500,000 people already, although the project has its critics.

In other aspects, urban planning amounts to very little planning at all. The city continues to expand north and west, taxing the environment and geography with unbridled growth.

Carnaval

Carnaval

Colorful, outrageous, hedonistic – words do little justice to this bacchanalian spectacle, for which the city is notorious. Visitors arrive in droves to join Cariocas as they drink, dance, celebrate and chalk up a few sins before Ash Wednesday brings it all to a close. Carnaval officially lasts from Friday to the Tuesday preceding Lent, but revelry begins well in advance. Rehearsals at the *escolas de samba* (samba schools) start around September.

Cariocas celebrate Carnaval in every form and fashion. Nightclubs and bars throw special costumed events, while formal balls draw an elegantly dressed (or costumed) crowd. Parks and plazas (Largo do Machado, Arcos do Lapa, Praça General Osório) often host free live concerts on Carnaval weekend, while many impromptu parties happen on street corners throughout town. The common denominators among them all are music, dancing and celebration.

Bandas, also called *blocos*, are another good way to celebrate à la Carioca. These consist of a procession of drummers and vocalists followed by anyone who wants to dance through the streets of Rio. Many of these encourage people to dress up, and drag is popular (among gays and straights alike).

The parade through the Sambódromo is the culmination of Carnaval, on Sunday and Monday nights. It's a spectacle that features thousands of costumed dancers, elaborate floats and exuberant fans cheering on their favorite schools.

Although there's a lot going on around town, don't expect the Carnaval to come to you. Many visitors show up with the expectation that the party will be all around them. Not so; you have to seek it out. See the Sights & Activities section (p26) to get some ideas on how to celebrate the return of King Momo, the lord of the Carnaval.

To get more information on events during Carnaval, check *Veja* magazine's Rio insert (sold on Sundays at newsstands) or visit **Riotur** (Map pp228-30; www.rio.rj.gov.br/riotur; 9th fl, Rua Assembléia 10; metro stop Carioca). They're the people in charge of Carnaval, by the way.

Street Carnaval (p27)

Carnaval Party Planner *Marcos Silviano do Prado*

Rio starts revving up for Carnaval long before the colorful parades take place, but the partying reaches boiling point from Friday to Tuesday. To make the most of your time, check out the range of long-standing *festas* (parties) listed below. You can dance through the streets in a *banda* (recommended) or party like a rock star at one of many dance clubs – Cine Ideal, Fundição Progresso – scattered throughout town (also recommended) or find your groove at one of the samba school rehearsals (highly recommended) listed on p139. Those looking for free, open-air, neighborhood-wide celebrations shouldn't miss Rio Folia in Lapa or the Cinelândia Ball in Centro. For up to date listings of what's on, visit www.ipanema.com.

Saturday Two Weeks Before Carnaval
- **Banda de Ipanema** (p27) at 4pm
- Rehearsals at samba schools

Weekend Before Carnaval
- **Banda Simpatia é Quase Amor** (p27) in Ipanema at 4pm Saturday
- Monobloco at 4pm Sunday, Leblon Beach
- Rehearsals at samba schools

Carnaval Friday
- Carnaval King Momo is crowned by mayor at 1pm
- Shows start at **Terreirão do Samba** (Samba Land; p29) and **Rio Folia** (in front of the Lapa Arches in Lapa) from 8pm
- **Cinelândia Ball** (p26) from 9pm
- Red and Black Ball at the **Scala** (p26), from 11pm
- Dance party at **Cine Ideal** (☎ 2252 7766; www.idealparty.com.br; Rua da Carioca 62, Centro)
- Gay balls at **Le Boy** (p140), Copacabana

Carnaval Saturday
- **Cordão do Bola Preta Street Band** (p27), Centro, from 9:30am
- Banda de Ipanema, from 4pm
- Competition of deluxe costumes at **Glória** (p175) from 7pm
- Parade of Access Group samba schools, from 7pm at the **Sambódromo** (p29)
- **Street Band Competition** (Av Rio Branco, Centro, admission free), from 8pm
- **Copacabana Palace Luxury Ball** (p26) from 11pm; costumes or black-tie are mandatory
- Off-Carnaval: X-Demente Party at **Fundição Progresso** (p87), Lapa
- Carnaval balls: Scala, **Help** (p140) and other venues, from 11pm
- Gay balls in Copacabana at Le Boy and **Incontrus** (☎ 2549 6498; Praça Serzedelo Correia 15, Copacabana)

- Off-Carnaval parties at **Bunker 94** (p138), and other dance clubs
- Shows start at Terreirão do Samba and Rio Folia, from 8pm

Carnaval Sunday
- Samba parade at the Sambódromo, from 9pm to 6am
- Carnaval balls from 11pm at Scala and Help
- Gay balls at Le Boy, Copacabana, and **Elite** (p137), Centro
- Rave party at theme park **Terra Encantada** (p92), Barra
- Off-Carnaval parties at Bunker 94, and other dance clubs
- Shows start at Terreirão do Samba and Rio Folia, from 8pm

Carnaval Monday
- Samba parade at the Sambódromo, from 9pm to 6am
- Carnaval balls from 11pm at Scala, Help and other venues
- Gay balls at Le Boy, Copacabana, and Elite downtown
- Off-Carnaval parties at Bunker 94, and other dance clubs
- Shows start at Terreirão do Samba and Rio Folia, from 8pm.

Carnaval Tuesday
- Banda de Ipanema, from 4pm
- Parade of Group B samba schools, Sambódromo, from 9pm
- Scala Gay Costume Ball, Leblon, from 11pm
- Carnaval balls from 11pm at Help and other venues
- Gay balls at Le Boy, Copacabana, and **Garden Hall** (☎ 2430 8400; Shopping Barra Garden, Av das Américas 3255, Barra da Tijuca)
- Off-Carnaval: X-Demente Party at Fundição Progresso
- Off-Carnaval parties at Bunker 94 and other dance clubs
- Shows start at Terreirão do Samba and Rio Folia, from 8pm.

HISTORY

Carnaval, like Mardi Gras, originated from various pagan spring festivals. During the Middle Ages, these tended to be wild parties, until tamed in Europe by both the Reformation and the Counter-Reformation. But not even the heavy hand of the Inquisition could squelch Carnaval in the Portuguese colony, where it came to acquire Indian costumes and African rhythms.

Some speculate that the word *carnaval* derives from the Latin *carne vale,* 'goodbye meat.' The reasoning goes something like this: for the 40 days of Lent, the nominally Catholic Brazilians give up liver and steak fillets, in addition to luxuries such as alcohol and pastries. To compensate for the deprivation ahead, they rack up sins in advance with wild parties in honor of King Momo.

SIGHTS & ACTIVITIES

There are dozens of ways to take part in Carnaval, from participating in a *banda* (street party), to attending one of the society balls, to watching the phantasmagoric parade live and up close at the Sambódromo. If you smile at the thought of putting on a costume and dancing before thousands (millions if you include the television audience), now's your chance – just pick out your favorite samba school and join up (see p139).

CARNAVAL BALLS

Carnaval balls are surreal and erotic events. The most famous one is held at the **Copacabana Palace** (p170). It's a formal affair, so you'll need a tux; there you'll have the opportunity to celebrate with Rio's glitterati as well as a few international stars in town. Tickets cost around US$200.

Other balls, which are decidedly less upper class, are held at **Scala** (Map pp236-8; Av Afránio de Melo Francoin, Leblon), at **Canecão** (p137) and at **Help** (p140). The most extravagant balls for gays are found at **Le Boy** (p140). The most popular ball is held in **Praça Floriano** (p83) in Cinelândia, which attracts around 60,000 revelers. Every night of Carnaval weekend (from 9pm on Friday to Tuesday), bands take the stage in front of the Câmara Municipal on the Praça Floriano. This ball is free.

Tickets go on sale roughly two weeks beforehand, and the balls are held nightly during Carnaval and the preceding week. Buy a copy of *Veja* magazine with the Veja Rio insert. It has details of all the balls.

Street Carnaval (p27)

SAMBA SCHOOL PARADES

The main parade takes place in the **Sambódromo** (Map p28; Rua Marquês do Sapuçai, near Praça Onze metro station), and it's nothing short of spectacular. Before an exuberant crowd of some 30,000, each of 14 samba schools has their hour and 20 minutes to dazzle the audience.

The parades begin in moderate mayhem and work themselves up to a higher plane of frenzy. The announcers introduce the school, the group's theme colors and number of wings. Far away the lone voice of the *puxador* (interpreter) starts the samba. Thousands more voices join him, and then the drummers kick in, 200 to 400 per school. The pounding drums drive the

Bandas: Carnaval on the Streets

Attending a *banda* is one of the best ways to celebrate Carnaval. *Bandas*, also called *blocos*, consist of a procession of drummers and singers followed by anyone who wants to dance through the streets. To join in, all you have to do is show up. Note that some *bandas* ask you to march in one of the *bandas* colors. Many sell shirts on the spot (around US$5) or you can just show up in the right colors. Dozens of *bandas* party through the streets before Carnaval. For complete listings, check **Riotur** (Map pp228-30; www.rio.rj.gov.br/riotur; 9th fl, Rua Assembléia 10; metro stop Carioca).

Banda Carmen Miranda (Praça General Osório, Ipanema; ☺ 4pm Carnaval Sun) A hilarious good time, Banda Miranda features lots of men decked out like the Brazilian bombshell. A lively mix of straights and gays parades through Ipanema's streets.

Banda de Ipanema (Praça General Osório, Ipanema; ☺ 4pm 2nd Sat before Carnaval & Carnaval Sat) This long-standing *banda* parades on the second Saturday before Carnaval, starting in Ipanema. It's a wild crowd, complete with drag queens and others in costume. Don't miss it.

Banda de Sá Ferreira (Av Atlântica & Rua Sá Ferreira, Copacabana; ☺ 3pm Carnaval Sat & Sun) This popular Copacabana *banda* marches along the ocean from Posto 1 to Posto 6.

Banda Simpatia é Quase Amor (Praça General Osório, Ipanema; ☺ 3pm 2nd Sat before Carnaval & Carnaval Sun) A big *bloco* with 10,000 participants and a 50-piece percussion band.

Barbas (cnr Rua Assis Bueno & Rua General Polidoro, Botafogo; ☺ 2pm Carnaval Sat) One of the oldest *bandas* of the Zona Sul parades through the streets with a 60-piece percussion band. A water truck follows along to spray the crowd of some 2500. Colors: red and white.

Bloco Cacique de Ramos (cnr Presidente Vargas & Rio Branco, Centro; ☺ 6pm Carnaval Sun) Participants in this *bloco* are expected to dress as Indians.

Bloco de Bip Bip (Rua Almirante Gonçalves 50, Copacabana; ☺ Carnaval Sat & 9:30pm Carnaval Tue) Has perhaps the best music of any *banda*, owing to the professional musicians who drop in from time to time. Leaves from the old samba haunt, **Bip Bip** (p133).

Bloco de Segunda (Cobal Humaitá, Rua Voluntários de Pátria 446, Botafogo; ☺ 5pm Carnaval Mon) Excellent percussion band joins 2000 or so revelers. T-shirt is obligatory; buy at the dance academy beforehand.

Cordão do Bola Preta (cnr Rua 13 de Maio & Rua Evaristo da Veiga, Centro; ☺ 10am Carnaval Sat) The oldest *banda* in action, features lots of straight men dressed as women, and a chaotic march that often leads the group to stop at bars along the way. Costumes always welcome – especially those with black and white spots.

Dois Pra Lá, Dois Pra Cá (Carlinho de Jesus Dance School, Rua da Passagem 145, Botafogo; ☺ 2pm Carnaval Sat) This fairly long march begins at the dance school and ends at the Copacabana Palace Hotel. Bring along your swimsuit for a dip in the ocean afterward.

Empurra Que Pega (Cnr Rua Carlos Góis & Rua Ataulfo de Paiva, Leblon; ☺ 6pm Carnaval Sat & Sun) A beautiful Leblon crowd of some 4000 take to the streets.

parade. Sambas, including the themes for each group, flood the airwaves for weeks before the beginning of Carnaval.

Next come the main wings of the school, the big allegorical floats, the children's wing, the drummers, the celebrities and the bell-shaped *baianas* (women dressed as Bahian aunts) twirling in elegant hoopskirts. The *baianas* honor the history of the parade itself, which was brought to Rio from Salvador da Bahia in 1877.

The *mestre-sala* (dance master) and *porta-bandeira* (flag bearer) waltz and whirl. Celebrities, dancers and tambourine players strut their stuff. The costumes are fabulously lavish: 1.5m feathered headdresses, long flowing capes, which sparkle with sequins, and rhinestone-studded G-strings.

More than an hour after it began, the school makes it past the arch and the judges' stand. The whole procession is also an elaborate competition. A hand-picked set of judges chooses the best school on the basis of many components, including percussion, the *samba do enredo* (theme song), harmony between percussion, song and dance, choreography, costumes, story line, floats and decorations. The championship is hotly contested, with the winner becoming the pride of Rio and all of Brazil.

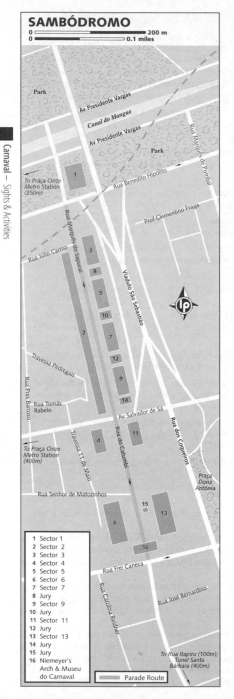

SAMBÓDROMO

0 ——————— 200 m
0 ——————— 0.1 miles

Park

Av Presidente Vargas

Canal do Mangue

Av Presidente Vargas

Park

Rua Marquês de Pombal

To Praça Onze
Metro Station
(250m)

Rua Benedito Hipólito

1

Prof Clementino Fraga

Rua Marquês do Sapucaí

Rua Júlio Carmo

3

8

5

10

2

7

12

9

14

Viaduto São Sebastião

Travessa Pedregais

Rua Frei Barroso

Rua Tomás
Rabelo

Av Salvador de Sá

Travessa 11 de Maio

4

11

Rua do Catumbi

Rua dos Coqueiros

To Praça Onze
Metro Station
(400m)

Praça
Dona
Antônia

Rua Senhor de Matozinhos

15

13

6

16

Rua Frei Caneca

Rua Catolina Reidher

Rua José Bernardino

To Rua Itapiru (100m);
Tunel Santa
Bárbara (400m)

1	Sector 1
2	Sector 2
3	Sector 3
4	Sector 4
5	Sector 5
6	Sector 6
7	Sector 7
8	Jury
9	Sector 9
10	Jury
11	Sector 11
12	Jury
13	Sector 13
14	Jury
15	Jury
16	Niemeyer's Arch & Museu do Carnaval

Parade Route

The Sambódromo parades start on Friday night with the *mirins* (young samba school members) and continue on through Saturday night when the Group A samba schools strut their stuff. Sunday and Monday are the big nights, when the Grupo Especial – the best 14 samba schools in Rio – parade: seven of them on Sunday night and into the morning, and seven more on Monday night. The following Saturday, the eight top schools strut their stuff once more in the Parade of Champions. Each event starts at 9pm and runs until 6am. If you go, you're allowed to bring in plastic bottles (two 500ml sizes per person), but no glass; a good option if you plan to drink while you're there.

Tickets

Getting tickets at legitimate prices can be tough. Many tickets are sold well in advance of the event. Check with **Riotur** (www.rio.rj.br/riotur) about where you can get them, as the official outlet can vary from year to year. People line up for hours, and travel agents and scalpers snap up the best seats. Riotur reserves seats in private boxes for tourists for US$200, but you should be able to pick up regular tickets for much less from a travel agent or from the **Maracanã stadium box office** (Map pp240-1; ☎ 2568 9962; for around US$40). Try to get seats in the center, as this is the liveliest section and has the best views.

By Carnaval weekend, most tickets will have sold out, but there are lots of scalpers. If you buy a ticket from a scalper (no need to worry about looking for them – they'll find you!), make sure you get both the plastic ticket with the magnetic strip and the ticket showing the seat number. The tickets for different days are color-coded, so double-check the date as well.

If you haven't purchased a ticket but still want to go, you can show up at the Sambódromo at around midnight, three or four hours into the show. This is when you can get grandstand tickets for about US$10 from scalpers outside the gate. Make sure you check which sector your ticket is for. Most ticket sellers will try to pawn off their worst seats.

And if you can't make it during Carnaval proper, there's always the cheaper (but less exciting) Parade of Champions the following Saturday.

Getting to the Sambódromo

Don't take a bus to or from the Sambódromo. It's much safer to take a taxi or the metro, which runs round the clock during Carnaval until 11pm Tuesday. This is also a great opportunity to check out the paraders commuting in costume.

Make sure you indicate to your taxi driver which side of the stadium you're on. If you decide to take the metro: what stop you get off at depends on where your seats are. For sectors 2, 4 and 6, exit at Praça Onze. Once outside the station, turn to the right, take another right and then walk straight ahead (on Rua Júlio Carmo) to Sector 2. For Sectors 4 and 6, turn right on Rua Carmo Neto and proceed to Av Salvador de Sá. You'll soon see the Sambódromo and hear the roar of the crowd. Look for signs showing the entrance to the sectors. If going to sectors on the other side (1, 3, 5, 7, 9, 11 and 13) exit at the metro stop Central. You'll then have to walk about 700m along Presidente Vargas until you see the Sambódromo.

Carnaval Parade (p26), Sambódromo

Carnaval – Sights & Activities

SAMBA LAND

The Sambódromo's latest addition, **Terreirão do Samba** (Samba Land), is an open-air courtyard next to Sector 1. Performances are presented the weekend before Carnaval, then continue the following Friday all the way through Tuesday. Samba Land also hosts a party the Saturday after Carnaval, which is the Champion's Parade.

Sambódromo Glossary

- **alas** Literally the 'wings.' These are groups of samba school members responsible for a specific part of the central *samba do enredo* (theme song). Special *alas* include the *baianas*, women dressed as Bahian 'aunts' in full skirts and turbans. The *abre ala* of each school is the opening wing or float.
- **bateria** The drum section. This is the driving beat behind the school's samba and the 'soul' of the school.
- **carnavalescos** The artistic directors of each school, who are responsible for the overall layout and design of the school's theme.
- **carros alegóricos** The dazzling floats, usually decorated with near-naked women. The floats are pushed along by the school's maintenance crew.
- **desfile** The procession. The most important samba schools *desfilar* (parade) on the Sunday and Monday night of Carnaval. Each school's *desfile* is judged on its samba, drum section, master of ceremonies and flag bearer, floats, leading commission, costumes, dance coordination and harmony.
- **destaques** The richest and most elaborate costumes. The heaviest ones usually get a spot on one of the floats.
- **diretores de harmonia** The school organizers, usually wearing white or the school colors; they run around yelling and 'pumping up' the wings and making sure there aren't any gaps in the parade.
- **enredo** The central theme of each school. The *samba do enredo* is the samba that goes with it. Themes vary tremendously.
- **passistas** A school's best samba dancers. They roam the parade in groups or alone, stopping to show their fancy footwork along the way. The women are usually scantily dressed and the men usually hold tambourines.
- **puxador** The interpreter of the theme song. He (a *puxador* is invariably male) works as a guiding voice leading the school's singers at rehearsals and in the parade.

Joining a Samba School

There's nothing to stop you from taking part in a Carnaval parade. Most samba schools are happy to have foreigners join one of the wings. Contact the **Liga Independente das Escolas de Samba** (League of Samba Schools; ☎ 2253 7409; www.liesa.com.br; 18th fl, Av Rio Branco 4, Centro) or write directly to one of the **samba schools** (p139) if you'd like to take part.

Fantasias (costumes) vary in price according to how elaborate they are, but they usually cost in the vicinity of US$200 to 300. If you don't want to buy online, it is always possible to get one by phoning the samba schools directly once you're in Rio, even as little as two weeks before Carnaval.

Those who would like a view of what it's like to join a samba school should read Alma Guillermoprieto's excellent book, *Samba*.

SAMBA SCHOOL REHEARSALS

Around August or September, rehearsals start at the *escolas de samba* (samba 'schools' or clubs). Rehearsals usually take place in the favelas and are open to visitors. They're fun to watch, but go with a Carioca for safety. Mangueira and Salgueira are among the easiest to get to, and are popular with a mix of Cariocas and tourists. See p139 for complete listings of samba schools.

DATES

The following are the Carnaval dates (Friday to Tuesday) in coming years:

2005 February 4-8

2006 February 24-28

2007 February 16-20

2008 February 1-5

Arts

Arts

Rio is stereotyped for being the land of beaches and football (by both foreigners and the assorted Paulistano detractors), but Rio's vibrant arts scene dwarfs that of many other cities. The city's musical contributions are its centerpiece. The birthplace of bossa nova today hosts samba, jazz, half a dozen regional styles, hip-hop (called 'black music'), reggae, funk, electronic music, Música Popular Brasileiro (MPB), and many fusions among them, such as samba-jazz, samba-funk, electro-samba and bossa-jazz. Vibrant samba clubs have emerged in some of Rio's most historic – but run-down – neighborhoods, mixing with 19th-century buildings and mid-20th-century decay reinvented by 21st-century musicians. In the Zona Sul, a broad range of musical styles – from jazz and classic bossa nova to drum 'n' bass and MPB – dominates in the bars, lounges and clubs scattered a few blocks from the beach.

Rio makes ample use of its tropical climate. Particularly in the summer, but throughout the year, open-air concerts are common (including in Glória Marina, on the beaches of Copacabana and Ipanema, and in the Jockey Club), as are small impromptu music jams all over the city – in sidewalk cafés, open-air bars, in parks and along Lagoa.

Rio isn't only about the music (although it may seem that way if you're just passing through). In recent years, museums have committed themselves to being at the vanguard of the visual arts – from hosting avant-garde exhibitions by Brazilian artists to attracting traveling international exhibitions. Some of the smaller cultural centers have more freedom to experiment and often attract the more daring exhibits.

The Greats Live On *Tom Phillips*

One morning in 1996 the community of Vila Isabel woke up to find one of the creators of samba sipping a beer and smoking a cigarette at a bar on 28 de Setembro. Strange, given that Noel Rosa had died of a heart attack in 1937, aged just 26. In fact, it was the first of an ever-growing number of interactive statues scattered around the city, paying homage to the great and the good in Carioca history.

The following year it was the turn of Pixinguinha. The saxophonist – praised by some as the 'father of Brazilian music' – can be found in Centro, Rio's downtown district. But it's not just musicians that are being honored: you can now take a rest on a Copacabana beach next to Mineiro writer Carlos Drummond de Andrade, who's permanently perched on a bench in front of his former residence (Av Rainha Elizabete). Or if you're near the **Jardim Botânico** (p61), how about getting to know journalist Otto Lara Resende, striking a pose on the street corner?

Soon you'll also be able to hum a tune with Cartola, the founder of the **Mangueira samba school** (p139) at the Morro de Mangueira. And as if that wasn't enough, Carnival-maestro Braguinha will still be waiting for you on Av Princesa Isabel in Copacabana. There are even plans for a sculpture of bossa nova icon Tom Jobim to welcome visitors at the Aeroporto Internacional Antonio Carlos Jobim.

Classical music, opera and dance are also well represented in the city – a perusal of *Veja*'s Rio insert reveals the range of offerings for any given week. Film is also experiencing a renaissance in Rio. Its many cinemas host a range of films from art-house cinema to foreign classics; and with a growing film industry, screen space is utilized by more and more Brazilian films each year. Like musical events, the city periodically uses its green space to host outdoor cinema.

The range of offerings in the city and its openness to experimentation are just several of the reasons why artists have been drawn to Rio (and there are plenty of other factors – the historical buildings, the nightlife, the natural beauty of the landscape...). In the past three decades, districts such as Santa Teresa – and more recently Laranjeiras – have drawn a mix of artists, writers and musicians, and the arts are flourishing. Rio feels as if it's on the edge of something big.

MUSIC & DANCE

Rio boasts the country's best music scene, and Brazil is at the forefront of the world music scene, which makes Rio...the center of the musical world? Although that's overstating things a bit, Rio has its musical contributions, its pioneers and virtuosos, and they are many. Samba clubs are widespread, as are jazz bars, lounges that showcase *pagode* (relaxed and rhythmic form of samba) and other regional styles, and concert halls, cultural centers and open-air spaces (beaches, parks, a street corner) also serve as settings for musical sessions.

Bip Bip (p133)

CLASSICAL

Brazil has several notable classical composers. Carlos Gomes (1836–96) was Brazil's first internationally known composer. Verdi was one of his greatest influences, and Gomes wrote nine operas throughout his career. His best known, *Il Guarany* (based on an Alencar novel), is still performed on stages in Rio and around the world. Heitor Villa-Lobos (1887–1959) is Brazil's other great composer (Alberto Nepomuceno is a third, though he is largely forgotten). He incorporated Brazilian folk themes into his compositions. His greatest symphonic works were *Floresta do Amazonas* and the music for the ballet *Uirapuru*.

TUDO DA SAMBA

In spite of early classical music, most Cariocas consider samba the birth of sound in their country – *tudo da samba*: Everything makes for a samba. The heart and soul of Brazilian music is the samba; all other styles that originated in Brazil can be traced back to its vibrant sound. Samba was first performed at the Rio Carnaval in 1917, though its origins go back much further. It is intimately linked with African rhythms the slaves brought with them to the sugar plantations. The most notable of these influences is the Angolan tam-tam, which was the basis for both the music and the distinctive dance steps. Samba caught on quickly after the advent of radio broadcasting and recorded music, and it has since become a national symbol. Samba's fast tempo speaks directly to the hips and feet; it is foremost a music to inspire dancing.

Samba is the most popular Brazilian rhythm; it's also the music of the masses. In Rio, samba is inextricably linked to Carnaval (see p24). The competing samba schools provide the structural backbone for the festivities, and the *batucada* (percussion ensembles) are almost – literally – its heartbeat. Each school parading in Carnaval has not only a theme, but also a theme samba, which is repeated constantly throughout the school's presentation. Samba could exist without Carnaval, but Carnaval could not continue without samba.

The 1930s are known as the golden age of samba. By this point, samba had evolved into many substyles. Samba *canção* and *chorinho* (which is played with a ukulele or guitar as its main instrument, and a recorder or flute accompanying) were romantic, intimate musical styles, very different from the loud percussive samba-school style of *samba-enredo*. Samba continues to develop: Today, *pagode* is a common form you'll hear in Rio bars. A new funk style of samba is also becoming popular, with many *funkeiros* joining samba schools.

Samba and *pagode* continue to be popular in Rio's poor outlying neighborhoods. Zeca Pagodinho and Bezerra da Silva are two popular artists who create alternatives to the high-gloss *pagode* from São Paulo that dominates the airwaves. Other longstanding favorites include Paulinho da Viola and Martino da Vila.

Related to samba, but with sounds of their own, are *timbalada* and *axê*, two musical percussion styles popular in the north.

The Dancehalls of Old *Carmen Michael*

If you're interested in Brazilian music and dance, shine up your dancing shoes and head for some of Rio's old-school-style dancehalls, known as *gafieiras*. Originally established in the 1920s as dancehalls for Rio's urban working class, *gafieiras* nowadays attract an eclectic combination of musicians, dancers, *malandros* (con men) and, of course, the radical chic from Zona Sul. Modern and sleek they are not. Typically held in the ballrooms of old colonial buildings in Lapa, the locations are magnificently old world. Bow-tied waiters serve ice-cold *cerveja* (beer) under low yellow lights and while it initially looks formal, give it a few rounds and it will dissolve into a typically raucous Brazilian evening.

Before *gafieiras* were established, Rio's different communities were polarized by their places of social interaction, whether it was opera and tango for the Europeans or street *choró* (romantic samba) for the Africans. Responding to a social need and in tandem with the politics of the time, they quickly became places where musicians and audiences of black and white backgrounds alike could mix and create new sounds. Through the *gafieiras*, street improvised *choró* formations became big-band songs and a new Brazilian sound was born. The best and oldest dancehalls are **Democraticus** (p136), attracting a young fashionably bohemian crowd on Wednesday, and **Estudantina** (p137) on Praça Tiradentes. Estudantina operates from Friday to Sunday.

The standard of dancing is outstanding in Brazil, so expect to see couples who would be considered professional in Europe or the US dancing unnoticed across the polished floors. While just about anything goes in Rio anywhere, it's an opportunity for the Cariocas to dress up a little, so you will see quite a few dresses and smart shoes. Don't be intimidated by the other dancers. Unlike the tango in Buenos Aires, Brazilians are pretty relaxed about newcomers dancing. For those traveling solo, *gafieiras* are fantastic places to meet some intriguing locals and learn a few steps. Dance around the edge of the dance floor with the rest of the dancers to get a closer look at how the dance works – if you are a woman, you won't wait long until someone asks you to dance. Alternatively, you can take a lesson and perhaps meet some fellow beginners to dance with. Estudantina has an in-house dance instructor with whom you can arrange lessons, otherwise head for one of the nearby dance schools, such as Nucleo de Dança on Rua Visconde do Rio Branco.

BOSSA NOVA: THE NEW SOUND

In the 1950s came bossa nova (literally, new wave), sparking a new era of Brazilian music. Bossa nova's founders – songwriter and composer Antônio Carlos (Tom) Jobim and guitarist João Gilberto, in association with the lyricist/poet Vinícius de Moraes – slowed down and altered the basic samba rhythm to create a more intimate, harmonic style. This new wave initiated a new style of playing instruments and singing.

Bossa nova was modern, sophisticated and intellectual. More than a musical style or movement, it immediately became associated with the new class of university-educated

Brazilians. It was also a musical response to other modernist movements that flourished during the optimistic administration of Juscelino Kubitschek (1956–61), which was the upbeat bridge between the postwar and the hippie eras.

By the 1960s, bossa nova had become a huge international success. The genre's initial development was greatly influenced by American jazz and blues, and over time, the bossa nova style came to influence those music styles as well. Bossa nova classics were adopted, adapted and recorded by such musical luminaries as Frank Sinatra, Ella Fitzgerald and Stan Getz, among others.

Great Brazilian bossa nova singers include Gal Costa and Beth Carvalho, with Elis Regina as the eternal queen. She was known to her public as *furacão* (hurricane), reflecting the intense emotion with which she sang (and lived). Regina's accidental death from an overdose in 1982, at the peak of her career, was regarded as a national tragedy.

10 Brazilian CDs – One for Every Taste

This list includes different types of Brazilian music, from classic samba and bossa nova to Música Popular Brasileiro (MPB) and electronic music. It will give you an introduction to the variety of Brazilian sounds.

- *Black Orpheus (Orfeu Negro)*, Antônio Carlos Jobim and Luiz Bonfá (1959) Bossa nova's introduction to the world.
- *Brasilidade*, Bossacucanova and Roberto Menescal (2001) Bossa nova classics remixed with DJ dance rhythms.
- *Brasil 2Mil: The Soul of Bass-O-Nova*, various artists (1999) Compilation of new happenings.
- *Getz/Gilberto* (1963) The famed collaboration that brought bossa's rhythms to the world stage.
- *Nova Bossa, Red Hot on Verve*, various artists (1996) Classic bossa nova stylings.
- *Red, Hot + Rio*, various artists (1996) Classics remixed and recorded by world-renowned musicians.
- *África Brasil*, Jorge Ben (1976) The mix of samba and funk made Ben's album an instant classic.
- *São Paulo Confessions*, Suba (2000) Modern ambient dance.
- *Tribalistas*, Marisa Monte, Carlinhos Brown and Arnaldo Antunes (2002) This exquisitely produced album combines MPB with bossa nova, samba and electronic beats.
- *Tropicalia: ou Panis et Circences*, Caetano Veloso, Gal Costa, et al (1968) This politically charged album is among the most important of its era.

TROPICALIA

A response to bossa nova, *tropicalia* was a late '60s and early '70s musical movement that incorporated American rock and roll, blues, jazz and British psychedelic styles into bossa nova and samba rhythms. The heart of the movement was in Bahia, propelled by Caetano Veloso and Gilberto Gil.

Tropicalia's break with the musical traditions of bossa nova and *choró* (romantic samba) was in part a response to the harsh political climate of the military dictatorship that took over in the '60s. Other *tropicalia* artists include Jorge Ben, Gal Costa, the psychedelic rock band Os Mutantes and the experimental Tom Zé.

FORRÓ

Forró is accordion-laced dance music from the Northeast, featuring syncopated rhythms similar to samba and Mexican mariachi music. The father of *forró* is Luiz Gonzaga, whose song 'Asa Branca' (*White Wing*) has become the theme song of *forró* and of the Northeastern *sertão* (interior). Asa Branca, incidentally, is also the name of a *forró* and samba club in Lapa.

Forró is high-octane dance music. Bands, musicians and singers take turns on the stage, and the *forró* dance party lasts for many hours. Legend has it that the name *forró* is a bastardization of the English words 'for all,' picked up when American GIs were stationed in Brazil. Other popular *forró* artists include Jackson do Pandeiro and the queen of *forró*, Elba Ramalho.

MPB, ELECTRONIC MUSIC & BEYOND

Música Popular Brasileira (MPB) is a catchphrase to describe all popular Brazilian music after bossa nova. It includes *tropicalia, pagoda,* and Brazilian pop and rock. All Brazilian music has roots in samba, and even in Brazilian rock, heavy metal, disco or dance, the samba sound is present.

Today, Marisa Monte is popular within Brazil and throughout the world, both for her fine songwriting and her smooth vocals. Her songs mix samba, *forró,* pop and rock sounds. Her collaboration with Arto Lindsay in 1994 helped to make her music popular throughout the world. More recently (in 2002), she teamed up with Arnaldo Antunes and Carlinhos Brown, both popular soloists in their own right, and produced the album *Tribalistas,* which has been a hit all over the world (especially after the trio performed at the Grammy Awards in 2003). It's easily Monte's best album since her 1996 release, *A Great Noise.*

Brazil has a wide variety of pop and rock favorites. The group Legião Urbana has been a national favorite for many years, even after the death of its lead singer, Renato Russo, in 1997. They have a smooth pop sound with poetic lyrics. Cidade Negra is a pop-reggae band from the north of Rio which features a rhythm section even Caribbeans would envy. Other big pop-rock bands include Skank, Paralamas do Sucesso and Lulu Santos. There's even in-your-face Brazilian punk, with artist Charlie Brown Jr making fun of the different styles of Brazilian music. Techno-funk is a techno-rap music style, which usually features one or two guys rapping over a techno beat; Bonde do Tigrão and Popozuda are two singers in this style.

From Recife, Chico Science and Nação Zumbi started the *manguebeat* style of music in the mid-1990s. They mixed funk, hip-hop, samba and *maracatu,* a musical style from Recife that has its history in black coronation pageants, to create a unique swamp groove. Sadly, Chico Science was killed in a car crash in 1997, but Lamento Negro continues to make music in the same style. From São Paulo comes the group Suba, which leans toward the ambient side of dance music, with dreamy vocals and heavy Brazilian rhythms. The trio Zuco 103 plays a mix of trip-hop, jazz and, of course, samba rhythms. The Six Degrees record label produces a lot of fabulous contemporary Brazilian music.

Gil *Tom Phillips*

Only in Brazil would you expect to find a pop star in government. Forget Silvio Berlusconi's crooning, or Tony Blair's attempts at Christian rock – Gilberto Gil has been one of Brazil's best-loved musicians since the 1960s.

Gil was always an *engajado* – during the 1960s he spent two years exiled in London after offending the dictatorship with his surreal, provocative lyrics. It's just that these days he's engaged in a different way, occupying an office in Brasília's Planalto, where he is the Minister of Culture in President Lula's cabinet.

A household name for decades, 'Gil' hails from the Northeastern state of Bahia. Born in 1942, he was raised in a middle-class family near Salvador. His career as a troubadour began in 1965, when he moved south to São Paulo with another Bahian musician Caetano Veloso. Between them they were responsible for *tropicalismo,* an influential though short-lived cultural movement that blended traditional Brazilian music with the electric guitars and psychedelia of The Beatles. Years later Veloso even recorded a Tupiniquim (an indigenous group in the Northeast) tribute to the Liverpool rockers – called *Sugar Cane Fields Forever.*

Over the decades Gil has notched up hit after hit – morphing from quick-footed *sambista* (samba dancer) to Stevie Wonder-esque balladeer to dreadlocked reggae icon. His latest album, *Kaya N'Gan Daya,* was a tribute to his idol Bob Marley. In 2003 he even took the stage with the United Nations secretary general in New York: Kofi Annan on bongos, Gil on guitar.

In between world tours, book launches and his ministerial duties, the slender 61 year old even finds time for the beach. Keep your eyes peeled – it's not uncommon to find Gil sunning himself at Ipanema's Posto 9.

Here is some essential listening:

- *Gilberto Gil,* Gilberto Gil
- *MTV Unplugged,* Gilberto Gil
- *Quanta,* Gilberto Gil
- *Refazenda,* Gilberto Gil
- *Tropicalia 2,* Gilberto Gil and Caetano Veloso
- *Tropicalia, ou Panis et Circencis,* Gilberto Gil, Caetano Veloso, Gal Costa and Os Mutantes

Baile Funk (p136)

Bebel Gilberto, the daughter of João Gilberto, has followed in her father's footsteps and gone beyond. Like many of the new Brazilian musicians, she has her roots in bossa nova, while incorporating rock techniques into many of her songs.

Recently, Brazil's music scene has experienced a resurgence of taking traditional bossa nova classics and remixing and rerecording them using dance, pop, jazz and rock techniques. It's the way Brazilian music has always redefined and reinvented itself. There's no doubt that Brazilians will always make music, and it will always make you want to move. For a more detailed history of Brazilian music, check out the book *The Brazilian Sound* by Chris McGowan and Ricardo Pessanha.

CINEMA

Rio has been the home of Brazilian cinema since the beginning of the 20th century, when, appropriately, the city itself starred in the first film made in the country – a slow pan of Baía de Guanabara, made in 1898.

From 1942 until 1962, Rio was the home of Atlântida Productions, which churned out musicals, comedies and romances. Neorealism was one of the earliest movements affecting Brazil cinema. *O Cangaceiro* (*The Brigand*; 1953) by Lima Barreto was one of the first Brazilian films to receive international recognition. The film chronicles the adventures of a roving band of outlaws, and was inspired by the Northeast's most infamous outlaw, Lampião.

Rio starred again in Marcel Camus' 1959 film *Orfeu Negro* (*Black Orpheus*), which opened the world's ears to bossa nova by way of the Jobim and Bonfá soundtrack. In the 1960s, several directors focused on Brazil's bleak social problems, and the Cinema Novo movement was born. One of the great films from this movement was the 1962 *O Pagador de Promessas* (*The Payer of Vows*), which garnered much international attention after winning the Palme D'Or at the Cannes Film Festival. Glauber Rocha was one of the great pioneers in Cinema Novo. In *Deus e o Diabo na Terra do Sol* (*Black God, White Devil*; 1963), he forged a polemical national style using Afro-Brazilian traditions in conscious resistance to the influences of Hollywood. His work touches on elements of mysticism without steering from political issues.

From Favela to Fame

In 1981 director Hector Babenco ignited a great deal of controversy after recruiting homeless children to star in his socially provocative film, *Pixote*. The 11-year-old prodigy Fernando Ramos da Silva was literally plucked from the streets to play the title role, and as the film screened worldwide, the expressive young actor brought attention to others just like him, living and dying in the inner city. Unfortunately, fame didn't stick for Fernando, and he soon returned to the streets, living in the same impoverished conditions he had when he played Pixote. Sadly, Fernando died at the hands of São Paolo police during a bungled robbery in 1987.

Fernando Meirelles also recruited a number of children from local favelas (shanty towns) to act in the powerful *Cidade de Deus* (City of God; 2002). Unlike Ramos da Silva before, many of them have gone on to play other roles. Two of the film's young stars – Douglas Silva and Darlan Cunha – were even invited to meet President Lula, who praised their work and recommended that every Brazilian see the film. Douglas Silva was able to move his family from the favela to an upscale neighborhood in Barra da Tijuca where, at last check, the 13-year-old actor was living the 'playboy lifestyle' he'd always wanted. More importantly, his parents envision him one day going to college – an impossibility before his fame.

The military dictatorship stymied much creative expression in the country – and the film industry was naturally affected. Since the end of the dictatorship, Brazil has enjoyed a film renaissance, although much of the money and talent these days is channeled into *telenovelas* (TV soap operas), which are followed religiously by much of the country. Most of the high-quality *telenovelas* are made at the Rio studios of Rede Globo.

The first major film produced after the end of the dictatorship was *Bye Bye Brasil* (1980) by Carlos Diegues. It chronicles the adventures of a theater troupe as they tour the entire country, performing in small villages and towns. Hector Babenco's *Pixote* (1981) came soon after, a powerful film that indicted Brazilian society for its indifference to the poor. It tells the story of a street kid in Rio, who gets swept along from innocent naïveté to murderer by the currents of the underworld.

Bruno Barreto's *O Que É Isso Companheiro* (released as *Four Days in September* in the US; 1998) is based on the 1969 kidnapping of the US ambassador to Brazil by leftist guerrillas. It was nominated for an Oscar in 1998.

Carla Camarut's *Carlota Joaquina – Princesa do Brasil*, a hilarious blend of fairy tale, satire and historical drama, is about a Spanish princess married to the Portuguese prince regent (later Dom João VI) when the entire Portuguese court fled to Brazil to escape Napoleon.

Walter Salles is one of Brazil's best-known directors. His first feature film *Terra Estrangeiro* (*Foreign Land*), shot in 1995, holds an important place in the renaissance of Brazilian cinema. The film won seven international prizes and was shown at over two dozen film festivals. It was named Best Film of the Year in Brazil in 1996, where it screened for over six months. Salles is also a great documentary filmmaker; *Socorro Nobre* (*Life Somewhere Else*) and *Krajcberg* (*The Poet of the Remains*), among others, won awards at many international festivals.

Central do Brasil (*Central Station*; 1998) is one of Salles' most famous films. It won an Oscar in 1998 for best foreign film. The central character is an elderly woman who works in the train station in Rio writing letters for illiterates with families far away. After a chance encounter with a young homeless boy, she accompanies him on a search for his father into the real, unglamorized Brazil. At the time of research, Salles was at Sundance screening his recently completed epic *Diarios de Motocicleta* (*The Motorcycle Diaries*), which details the historic journey of Che Guevara and Alberto Granada across South America, and stars Johnny Depp.

Eu, Tu, Eles (*Me, You, Them*), Andrucha Waddington's social comedy about a Northeasterner with three husbands, was also well received when it was released in 2000. It has beautiful cinematography and a score by Gilberto Gil (currently President Lula's Minister of Culture), which contributed to the recent wave of popularity for that funky Northeastern music, *forró*.

Fernando Meirelles is one of Brazil's most talented young directors. His first feature-length film, *Domésticas* (*Maids*; 2001) gives an insight into the millions of domestic servants who work in Brazil. His latest film, *Cidade de Deus* (*City of God*), is based on a true story by Paolo Lins. It gives an honest and heart-wrenching portrayal of life in a Rio favela (shanty town). After its release in 2002, it brought much attention to the plight of the urban poor, and director Fernando Meirelles was nominated for an Oscar (Best Director) in 2004. It also spawned many spin-offs, including *Cidade de Homens*, a popular TV series about Rio's favela gangs, also directed by Meirelles.

LITERATURE

Since the mid-1990s Brazilians have been buying books in record numbers, and good Brazilian novels are increasingly being translated into English. Best-selling author Paolo Coelho, a Carioca, has sold more than 10 million books (among his 12 titles) in Brazil alone. He's Latin America's second most read novelist (after Gabriel García Márquez). Coelho's more recent efforts, such as *Veronika Decides to Die*, about a writer committed to a mental hospital after a suicide attempt, and *The Fifth Mountain*, a fictionalized tale about the prophet Elijah, are more sophisticated than the New-Age spiritual fables with which he sprang to fame in the mid-1990s in books, such as *The Alchemist* and *The Pilgrimage*.

Going back in history, José de Alencar is one of Brazil's famous 19th-century writers. Many of his works are set in Rio, including *Cinco Minutos* and *Senhora*, both published in 1875. Joaquim Manoel de Macedo was a great chronicler of the customs of his time. In addition to such romances as *A Moreninha*, he also wrote *Um Passeio pela Cidade do Rio de Janeiro*, published in 1863, and *Memórias da Rua do Ouvidor*, published in 1878.

Joaquim Maria Machado de Assis (1839–1908), another Carioca, is widely regarded as Brazil's greatest writer. The son of a freed slave, Assis worked as a typesetter and journalist in late 19th-century Rio. A tremendous stylist with a great command of humor and irony, Assis had an understanding of human relations, which he tweaked into his brilliantly cynical works. He used Rio as the background for most of his works in the late 19th century, in books such as *The Posthumous Memoirs of Bras Cubas* and *Quincas Borba* (previously published as *Epitaph of a Small Winner* and *Philosopher or Dog?*, respectively). The excellent new translations by Rabassa capture the essence of this great writer. Machado's other major novel was *Dom Casmurro*.

Arts – Literature

Toca do Vinícius (p59)

Brazil's most famous writer is Jorge Amado, who died in August 2001. Born near Ilhéus in 1912, and a long-time resident of Salvador, Amado wrote colorful romances of Bahia's people and places, with touches of magical realism. His early work was strongly influenced by communism. His later books are lighter in subject, but more picturesque and intimate in style. The two most acclaimed are *Gabriela, Clove and Cinnamon*, which is set in Ilhéus, and *Dona Flor and Her Two Husbands*, which is set in Salvador. The latter relates the tale of a young woman who must decide between two lovers – the first being the man she marries after her first husband drops dead at Carnaval, the second being her deceased husband who returns to her as a ghost. The ensuing ménage à trois is delightfully portrayed. His other works include *Tent of Miracles*, which explores race relations in Brazil, and *Pen, Sword and Camisole*, which exposes the petty political maneuverings in the realm of academic and military politics. *The Violent Land* is an early Amado classic – something of a dark frontier story novel. *Shepherds of the Night*, three short stories about a group of Bahian characters, provides another excellent and witty portrait of Bahia.

Mario de Andrade (1893–45) is another great Brazilian writer. He led the country's artistic renaissance in the 1920s, and became one of the leading figures in the modernist movement. In works such as *Macunaíma* he pioneered the used of vernacular language in national literature. He stressed the importance of Brazilian writers to draw from their own rich heritage. At the same time, his work showed elements of surrealism and was later seen as a precursor to magical realism.

Existentialist-influenced Clarice Lispector (1925–77) wrote several collections of short stories, focusing on human isolation, alienation and moral doubt. *Family Ties* and *Soulstorm* are among her best works.

Themes of repression and violence began appearing at the end of the 1960s with the advent of the military dictatorship. The bizarre and brutal *Zero*, by Ignácio de Loyola Brandão, was banned by the government until a national protest helped lift the prohibition. For a glimpse of Rio's big-city rival, take a look at Ivan Ângelo's *Tower of Glass*, five absurdist stories that paint a cynical portrait of São Paolo.

Dinah Silveira de Queiroz's *The Women of Brazil* is about a Portuguese girl who goes to 17th-century Brazil to meet her betrothed. Another excellent writer is Joyce Cavalcante who emerged in the 1990s as a writer able to express the experience of women in modern Brazil as well as the enduring social problems of the Northeast. *Intimate Enemies*, a tale of corruption, violence and polygamy, is her best-known work.

Contemporary Brazilian writers who have found inspiration in Rio include Manuel Bandeira, and Nelson Rodrigues, whose *A Vida Como Ela É...* is a selection of short stories that provides a fascinating insight into what makes Cariocas tick.

ARCHITECTURE

Rio contains a rich array of architectural styles from the 17th, 18th, 19th and 20th centuries, all cobbled together in Rio's downtown district (Centro).

The most impressive edifices remaining from the 17th century are the churches built by the Jesuits, the **Convento de Santo Antônio** (p81) and the **Monasteiro de São Bento** (p81), both good examples of the religious baroque style. They are typified by their ornate use of gold throughout the interior of the churches.

With the arrival of a French artistic mission in 1816, neoclassicism became the official style of the empire. French architect Victor Grandjean de Montigny planned many buildings around the city and introduced the official study of architecture to Brazilian students. Constructions became grandiose and monumental, dominated by classical features, such as columns and smooth walls. The **Museu Nacional de Belas Artes** (p82) and the **Teatro Municipal** (p82), which was modeled after the Paris Opéra, are two fine examples from this period.

By the beginning of the 20th century, art nouveau, again influenced by French taste for curved lines and natural themes, appeared in Rio. An excellent example is the interior of the **Confeitaria Colombo** (p120).

Between 1903 and 1906, Rio's mayor Pereira Passos instituted a major remodeling of the city, with the construction of grand avenues, tunnels, parks and an extensive urban sanitation system. Although some of Rio's colonial buildings were destroyed in the process, the mayor did create the city's main boulevard (now Av Rio Branco) in order to showcase the Teatro Municipal, the **Biblioteca National** (p79), and dozens of other stately buildings that lined the avenue.

The art deco movement influenced Brazil in the 1930s, and good specimens include the central train station and the **statue of Cristo Redentor** (p76) on Corcovado.

Brazilian architecture didn't develop its own style until 1930. Influenced by the modernist ideas of Le Corbusier, a new generation of Brazilian architects, notably Lúcio Costa and Oscar Niemeyer, adopted and developed the functional style, with its extensive use of steel and glass, and lack of ornamentation. The **Museu de Arte Moderna** (inaugurated in 1958) and the **Catedral Metropolitana** (begun in 1964; p86) are good examples of this style. You can also see Corbusier-influenced design at work in the Aeropuerto Santos Dumont (completed in 1937).

One of the most fascinating modern buildings close to Rio is the Niemeyer-designed **Museu do Arte Contemporânea** (MAC; p90) in Niterói. Its fluid form and delicate curves are reminiscent of a flower in bloom. It also showcases the natural setting and offers stunning views of Rio.

For additional information on Rio's landmark buildings, turn to the Neighborhoods chapter (p51).

Museu de Arte Moderna (p87)

VISUAL ARTS

Rio has always inspired landscape painters, which is easy to understand. The 19th-century French artists Jean-Baptiste Debret and Nicolas Taunay made good use of the exuberant landscape around the city. They arrived with a French artistic mission to the city in 1816, and taught in the Academía de Belas Artes, which organized classes, expositions and art awards. Debret's and Taunay's works in oil and watercolors are some of the first visual records of life in the colony.

The French influence remained strong and neoclassicism dominated in the 19th century. During this period Victor Meirelles (1832–1903) emerged as Brazil's best-known painter of the time. One of his most famous works is *A Primeira Missa*, painted in 1861. It depicts the first Mass celebrated in the new colony, with Pedro Álvarez Cabral (Portuguese discoverer of Brazil) and his men in attendance. Meirelles' most important works hang in the **Museu Nacional de Belas Artes** (p82). Eliséu d'Angelo Visconti (1866–1944) is another of the early artists converted by neoclassicism. His most important work was for the **Teatro Municipal** (p82), for which he painted the frieze and ceiling.

Modernism arrived in Brazil when the painter Anita Malfatti (1889–1964) returned from Paris and began executing works that showed strong influences from the European avant-garde. Although Brazilian artists of that time showed traces of cubism and futurism – and other European currents – in their work, they still imbued their canvases with uniquely Brazilian subject matter. A number of other important painters and sculptors emerged from that time: Osvaldo Goeldi, John Graz, Emiliano di Cavalcanti (who painted scenes from Carnaval; 1897–1976) and the sculptor Victor Brecheret.

In the 19th and 20th centuries, Brazilian artists followed international trends, such as neoclassicism, romanticism, impressionism and modernism. Internationally, the best-known Brazilian painter is Cândido Portinari (1903–62). Early in his career he made the decision to paint only Brazil and its people. Strongly influenced by the Mexican muralists, such as Diego Rivera, he managed to fuse native, expressionist influences into a powerful, socially conscious and sophisticated style. His best-known work is a fresco inside Oscar Niemeyer's chapel of São Francisco in Belo Horizonte.

Teatro Municipal (p82)

THEATER & DANCE

Following Brazil's independence in 1822, the first Brazilian theater troupes were formed, and playwrights soon developed a national style. The poet and writer Gonçalves Dias (1823–64) was among the first Brazilians to write plays. Only a handful of Dias' work remains, and the romantic figure (who later died in a shipwreck) is more known for his poetry. His lyric 'Cançao do Exílio' is his dedication to Brazil's natural beauty.

During the days of the early Republic, other great works were produced. Well-known writers, such as José de Alencar, Machado de Assis and Artur Azevedo, wrote plays in addition to literary works, which expanded the national repertoire of Brazil's growing theaters.

In the 1940s, Nelson Rodrigues (1912–80) was instrumental in transforming Brazilian theater. His socially conscious plays revealed the moral hypocrisy of upper-class Brazilian families. The 1950s saw a flourishing of the theater arts. Playwrights, such as Gianfranco Guarnieri, Jorge Andrade and Ariano Suassuna, created more experimental works, and a dynamic theater scene emerged in Rio and São Paolo.

The 1964 military coup stifled creative works across the arts. Censorship remained in force until 1979 when the country returned to democracy. Since then, things have slowly revitalized on stage. New playwrights are emerging, just as old classics are being reinvestigated. The works of Nelson Rodrigues are still commonly performed by Rio's theater companies.

The magnificent **Teatro Municipal** (p82) in Centro is reserved for the higher performing arts, and is home for the city's world-class ballet troupe, opera company and orchestra.

There are dozens of other theaters in Rio, which put on anything from international musicals to plays with Brazilian themes (p124).

History

History

THE RECENT PAST

Today Rio is more full of optimism and hope than it has been in years. The city buzzes with an unstoppable creative energy, and long-awaited projects are finally being financed. The biggest is the controversial Favela-Bairro project, which strives to integrate favelas (shanty towns) into the rest of the city by providing basic sanitation and planning leisure areas, health clinics, schools, preschools and community centers. At the same time, some of Rio's aging colonial gems are being revitalized, and businesses are springing up all over town. As a result, Rio looks better than it has in quite some time and Cariocas (residents of Rio) seem to be hopeful about the future. Other projects that mayor Cesar Maia has helped bring to Rio include the 2007 Pan-American Games and a branch of the Guggenheim museum, the first ever in Latin America.

FROM THE BEGINNING

Archaeological evidence shows that humans have lived around the Baía de Guanabara (Guanabara Bay) for at least 10,000 years. Some even speculate that humans have been in the area for as long as 50,000 years. The oldest remains are found in high columns of shell deposits called *sambaquis*. These mounds also contain burial remains, traces of old cooking fires, and bones transformed into utensils and ornaments, such as needles, arrowheads, knives and necklaces of fish vertebrae.

Higher in the strata, ceramics are found, indicating a more settled lifestyle. Many shell mounds are located along the coast of Rio State: Baía de Sepetiba, the Restinga da Marambaia, Guaratiba, around Baía de Guanabara, Saquarema and Cabo Frio. When the Portuguese arrived, the region was home to two main Indian groups: the Temiminós and their rivals, the bellicose and powerful Tamoios.

Gaspar de Lemos set sail from Portugal for Brazil in May 1501 and entered a huge bay in January 1502. Mistaking the bay for a river, he named it Rio de Janeiro. It was the French, however, who became the first Europeans to settle along the great bay. Like the Portuguese, the French had been harvesting dyewood along the Brazilian coast, but unlike the Portuguese they hadn't attempted any permanent settlements in this region until Rio de Janeiro.

As the Portuguese colonization of Brazil began to take hold, the French became concerned that they'd be pushed out of the colony. Three ships of French settlers reached the Baía de Guanabara in 1555. They settled on a small island in the bay and called it Antarctic France.

The town seemed doomed to failure almost from the start. It was torn by religious divisions and demoralized by the puritanical rule of the French leader Nicolas de Villegagnon. Antarctic France was weak and disheartened when the Portuguese, led by Estácio de Sá (nephew of Mem de Sá, governor of Brazil), attacked in 1565.

Allied with the French during this period were the Tamoio Indians, led by their fierce chief, Cunhambebe. The Tamoio hated the Portuguese for the cruelty the colonizers had already displayed, and they had also entered into a relatively profitable barter trade with the French. A series of battles occurred, but the Portuguese were better armed and better supplied than the French, who were finally expelled in 1567. Estácio de Sá himself was among those killed. The victors then drove the Tamoio from the region in another series of bloody battles.

TIMELINE	8000 BC	1502	1567
	Ancestors of Tamoio living along Baía de Guanabara (Guanabara Bay)	Portuguese explorer Gaspar de Lemos sails into Baía de Guanabara after an eight-month voyage	Portuguese set up the first settlement on Morro do Castelo

By the 17th century, the Tamoio had been wiped out. Those who weren't taken into slavery were depleted by disease or killed by colonists. Other Indians were 'pacified' and forced to live in settlements organized by the priests. Many of today's Cariocas are descended from these first inhabitants.

THE FIRST TOWN

The Portuguese set up a fortified town on Morro do Castelo in 1567 to maximize protection from European invasion by sea and Indian attack by land. They named their town São Sebastião do Rio de Janeiro, in honor of King Sebastião of Portugal.

The 500 founding Cariocas built a typical Brazilian town: poorly planned, with irregular streets in the medieval Portuguese style. By the end of the century, the small settlement was, if not exactly prosperous, surviving on the export of brazilwood and sugarcane, and from fishing in Baía de Guanabara.

In 1660 the city had a population made up of 3000 Indians, 750 Portuguese and 100 blacks. It grew along the waterfront and what is now Praça 15 de Novembro. Next came the religious orders – the Franciscans, the Jesuits and the Benedictines – all of whom built austere, closed-in churches, some of which survive today.

Praça XV de Novembro (p82)

ECONOMIC GROWTH

With its excellent harbor and good lands for sugarcane, Rio became Brazil's third most important settlement (after Salvador da Bahia and Recife-Olinda) in the 17th century. Huge numbers of slaves were brought from Africa and the sugar plantations thrived. The owners of the sugar estates lived in the protection and comfort of the fortified city.

The gold rush in Minas Gerais had a profound effect on Rio and caused major demographic shifts on three continents. The rare metal was first discovered by *bandeirantes* in the 1690s, and as word spread gold seekers arrived in droves. Over the next half century, an estimated 500,000 Portuguese arrived in Brazil just as many thousands of African slaves were imported. Rio served as the natural port of entry for this flow of people and commerce to and from the Minas Gerais goldfields.

As a result of all the wealth passing through the city, Rio's population and economy grew rapidly, and the city became the prize of Brazil. In 1710 the French, who had extended their wars with Portugal to the colonies, attacked the city. The French were initially defeated, but a second expedition succeeded, forcing the entire population to abandon the city by cover of night.

The occupying French forces threatened to level the city unless a sizable ransom in gold, sugar and cattle was paid. The Portuguese obliged. During the return voyage to an expected heroes' welcome in France, the victors lost two ships and most of the gold.

1570	1599	1690s	1763
Portuguese begin importing slaves into Brazil	All of the Tamoios have been wiped out by smallpox and other diseases	Gold is discovered in Minas Gerais	Rio's population swells to 50,000 and the capital of Brazil moves from Salvador to Rio

Rio quickly recovered from the setback. Its fortifications were improved, many richly decorated churches were built, and by 1763 its population had reached 50,000. With international sugar prices slumping and the sugar economy in the doldrums, Rio replaced the more sugar-dependent Salvador da Bahia as the colonial capital. The city expanded south toward Botafogo and north to São Cristóvão. Main streets were paved and swampy areas were filled.

GROWTH OF THE MODERN CITY

In 1807 Napoleon's army marched on Lisbon. Two days before the invasion, 40 ships carrying the Portuguese prince regent (later known as Dom João VI) and his entire court of 15,000 had set sail for Brazil under the protection of British warships. When the prince regent arrived in Rio, his Brazilian subjects celebrated wildly, dancing in the streets. He immediately took over rule of Brazil from his viceroy.

As foreigners have been doing ever since, Dom João VI fell in love with Brazil. A great admirer of nature, he founded Rio's botanical gardens and introduced the habit of sea

Igreja de Nossa Senhora da Glória de Outeiro (p78)

bathing to the water-wary inhabitants of Rio. With the court came an influx of money and talent that helped build some of the city's lasting monuments, such as the palace at the Quinta da Boa Vista.

Within a year of his arrival, Dom João VI also created the School of Medicine, the Bank of Brazil, the Law Courts, the Naval Academy and the Royal Printing Works. Talented French exiles, such as the architect Victor Grandjean de Montigny and the painters Jean-Baptiste Debret and Nicolas Antoine Taunay, also had a profound influence on Rio's cultural life.

Dom João VI was expected to return to Portugal after Napoleon's Waterloo in 1815, but instead stayed in Brazil. The following year his mother, mad queen Dona Maria I, died, and Dom João VI became king. He refused demands to return to Portugal to rule, and he declared Rio the capital of the United Kingdom of Portugal, Brazil and the Algarves. Brazil became the only New World colony to ever have a European monarch ruling on its soil.

Five years later Dom João VI finally relented to political pressures and returned to Portugal, leaving his son Pedro in Brazil as prince regent. According to legend, in 1822 Pedro pulled out his sword and yelled 'Independência ou morte!' ('Independence or death!'), putting himself at the country's head as Emperor Dom Pedro I. Portugal was too weak to fight its favorite son, not to mention the British, who had the most to gain from Brazilian independence and would have come to the aid of the Brazilians. The Brazilian Empire was born. Without spilling blood, Brazil had attained its independence and Dom Pedro I became the first emperor of Brazil.

1807	1815	1816	1820
Napoleon invades Portugal and the Portuguese prince regent (later known as Dom João VI) gets the hell out of Dodge	Napolean has his Waterloo; Dom João VI decides he'd rather stay in the tropics than return to Portugal	Dom João VI declares Rio the capital of the United Kingdom of Portugal, Brazil and the Algarves	Portuguese Parliament threaten to curtail Dom João VI's power, so he returns to Portugal, leaving his son Dom Pedro I in charge

The Once and Future Dom

When Pedro I declared independence from Portugal in 1822, he had the whole country behind him. Yet as he continued governing Brazil in the same imperial manner as it had been governed previously, the citizens grew discontented. His involvement in a war with Argentina made him unpopular, as did his prolific extramarital affairs. The most torrid of these affairs involved Domitila de Castro, the wife of an army officer, who bore him several children. His growing unpopularity and the death of his father in Portugal forced him to abdicate the throne and return to Lisbon. Pedro left his eldest son, Pedro II, to take his place.

Pedro II seemed an unlikely candidate for success – especially given that he was only five years old and virtually orphaned by his father and mother. Yet, unlike his bumbling father, Pedro II blossomed. The country's best tutors taught him Latin, Greek, French, German, Spanish and English, and he received a broad education in the arts and sciences. Inspired by his tutors, he developed a cunning intelligence and a deep curiosity that would remain with him throughout his life. In some ways, he became the enlightened monarch envisioned by 18th-century thinkers.

While he grew up, a council of regents appointed by parliament ruled the country. Bitter power struggles resulted from the sharing of power, and civil revolts threatened the unity of the young nation. Although the constitution did not allow him to be coronated until his 18th birthday, the parliament, seeing the boy's maturity and hoping to bring an end to the country's strife, offered him the crown in 1840 when he was just 14 years old.

His rule for the next 49 years would be one of the most prosperous epochs in the country's history. In contrast to the instability plaguing other Latin American countries, Brazil remained a peaceful nation with power shared between liberals and conservatives. Pedro II oversaw the end of slavery (without bloodshed) and kept the military intentionally weak (contrasting again with other Latin American nations), at least until he was drawn into a conflict with Paraguay.

As Pedro II grew older, he fell out of favor with certain key support groups, and in 1889, after almost 50 years in power, he was toppled by a group of conspirators in a coup d'état. The move caught Pedro II off guard, and with little support around him, he chose to go into exile.

On the following day, the royal family set sail for Europe. The journey must have been hard on the empress, who died within a month. Pedro II never recovered from the loss of his country and then his wife. He died two years later (1891) in a hotel in Paris. Still banned from Brazil, his body was laid in the royal mausoleum in Portugal beside his father and grandfather. But in 1922, during the celebration of Brazil's centennial of independence, the bodies of Pedro II and the empress were returned to the country they loved for reburial.

Dom Pedro I ruled for only nine years. From all accounts, he was a bumbling incompetent who scandalized even the permissive Brazilians by siring several soccer teams of illegitimate children. He also strongly resisted any attempts to weaken his power by constitutional means. In 1831 he surprised everyone by abdicating, paving the way for his five-year-old, Brazilian-born son to become emperor.

Until Dom Pedro II reached adolescence, Brazil suffered through a turbulent period of unrest under the rule of a weak triple regency. In 1840, at the age of 14, Dom Pedro II took the throne. During his reign he nurtured an increasingly powerful parliamentary system, went to war with Paraguay, meddled in Argentine, Paraguayan and Uruguayan affairs, encouraged mass immigration, abolished slavery, and became the first man in Brazil to have his photograph taken and to speak on the telephone (though not at the same time). The nation rallied behind the young emperor, and his 49-year reign is regarded as the most prosperous period in Brazilian history. Ultimately, he forged a nation that would do away with the monarchy forever.

The coffee boom in the mountains of São Paulo and Rio revitalized Brazil's economy during the 19th century. Rio took on a new importance as a port and commercial center, and coffee commerce modernized the city. Regular passenger ships began sailing to London (1845) and Paris (1851), and the local ferry service to Niterói began in 1862. A telegraph system and gas streetlights were installed in 1854. By 1860 Rio had a population of more than 250,000 inhabitants making it the largest city in South America.

1822	1831	1840	1888
Dom Pedro I declares independence from Portugal and crowns himself emperor	The Brazilians realize Dom Pedro I is incompetent and he is forced to abdicate the throne	After a long period of instability, Dom Pedro I's 14-year-old son takes the throne	Slavery abolished

As Rio's population grew, so too did the number of slaves imported to meet the labor needs of the expanding coffee plantations on the slopes of the Paraíba Valley. By the early 19th century, African slaves made up two-thirds of Rio's population. The abolition movement in Europe brought pressure on the Brazilian government, which outlawed the trade in 1830. However, illegal trade continued well into the 1850s, when the British took it upon themselves to suppress it with their naval squadrons.

Eliminating slavery in Brazil was a pet project of the enlightened Dom Pedro II. By the mid-1880s, the abolition movement in Brazil, led by Joaquim Nabuco, became a popular crusade. On May 13, 1888, the National Assembly passed the abolition decree, which was approved and announced by Princesa Isabel, acting as regent for her father who was in Europe. No compensation was offered to slave owners, and their plotting eventually led to the downfall of the monarchy and proclamation of the new Brazilian Republic in 1889.

Positivism and the Young Republic

In 1891, two years after Pedro II abdicated, Brazil adopted a constitution, modeled on the US charter. The fledgling republic also designed a new flag, with the slogan 'Order and Progress.' This phrase came from French philosopher Auguste de Comte (1797–1857), whose ideas were extremely influential on the thinking of the early Republicans. His philosophy, known as positivism, glorified reason and scientific knowledge and rejected traditional religious beliefs. De Comte believed that humanity would one day overcome its superstitions of the past and with the help of science, or positive knowledge, enter a new era – one where specialists would run an authoritarian republic to achieve true progress. He summed up his ideas in the following lines: 'Love as the principle. Order as the base. Progress as the goal.' Unfortunately for its citizens, the Brazilian Republic's early leaders left love out of the equation.

POPULATION EXPLOSION & THE 20TH CENTURY

At the end of the 19th century, the city's population exploded because of European immigration and internal migration (mostly ex-slaves from the declining coffee and sugar regions). By 1890 Rio boasted more than a million inhabitants, a quarter of them foreign-born.

The city spread rapidly between the steep hills, bay and ocean. The first tunnel through the mountains to Copacabana was built in 1892, and the Leme Tunnel was completed in 1904. The rich started to move further out, a pattern that continues today.

Radical changes took place in the city center. In 1904 almost 600 buildings were cleared to make way for Ave Central (later renamed Rio Branco), which became the Champs Élysées of Rio, an elegant boulevard full of sidewalk cafés and promenading Cariocas.

The early 1920s to the late 1950s are remembered by many as Rio's golden age. With the inauguration of the grand luxury resort hotels (the Glória in 1922 and the Copacabana Palace in 1924), Rio became a romantic, exotic destination for Hollywood celebrities and international high society. They came to play and gamble at the casinos and dance or perform in the nightclubs.

Visitors included Lana Turner, Jayne Mansfield, Josephine Baker, Eva Perón, Maurice Chevalier and Ali Khan. Orson Welles stayed at the Copacabana Palace in 1942 and partied hard. He even threw furniture out the window in a jealous rage – years before rock stars were to follow the trend.

Rio continued to change. Three large landfill projects were undertaken to ease the strain on a city restricted by its beautiful surroundings. The first was to become Aeroporto Santos Dumont, near Centro. The second resulted in Parque do Flamengo, and the third was used to widen the shore along Copacabana and create Av Atlântica.

1889	1892	1950	1960
Brazilian Republic declared	Tunnel into Copacabana built; the upper classes begin moving south	Pelé plays his last match at Maracanã; 200,000 fans come to watch	The capital of Brazil transfers from Rio to Brasília

Rio's Malandros *Carmen Michael*

In the suffocating heat of a Rio afternoon sometime in the 1930s, João Francisco dos Santos walked into the shabby, corrupt Lapa police station with a depthless rage against a discriminatory society and retribution on his mind. With a silk shirt stretched across his taut frame and a gold ring engraved with St George on his long-nailed hands, he allegedly assaulted five policemen who had previously assaulted his transvestite friends. Well that's the story they tell in the more notorious drinking dens of Lapa anyway. Born to slaves in the impoverished Northeast of Brazil, swapped at eight years old for a horse, and later emerging as a flamboyant transvestite cabaret performer and formidable *capoeirista* (*capoeira* practitioner) on the streets of Lapa, João Francisco dos Santos (or Madam Satã as he was later called) became the first of a new breed of social misfits known in Rio as *malandros*. In 2002, his life was immortalised in the feature film *Madame Satã*, which screened at the Cannes Film Festival and achieved art-house circulation.

In the tumultuous post-slavery era of the 1930s, Lapa emerged as a seedy bohemian enclave of gambling houses, cabaret and brothels. In this environment *malandros* consorted with a cast of exotic dancers, transvestites, penniless musicians and angst-ridden poets. Listen to the music of Noel Rosa, Wilson Batista and Nelson Gonçalves and you will discover the stories of characters such as Meia Noite, Camisa Preta and Miguel Zinho. Originally portrayed as a paradoxical Robin Hood type, the *malandro* today is more likely to be described as a sly con artist.

'First samba, then make love and then sleep,' wrote Chico Buarque (one of Brazil's most talented musicians), summing up the idle *malandro* philosophy of life in one of his many odes to Malandragem. Through their dubious eking out of an existence on the shady fringes of society, *malandros* have never been the toast of conservative Rio society. And yet, there is a tenuous but popular argument that it was the social and economic inequality of this society that gave rise to the *malandro*. For the victims of poverty and discrimination, *malandros* became a symbol of rebellion and the lower classes protected and promoted the myths of their exploits. The *malandro* was seen as a person whom society had failed dismally and his refusal to become a victim had glamorous appeal. Carefully dodging the title of thief or gigolo, *malandros* used charm, persuasion and manipulation to fund their flamboyant lifestyle of samba, gambling and beautiful women or men. Their satirical adoption of the clothes of the wealthy, from the white patent shoes to the silk shirt and scarf, was as much of a moral statement as a means of diverting police attention from their dubious connections to the criminal underworld.

The legends of Rio's *malandros* have recently experienced a revival of interest with the sell-out performance of Chico Buarque´s *Opera do Malandro*. He laments their disappearance in 'Homage to the Malandro' in which he sings that the only *malandros* nowadays are officials with political candidacy and neckties, promoting themselves through the social pages. Inequality still exists in Rio, but unfortunately the *malandro* culture of intelligent protest has disappeared – along with bohemia – leaving in its place apathy, or worse, trapping the rage of the impoverished classes in a vicious cycle of escalating crime. Although some would argue that a new breed of *malandro* has emerged on the street, playfully targeting Western tourists who possess money and naïveté in equal and abundant quantities. When Brazilians talk about *malandros* today, mostly they mean that unnaturally good-looking *capoeirista*, *sambista* (samba dancer) or surfer who offers to 'show you around' and who will spend your money so fast it will make your head spin. And then, as all good *malandros* should do, he will disappear into the night to the local *botequim* (bar with table service), ensuring his exploits are well known in the barfly history books. As they say in Rio: as long as *otários* (the gullible) exist, there will always be *malandros*.

1960 TO THE PRESENT

Rio remained the political capital of Brazil until 1960, when the capital was moved to Brasília (and thousands of public servants went into deep depression). Rio became the city-state of Guanabara, before merging with the state of Fluminense in 1975 to form the state of Rio de Janeiro, of which Rio is the regional capital.

During the 1960s, lots of modern skyscrapers went up in the city, and some of Rio's most beautiful buildings were lost. A hotel-building boom along the beaches saw the rise of the big hotels like the Sheraton, Rio Palace and Le Meridien.

1964	1968	1970s	1985
President Goulart overthrown by a military coup and the era of heightened repression begins	Military regime is at its worst: political parties outlawed, murder of opponents widespread	The generals' heavy borrowing leads to 'Brazilian economic miracle'; the economy grows 10% annually	Civilian rule returns to Brazil under José Sarney

Carnaval Scandals

In 1994 President Itamar Franco caused a great deal of gossip around Rio – and the country – after an incident during the Carnaval parade. Apparently, the 63-year-old president was introduced to young samba dancer and model Lilian Ramos, who had just performed with one of the schools. She was exuberantly excited about meeting the president and stood by his side, waving her arms in the air and dancing, heedless of her shirt bouncing above her waist, as the *bateria* (drum section) rolled by. This, of course, would hardly have made the news had it not been for the fact that Lilian Ramos wasn't wearing anything besides her T-shirt (after she had changed out of her costume, she had apparently neglected to put on a few articles of clothing). The national magazines *Veja* and *Isto É* were both on hand, snapping photos of the spectacle – the indiscrete footage of which appeared on newsstands the next day. When the president was later criticized, he told his detractors, 'How am I supposed to know if people are wearing underwear?'

During the same period, the favelas of Rio were becoming overcrowded with immigrants from poverty-stricken areas of the Northeast and interior, who swelled the number of urban poor in the city. The 'Cidade Maravilhosa' (Marvelous City) began to lose its gloss as crime and violence increased.

The final decade of the military dictatorship that ruled Brazil from 1964 to 1985 was not kind to Rio. There were numerous protests during that period (notably in 1968 when some 100,000 marched upon the Palácio Tiradentes). And even Rio's politicians opposed the military regime, which responded by withholding vital federal funding. The administration was forced to tighten its belt, and infrastructure deteriorated as decay set in.

A turning point for Rio came when it was chosen as host city for Eco 92, the United Nations Conference on Environment and Development. In the buildup to the conference, the federal government poured in almost US$1 billion to improve Rio's infrastructure. Approximately US$18 million was spent on satellite communications alone, and Riocentro, a huge convention center, was built. Rio remains the cultural and tourist capital of Brazil. It still sets the fashion and the pace for the rest of the nation, and it should continue to do so for many years to come.

1992	1994	2002	2007
Rio hosts Eco 92, the United Nations Conference on Environment and Development	The Favela-Bairro project is unveiled; Brazil wins its fourth World Cup	After four unsuccessful attempts, Lula is elected president; Brazil wins its fifth World Cup	Rio to host the Pan-American Games

Neighborhoods

Neighborhoods

Lying just north of the Tropic of Capricorn, Rio de Janeiro is a city of unusual urban diversity, with beaches, mountains, skyscrapers and the omnipresent favelas (slums) all woven into the fabric of the landscape. The city itself can be divided into two zones: the Zona Norte (North Zone), which consists of industrial, working-class neighborhoods, and the Zona Sul (South Zone), full of middle- and upper-class neighborhoods and the well-known beaches. Centro, Rio's business district and the site of its first settlement, marks the boundary between the two.

The Zona Sul contains some of Rio's loveliest neighborhoods and its most famous beaches. We begin with beach-fronting Ipanema and Leblon, which border Lagoa and Jardim Botânico. As we travel north, we reach Copacabana, Leme and Urca, where the striking peak of Pão de Açúcar (Sugar Loaf) dominates the landscape. Continuing north toward Centro, we encounter the older, working-class neighborhoods of Botafogo and the villagelike setting of Urca, just opposite. Next we reach Flamengo, Laranjeiras and Cosme Velho, above which looms one of Rio's most well-known sites, Cristo Redentor (Christ the Redeemer) atop Corcovado. Catete and Glória follow, then bustling Centro and cinematic Cinelândia, all of which host some of Rio's most important museums and colonial buildings. Working our way inland, we cover the bohemian hoods of Lapa and Santa Teresa, then move to Greater Rio, which includes São Cristóvão, the Bay, Niterói and the eastern beaches. We end by heading further south of Ipanema to Barra da Tijuca and the lovely western beaches. See each section and the Directory (p194) for transportation details.

ITINERARIES

One Day

If you have only one day in Rio, head to Ipanema and take in the beach, where you can be both a spectator (people watching) and participant (*futebol*, surfing, *frescobol*, wave frolicking). When you've had enough sun, grab a cab (time is of the essence!) and head to Centro for lunch at one of the excellent lunchtime restaurants there, such as **Cais do Oriente** (p120) and **Bar Luiz** (p119). Walk off those *chopes* (draft beers) in the pedestrian shopping area surrounding Río Branco. As afternoon wanes, head to Urca and take the cable car to **Pão de Açúcar** (p65), where you can watch a spectacular sunset over the Cidade Maravilhosa. For dinner, glammy Leblon is tops. There you can sample some of the city's best cuisine at **Sushi Leblon** (p109) and **Satyricon** (p108), have a fruit-infused *caipirinha* at **Academia da Cachaça** (p125) before heading to Lapa for serious beats at one of the numerous samba clubs in the neighborhood, such as **Río Scenarium** (p137) and **Democraticus** (p136).

Three Days

If you spent the previous night dancing (see above), on your second day you may need a slow morning to come to life. Take in an exhibition at one of Centro's cultural centers, such as **Centro Cultural Justiça Federal** (p80), or at the forward-thinking **Museu de Arte Moderna** (MAM; p87). As lunchtime nears, take the *bonde* (tram) to Santa Teresa and sample traditional cuisine at **Bar do Mineiro** (p121) or **Sobrenatural** (p122). Afterward, walk the historic streets before reaching **Parque das Ruínas** (p86), with its fine views over the city. From there, a short stroll leads to Lapa, where you can shop (records, used books, antiques) among narrow, cinematic streets. Grab dinner at **Porcão Río's** (p117) or **Marius** (p113), two of Rio's famed *churrascarias* (traditional barbecue restaurants). For a fine cap to the day, go to the **Casa Cavê** (p121) in Cosme Velho, where you can hear some excellent jazz. By the third day, it's time to see one of Brazil's wild football matches at Maracanã. Following the game, take the cog train up Corcovado to **Cristo Redentor** (p76), where the city unfolds beneath Christ's outstretched arms. Lagoa makes a fine setting to the day's end. Stroll along the lakeside promenade and dine at one of the many open-air kiosks perched on the shore.

One Week

By the fourth day, it's time for adventure of the non-urban variety. Book a tandem hang-gliding flight – 15 minutes of airborne exhilaration before landing on the beach near São Conrado. Afterward, it's on to **Parque Nacional da Tijuca** (p56), for a hike through tropical rain forest. By day's end, enjoy a much-deserved *chope* at **Devassa** (p126) in Leblon and scrumptious Bahian cuisine at **Yemanjá** (p109) in Ipanema. By the fifth day, you'll probably need a respite from Rio's intensity. The untouched beauty of **Ilha Grande** (p184), two hours west of Rio, offers a mix of lush forests and breathtaking beaches. Further east lies Paraty, whose charming colonial streets make for fine evening strolls after a day exploring the region's natural wonders – beaches, forests, waterfalls. Spend two days in either location (the manic can opt for a day in each), then return for a final day in Rio. On your last day, load up on handicrafts and Northeastern cuisine at the action-packed **Feira Nordestina** (p159). Before sunset make it to Praia Vermelha in Urca, where you can listen to musicians play sad tunes before you bid the city farewell. If you don't want to end the night quietly, cross town to Praça Santos Dumont in Gávea, where young revelers spill out onto the streets most nights of the week. Dance one last night away at nearby **Melt** (p140), and if you're still standing at six in the morning, go to Ipanema beach and watch a sure-to-be-memorable sunrise.

ORGANIZED TOURS

Bay Tours

SAVEIROS TOURS Map pp228-30

☎ 2224 6990; saveiros@saveiros.com.br; Rua Conde de Lages 44s 1001, Glória; ⏰ 9:30-11:30am Tue-Sun

Saveiros leads two-hour cruises out over Baía de Guanabara in large schooners. The route follows the coastline of Rio and Niterói and you'll get excellent views of **Pão de Açúcar** (p65), the MAC, Ilha Fiscal and the old fort of Urca. You'll also sail under the Niterói bridge. You can purchase tickets in advance at the Marina de Glória from 8am to 6pm Monday to Friday.

City Bus Tours

GRAY LINE TOURS

☎ 2512 9919; www.grayline.com.br; Av Niemeyer 121, Leblon

The Rio-based branch of the international chain offers a range of sightseeing tours in and around Rio. Tours cover the usual tourist destinations – with four-hour trips to Corcovado, Historic Centro and Baía de Guanabara, all of which cost around US$30. It also has day trips to Buzios (US$28) and Petropólis (US$22). Look for its brochures on the reception desks of most hotels or check its website for more details. Some readers have complained of spending more time on the bus (while it picks up passengers from other hotels) than on the actual tour itself.

Favela Tours

MARCELO ARMSTRONG

☎ 3322 2727, 9989 0074; www.favelatour.com.br; per person US$20

Marcelo is the pioneer of favela tourism, and takes small groups to visit the favelas of Rocinha and Vila Canoas near São Conrado. His tours include a visit to a school, a medical center and private houses, and guides make an effort to explain the social and political context of the favela in relation to greater Rio de Janeiro. Although Marcelo was the first to lead a favela tour, in recent years some readers have complained that the quality of his tours isn't what it used to be.

PAULO AMENDOIM

☎ 3322 8498, 9747 6860; pauloamendoim@hotmail .com; per person US$20

President of Rocinha's resident association, Paulo leads tours through Rio's biggest favela and offers visitors the chance to see beneath the gross stereotypes of favela life. Paulo picks up visitors at their hotel, takes them to the top of Rocinha, then leads a guided walking tour downhill through the favela. He stops often to talk to locals and explain the structure of the community, and he seems well liked by many there, perhaps owing to his involvement in a Rocinha childcare project. Paulo speaks English and has been described as enormously funny. Trips run from two to three hours.

Rocinha: Rio's Largest Favela *Tom Phillips*

Rocinha wasn't the first of Rio de Janeiro's favelas (that honor falls to the Morro da Providência, founded in 1897 by slaves migrating from the Northeast's sugar plantations after the abolition of slavery), but it is now indisputably the largest, with over 127,000 inhabitants. It is also one of the most developed, elevated to *bairro* (district) status in 1992 by the controversial government Favela-Bairro project. Manhole covers, electricity cables and Internet cafés all pay testament to the fact that Rocinha is no ordinary 'slum.' In fact, to dismiss it as such is to rather miss the point.

From the patio of Rocinha's Casa de Cultura on Rua 1, the vast *comunidade* (community) spreads out before the eye; a mishmash of redbrick housing stretches down toward the affluent beachside district of São Conrado. It's not just an architectural patchwork. Split into various boroughs, the area is a complex web of social groups and people. Many occupants hail originally from the northeastern state of Paraíba, while there are several foreign students to whom the area is home, too. There is a community of transvestites (generally well respected by locals) and even a man who lives in a cave with running water, electricity, 12 dogs and a cell phone. There are evangelists clad in suits, who clasp copies of the Nova Testemunha (New Testament) as they march home from *cultos* (church services). Doctors, lawyers and maids all live here alongside the unemployed and impoverished.

According to a survey carried out by Rocinha's local TV channel last year, 56% of inhabitants use the local shopping mall, 23% have a credit card and 93% have at least one television at home. It's perhaps not what you would expect from what is so often referred to as 'South America's largest slum.'

In many ways Rocinha is a normal, safe and welcoming place; a reality underlined by the increasing number of tourists making the pilgrimage to the Estrada de Gávea to photograph stunning views of Corcovado, and to glimpse the *other* side of Rio life. Yet it remains one of the more deprived parts of the city, with widespread unemployment.

The favela – once one of the most dangerous parts of the city – has mellowed considerably in the last decade. Part of the reason for this is the drug traffickers, whose deadly style of community policing serves as a brutal but effective deterrent. People here live by a strict code. It is forbidden to talk to the few police that can be found here in two tiny stations. Problems are resolved within the community.

Yet due to the presence of *tráfico* a fundamental tension exists here. One of the community's former drug-lords is looking to retake Rocinha, and is reported to be preparing an invasion. Teenage boys, linked to the Comando Vermelho, a drug gang, can be seen patrolling the streets with automatic weapons just a few hundred meters away from where tourists are busy snapping away. 'Roça' is a lively, tight-knit and fascinating community, which desperately needs normalizing. The trouble is, it's not normal yet.

Helicopter Tours
HELISIGHT

☎ 2511 2141; www.helisight.com.br; Rua Conde Bernadotte 26, loja 119, Leblon; ⏲ 9am-6pm

In business since 1991, Helisight offers eight different tours, lasting from six to 60 minutes. From one of its four helipads, helicopters travel around Cristo Redentor, from which you can glimpse the statue's excellent craftsmanship. Helisight also has flights over the **Parque Nacional da Tijuca** (p56) and above the mountains and beaches woven into Rio's lush landscape. Helipad locations are in Parque Nacional da Tijuca facing Corcovado; on Morro da Urca, the first cable-car stop up **Pão de Açúcar** (p65); on the edge of Lagoa; and Pier Mauá downtown at the docks. Sample prices are US$43 per person for a six-minute flight and US$148 for a 30-minute one (three-person minimum).

Hiking Tours
RIO HIKING

☎ 2552 9204, 9721 0594; www.riohiking.com.br

Led by Denise Werneck and her son Gabriel, tours range from easy to strenuous and cover a variety of terrains in and around Rio. Popular treks include hikes up Pico da Tijuca (the highest point in the national park), Pedra da Gávea, Pão de Açúcar and Corcovado, most of which cost around US$40. They also arrange cycling and diving adventures, surfing and rappelling. Both speak English and are excellent sources of information about nightlife in the city.

TANGARA ECOLOGICAL HIKES

☎ 2252 8202, 9656 1460; www.tangarapasseios.com.br

Run by two Brazilians who love the outdoors, Tangara offers an enormous variety of excursions, from kayaking excursions off Praia

Vermelha to climbs up Pedra da Gavéa, while hang gliders soar nearby. They also have two-day trips: exploring Ilha Grande, rafting excursions in Mont Serrat and climbing treks up Pedra do Baú. They rate hikes according to level of difficulty (easy, moderate and hard), and their outings remain popular with young Brazilians. Guides speak English, Spanish and Portuguese.

TRILHARTE ECOTURISMO
☎ 2245 5626; www.trilharte.com.br
Although the guides don't speak Portuguese, this ecologically minded organization offers exceptional excursions, catering to adventurers 'with a passion for photography.' It offers hiking, rappelling, rafting and horseback riding trips, which range in price from US$10 to US$50. It also hosts photographic safaris, where participants study under a professional photographer on a day- or weekend-long excursion. Past trips have ranged from the aesthetic (Holy Week in Ouro Preto) to the far out (nudes in nature). For a list of scheduled excursions, visit its website (click on 'programa de trilhagem'). Most activities are held on weekends. (See also Courses, p198.)

Jeep Tours
JEEP TOUR
☎ 2589 0883; www.jeeptour.com.br
Travel to the lush Parque Nacional da Tijuca in a large, convertible jeep. Four-hour tours, which cost around US$40 per person, consist of a stop at the Vista Chinesa, then on to the forest for an easy hike, and a stop for a swim beneath a waterfall, before making the return journey. On the way back, you'll stop at Pepino Beach, the landing strip for hang gliders from nearby Pedra Bonita. Other excursions offered by Jeep Tour include trips to Angra dos Reis (where forest meets sea) and a coffee *fazenda* (plantation). The price of all tours includes pickup and dropoff at your hotel.

Motorcycle Tours
ROUGH TRIP
☎ 2572 9991; www.roughtrip.com.br
Head off-road on a 200cc motorcycle on one of Rough Trip's tours of Rio's beaches, forests and mountains. Guides are provided (as are helmets and gloves). In addition to its Rio tour, Rough Trip also offers excursions to Buzios or will custom-design a tour to your liking.

Samba School Tours
ANGRAMAR TURISMO
☎ 2235 1989; angramar2000@yahoo.com.br; Av NS de Copacabana 534
During Carnaval season (September until February or March), Angramar offers regular trips to some of the better-known samba schools, providing visitors with the opportunity to see a live rehearsal and party with the school participants. Angramar has regular departures to Viradouro (8:30pm Tuesday), Salgueiro (7:30pm Wednesday), Beija Flor (10pm Thursday), Grande Rio (10pm Friday) and its most popular destination, Mangueiro (10pm Saturday). Most trips cost around US$15, which includes round-trip transportation and entrance fee.

Tram Tours
BONDE HISTORICO
☎ 2242 2354, 2524 2508; per person US$3.50
Run by the **Museu do Bonde** (Tram Museum; p85), guided tours of the Santa Teresa neighborhood illuminate historic points along the journey from downtown to Silvestre and back, with a stop at the Museu do Bonde. Trains depart every Saturday at 10am, from the tram station on Rua Profesor Lélio Gama, Centro.

Bonde (p84), Santa Teresa

Climbing Pão de Açúcar (p54)

Walking Tours

CULTURAL RIO

☎ 3322 4872, 9911 3829; www.culturalrio.com.br

Run by art historian Professor Carlos Roquette, who speaks English and French as well as Portuguese, Cultural Rio offers visitors an in-depth look at social and historical aspects of Rio de Janeiro. Roquette has a wealth of Carioca knowledge (and a quirky sense of humor), and he feels as comfortable discussing Jobim and the bossa nova scene as he does the sexual indiscretions of the early Portuguese rulers. Itineraries include a night at the **Teatro Municipal** (p125), colonial Rio, baroque Rio, imperial Rio and a walking tour of Centro. In business for over 20 years, Professor Roquette charges US$50 for a four-hour tour and US$10 for each additional hour.

FABIO SOMBRA

☎ 2275 8605; www.fasombra.cjb.net

A multilingual artist still active as an arte naïf painter, Fabio leads tours highlighting historical and cultural Centro and Santa Teresa. His

Parque Nacional & Floresta da Tijuca   Map p239

The Tijuca is all that's left of the Atlantic rain forest that once surrounded Rio de Janeiro. In just 15 minutes you can go from the concrete jungle of Copacabana to the 120-sq-km tropical jungle of the Parque Nacional da Tijuca. A more rapid and dramatic contrast is hard to imagine. The forest is an exuberant green, with beautiful trees, creeks and waterfalls, mountainous terrain and high peaks. It has an excellent, well-marked trail system. *Candomblistas* leave offerings by the roadside, families have picnics and serious hikers climb the 1012m to the summit of **Pico da Tijuca**.

The heart of the forest is the **Alto da Boa Vista** area in the Floresta (Forest) da Tijuca, with many lovely natural and manmade features. Among the highlights of this beautiful park are several waterfalls (**Cascatinha Taunay, Cascata Gabriela** and **Cascata Diamantina**), a 19th-century chapel (**Capela Mayrink**) and numerous caves (**Gruta Luís Fernandes, Gruta Belmiro, Gruta Paulo e Virgínia**). Also in the park is a lovely picnic spot (**Bom Retiro**) and several restaurants (**Restaurante Os Equilos** and **Restaurante a Floresta**, which is near the ruins of Major Archer's house – **Ruínas do Archer**). A recommended culinary experience is dining at the open-air brunch at the **Museu do Açude** (p122), held the last Sunday of the month.

The park is home to many different bird and animal species, including iguanas and monkeys, which you might encounter on one of the excellent day hikes you can make here (the trails are well-signed). Maps can be obtained at the small artisan shop just inside the park entrance, which is open from 7am to 9pm.

The entire park closes at sunset. It's best to go by car, but if you can't, catch a No 221, 233 or 234 bus. Alternatively, take the metro to Saens Peña then catch a bus going to Barra da Tijuca and get off at Alta da Boa Vista.

The best route by car is to take Rua Jardim Botânico two blocks past the Jardim Botânico (heading east from Gávea). Turn left on Rua Lopes Quintas and then follow the Tijuca or Corcovado signs for two quick left turns until you reach the back of the Jardim Botânico, where you turn right. Then follow the signs for a quick ascent into the forest and past the **Vista Chinesa** (get out for a good view) and the **Mesa do Imperador**. As soon as you seem to come out of the forest, turn right onto the main road and you'll see the stone columns to the entrance of Alto da Boa Vista on your left after a couple of kilometers. You can also drive up to Alto da Boa Vista by heading out to São Conrado and turning right up the hill at the Parque Nacional da Tijuca signs.

Warning: there have been occasional reports of robbery within the park. Most Cariocas recommend going on weekends when there are more people around. Ask at Riotur of the present situation.

most popular tour covers the ruins of the old port and historical sites around Praça 15 de Novembro, the monastery of **São Bento** (p81) and the **Catedral Metropolitana** (p86), passing through Lapa and ending in Santa Teresa. This tour costs US$70 for four people. Fabio also enjoys having visitors to his studio at Rua Dr Xavier Sigaud 205 (10 minutes' walk from Pão de Açúcar in Urca), where he gives a colorful slide show called 'Rio Fold Experience.' Call in advance before you drop by.

LUIZ AMARAL TOURS
☎ 2259 5532; www.travelrio.com

Luiz strives to lead small groups (maximum of four people) that make participants feel less like they're on a tour and more like they're on an outing among friends. A friendly, well-traveled Carioca with a good command of English, Luiz can put together a tour to do whatever you want. His more unique excursions include a combined hike/climb up Pão de Açúcar (US$30 per person for groups of two), an exploration of beaches south of Barra (US$27 per person for groups of four), and nightlife tours in Rio (US$20 per person for two or more).

QUALITOURS
☎ 2232 9710; www.privatetours.com.br

Recommended for his tailor-made tours, Pedro Novak has been leading excursions around the city and further afield since 1992. One of his more unique offerings is his sunset tour, where you watch the sun set over Rio and the bay from atop the 270m-high Niterói city park. The trip also includes a visit to the old Santa Cruz fortress (constructed in 1567), followed by dinner at a restaurant overlooking the bay.

IPANEMA & LEBLON

Eating p104 ; Shopping p153; Sleeping p166

Boasting a magnificent beach and tree-lined streets full of boutiques, restaurants and colorful bars and cafés, Ipanema and Leblon are Rio's loveliest destinations, and the favored residence for young, beautiful (and wealthy) Cariocas. Populated by a mix of well-to-do families, models and hipsters of both the gay and straight variety, the twin neighborhoods boast some of the city's highest rents, the result no doubt of their appeal.

Ipanema acquired international fame in the early '60s as the home of the bossa nova character 'Girl from Ipanema.' It became the hangout of artists, intellectuals and wealthy liberals, who frequented the sidewalk cafés and bars. After the 1964 military coup and the resulting crackdown on liberals, many of these bohemians were forced into exile. Today, Ipanema continues to be a center of Carioca chic and remains one of the most animated and exciting neighborhoods of Rio.

During the '70s, Leblon became the nightlife center of Rio. The restaurants and bars of Baixo Leblon, on Av Ataulfo de Paiva between Ruas Aristídes Espínola and General Artigas, were the meeting point for a new generation of artists and musicians. Nightlife today continues to be very animated here.

Orientation

Situated in the Zona Sul, Ipanema and Leblon face the same stretch of beach and are separated by the Jardim de Alah, a canal and adjacent park. A few blocks to the north lies Lagoa Rodriga de Freitas, while the rocky outcropping of Ponta do Arpoador (a surfer favorite) forms the eastern boundary. To the west looms the Morro (mountain) Dois Irmãos, nicely framing the already lovely stretch of sand.

Ipanema & Leblon Top Five

- Drinking *água de coco* (coconut water) while people-watching on **Posto 9** (p58).
- Dining at one of the many restaurants on the stylish Rua Dias Ferreira in **Leblon** (p104).
- Browsing the colorful **Feira Hype market** (p159) at Praça General Osório on Sunday.
- Sipping cocktails at **Bar D'Hotel** (p126).
- Watching the sun set from Arpoador.

Transportation

Bus Each of these lines stop in Ipanema and Leblon: Botafogo Metro No 503; Corcovado train station Nos 583 and 584; Urca Nos 511 and 512; São Conrado Nos 591 and 592; Largo Machado Nos 569 and 570; Praça XV de Novembro No 415; Novo Rio bus terminal Nos 128 and 172; Centro (Rio Branco) No 132 (many buses go to Centro); Copacabana Nos 503, 569, 570, 583, 584, 591 and 592.

Metro Although the new stations in Ipanema aren't completed, there is a special metro-bus connection that runs between Siqueira Campos station and Ipanema and Leblon. The gray buses with the metro logo run along two lines: Ipanema (which terminates at Praça General Osório) and Gávea (which stops at Praça General Osório, Praça NS de Paz, Praça Antero de Quental in Leblon and finally Rua Padre Leonel França in Gávea). You can only get on and off the bus at these points. Integrated bus-metro tickets are available at all metro stations except for Siqueira Campos (US$1).

IPANEMA & LEBLON BEACH Map pp236-8
Av Delfim Moreira & Av Viera Souto

Although the beaches of Ipanema and Leblon are really one long beach, the *postos* (posts) along them subdivide the beach into areas as diverse as the city itself. Posto 9, right off Rua Vinícius de Moraes, is Garota de Ipanema, which is where Rio's most lithe and tanned bodies tend to migrate. The area is also known as the Cemetério dos Elefantes because of the old leftists, hippies and artists who hang out there. In front of Rua Farme de Amoedo the beach is known as Bolsa de Valores or Crystal Palace (this is the gay section), while Posto 8 further up is mostly the domain of favela kids. Arpoador, between Ipanema and Copacabana, is Rio's most popular surf spot. Leblon attracts a broad mix of single Cariocas, as well as families from the neighborhood.

Whatever spot you choose, you'll enjoy cleaner sands and sea than those found in neighboring Copacabana. Keep in mind that if you go on Saturday or Sunday, the sands get fearfully crowded. Go early to stake out a spot.

Incidentally, the word *ipanema* is Indian for 'bad, dangerous waters' – not so far off given the strong undertow and often oversized waves crashing on the shore. Be careful, and swim only where the locals do.

MIRANTE DO LEBLON Map pp236-8
Av Niemeyer

A few fisherman, casting out to sea, mingle with couples admiring the view at this overlook at the western end of Leblon Beach, stretching down Leblon and Ipanema Beaches. The luxury Sheraton Hotel looms to the west, with the not so luxurious favela of Vidigal nearby.

Ipanema Beach (above)

MUSEU H STERN Map pp236-8

☎ 2259 7442; hstern@hstern.com.br; Rua Garcia D'Ávila 113; admission free; ☻ 8:30am-6pm Mon-Fri, 8:30am-noon Sat

The headquarters of the famous jeweler H Stern incorporates a museum displaying a permanent exhibition of fine jewelry, some rare mineral specimens and a large collection of tourmalines. There is a 12-minute tour, which displays the process of turning the rough stones into flawlessly cut jewels as the gems pass through the hands of craftsmen, cutters, goldsmiths and setters. With a coupon, you can get a free cab ride to and from the shop and anywhere in the Zona Sul. Call them at ☎ 2274 6171 and they'll come and pick you up.

MUSEU AMSTERDAM SAUER
Map pp236-8

☎ 2512 1132; www.amsterdamsauer.com; Rua Garcia D'Ávila 105; admission free; ☻ 9:30am-2:30pm Mon-Fri, 10am-2pm Sat

Next door to **H Stern** (above), the Amsterdam Sauer Museum also houses an impressive collection of precious stones – over 3000 items in all. In addition to gemstones and minerals, visi-tors can also take a peek at the two life-sized replicas of mines.

PARQUE GAROTA DE IPANEMA
Map pp236-8

Off Rua Francisco Otaviano near Rua Bulhões Carvalho; ☻ 7am-7pm

This small park next to the Arpoador rock features a tiny playground and a small concrete area popular with skaters, as well as a lookout with a good view of Praia de Ipanema. On weekends in the summer, concerts are sometimes held here.

TOCA DO VINÍCIUS Map pp236-8

☎ 2247 5227; www.tocadovinicius.com.br; Rua Vinícius de Moraes 129; ☻ 9am-9pm Mon-Fri, 10am-5pm Sun

A quintessential stopoff for bossa nova fans, Toca do Vinícius is a **music store** (p155) named in honor of the famous Brazilian musician, Vinícius de Moraes. The 1st floor has a good selection of bossa, while upstairs a tiny museum displays original manuscripts and photos of the great songwriter and poet. Live bossa nova concerts are held in the small space several nights a week.

GÁVEA, JARDIM BOTÂNICO & LAGOA

Eating p110; Shopping p156

Just north of Ipanema, the well-to-do suburbs of Gávea, Jardim Botânico and Lagoa comprise a mix of eclectic restaurants, stylish bars, attractive parks and country clubs. Jardim Botânico gets its name from the lush botanical gardens at

its edge, and owing to ongoing gentrification, its residents comprise more and more young professionals on the make.

Like Jardim Botânico, Lagoa also earns its moniker from one of the Zona Sul's natural attractions, a saltwater lagoon. With lovely views of Corcovado and the mountains surrounding it, the lake is one of Rio's gems. By day, joggers and cyclists circle its shores, while at night music-filled restaurants serve diners under the open sky.

Natives dubbed this body of water Sacopenapã, meaning 'place of the socó birds,' but it was later changed to Rodrigo de Freitas, named after the Portuguese settler who made his fortune off the sugarcane fields surrounding the lake in the 16th century. Lagoa has also benefited from redevelopment, and although the lake is still too polluted for swimming, some wildlife has returned, and visitors are now likely to see egrets fishing in the lake. In the late '90s the lake was declared a national landmark by the Historical Patrimony.

Gávea is among Rio's more upscale neighborhoods. The biggest landmark in the area is the Hipódromo de Gávea, Rio's premier horseracing track. Near the hipódromo, Gávea's most privileged residents enjoy a membership at one of the several private country clubs along the lake, while the younger set prefers mixing it up over *caipirinhas* at neighborhood bars, like the lively scene at **Hipódromo** (p128) on Praça Santos Dumont.

Orientation

In back of Ipanema, Lagoa Rodrigo de Freitas forms the centerpiece to these three charming neighborhoods. The lake itself, with a path looping around it, is a fine place for strolling. At night, kiosks on the western and eastern sides of Lagoa draw diners from all over the city. Two small islands in the lake, Ilha Piraqué and Ilha dos Caiçaras, are private country clubs.

The district of Lagoa itself, with high-rise condominiums fronting the lake, extends along the northern shores. The tropical acreage of the Jardim Botânico lies to the west of the lake, and its residents live just north of there. South of the gardens lies Praça Santos Dumont, a small plaza at the intersection of three busy streets that forms the backdrop to Gávea's most active bar scene. Across busy Rua Jardim Botânico lies the country club Joquei Clube.

Traffic around the lake can be a headache. Av Epitácio Pessoa, the wide boulevard on the eastern side of the lake, leads to the Túnel Rebouças, which connects Lagoa to downtown or the Linha Vermelha, the northern highway out of town. The major thoroughfare on the western edge of the lake, Rua Jardim Botânico, continues north around the lake turning into Rua Humaitá once it crosses Av Epitácio Pessoa. This is a handy shortcut to get to Botafogo or Leme.

Av Padre Leonel Franca, which divides Gávea from Leblon to the south, turns into the Lagoa-Barra Highway as it heads west, passing through São Conrado before reaching Barra.

Transportation

Bus The following buses leave from Jardim Botânico: No 170 to Centro (Av Rio Branco); No 571 to Botafogo, Flamengo and Glória; No 572 to Leblon, Ipanema and Copacabana. Departing from Rua Padre Leonel Franco, Gávea bus lines are Centro (Nos 176 and 178) and Copacabana (Nos 591 and 592). From Leblon Nos 460A, 461 and 476 travel along the western side of the lake (Av Borges). From Copacabana Nos 462 and 433 travel along the eastern side (Av Epitácio Pessoa).

Metro-Bus A special metro-bus connection runs between Siqueira Campos station and Gávea. The gray buses with the metro logo run has a Gávea line which stops at Praça General Osório, Praça NS de Paz, Praça Antero de Quental in Leblon, then stops twice in Gávea at Rua Padre Leonel França and Rua Marques de São Vicente. You can only get on and off the bus at these points. Integrated bus-metro tickets available at all metro stations except for Siqueira Campos (US$1).

GÁVEA

MUSEU HISTÓRICO DA CIDADE

Map pp236-8

☎ 2512 2353; www.rio.rj.gov.br/cultura in Portuguese; Estrada de Santa Marinha 505; admission US$2; ☾ 10am-4pm Tue-Sun

The 19th-century mansion located on the lovely grounds of the Parque da Cidade now houses the City History Museum. In addition to its permanent collection, which portrays Rio from its founding in 1565 to the mid-20th century, the museum has exhibitions of furniture, porcelain, photographs and paintings by well-known artists. The park itself is free, open from 7am to 6pm.

INSTITUTO MOREIRA SALLES

Map pp236-8

☎ 3284 7400; www.ims.com.br in Portuguese; Rua Marquês de Sao Vicente 476; admission free; ☾ 1-8pm Tue-Sun

This beautiful cultural center is next to the Parque da Cidade and contains an archive of more than 80,000 photographs, many portraying old streets of Rio as well as the urban development of other Brazilian cities over the last two centuries. It also hosts impressive exhibitions, often showcasing the works of some of Brazil's best photographers and artists. Check its website for details of what's on when you're in town.

The gardens, complete with artificial lake and flowing river, were designed by eminent

---

Gávea, Jardim Botânico & Lagoa Top Five

- Picnicking at the lush **Jardim Botânico** (opposite).
- Participating in the festive bar scene at **Hipódromo** (p128).
- Catching electro-bossa at one of **00's** (p138) rotating parties in the Planetário.
- Dining at one of the scenic **kiosks** (p110) on the lake.
- Catching an exhibit at the **Instituto Moreira Salles** (oppostie).

Brazilian landscaper Burle Marx. There's also a craft shop and a quaint café that serves lunch or afternoon tea.

PLANETÁRIO Map pp236-8

☎ 2274 0096; www.rio.rj.gov.br/planetario in Portuguese; Rua Padre Leonel Franca 240; museum admission free, domes $2; ☺ 10am-5pm Tue-Sun (museum); bus 174 from Centro, 593 from Copacabana, 558 from Ipanema

Gávea's stellar attraction, the Planetário (Planetarium) features a museum, a *praça dos telescópios* (telescopes' square) and a couple of state-of-the-art operating domes, each capable of projecting over 6000 stars onto its walls (40-minute sessions in the domes are at 4pm, 5:30pm and 7pm Saturday, Sunday and holidays; admission US$2). Visitors can take advantage of free guided observations through the far-seeing telescopes on Monday, Wednesday and Thursday from 6:30pm to 8:30pm. The hyper-modern Museu do Universo (Universe Museum) houses permanent exhibitions, sundials and a Foucault's Pendulum, as well as good temporary ones – the recent Mars exhibit garnered much attention. Periodically, the planetarium hosts live *chorinho* concerts on weekends. Check the website or the newspaper for information.

JARDIM BOTÂNICO

JARDIM BOTÂNICO Map pp236-8

☎ 2294 9349; www.jbrj.gov.br in Portuguese; Rua Jardim Botânico 920; admission US$2; ☺ 8am-5pm; any bus marked 'Jardim Botânico' or 'via Jóquei,' or bus 571, 572, 594 from Zona Sul, 170 from Centro

This exotic 1.41-sq-km garden, with over 5000 varieties of plants, was designed by order of the Prince Regent Dom João in 1808. It's quiet and serene on weekdays and blossoms with families and music on weekends. The row of palms (planted when the garden first opened), the Amazonas section and the lake containing the huge Vitória Régia water lilies are some of the highlights. A pleasant outdoor café overlooks the gardens in back. Take insect repellent.

PARQUE LAGE Map pp236-8

☎ 2538 1091; www.eavparquelage.org.br in Portuguese; Rua Jardim Botânico 414; ☺ 7am-6pm; any bus marked 'Jardim Botânico'

This is a beautiful park at the base of Parque Nacional da Tijuca, about a kilometer from the Jardim Botânico. It has English-style gardens, little lakes and a mansion that now houses the Instituto Nacional de Belas Artes, which often hosts art exhibitions and occasional performances. The park is a tranquil place – a favorite of families with small children. Native Atlantic rain forest surrounds Parque Lage. This is the starting point for challenging hikes up Corcovado (not recommended alone).

LAGOA

FUNDIÇÃO EVA KLABIN RAPAPORT
Map pp236-8

☎ 2523 3471; Av Epitácio Pessoa 2480, Lagoa; ☺ 1-5pm Wed-Sun

An old mansion full of antiques, the former residence of Eva Klabin Rapaport houses the works of art she collected for 60 years. Reflecting Eva's diverse interests, the collection contains 1100 pieces from the ancient Egypt, Greece and China. Paintings, sculptures, silver, furniture and carpets are also on display.

LAGOA RODRIGO DE FREITAS
Map pp236-8

One of the city's most picturesque spots, Lagoa has 7.2km of cycling/walking path around the lake. Bikes (p145) are available for hire near Parque Brigadeiro Faria Lima. Although it sounds cheesy, hiring a paddle boat is another way to enjoy the lake, especially when the Christmas tree is lit up across the water (December through early January). For those who prefer *caipirinhas* to plastic swan boats, the kiosks (p110) in Parque dos Patins offer lakeside dining al fresco, often accompanied by live *forró* (traditional music from the Northeast).

PARQUE DA CATACUMBA Map pp236-8

Av Epitácio Pessoa; ☺ 8am-7pm

Inaugurated in 1979, Catacumba is the site of Brazil's first outdoor sculptural garden. The site of a former favela (which was demolished to create the park) Catacumba sits atop the Morro dos Cabritos, which rises from the Lagoa Rodrigo de Freitas. It's a choice place to escape the heat while strolling through some fascinating works by artists such as Roberto Moriconi and Bruno Giorgi. Superb views await those willing to climb to the top of the hill (130m). During the summer, Catacumba hosts free Sunday-afternoon concerts featuring top performers in its outdoor amphitheater. Check *O Globo*'s weekend listings for details.

COPACABANA & LEME

Eating p111; Shopping p156; Sleeping p169

Fronted by sea and backed by steep hills, the neighborhoods of Copacabana and Leme harbor one of the world's most well-known beaches, stretching 4.5km from end to end. Copacabana is also one of the planet's most densely populated areas, with over 25,000 people per square kilometer crammed into the narrow strip of land.

The name Copacabana comes from a small Bolivian village on Lake Titicaca. Historians believe a statue of the Virgin Mary (Our Lady of Copacabana) was brought to Rio and consecrated inside a small chapel near Arpoador. Copacabana remained a small fishing village until Túnel Velho opened in 1891, connecting Copacabana with the rest of the city.

The construction of the neoclassical Copacabana Palace Hotel in 1923 heralded a new era for Copacabana – and Rio – as South America's premier destination for the rich and fabulous. Copacabana remained Rio's untarnished gem until the 1970s, when the area began to fall into decline. Today, the neighborhood is a mix of chaos and beauty, gorgeous beaches fronted by luxury hotels, and the favelas ever present along the perimeters. Copacabana is also the heart of Rio's red-light district. After dark, prostitutes troll the restaurants along Av Atlântica while over-stimulated foreigners wander the strip clubs around Av Princesa Isabel.

Transportation

Bus Along Av NS de Copacabana, you can take Nos 119, 154, 413, 415, 455 and 474. You can also look for the signs in the windows: 'Praça XV,' 'Castelo,' and 'Praça Mauá' all head there. Buses with signs saying 'via Aterro' take the expressway (closed Sunday) between Botafogo and Centro, meaning they don't stop anywhere along the way. Buses to Ipanema and Leblon are also plentiful. Leblon buses are clearly marked, while for Ipanema buses, you'll need to look for signs that indicate 'Praça General Osório.'

In spite of its chaotic streets and seedy elements, Copacabana still has charm beneath its theatrical facade. Old-school *botecos* (open-air bar), eclectic restaurants and nightclubs, myriad shops selling everything under the tropical sun, and of course the handsome beach still cast a spell on many visitors. In spite of naysayers, Copacabana will continue to be the archetype for Brazil's growing tourism in the years to come.

Orientation

Bordered by mountains on three sides and ocean to the east, congested Copacabana contains only three parallel streets traversing its entire length. Av Atlântica runs along the ocean. The one-way Av NS de Copacabana is two blocks inland, and runs east. One block further inland, Rua Barata Ribeiro is also one-way, running west (toward Ipanema and Leblon). The names of all these streets change when they reach Ipanema. As in Ipanema, part of the beachside street (Av Atlântica in this case) closes on Sundays and holidays (until 6pm), giving freer reign to the joggers, cyclists and rollerbladers normally jostling for space on the sidewalks. Av Princesa Isabel, which serves as the boundary between Copacabana and Leme, is the principal thoroughfare to Botafogo, Centro and points north.

MUSEU HISTÓRICO DO EXÉRCITO E FORTE DE COPACABANA

Map pp234-5

☎ 2521 1032; Av Atlântica & Rua Francisco Otaviano; admission US$2; ☼ 10am-4pm Tue-Sun

Built in 1914 on the promontory of the old Our Lady of Copacabana chapel, the fort of Copacabana was one of Rio's premier defenses against attack. You can still see its original features, including walls up to 12m thick, defended by Krupp cannons. The several floors of exhibits tracing the early days of the Portuguese colony to the mid-19th-century aren't the most tastefully done, but the view alone is worth a visit. Be sure to stop in the recently opened **Confeitaria Colombo** (p113).

MORRO DO LEME Map pp234-5

☎ 2275 7696; admission US$1; ☀ 9am-noon Sat & Sun, reservations required

East of Av Princesa Isabel, Morro do Leme contains an environmental protection area. The 11 hectares of Atlantic rain forest are home to numerous species of birds, such as the saddle and bishop tanagers, thrushes and the East Brazilian house wren. An hour-long tour is available by booking ahead.

COPACABANA & LEME BEACH

Map pp234-5

A magnificent confluence of land and sea, the long, scalloped beach of Copacabana and Leme runs for 4.5km, with a flurry of activity always stretching along its length: over-amped footballers singing their team's anthem, Cariocas and tourists lining up for *caipirinhas* at kiosks, favela kids showing off their football skills, beach vendors shouting out their wares among the beached and tanned bodies.

As in Ipanema each group stakes out their stretch of sand. Leme is a mix of older residents and favela kids, while the area between the Copacabana Palace Hotel and Rua Fernando Mendes is the gay and transvestite section, known as the Stock or Stock Market –

easily recognized by the rainbow flag. Young football and *futevôlei* (soccer volleyball) players hold court near Rua Santa Clara. Posts five and six are a mix of favela kids and Carioca retirees, while the beach next to the Forte de Copacabana is the fishermen's community beach. In the morning, you can buy a fresh catch for the day.

The beach is lit at night and there are police in the area, but it's still not wise to walk there after dark – stay on the hotel side of Av Atlântica if you take a stroll. Av NS de Copacabana is also dangerous – watch out on weekends, when the shops are closed and there are few locals around.

Neighborhoods – Botafogo & Urca

BOTAFOGO & URCA

Eating p115; Shopping p157; Sleeping p173

A largely middle-class residential area, Botafogo lacks the sensuality of Ipanema and the decadence of Copacabana, but it's one of Rio's most traditional neighborhoods. With small museums, excellent theaters, quaint bookstores, neighborhood bars and a welcome shortage of high-rises, Botafogo is an excellent place to get acquainted with an authentic side of Rio.

Named after the Portuguese settler João Pereira de Souza Botafogo, the area attained prominence in the late 1800s when the Portuguese Court arrived in Brazil. Dom João VI's wife, Carlota Joaquina, had a country villa, and she used to bathe in the Baía de Guanabara. With royalty established in the area, many mansions were constructed, some of which still stand – as schools, theaters and cultural centers.

In the 19th century, development was spurred by the construction of a tram that ran to the botanical garden (Jardim Botânico), linking the bay with the lake (Lagoa). This artery still plays a vital role in Rio's traffic flow, though, even so, Botafogo's streets are extremely congested. Several palatial mansions left over from Joaquina's days housed foreign consulates when Rio was still the capital of Brazil.

The tranquil, shady streets of Urca offer a pleasant escape from the urban bustle of other parts of the city. An eclectic mix of building styles and manicured gardens line its streets, with local residents strolling among them. Along the seawall, which forms the northwestern perimeter of **Pão de Açúcar** (p65), fishermen cast for dinner as couples lounge beneath palm trees, taking in views of Baía de Guanabara and **Cristo Redentor** (p76) off in the distance. Tiny Praia Vermelha in the south has one Rio's finest beach views. A lovely walking trail begins from there.

Although it was the site of one of the first Portuguese garrisons in the region, almost 300 years elapsed before Urca developed into a residential neighborhood. Today it holds the distinction of being one of the safest and – in spite of the Pão de Açúcar cable car in its midst – least discovered by foreign visitors.

Orientation

Botafogo lies just north of Copacabana and borders the Baía de Guanabara to the east. A small beach faces the bay, but unlike in Dona Carlota Joaquina's time, the water here is now too polluted for swimming. To the north lies the Flamengo district, while heading west, along Rua Humaitá leads to Lagoa. Rua Voluntários da Patria, which runs the length of Botafogo, is one of the main thoroughfares in the region. The region's eastern boundary is Av Lauro Sodré, the chaotic artery that feeds into Copacabana. Along this stretch are some of Botafogo's more mammoth attractions: **Canecão** (p137), the large concert hall; **Rio Sul** (p158), an enormous shopping mall; and **Rio-Off Price Shopping** (p158), a discount mall.

To the east of Av Laura Sodré runs Av Pasteur. This is the only road into Urca. It continues past the Praça Euzebio Oliveira to the Pão de Açúcar cable car, which is a stone's throw from Praia Vermelha. Northeast from there is the pleasant neighborhood, which consists of only a handful of quiet streets – all built on landfill. The neighborhood's most prominent features are visible from the other side of the city. Morro da Urca and Morro de Pão de Açúcar loom majestically overhead, while Morro de Cara de Cão (Face of the Dog Mountain) lies hidden behind them (to the northeast). At the tip of this hill lies Fortaleza de São João, site of one of Rio's first settlements.

Museu do Índio (p65)

BOTAFOGO

MUSEU CASA DE RUI BARBOSA
Map pp232-3

☎ 2537 0036; www.casaruibarbosa.gov.br in Portuguese; Rua São Clemente 134; admission US$0.50; ⏱ 9:30am-5pm Tue-Fri, 2-5pm Sat & Sun

The former mansion (completely restored in 2003) of famous Brazilian journalist and diplomat Rui Barbosa is now a museum housing his library and personal belongings, along with an impressive archive of manuscripts and first editions of other Brazilian authors, such as Machado de Assis and José de Alençar. Barbosa played a major role in shaping the country's socio-economic development in the early 20th century.

MUSEU DO ÍNDIO Map pp232-3

☎ 2286 8899; www.museudoindio.org.br; Rua das Palmeiras 55; admission US$2; ⏱ 9:30am-5:30pm Tue-Fri, 1-5pm Sat & Sun

Featuring multimedia exhibitions on Brazil's northern tribes, the small Museu do Índio provides an excellent introduction to the economic, religious and social life of Brazil's indigenous people. Next to native food and medicinal plants, the four life-sized dwellings in the courtyard were actually built by four different tribes. As a branch of Funai (the National Indian Foundation), the museum contains an excellent archive of 14,000 objects, 50,000 photographs and 200 sound recordings. Its indigenous ethnography library containing 16,000 volumes by local and foreign authors is open to the public during the week.

MUSEU VILLA-LOBOS Map pp232-3

☎ 2266 3845; Rua Sorocaba 200; admission free; ⏱ 10am-5:30pm Mon-Fri

Housed in a century-old building, the modest museum is dedicated to the memory of Brazil's greatest classical composer – and founder of the Brazilian Academy of Music – Heitor Villa-Lobos. In addition to scores, musical instruments – including the piano on which he composed – and personal items, the museum contains an extensive sound archive. The gardens were designed by landscape architect Burle Marx.

PASMADO OVERLOOK Map pp232-3
Rua Bartolomeu Portela

Sweeping views of Enseada de Botafogo (Botafogo Inlet), Pão de Açúcar and Corcovado await visitors who make the journey up

---

Botafogo & Urca Top Five

- Ascending **Pão de Açúcar** (below).
- Taking in the live samba beats to the backdrop of crashing waves at **Praia Vermelha** (p115).
- Strolling along **Pista Cláudio Coutinho** (p66).
- Dining on *moqueca* at **Yorubá** (p116).
- Listening to Amazonian bird calls at the **Museu do Índio** (opposite).

Pasmado. It's best reached in early morning or late afternoon, when the light is at its best for capturing the postcard panorama. Visitors will also be able to see details of a favela from above. The overlook is best reached by taxi via Rua General Severiano.

URCA

PÃO DE AÇÚCAR Map pp232-3

☎ 2546 8400; Praça General Tibúrcio; admission US$10; ⏱ 8am-10pm; bus 107 from Centro, 500, 511 or 512 from Zona Sul

Pão de Açúcar is dazzling. Seen from its peak, Rio is undoubtedly the most beautiful city in the world. There are many good times to make the ascent, but sunset on a clear day is the most rewarding.

Everyone must go to Pão de Açúcar, but if you can, avoid it from about 10am to 11am and 2pm to 3pm, which is when most tourist buses arrive. Avoid cloudy days as well.

To reach the summit, 396m above Rio and the Baía de Guanabara, you have to take two cable cars. The first ascends 220m to Morro da Urca. From here, you can see Baía de Guanabara and along the winding coastline. On the ocean side of the mountain is Praia Vermelha, in a small, calm bay. Morro da Urca has its own restaurant, souvenir shops, a playground, an outdoor theater and a **helipad** (p54).

The second cable car goes up to Pão de Açúcar. At the top, the city unfolds beneath you, with Corcovado mountain and Cristo Redentor off to the west, and the long curve of Copacabana Beach to the south. If the breathtaking heights unsteady you, a drink stand is on hand to serve *caipirinhas* or cups of Skol (beer). The two-stage cable cars depart every 30 minutes.

Those who'd rather take the long way to the summit should sign up with one of the granite-hugging climbing tours offered by various outfits in Rio (p54).

MUSEU DE CIÊNCIA DA TERRA

Map pp232-3

☎ 2546 0200; Av Pasteur 404; admission free;
☪ 10am-4pm Tue-Sun

With curved staircases and looming statues out front, this majestic building went through a number of incarnations before it finally ended up housing the Earth Science Museum. The museum appeals mostly to children, who still marvel at some of the life-sized dinosaurs on display. The four-room exhibit gives a quick overview of the natural history of Brazil since the Big Bang. Other rooms showcase the museum's extensive collection of minerals, rocks and meteorites – 5000 pieces in all.

PRAIA DA URCA Map pp232-3

This tiny beach is popular with neighborhood kids who gather here for pickup football games when school is not in session (and sometimes when it is). A small restaurant, **Garota da Urca** (p116), lies near the beach.

PRAIA VERMELHA Map pp232-3

Beneath Morro da Urca, the narrow Praia Vermelha has superb views of the rocky coastline from the shore. Its coarse sand gives the beach the name *vermelha* (red). Because the beach is protected by the headland, the water is usually calm.

PISTA CLÁUDIO COUTINHO Map pp232-3

☪ 6am-sunset

All day walkers and joggers course along this paved 2km trail winding along the southern contour of Morro do Urca. It's a lush area, shaded by trees, with the waves crashing on the rocks below. Keep an eye out for families of *micos* – small, coastal-dwelling monkeys with gray fur, striped tails and tiny scrooge-like faces. About 300m along the path, there's a small unmarked trail leading off the path. This leads up to Morro da Urca. From there you can continue up to **Pão de Açúcar** (p65) by cable car, saving a few *reais*. Pão de Açúcar can also be climbed – but it's not recommended without climbing gear.

FLAMENGO, LARANJEIRAS & COSME VELHO

Eating p116; Shopping p158; Sleeping p174

Flamengo was once Rio's finest residential district – some believe the first Portuguese house was constructed here – but when the tunnel to Copacabana was completed in 1904, the upper classes began moving to the unblemished shoreline to

the south. Today, Flamengo maintains its largely residential roots, and owing to ongoing gentrification, the residents are increasingly comprised of younger, single Cariocas. Like Botafogo, the neighborhood provides a fine window into a part of Rio that is unadorned – but no less disarming. Along tree-shaded sidewalks, old-school restaurants and historic bars lie beside fragrant juice bars and MPB-playing Internet cafés. Flamengo also boasts one of the world's largest urban parks, **Parque do Flamengo** (p75), fronting a scenic beach (too polluted for swimming).

Bordering Flamengo to the west, Laranjeiras is among the most tightly interwoven communities of the Zona Sul. The connected backyards, small businesses and chatter among neighbors on the streets bring a small-town feel to the district. Ironically, this familial atmosphere was once the site of a famous brothel at the beginning of the 20th century. **Casa Rosa** (p136), situated on Rua Alice, once attracted a clientele of intellectuals and artists – today it hosts one of Rio's best nightclubs and is still popular with the kind of people who might have patronized it a century ago.

Transportation

Flamengo

Bus From Leblon, Ipanema and Copacabana take No 571 or 572, which travel north along Rua Sen Vergueiro and south along Rua Marques de Abrantes.

Metro Flamengo, Largo do Machado.

Laranjeiras

Bus From Ipanema (Praça General Osório), bus No 456 travels through Copacabana and along Rua das Laranjeiras; from Largo do Machado take No 406A.

Cosme Velho

Bus From Centro, Glória or Flamengo take No 180; from Copacabana, Ipanema or Leblon take No 583 or 584.

(Continued on page 75)

1 Street Carnaval (p23),
Ipanema 2 Carnaval (p23),
Sambódromo 3 Street Carnaval
(p23), Ipanema 4 Trumpeter,
street Carnaval (p23), Ipanema

1 View of Arpoador Beach, from Arpoador Inn (p166) *2* Boy, Ipanema Beach (p58) *3* Surfer, Arpoador (p92) *4* Nam Thai (p108)

1 *Ipanema Beach (p58)* 2 *Cyclist,*
Lagoa Rodrigo de Freitas (p61)
3 *Streetscape, Leblon (p57)*
4 *Somersault, Ipanema Beach (p58)*

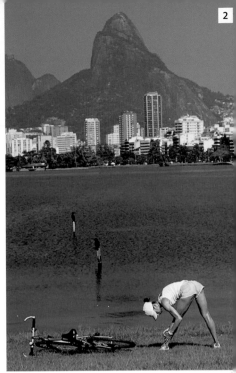

1 *Diver, Copacabana (p63)*
2 *Children, Botafogo (p63)* 3 *Tourist boat (p53), Flamengo Beach*
4 *Boardwalk, Copacabana (p62)*

1 *Parque Guinle (p76)* 2 *Joggers, Urca (p65)* 3 *Bip Bip (p133)*
4 *Fisherman, Fishermen's Community Beach (p63)*

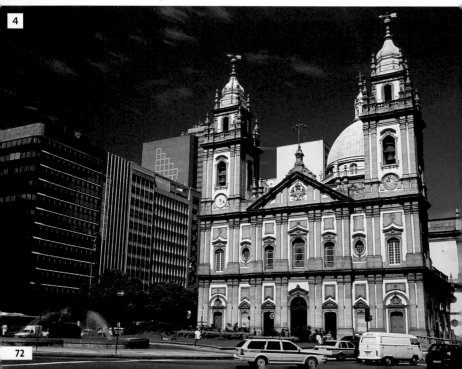

1 *Escadaria Selarón (p87)* 2 *Samba club (p134), Lapa* 3 *Cais do Oriente (p120)* 4 *Igreja de Nossa Senhora de Candelária (p81)*

1 Boys, Santa Teresa (p83) 2 Rio Scenarium (p137) 3 Tram, Arcos do Lapa (p86) 4 Museu da República (p77)

1 *Rua da Lapa, Paraty (p182)*
2 *Fisherman, Búzios (p186)* 3 *Museu do Arte Contemporânea (p90)*
4 *Catedral São Pedro de Alcântara (p190), Petrópolis*

(Continued from page 66)

Cosme Velho lies west of Laranjeiras and is one of the city's most visited neighborhoods – if only for the statue of Cristo Redentor soaring above its curvy streets. The district also contains a museum of arte naïf and the charming **Largo do Boticário** (p76), a preserved plaza that gives onlookers a glimpse of 19th-century Rio. Cosme Velho and Laranjeiras both have their share of nightlife options; their jazz cafés and discreet dance clubs cater to Cariocas tired of the Zona Sul scene.

Flamengo, Laranjeiras & Cosme Velho Top Five

- Sharing **Cristo Redentor's** (p76) panoramic gaze atop Corcovado.
- Dancing until daybreak at **Casa Rosa** (p136).
- Bike riding lazily through **Parque do Flamengo** (below).
- Listening to laidback *chorinho* at **Clan Café** (p133).
- Indulging in *churrasco* to **Porção Rio's** (p117) stunning view.

Orientation

The small neighborhood of Flamengo lies north of Botafogo overlooking the bay. Its eastern boundary is formed by several wide roads – Praia do Flamengo and Av Infante Dom Henrique – leading north and south. The verdant Parque do Flamengo begins just across these roads and contains a restaurant, museum, sports fields, and many paths winding along the manicured landscape as it parallels the Flamengo beach. Southward-running Rua Marques de Abrantes is Flamengo's main street and site of its most prominent restaurant scene. Inland, the Praça São Salvador is one of Flamengo's small, charming parks worth a stroll for those interested in taking in the neighborhood. A few blocks north of this park is the bigger **Parque Guinle** (p76) containing the **Palácio de Laranjeiras** (p76), seat of the state government. Between the two parks is Rua das Laranjeiras, a thoroughfare that runs west, eventually becoming Rua Cosme Velho as it leads into the neighborhood of the same name. Off this main road you'll reach the cog railway station of Corcovado, the **Museu Internacional de Arte Naïf do Brasil** (p76) beyond it, and the Largo do Boticário a few blocks further west.

North of Laranjeiras is the picturesque neighborhood of Santa Teresa, though access to its tortuous roads is difficult from here owing to the Morro So Judas Tadeu separating the two neighborhoods.

FLAMENGO

ARTE-SESC CULTURAL CENTER
Map pp232-3

☎ 3138 1343; Rua Marquês de Abrantes 99; admission free; ☽ noon-6pm Tue & Wed, noon-8pm Thu-Sat, 11am-5pm Sun

This small cultural center is housed in an early 20th century mansion built by Czech entrepreneur Frederico Figner. Figner's record company is better known than he is – Odeon records being one of the top labels in the country. The small gallery features good exhibits, often highlighting Rio's development in the early 20th century. Downstairs is the excellent **Senac Bistro** (p117).

MUSEU CARMEN MIRANDA Map pp232-3

☎ 2551 2597; facing Av Rui Barbosa 560; admission US$0.50; ☽ 10am-5pm Tue-Fri, noon-5pm Sat & Sun

At one time Carmen Miranda was the highest-paid entertainer in the USA. She is also the only Brazilian to leave her prints in Hollywood's Walk of Fame. Although she's largely forgotten there, the talented Brazilian singer still has her fans in Rio, and has become a cult icon among the gay community. For those interested in getting to know one of Brazil's stars of the '40s, the small museum dedicated to her is an excellent starting point. In addition to photographs and music of that era, the museum showcases the starlet's iconographic costumes and jewelry.

PARQUE DO FLAMENGO
Map pp232-3 & Map pp228-30

Officially called Parque Brigadeiro Eduardo Gomes, Parque do Flamengo was the result of a landfill project that leveled the São Antônio hill in 1965, and now spreads all the way from downtown Rio through Glória, Catete and Flamengo, and on around to Botafogo. The 1.2 million sq meters of land reclaimed from the sea now stages every manner of Carioca outdoor activity. Cyclists and rollerbladers glide along the myriad paths winding through the park, while the many football fields and sports courts are framed against the sea. On Sundays and holidays, the avenues through the park are closed (from 7am to 6pm), and a welcome calm descends on the verdant park.

Designed by famous Brazilian landscaper Burle Marx (who also landscaped Brasília), the park features some 170,000 trees of 300 different species. In addition there are three museums in the park: the **Museu de Arte Moderna** (p87), the **Monumento Nacional dos Mortos da II Guerra Mundial** (p87) and the **Museu Carmen Miranda** (p75).

LARANJEIRAS

MARACATU BRASIL Map pp232-3

☎ 2557 4754; www.maracatubrasil.com.br; Rua Ipiranga 49, 2nd fl, Laranjeiras; 🕑 10am-6pm Mon-Sat

One of Rio's best places to study percussion, Maracatu Brasil is very active in music events throughout the city. Instructors here offer courses in a number of different drumming styles: zabumba, pandeiro, symphonic percussion, and others. You can arrange for private lessons (US$30 per hour) or sign up for group classes if you plan to stick around a while (US$20 to US$60 a month). On the 1st floor of the lime-green building, Maracatu sells instruments (p159).

PARQUE GUINLE & THE PALÁCIO DE LARANJEIRAS Map pp232-3

☎ 2299 5233; Rua Paulo Cesar de Andrade 407; palace guided visits 1pm, 2pm & 3pm Mon & Fri

Designed by French landscaper Gochet, the park has a European air, and has a small lake, lanes and lawns. Overlooking the park is the resplendent **Palácio da Laranjeiras**, built between 1909 and 1914 by architect Silva Telles. Today it is the official residence in Rio of the state governor, and contains the same artwork, furniture and ornamental objects found when the palace was built. You can tour parts of the palace by guided appointments (by advance notice only).

COSME VELHO

CRISTO REDENTOR Map pp226-7

☎ 2558 1329; www.corcovado.com.br; Rua Cosme Velho 513 (cog station); admission US$10; 🕑 8:30am-6:30pm; bus 180, 184, 583 or 584

Atop Corcovado, which means 'hunchback,' Cristo Redentor (Christ the Redeemer) gazes out over Rio, a placid expression on his well-crafted face. The mountain rises straight up from the city to a height of 710m, and at night, the brightly lit, 38m-high statue is visible from nearly every part of the city – all 1145 tons of the open-armed redeemer.

The view from the top of Corcovado provides a spectacular panorama of Rio and its surroundings. With his visage turned to **Pão de Açúcar** (p65), Christ's left arm points toward the Zona Norte, and Maracanã, the world's largest soccer stadium, crowds the foreground. You can also see the international airport on Ilha do Governador just beyond and the Serra dos Órgãos mountain range in the far distance. Beneath Christ's right arm is the Lagoa Rodrigo de Freitas, 'Hipódromo de Gávea,' Jardim Botânico, and over to Ipanema and Leblon.

Corcovado lies within the **Parque Nacional da Tijuca** (p56). You can get here by car or by taxi, but the best way is to go up in the cog train (departures every 30 minutes). For the best view, sit on the right-hand side going up. You can also drive to the top. Taxi drivers typically charge around US$20 for return trips with waiting time.

A word of advice: choose a clear day to come up to the top or you'll be disappointed. It might be clear at sea level and cloudy up high, so check the mountains before you make a move.

LARGO DO BOTICÁRIO Map pp232-3

Rua Cosme Velho 822

The brightly painted houses on this picturesque square date from the early 19th century. Largo do Boticário was named in honor of the Portuguese gentleman – Joaquim Luiz da Silva Souto – who once ran an apothecary, or *boticário*, utilized by the royal family. The sound of a brook coming from the nearby forest adds to the square's charm. Occasional art and cultural events are hosted here.

MUSEU INTERNACIONAL DE ARTE NAÏF DO BRASIL Map pp232-3

☎ 2205 8612; www.museunaif.com.br; Rua Cosme Velho 561; admission US$2.50; 🕑 10am-6pm Tue-Fri, noon-6pm Sat & Sun; bus 180, 184, 583 or 584

Vivid color and a playful perspective are two of the characteristics of arte naïf paintings, and many of the artists of this style came from outside the academy. Also known as primitivist, arte naïf paintings in this permanent collection are extensive: over 8000 pieces, executed by artists from 130 countries, dating from the 15th century to the present. This makes it the largest museum of its kind in the world. Visitors receive a 20% discount by showing a ticket stub to the Corcovado cog train – one block away.

CATETE & GLÓRIA

Eating p117; Shopping p160; Sleeping p175

An aura of faded splendor pervades the neighborhoods of Catete and Glória. Like Flamengo, these twin districts flourished in the mid-19th century, when their location at the outskirts of the city made them among the most desirable places to live. Many noblemen and merchants built stately homes in this district, including the Barão de Novo Friburgo, who built the stately Palácio do Catete. By the end of the century, though, the aristocracy had moved further out as the inner city expanded – a trend that in some ways continues today.

The **Palácio do Catete**, which once served as the republic's seat of power, remains the jewel of the neighborhood, and its attached gardens are a peaceful refuge from the often chaotic streets outside. Another place of historic interest lies a few blocks north. Atop a small hill overlooking the bay, the baroque **Igreja de Nossa Senhora da Glória de Outeiro** (p78) dates from the 18th century and was a favorite of Dom Pedro II and the royal family.

Aside from these vestiges of the past, most of the area is now an area of small-scale commerce. A handful of working-class restaurants, unkempt juice bars and a movie theater lie scattered among office-supply stores, clothing shops and hardware and plumbing-supplies stores.

Today, a number of the former mansions have become hotels – some in serious need of a paint job. With many budget options among these crumbling buildings, Glória and Catete attract a number of shoestring travelers who don't mind the workaday bustle of the district – or mind it, but stay there nonetheless.

Transportation

Bus To Rua da Glória: from Leblon take No 571; from Copacabana take No 572; from Largo do Machado No 569 goes to Leblon via Jóquei, while No 570 also goes there via Copacabana.

Metro Largo do Machado, Catete, Glória.

Orientation

Catete and Glória lie just west of the Baía de Guanabara. Glória is the northernmost neighborhood of the two. Rua do Catete, which runs north, is the main thoroughfare, and it connects the area with Flamengo to the south and Lapa to the north. Busy Praia do Flamengo, separates the neighborhood from Parque do Flamengo, although there are a number of pedestrian overpasses to reach the park.

CATETE

MUSEU DA REPÚBLICA Map pp232-3

☎ 2558 6350; www.museudarepublica.org.br; Rua do Catete 153; admission US$2; ☯ noon-5pm Tue & Thu-Fri, 2-5pm Wed & Sat-Sun; bus 571, metro Catete

The Museu da República, which is located in the Palácio do Catete, has been wonderfully restored. Built between 1858 and 1866 and easily distinguished by the bronze condors on the eaves, the palace was home to the president of Brazil from 1896 until 1954, when President Getúlio Vargas committed suicide here.

Vargas had made powerful enemies in the armed forces and the political right wing and was attacked in the press as a communist for his attempts to raise the minimum wage and increase taxes on the middle and upper classes. Tensions reached a critical level when one of Vargas' bodyguards fired shots at a journalist. Although the journalist was unharmed, an air force officer guarding him was killed, giving the armed forces the pretext they needed to demand the resignation of Vargas. In response, Vargas committed suicide, and his emotional suicide note read, 'I choose this means to be with you (the Brazilian people) always...I gave you my life; now I offer my death.' The bedroom in which the suicide occurred is eerily preserved on the 3rd floor.

The museum has a good collection of art and artifacts from the Republican period, and also houses a good lunch restaurant, art-house cinema and bookstore.

Catete & Glória Top Five

- Wandering through the eerie rooms on the 3rd floor of the **Museu da República** (p77), housed in the Palácio do Catete.
- Enjoying afternoon tea at **Bistro Jardins** (p118) overlooking the gardens behind Palácio do Catete.
- Absorbing colorful folk art at the **Museu de Folclórico Edson Carneiro** (below).
- Dancing to electronic beats at one of **Nautillus's** (p140) rotating parties.
- Praying for good weather in the cool splendor of the **Igreja de NS da Glória de Outeiro** (opposite).

MUSEU DE FOLCLÓRICO EDSON CARNEIRO Map pp232-3

☎ 2205 0090; Rua do Catete 181; admission US$1; ☽ 11am-6pm Tue-Fri; 3-6pm Sat & Sun; bus 571, metro Catete

Created in 1968, the museum is an excellent introduction to Brazilian folk art, particularly from the Northeast. Its permanent collection comprises 1400 pieces, and includes Candomblé costumes, ceramic figurines and religious costumes used in festivals. The museum also features a folklore library and a small shop, selling handicrafts, books and folk music. The museum lies next door to the Palácio do Catete.

PARQUE DO CATETE Map pp232-3

☎ 2205 0090; Rua do Catete 181; admission US$1; ☽ 11am-6pm Tue-Fri; 3-6pm Sat & Sun; bus 571, metro Catete

The small landscaped park on the grounds of the Palácio do Catete provides a quiet refuge from the city. Its pond and shade-covered walks are popular with neighborhood strollers and children. Special performances in the park include concerts and plays. The **Bistro Jardins** (p118), overlooking the park, makes a fine spot for afternoon tea.

GLÓRIA

IGREJA DE NOSSA SENHORA DA GLÓRIA DE OUTEIRO Map pp228-30

☎ 2557 4600; www.outeirodagloria.org.br; Praça Nossa Senhora da Glória 135; ☽ 9am-5pm Tue-Fri, 9am-noon Sat & Sun; guided visits first Sun of month; bus 119 or 571

This tiny church atop Ladeira da Glória commands lovely views out over Parque do Flamengo and the bay. Considered one of the finest examples of religious colonial architecture in Brazil, the church dates from 1739 and became the favorite of the royal family upon their arrival in 1808. Some of the more fascinating features of the church are its octagonal design, its single tower (through which visitors enter), the elaborately carved altar (attributed to the artist Mestre Valentim) and its elegant, 18th-century tiles.

CENTRO & CINELÂNDIA

Eating p118; Shopping p160; Sleeping p176

Rio's bustling commercial district, Centro is the city's business and finance hub. By day, the wide avenues and narrow lanes adjoining them fill with lawyers and bankers, temps and delivery boys, all making their way through the crowded, noisy streets. Although hyper-modern on one hand, among Centro's numerous high-rise office buildings are remnants of its once-magnificent past. Looming baroque churches, wide plazas and cobblestone streets lined with colorful colonial buildings lie scattered throughout the district.

Many pedestrian-only areas crisscross Centro. The most famous of these is known as Saara, a giant street bazaar crammed with discount stores. In the last century, Saara attracted an influx of immigrants from the Middle East, and if you're in search of authentic Lebanese cuisine, this is the place to go.

Centro has restaurants to suit every taste and budget, from greasy diners to elegant French restaurants overlooking the bay. After lunch, Cariocas browse the district's bookstores, music shops, galleries and curio shops. By workday's end (5pm or 6pm), the pubs and streetside cafés buzz with life as Cariocas unwind over draughts or cocktails.

In addition to its culinary attractions, Centro has a number of museums, historic churches and attractive cultural centers featuring changing exhibitions. Visitors to the area will also find essential services: the main airline offices are here, as are foreign consulates, Brazilian government agencies, money-exchange houses, banks and travel agencies.

At the southern edge of the business district, Cinelândia's shops, bars, restaurants and movie theaters are popular day and night. The bars and restaurants get crowded at lunch and after work, when street musicians sometimes wander the area. There's a greater mix of Cariocas here than in any other section of the city. Several gay and mixed bars stay open until late.

Orientation

Av Rio Branco is the wide, chaotic boulevard that connects Centro to the Zona Sul. In addition to banks and travel agents, the street harbors several museums, theaters and cultural centers, most near Praça Floriano at the southern end of Centro. Many blocks north of there, Av Presidente Vargas intersects Rio Branco at Praça Pio X, which fronts the impressive **Igreja Nossa Senhora de Candelária** (p81) – one of the city's more ornate churches. The metro travels beneath both Rio Branco (to the Zona Sul) and Presidente Vargas (to the Sambódromo and points west) as it travels in and out of Centro. Most buses leave for the Zona Sul along Rio Branco.

The Saara Bazaar lies west of Rio Branco along Rua da Alfândega, Rua Senhor dos Passos, Rua de Buenos Aires and Av Passos. Other pedestrian streets lie west of Rio Branco. Cobbled Travessa do Comércio, becomes a lively scene weekday evenings. South of there is Praça 15 de Novembro, which lies just east of the breezy Praça Mercado Municipal, the departure point for ferries to Niterói and Paquetá. Just south of there is the Santos Dumont area, at Centro's eastern edge.

Cinelândia is a small area bounded by Praça Floriano at its eastern edge, Rua Evaristo da Veiga to the north Rua Republica de Paraguai to the west and the Passeio Público to the south. Its narrow pedestrian streets are lined with cheap restaurants and bars spilling onto the sidewalk.

Transportation

Bus Numerous buses travel to Centro and Cinelândia. From the Zona Sul look for the following destinations printed in the window: 'Rio Branco,' 'Praça XV,' 'Praça Tiradentes,' 'Castelo' and 'Praça Mauá.' The following buses also go there: Nos 119, 154, 413, 415, 455 and 474.

Metro Cinelândia, Carioca, Uruguaiana, Presidente Vargas.

CENTRO

BIBLIOTECA NACIONAL Map pp228-30

☎ 2262 8255; Av Rio Branco 219; admission free; ☽ 9am-8pm Mon-Fri, 9am-3pm Sat, free guided visits 11am, 1pm & 4pm Mon-Fri; metro Cinelândia

Inaugurated in 1910, the national library is the largest in Latin America, with more than 8 million volumes. Designed by Francisco Marcelino de Souza Aguiar, the building is neoclassical, surrounded by Corinthian columns. On the ground floor, the periodical section is to the left, and general works are to the right. On the 2nd floor are many rare books and manuscripts, including two copies of the precious Mainz Psalter Bible, printed in 1492. Owing to their fragility, most of these rare books can be viewed only on microfilm.

CAMPO DE SANTANA Map pp240-1

Campo de Santana is a pleasant park that, on 7 September 1822, was the scene of the proclamation of Brazil's independence from Portugal by Emperor Dom Pedro I of Portugal. The landscaped park with artificial lake and swans is a fine place for a respite from the chaotic streets, and you're liable to see a few *agoutis* (a rodent native to Brazil) running wild here.

CASA FRANÇA-BRASIL Map pp228-30

☎ 2253 5366; www.casafrancabrasil.rj.gov.br in Portuguese; Rua Visconde de Itaboraí 78; admission free; ☽ noon-8pm Tue-Sun

In a neoclassical building dating from 1820, the Casa França-Brasil opened in 1990 for the purpose of advancing cultural relations between France and Brazil. The main hall features changing exhibitions often dealing with political and cultural facets of Carioca society. The building is considered the most important Classical Revival structure in Brazil, and once served as a customs house.

Centro & Cinelândia Top Five

- Dining in the converted mansion **Cais do Oriente** (p120).
- Attending the opera or ballet at the lavish **Teatro Municipal** (p125).
- Drinking early evening cocktails on quaint **Travessa do Comércio** (p83).
- Picking through shops at the **Saara Bazaar** (p79), followed by lunch at **Cedra do Líbano** (p121).
- Catching an exhibition at **Banco do Brasil Centro Cultural** (below).

CENTRO CULTURAL BANCO DO BRASIL Map pp228-30

☎ 3808 2000; www.cultura-e.com.br in Portuguese; Rua Primeiro de Março 66; admission free (exhibitions US$2-4); ⏰ noon-8pm Tue-Sun

Reopened in 1989, the Centro Cultural do Banco do Brasil (CCBB) is housed in a beautifully restored building dating from 1906. The CCBB is now one of Brazil's best cultural centers, with more than 120,000 visitors per month. Its facilities include a cinema, two theaters and a permanent display of the evolution of currency in Brazil. In addition, CCBB hosts excellent exhibitions that are among the city's best. A recent exhibition of African art garnered international attention.

There's always something going on at CCBB – exhibitions, lunchtime and evening concerts, film screenings – so have a look at *O Globo*'s entertainment listings before you go. Don't miss this place, even if you only pass through the lobby on a walking tour.

CENTRO CULTURAL CARIOCA Map pp228-30

☎ 2242 9642; www.centroculturalcarioca.com in Portuguese; Rua do Teatro 37, Centro; ⏰ noon-8pm Tue-Sun

This restored theater on Praça Tiradentes is once again a major contributor to the arts in downtown Rio. Its exposed brick walls and large wood-framed windows form the backdrop to superb musical groups – often samba – performing throughout the week (p136), and also has dance recitals, book releases and ongoing exhibitions. They also teach dance classes here (p149).

CENTRO CULTURAL JUSTIÇA FEDERAL Map pp228-30

☎ 2510 8846; Av Rio Branco 241; admission free; ⏰ noon-7pm Tue-Sun; metro Cinelândia

The stately building overlooking the Praça Floriano served as the headquarters of the Supreme Court (Supremo Tribunal Federal) from 1909 to 1960. Following its recent restoration, it's become the Federal Justice Cultural Center, featuring exhibitions focused above all on photography and Brazilian art.

Convento de Santo Antônio (opposite)

In recent years, its three floors of exhibition space has covered photographs from the Depression era in the USA to posters and movie stills from the cinema of Frederico Fellini, displayed in a dreamlike sequence. The bookstore on the 1st floor contains a wide array of books dealing with Rio and the history of its neighborhoods.

IGREJA SÃO FRANCISCO DA PENITÊNCIA & CONVENTO DE SANTO ANTÔNIO Map pp228-30

☎ 2262 0197; Largo da Carioca 5; admission free; ☺ 9am-noon & 1-4pm Tue-Fri (convent), guided visits only to the church

Overlooking the Largo da Carioca is the baroque Igreja São Francisco da Penitência, dating from 1726. Recently restored to its former glory, the church's sacristy, which dates from 1745, has blue Portuguese tiles and an elaborately carved altar made out of jacaranda wood. It also has a roof panel by José Oliveira Rosa depicting St Francis receiving the stigmata. The church's **statue of Santo Antônio** is an object of great devotion to many Cariocas in search of a husband or wife.

A garden on the church grounds leads to the **catacombs**, used until 1850. Visits must be arranged in advance.

Next door, the **Convento de Santo Antônio** was built between 1608 and 1615. It contains the chapel of **Nossa Senhora das Dores da Imaculada Conceição**. Fabiano de Cristo, a miracle-working priest who died in 1947, is entombed here.

IGREJA DE NOSSA SENHORA DE CANDELÁRIA Map pp228-30

☎ 2233 2324; Praça Pio X; admission free; ☺ 8am-4pm Mon-Fri, 8am-1pm Sat, 9am-1pm Sun

The construction of the original church (dating from the late 16th century) on the present site was credited to a ship's captain who had nearly been shipwrecked at sea. Upon his safe return he vowed to build a church to Nossa Senhora de Candelária. A later design led to its present-day grandeur. Built between 1775 and 1894, Nossa Senhora de Candelária was the largest and wealthiest church of imperial Brazil. The interior is a spectacular combination of baroque and Renaissance styles. The ceiling above the nave reveals the origin of the church. The cupola, fabricated entirely from limestone shipped from Lisbon, is one of its most striking features. Mass is said at 9am, 10am and 11am on Sunday. Watch out for the traffic as you cross to the church.

MOSTEIRO DE SÃO BENTO Map pp228-30

☎ 2291 7122; Rua Dom Gerardo 68; admission free; ☺ 8am-11am & 2:30-6pm

This is one of the finest colonial gems in Brazil. Built between 1617 and 1641 on Morro de São Bento, one of the four hills that once marked colonial Rio, the monastery has a fine view over the city. The simple facade hides a baroque interior richly decorated in gold. Among its historic treasures are wood carvings designed by Frei Domingos da Conceição (and made by Alexandre Machado) and paintings by José de Oliveira Rosa. On Sunday, the High Mass at 10am includes a choir of Benedictine monks singing Gregorian chants.

Mass is also said at 7:15am Monday to Saturday, and at 8am, 10am and 6pm on Sunday. To reach the monastery from Rua Dom Gerardo, go to No 40 and take the elevator to the 5th floor.

MUSEU HISTÓRICO E DIPLOMÁTICO Map pp228-30

☎ 2253 7961; Av Marechal Floriano 196; ☺ 2pm, 3pm, 4pm Mon, Wed & Fri (guided visit only); metro Presidente Vargas

Housed in the neoclassical **Palácio Itamaraty**, the Museum of History and Diplomacy served as the private presidential home from 1889 until 1897. The museum has an impressive collection of art, antiques and maps. Visits are by guided 45-minute tours. Call ahead to ensure you get an English- or French-speaking guide. The museum is just a short walk west from Presidente Vargas metro station.

MUSEU HISTÓRICO NACIONAL Map pp228-30

☎ 2550 9224; www.museuhistoriconacional.com.br; off Av General Justo near Praça Marechal Âncora; admission US$1.50; ☺ 10am-5:30pm Tue-Fri, 2-6pm Sat & Sun

Housed in the colonial arsenal, which dates from 1764, the large national history museum contains over 250,000 historic relics relating to the history of Brazil from its founding to its early days as a republic. Its extensive collection includes a full-sized model of a colonial pharmacy and the writing quill that Princesa Isabel used to sign the document abolishing slavery in Brazil.

MUSEU NACIONAL DE BELAS ARTES
Map pp228-30

☎ 2240 0068; Av Rio Branco 199; admission US$1.50; ⏰ 10am-6pm Tue-Fri, 2-6pm Sat & Sun; metro Carioca

Rio's fine art museum houses more than 800 original paintings and sculptures ranging from the 17th to the 20th century. One of its most important galleries is the **Galeria de Arte Brasileira**, with 20th-century classics such as Cândido Portinari's *Café*. Other galleries display Brazilian folk-art, African art and furniture, as well as contemporary exhibits. Guided tours available in English (call ahead).

MUSEU NAVAL E OCEANOGRÁFICO
Map pp228-30

☎ 2533 7626; Rua Dom Manuel 15, Praça 15 de Novembro; admission free; ⏰ noon-4:30pm

Chronicling the history of the Brazilian navy from the 16th century to the present, the museum also has exhibitions of model warships, maps and navigational instruments.

Naval enthusiasts should also visit the nearby **Espaço Cultural da Marinha** (ECM; Map pp228-30; admission free; ⏰ noon-5pm Tue-Sun), on the waterfront near the eastern end of Av Presidente Vargas. It contains the *Riachuelo* submarine, the *Bauru* (a WWII torpedo boat) and the royal family's large rowboat. The boat tour to **Ilha Fiscal** (p89) leaves from the docks here.

PAÇO IMPERIAL Map pp228-30

☎ 2533 4407; Praça 15 de Novembro; admission free; ⏰ noon-6:30pm Tue-Sun

The former imperial palace was originally built in 1743 as a governor's residence. Later it became the home of Dom João and his family when the Portuguese throne transferred the royal seat of power to the colony. In 1888, Princesa Isabel proclaimed the Freedom from Slavery Act from the palace's steps. The building was neglected for many years but has been restored and is used for exhibitions and concerts; its cinema frequently screens foreign and art-house films. Be sure to visit the charming bookshop and the bistro, **Bar das Artes** (p119) on the 1st floor.

PALÁCIO TIRADENTES Map pp228-30

☎ 2588 1411; Rua Primeiro de Março; ⏰ 10am-5pm Mon-Sat, noon-5pm Sun

In the looming building overlooking the bay, the Tiradentes Palace today houses the seat of the legislative assembly. Atop the steps, the statue of Brazil's independence martyr Tiradentes graces the archway. Today, the palace features a permanent multimedia exhibition titled 'Palácio Tiradentes: Site of Legislative Power.'

PASSEIO PÚBLICO Map pp228-30

Rua do Passeio; admission free; ⏰ 9am-5pm; metro Cinelândia

The oldest park in Rio, the Passeio Público was built in 1783 by Mestre Valentim, a famous Brazilian sculptor, who designed it after Lisbon's botanical gardens. In 1860 the park was remodeled by French landscaper Glaziou. The park features some large trees, a pond with islands and an interesting crocodile-shaped fountain. The entrance gate was built by Valentim. Before the Flamengo park landfill, the sea came right up to the edge of the park.

PRAÇA XV DE NOVEMBRO Map pp228-30

Near Rua Primeiro de Março

The first residents on this historic site were Carmelite fathers who built a convent here in 1590. It later came under the property of the Portuguese crown and became Largo do Paço, which surrounded the royal palace (Paço Imperial). A number of historic events took place here: the coronation of Brazil's two Emperors (Pedro I and Pedro II), the Abolition of Slavery and the overthrow (deposition) of Emperor Dom Pedro II in 1889.

REAL GABINETE PORTUGUÊS DE LEITURA Map pp228-30

☎ 2221 3138; Rua Luís de Camões 30; admission free; ⏰ 9am-6pm

Built in the Manuelin Portuguese style in 1837, the górgeous Portuguese Reading Room houses over 350,000 works, many dating from the 16th, 17th and 18th centuries. It also has a small collection of paintings, sculptures and ancient coins.

TEATRO MUNICIPAL Map pp228-30

☎ general info 2299 1716, booking 2262 3501; Rua Manuel de Carvalho; guided tour US$2 ⏰ 9am-5pm Mon-Fri; metro Cinelândia

Built in 1905 in the style of the Paris Opera, the magnificent Municipal Theater is the home of

Rio's opera, orchestra and ballet. Its lavish interior contains many beautiful details – including the stage curtain painted by the Italian artist Eliseu Visconti, which contains portraits of 75 major figures from the arts: Carlos Gomes, Wagner and Rembrandt among others. Bilingual guided tours are a worthwhile investment (call ☎ 2544 2900 to book one). If you get a chance, come to a performance here (p125).

TRAVESSA DO COMÉRCIO Map pp228–30
Near Praça XV de Novembro
Beautiful two-story colonial townhouses line this narrow cobblestone street leading off of Praça XV de Novembro. The archway, **Arco de Teles**, leading into the area was once part of an old viaduct running between two buildings. Today, the street contains half a dozen restaurants and drinking spots that open onto the streets. It's a favorite spot for Cariocas after work.

CINELÂNDIA
PRAÇA FLORIANO Map pp228–30
Av Rio Branco
The heart of modern Rio, the Praça Floriano comes to life at lunchtime and after work when the outdoor cafés are filled with beer drinkers, samba musicians and political debate. The square is also Rio's political marketplace. There are daily speechmaking, literature sales and street theater. Most city marches and rallies culminate here on the steps of the old **Câmara Municipal** (Town Hall) in the northwestern corner of the plaza.

SANTA TERESA & LAPA
Eating p121; Shopping p162; Sleeping p177

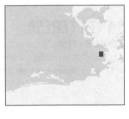

Set on a hill overlooking the city, Santa Teresa, with its cobbled streets and aging mansions, retains the charm of days long past. Originally named after the Carmelite convent founded here in 1750, Santa Teresa was the uppermost residential neighborhood in the 19th century, when Rio's upper class lived here and rode the *bonde* (tram) to work in Centro. Many beautiful colonial homes stretch skyward, their lush gardens hidden behind gabled fences. Like other areas near Centro, the neighborhood fell into neglect in the early 20th century as the wealthy moved further south. During the 1960s and 1970s many artists and bohemians moved into Santa Teresa's mansions, initiating a revitalization process that still continues. Today, Santa Teresa is experiencing a tremendous renaissance, and the neighborhood has become synonymous with Rio's vibrant art and music scene. Throughout the year, impromptu festivals and street parties fill the air, ranging from Maracatu drumming along Rua Joaquim Murtinho to live jazz at the Parque Ruinas to the annual Portas Abertas event, where dozens of the artists open their studios and cover the streets with living installations.

The neighborhood's ongoing restoration has led to an influx of restaurants, bars and cultural centers, and some have even compared Santa Teresa to Paris' Montmartre. Yet this unpolished gem is unlikely to ever completely lose its edginess, if only for the omnipresent favelas spreading down the hillsides. Be cautious when walking around Santa Teresa.

The streets of Lapa lie down the hill from Santa Teresa and south of Cinelândia. Formerly a residential neighborhood of the wealthy, Lapa's best days came and went before 20th century, and its mansions are now sadly neglected. Although Lapa still recalls decades of dereliction in the minds of many Cariocas, the district has recently experienced a cultural revival, and its old buildings are slowly being restored. Lapa is the center of a vibrant bohemian scene in Rio, and the setting for many Brazilian novels.

At night, Lapa is the setting for one of Rio's most vibrant street parties as revelers from all over the city mingle among its samba clubs and music-filled bars. On weekends it gets fearfully crowded here as thousands gather for the chaotic street scene. In spite of some restoration, this neighborhood, like Santa Teresa, still maintains its edgy side. Take care when strolling around here.

Lapa's landmark aqueduct, **Arcos do Lapa** (Lapa Arches), is one of the neighborhood's most prominent features. Narrow tracks course over the 64m-high structure, carrying the famous *bonde* to and from Santa Teresa.

Orientation

Santa Teresa lies atop a hill overlooking Centro and the Zona Norte. The *bonde*, which rattles through the district, begins at the station on Rua Professor Lélio Gama off Rua Senador Dantas, then travels over the Arcos do Lapa and up into Santa Teresa.

Lapa is north of Santa Teresa and south of Cinelândia. (The boundary between Lapa and Cinelândia is marked by the modern Catedral Metropolitana and the Arcos do Lapa.) Rua do Lavradio, to the west of the cathedral, is one of Lapa's most charming streets with its antique shops and bars. South of the arches is Rua Joaquim Silva, site of Rio's burgeoning samba street scene on weekends. Its crumbling buildings also contain clubs and music halls. Parallel to this street is the much larger Rua da Lapa, which runs south to Glória and toward the Zona Sul. The tram leads up to Santa Teresa, as do the windy streets throughout Lapa.

Transportation

Santa Teresa

Bus To get to Santa Teresa from Centro, take No 206A, 206B or 214, all of which travel along Av Almirante Barroso and Rua do Lavradio.

Bonde Paula Matos, Dois Irmãos.

Lapa

Bus No 571 travels between Largo da Lapa and Leblon via Jóquei; No 572 travels between the same points, going via Copacabana.

Metro Cinelândia.

SANTA TERESA

BONDE (TRAM) Map pp228-30

☎ 2240 5709; station at Rua Lélio Gama 65; fare US$0.65; ☼ departures every 30min

The *bonde* that travels up to Santa Teresa from Centro is the last of the historic streetcars that once crisscrossed the city. Its romantic clatter through the cobbled streets has made it the archetype for bohemian Santa Teresa. The two routes currently open have been in operation since the 19th century. Both travel high atop the narrow **Arcos do Lapa** (p86) and along curving Rua Joaquim Murtinho before reaching **Largo do Guimarães** (opposite). From there, one line (Paula Matos) takes a north-western route, terminating at **Largo das Neves** (opposite). The longer route (Dois Irmãos) continues from Largo do Guimarães uphill and southward before terminating near the water reservoir at Dois Irmãos (Two Brothers – named after the twin stone pyramids used to collect water from the Carioca River).

Santa Teresa & Lapa Top Five

- Riding the **bonde** (above) up to Santa Teresa.
- Dancing to samba at the magical **Río Scenarium** (p137).
- Eating Saturday *feijoada* at **Bar do Mineiro** (p121).
- Admiring the stunning views from **Parque das Ruinas** (p86).
- Browsing the antique shops along **Rua do Lavradio** (p152).

Although a policeman often accompanies the tram, the favelas down the hillsides still make this a high-crime area. Go by all means, but don't bring any valuables. Local kids jumping on and off the train lend a festive air to the journey. An unspoken tradition states that those who ride on the running board ride for free.

Tram tours depart every Saturday, highlighting historic points in the neighborhood (p55).

CASA DE BENJAMIN CONSTANT

Map p231

☎ 2509 1248; Rua Monte Alegre 255; admission free; ☼ guided appointment only 1-5pm, gardens open 8am-6pm

This country estate served as the residence for one of Brazil's most influential politicians in the founding of the young Republic. Benjamin Constant (1837–91) was an engineer, military officer and professor before taking an active role in the Provisional Government. He is also remembered for founding a school for blind children. Painstakingly preserved, his house provides a window into his life and times. The lush gardens surrounding his estate provide a fine view over Centro and the western side of Santa Teresa.

CENTRO CULTURAL LAURINDA SANTOS LOBO Map p231

☎ 2224 3331; Rua Monte Alegre 306; admission free; ☼ 8am-5pm

The large mansion built in 1907 once served as a salon for artists from Brazil and abroad as socialite Laurinda Santos hosted her parties there. Villa-Lobos and Isadora Duncan among others attended. Today, the cultural center still plays an active role in the neighborhood by hosting exhibitions and open-air concerts throughout the year.

LARGO DAS NEVES Map p231
End of Rua Progresso

A slice of small-town life in the city, this small square is the gathering point of neighborhood children and families who lounge in the benches by day. At night, the bars surrounding the square come alive with revelers crowding the walks. At times, MPB bands perform to a young crowd here. Largo das Neves is the terminus of the Paula Matos *bonde* line.

LARGO DO GUIMARÃES Map p231
Rua Almirante Alexandrino

The square named after Joaquim Fonseca Guimarães (a local resident whose house became the Hotel Santa Teresa just up the road) now forms the center of bohemian Santa Teresa. A festive Carnaval street party originates here, and a number of restaurants, handicrafts and thrift shops lie within a short distance of here.

MUSEU CHÁCARA DO CÉU Map p231
☎ 2507 1932; Rua Murtinho Nobre 93; admission US$3; ☺ noon-5pm closed Tue

The former mansion of art patron and industrialist Raymundo Ottoni de Castro Maya, the museum contains a small but diversified collection of modern art – formerly Ottoni's private collection, which he bequeathed to the nation. In addition to works by Portinari, Di Cavalcanti, Picasso, Matisse and Salvador Dalí, the museum displays furniture and Brazilian maps dating from the 17th and 18th century. Beautiful gardens surround the museum, and a panoramic view of Centro and Baía de Guanabara awaits visitors.

MUSEU DO BONDE Map p231
☎ 2242 2354; Rua Carlos Brant 14; admission free; ☺ 9am-4:30pm

The tiny one-room Tram Museum at the depot close to **Largo do Guimarães** offers a history of Rio's tramways since 1865 – when the trams were pulled by donkeys. A few photographs, trip-recorders and conductor uniforms are just about the only objects documenting their legacy. Uplifting music plays overhead. The term *bonde* incidentally means just that – bond –

Neighborhoods – Santa Teresa & Lapa

Bonde (opposite)

Living in Santa Teresa *Carmen Michael*

The house I live in is one of the most important colonial houses in Santa Teresa. I know this because it was featured in an important-looking book called *Arquitectura na Joaquim Murtinho*. There have been whisperings that the selection of the house for this book was tainted by politics, but this is hotly refuted by Gustavo, patron of the property and an upstanding local citizen.

The house is an ostentatious canary-yellow, with a white candy-box trim and a magnificent black-marble statue of a naked woman on the front veranda. I came to live in this house after sauntering up Joaquim Murtinho one lazy Rio afternoon. I was in the middle of a daydream, when the house stopped me dead. I smiled at the guy swinging in the hammock on the balcony and said deadpan that the house was mine. He beamed, and played along, shouting that I had better come in then. He gave me the grand tour of the dreamy, creaky mansion; I saw my future rooms complete with Chinese canopy bed; and following two discreetly inquiring dinners with Gustavo, I became a resident of Santa Teresa.

Gustavo is 57 years old, immaculately upper class and the self-appointed custodian of my welfare here in Brazil. Each day, as we take coffee together overlooking the garden at the back of the house, I received instruction on Brazilian etiquette. Upon moving in, I received a reception to Brazilian high society akin to one of those memoirs of an English lady traveling to the colonies in the 1800s. I was slipped into glamorous society parties and introduced to the eligible bachelors of Santa Teresa, while middle-aged women tittered information about their wealth, social status and history of scandal behind me. It was fascinating, although to the dismay and derision of my housemates, who envisaged me *marrying up*, I ended up with a local *sambista* (samba performer) from Lapa. So now I divide my life between arty cocktail parties in Santa Teresa and raucous street parties in Lapa, or the 'gutter' as Gustavo calls it, in a flurry of white kaftan, because it is full of *malandros* (con men), drunks and loose women.

Tucked away from the city between the jungles of Corcovado and the seediness of Lapa, people are able to live a village life in Santa Teresa. They sit on the benches at corners gossiping, drag tables outside at sunset to entertain friends or loiter in doorways to sing an old tune that lifts the spirit. Sometimes it can take a whole evening to walk up the street if you let yourself wander from bench to table to doorway.

Gustavo is a fabulous chef, so at other times we have parties in the house, to which an eclectic mix of musicians, acrobats, artists and assorted vagabonds turn up. (They always come a minimum of four hours late and stay until morning.) Even when we stay in, we're accustomed to unannounced visits from Santa Teresa's ragged jagged characters.

I don't know if it is the steamy heat, the tumultuous history, the burning *cachaça*, the heartbeat of samba, or simply the fact that I am traveling, but Rio seems to be the most extraordinary place. I came for one week. I have been here six months, and keep extending my stay for one reason or another: Jambeiros´s exhibition opens Tuesday, the Chilean acrobats are playing Fundição Progresso, 80-year-old Madrugada is recording his first CD at Rua do Mercado... I guess it will just have to be *amanhã* (tomorrow), as the Latin Americans say, or next week, as they say in Santa Teresa.

To stay in the area, see **Rio Hostel** (p177) or **Cama e Café** (p177), or hit the pavements like I did.

---

indicating the way in which the first electric trams were financed – through public bonds. While you're at the museum, wander down to the old workshop that houses the trams. Cineastes may remember the depot from the opening sequence of the film *Orfeu Negro*.

PARQUE DAS RUINAS Map p231

☎ 2252 1039; Rua Murtinho Nobre 169; admission free; ☻ 10am-8pm Tue-Sun

Connected to the **Museu Chácara do Céu** (p85) by a walkway, this park contains the ruins of the mansion belonging to Brazilian heiress Laurinda Santos Lobo. Her house was a meeting point for Rio's artists and intellectuals for many years until her death in 1946. Today, the park often stages open-air concerts and performances for children on Sunday mornings (readings, puppet shows). Don't miss the excellent view from the top floor.

LAPA

ARCOS DO LAPA Map pp228-30

Near Av Mem de Sá

The landmark aqueduct dates from the mid-1700s when it was built to carry water from the Carioca River to downtown Rio. In a style reminiscent of ancient Rome, the 42 arches stand 64m high. Today, it carries the famous *bonde* to and from Santa Teresa atop the hill.

CATEDRAL METROPOLITANA

Map pp228-30

☎ 2240 2669; Av República do Chile 245; admission free; ☻ 7am-5:30pm

The enormous cone-shaped cathedral was inaugurated in 1976 after 12 years of construction. Among its sculptures, murals and other works of art, the four vivid stained-glass windows, which stretch 60m to the ceiling, are breathtaking. The **Museu de Arte Sacra** (Museum of Sacred Art) in the basement contains a number of historical items, including the baptismal font used at the christening of royal princes, the throne of Dom Pedro II. The cathedral can accommodate up to 20,000 worshippers.

ESCADARIA SELARÓN Map pp228-30
Stairway btwn Rua Joaquim Silva in Lapa & Rua Pinto Martins in Santa Teresa

An ever expanding installation, the staircase leading up to the Convento de Santa Teresa from Rua Joaquim Silva became a work of art when Chilean-born artist Selarón decided to cover the steps with colorful mosaics. Originally a homage to the Brazilian people, the 215 steps feature ceramic mosaics in green, yellow and blue. He uses mirrors as well as tiles collected from around the world to create the illustrious effects. A hand-painted sign in English and Portuguese explains Selarón's vision. Recently, the artist has expanded his artistry to include mosaics near the **Arcos do Lapa** (opposite).

FUNDIÇÃO PROGRESSO Map pp228-30
☎ 2220 5070; Rua dos Arcos 24; admission free; ⏰ 9am-6pm Mon-Fri

Once a foundry for safes and ovens, the building today hosts avant-garde exhibitions, performances and its popular samba parties during the summer. It is one of the few buildings in the area that survived the neighborhood redistricting project in the 1950s to widen the avenue.

MONUMENTO NACIONAL AOS MORTOS DA II GUERRA MUNDIAL
Map pp228-30

☎ 2240 1283; Av Infante Dom Henrique 75; admission free; ⏰ 10am-4pm Tue-Sun

This delicate monument to the soldiers who perished in WWII contains a **museum**, a **mausoleum** and the **Tomb of the Unknown Soldier**. The museum exhibits uniforms, medals and documents from Brazil's Italian campaign. There's also a small lake and **sculptures** by Ceschiatti and Anísio Araújo de Medeiros.

MUSEU DE ARTE MODERNA
Map pp228-30

☎ 2240 4944; http://mamrio.org.br in Portuguese; Av Infante Dom Henrique 85; admission US$5; ⏰ noon-6pm Tue-Fri, noon-7pm Sat & Sun; metro Cinelândia, bus 154, 401, 422, 472 & 438

At the northern end of Parque do Flamengo, the Museu de Arte Moderna (MAM) is immediately recognizable by the striking postmodern edifice designed by Alfonso Eduardo Reidy. The landscaping of Burle Marx is no less impressive.

After a devastating fire in 1978 that consumed 90% of its collection, the museum is finally back on its feet, and now houses 11,000 permanent works, including pieces by Brazilian artists Bruno Giorgi, Di Cavalcanti and Maria Martins. Curators often bring excellent photography and design exhibits to the museum, and the cinema hosts regular film festivals throughout the year. Check the website for details.

GREATER RIO
Eating p122; Shopping p163

Although visitors tend to stick to the Zona Sul and Centro, Rio's outer regions offer a variety of attractions from sweeping views from the other side of the bay to football rowdiness at Maracanã.

São Cristóvão encompasses the **Quinta da Boa Vista** (p89), a large park containing the **Museu Nacional** (p89) and the **zoo** (p88). It's also the site of the football stadium and the Feira Nordestina, one of Brazil's wildest weekend markets. In the 19th century the suburb was the home of the nobility, including the monarchs themselves. It has since become one of the most populous suburbs in Rio.

To the east of Centro lies Rio's lovely bay. Unfortunately, it's too polluted for swimming, but it makes a fine setting for a cruise to either **Ilha de Paquetá** (p89) or **Niterói** (p90). The bay has a prominent place in Rio's history. In 1502 Portuguese explorers sailed into the bay and, mistaking it for the entrance to a large river, named it Rio de Janeiro (River of January). Even though they were mistaken in their geography, the name stuck and was later extended to the new settlement as a whole. Of course, the history doesn't begin with the Portuguese arrival. The indigenous Tamoio people lived peacefully along the shore long before their arrival; and the bay provided much of their sustenance – they were also the ones who named the bay 'Guanabara,' which means 'arm of the sea.' In those days it was a tropical wilderness teeming with tapirs and jaguars. Today the wild animals (and much of the aquatic life as well) have disappeared from Baía de Guanabara. Much of its area has also disappeared. Owing to several landfill projects – which created **Parque do Flamengo** (p75) and Santos Dumont airport – the bay is also disappearing. The best way to experience the bay is to sail around it. Take a ferry ride to **Niterói** (p90) or go on a three-hour cruise (p53).

Orientation

São Cristóvão lies a few metro stops west of Centro, and is bordered by a number of suburbs and favelas, which extend in all directions. Rio and Niterói face each other across the Baía de Guanabara. In addition to the landfill that was added to the bay to create the Santos Dumont airport and the Parque do Flamengo, there are a number of natural islands. Ilha Fiscal, just off Centro is among the smallest. The largest is Ilha do Governador, which is the site of the international airport.

SÃO CRISTÓVÃO

FEIRA NORDESTINA Map pp240-1
☎ 3860 9976; www.feiradesaocristovao.art.br; Campo de São Cristóvão, São Cristóvão; Fri-Sun

This enormous fair (32,000 sq meters with 658 stalls) is not to be missed. The fair showcases the culture from the Northeast, with *barracas* (stalls) selling Bahian dishes as well as beer and *cachaça*, which flows in great abundance here. Bands play throughout the weekend – accordion, guitar and tambourine players performing *forró*, samba groups and comedy troupes, MPB and *rodas de capoeira* (capoeira circles). The vibrant scene starts around 8pm on Friday and continues nonstop through Sunday evening. (Many club kids stop by here just before sunrise). In addition to the food and drink you can stock up on secondhand clothes, some well-priced hammocks and a few good Northeastern gifts such as leather *vaqueiros* (cowboys).

JARDIM ZOOLÓGICO Map pp240-1
☎ 2569 2024; Quinta da Boa Vista; admission US$2; 9am-4:30pm Tue-Sun

Covering over 120,000 sq meters, the zoo at **Quinta da Boa Vista** (opposite) has a wide variety of reptiles, mammals and birds – mostly indigenous to Brazil. Special attractions include the large, walk-through aviary and the night house, which features nocturnal animals. The monkey house is also a crowd favorite.

MARACANÃ Map pp240-1
☎ 2568 9962; gate 18, Rua Professor Eurico Rabelo; 9am-5pm Mon-Fri; metro Maracanã

Brazil's temple of soccer easily accommodates more than 100,000 people. On certain occasions, such as the World Cup match of 1950 or Pelé's last game, it has squeezed in close to 200,000 crazed fans – although it's now been modified to hold fewer.

If you like sports, if you want to understand Brazil, or if you just want an intense, quasi-psychedelic experience, then by all means go see a game of *futebol* – preferably a championship game or one between local rivals Flamengo, Vasco, Fluminense or Botafogo. See p144 for details.

There's a **sports museum** (🕙 9am-5pm Mon-Fri) inside the stadium. It has photographs, posters, cups and the uniforms of Brazilian sporting greats, including Pelé's famous No 10 shirt. There's also a store where you can buy football shirts. Enter through gate No 18 on Rua Professor Eurico Rabelo.

MUSEU DO PRIMEIRO REINADO
Map pp240-1

Av Dom Pedro II 293; admission US$2; 🕙 11am-5pm Tue-Fri

Housed in the former mansion of the Marquesa de Santos, this museum depicts the history of the First Reign (the reign of bumbling Dom Pedro I before he was driven out of the country). The collection includes documents, furniture and paintings, but the main attraction is the building and its interior, with murals by Francisco Pedro do Amaral.

MUSEU NACIONAL Map pp240-1

☎ 2568 8262; Quinta da Boa Vista; admission US$1; 🕙 10am-4pm Tue-Sun

This museum and its imperial entrance are still stately and imposing, and the view from the balcony to the royal palms is majestic. However, the graffitied buildings and unkempt grounds have clearly declined since the fall of the monarchy.

There are many interesting exhibits: dinosaur fossils, saber-toothed tiger skeletons, beautiful pieces of pre-Columbian ceramics from the littoral and high plains of Peru, a huge meteorite, hundreds of stuffed birds, mammals and fish, gruesome displays of tropical diseases, and exhibits on the peoples of Brazil.

The back end of the collection is the most interesting. Rubber-gatherers and Indians of the Amazon, lace-workers and jangadeiros (traditional sailboat fishermen from the Northeast), *Candomblistas* of Bahia, gaúchos (residents of Rio Grande do Sul) and *vaqueiros* (cowboys) of the *sertão* are all given their due.

QUINTA DA BOA VISTA Map pp240-1

☎ 2234 1609; São Cristóvão; 🕙 9am-5pm; metro São Cristóvão, bus 472 or 474

Quinta da Boa Vista was the residence of the imperial family until the Republic was proclaimed. Today, it's a large and busy park with gardens and lakes. On weekends it's crowded with soccer games and families from the Zona Norte. The former imperial mansion houses the **Museu Nacional** (above) and **Museu da Fauna**. The **Jardim Zoológico** (opposite), Rio's zoo, is 200m away.

BAÍA DE GUANABARA & NITERÓI

ILHA DE PAQUETÁ

☎ ferry 2533 6661, hydrofoil 2533 7524

This island in the Baía de Guanabara was once a very popular tourist spot and is now frequented mostly by families from the Zona Norte. There are no cars on the island. Transport is by foot, bicycle (with literally hundreds for rent) or horse-drawn cart. There's a certain dirty, decadent charm to the colonial buildings, unassuming beaches and businesses catering to local tourism. The place gets crowded on weekends.

Go to Paquetá for the boat ride through the bay and to see Cariocas at play – especially during the **Festa de São Roque**, which is celebrated over five days in August.

Boats leave from near the **Praça XV de Novembro** (p82) in Centro. The regular ferry takes an hour and costs US$.50. The more comfortable hydrofoil takes only 25 minutes and costs US$5. Ferry service goes from 5:30am to 11pm, leaving every two to three hours. During the week, the hydrofoil leaves at 10am, noon, 2pm and 4pm and returns at 7:40am and 11:40am and 12:30pm, 2:30pm and 4:30pm. On weekends, it leaves Rio every hour on the hour from 8am to 4:30pm and returns hourly from 8:30am to 5:30pm.

ILHA FISCAL Map pp228-30

☎ 3870 6992; admission US$3; 🕙 1pm, 2:30pm & 4pm Thu-Sun except on the second weekends of each month

This lime-green, neogothic palace sitting in the Baía de Guanabara looks like something out of a fairy tale. It was designed by engineer Adolfo del Vecchio and completed in 1889. Originally used to supervise port operations, the palace is famous as the location of the last Imperial Ball on 9 November 1889. Today it's open for guided tours three times a day from Thursday to Sunday; tours leave from the dock near Praça XV.

Transportation

Bus To cross the bridge into Niterói, you can take bus No 999 from Rua Senador Dantas and Av Beira Mar.

Ferry All boats to Paquetá and Niterói depart from the ferry terminal near Praça XV de Novembro; ferries to Ilha Fiscal depart from the dock further north from the Cais Pharoux.

MUSEU DO ARTE CONTEMPORÂNEA

☎ 2620 2400; www.macniteroi.com in Portuguese;
Mirante da Boa Viagem s/n, Niterói; admission
US$1.75; 11am-7pm Tue-Sun; bus 47B

Designed by Brazil's most famous architect,
Oscar Niemeyer, the MAC has been likened
to a flying saucer. Its sweeping curvilinear
design, however, is much more breathtaking
than that. The views from here are splendid.
The expositions inside the museum, on the
other hand, are a mixed bag. To get to the
MAC from the Niterói ferry terminal, turn right
as you leave and walk about 50m across to the
bus terminal in the middle of the road; a 47B
minibus will drop you at the museum door.

NITERÓI

Niterói's principal attraction is the famous
Museu do Arte Contemporânea (above). The cruise
across the bay, however, is perhaps just as
valid a reason for leaving Rio. Out on the
water, you'll have impressive views of downtown, **Pão de Açúcar** (p65) and the other green
mountains rising up out of the city; you'll also
see planes (quite close) landing and taking off
at Santos Dumont. Try to be on the water at
sunset when Centro glows with golden light.
The ferry costs about US$0.75 and leaves from
Praça XV de Novembro (p82) in Centro; it's usually
quite full of commuters. The faster and more
comfortable alternative is the jumbo catama-
ran, which runs every 15 minutes from 7am
to 4pm and costs US$2. Once you reach the

> ## The Beaches East of Niterói
>
> A number of beaches lie just east of Niterói. The ones
> closest to town are too polluted for swimming, but as
> you continue out, you'll reach some pristine beaches –
> **Piratininga, Camboinhas, Itaipu** and finally **Ita-
> coatiara**, which is the most fabulous of the bunch. With
> vegetation at the back and looming hills on either side,
> the white sands of Itacoatiara seem a world removed
> from the urban beaches of Rio. *Barracas* (stalls) sell
> scrumptious plates of fish from time to time, and
> there are also food stands overlooking the beach (try
> Sanduiches Onda for a *natural*). The surf is strong out
> here – as evidenced by the abundance of surfers – so
> swim with caution. To get there, you can take bus 38
> from the ferry terminal (US$1, 50 minutes) or any bus
> labeled 'Itacoatiara.' If you're traveling in a group, you
> can negotiate a return fare with a taxi driver.

dock, there isn't much to see in the immediate area. It's a busy commercial area, full of
pedestrians, and crisscrossing intersections.
From here catch a bus to the MAC or to one
of the beaches.

PONTE RIO-NITERÓI

The Ponte (bridge) Rio-Niterói offers spectacular views of Baía de Guanabara. It is
15.5km long, 60m high and 26.6m wide, with
two three-lane roads. There's a tollbooth 3km
from the Niterói city center.

BARRA DA TIJUCA & WEST OF RIO

Eating p122; Shopping p163; Sleeping p178

Barra is the Miami of Rio, with malls and shopping centers
set against the tropical landscape. The beach here is lovely
and the city's longest at 15km wide. The commercial area has
a different feel to other parts of Rio owing to its fairly recent
founding. The middle classes first began moving here in the 1970s, when the situation in
urban Rio seemed as if it had reached boiling point. Cariocas fled the crime and the crowded
city to live on a gorgeous stretch of sand. Today, Barra is still a safe neighborhood, but the
influx of new residents has created crowded conditions once again.

Barra da Tijuca is no longer fashionable. It's too far from anywhere and suffers huge
traffic bottlenecks and a chronic shortage of water. The upper classes have begun moving
back to Ipanema, Leblon, and the traditional Av Osvaldo Cruz area of Flamengo. Barra now
caters to *emergentes*, the nouveaux riches from the towns west of Rio.

At the southern tip of Barra, Recreio is being built up fast. It's full of gated communities,
modern shopping centers and giant supermarkets. There are also some fine beaches and
a very interesting museum. Beyond this, the region gets less and less urban. Some of Rio's
loveliest beaches lie out this way (p92). Further west lies Brazil's gorgeous coastal road,
which travels through the region known as the **Costa Verde** (p181).

Orientation

Barra da Tijuca lies 10km west of Leblon, reached by a scenic stretch along the coast. The major roads that pass through Barra are the east-west Av das Américas and the north-south Av Ayrton Senna. At the intersection of these two roads is the major commercial area, where *shoppings* (shopping malls) bloom like wildflowers. Av Ayrton's southern terminus is the beach (Praia da Tijuca). Av Sernambetiba runs along the beach (east-west) – as it heads east it eventually turns into Av Niemeyer; heading west, it leads to Recreio dos Bandeirantes and other beaches.

Transportation

Bus From Copacabana via Leblon take No 523. From Centro take No 175, which travels down Rio Branco and through Copacabana. Another Centro option is No 268, which goes from Praça XV to Riocentro. Bus No 179 travels from Botafogo and Praia de Flamengo.

Taxi A taxi from the Zona Sul to Barra costs around US$16, more in the evening.

BOSQUE DA BARRA Map p239

☎ 3325 6519; Km 7, Av das Américas (intersection of Av Ayrton Senna); ☻ 7am-6pm

Covering 500,000 sq meters of salt-marsh vegetation, the park provides a refuge and breeding area for many small birds and animals. The woods have a jogging track and bicycle path. For guided visits, phone ☎ 2509 5099.

MUSEU AEROSPACIAL Map pp226-7

☎ 3357 5212; www.musal.aer.mil.br in Portuguese; Av Marechal Fontenele 2000, Campo dos Afonsos; admission free; ☻ 9am-3pm Tue-Fri , 9:30am-4pm Sat & Sun; bus 701, 702 or 703 from Centro

This museum maintains expositions on Santos Dumont (the Brazilian father of aviation), Air Marshal Eduardo Gomes, the history of Brazilian airmail and the role of Brazil's air force in WWII. There are lots of old planes, motors and flying instruments. Highlights are replicas of Santos Dumont's planes, the *14 Bis* and the *Demoiselle*. You can also arrange guided visits if you call at least three days in advance.

MUSEU CASA DO PONTAL

☎ 2490 4013; Estrada do Pontal 3295, Recreio dos Bandeirantes; admission US$4, children under 5 free; ☻ 9am-5:30pm Tue-Sun; bus 175 to Barra Shopping, then 702 or 703

Owned by French designer Jacques Van de Beuque, this impressive collection of over 4500 pieces is one of the best folk-art collections in Brazil. The assorted artifacts are grouped according to themes, including music, Carnaval, religion and folklore. The grounds of the museum are surrounded by lush vegetation, which alone makes it worth the trip out here.

PARQUE DO MARAPENDI Map p239

Av Sernambetiba, Recreio dos Bandeirantes; ☻ 8am-5pm

At the end of Av Sernambetiba in Recreio dos Bandeirantes, this biological reserve sets aside 700,000 sq meters for study and has a small area for leisure, with workout stations and games areas.

PARQUE ECOLÔGICO MUNICIPAL CHICO MENDES Map p239

☎ 2437 6400; Km 17, Av das Américas, Recreio dos Bandeirantes; ☻ 8:30am-5:30pm; bus 387 Castelo-Marambaia

This 400,000-sq-meter park was created in 1989 and named after the Brazilian ecological activist who was murdered for his work. The park protects the remaining sand-spit vegetation from real estate speculators. The facilities include a visitors center and ecological trails leading to a small lake. Animals protected in the park include butterflies, lizards, tortoises and the broad-nosed caiman.

PRAIA DA BARRA DA TIJUCA Map p239

The best thing about Barra is the beach. It's 12km long, with the lovely blue sea lapping at the shore. The first few kilometers of the beach are filled with bars and seafood restaurants.

Barra da Tijuca & West of Rio Top Five

- Soaking up rays at **Praia da Barra da Tijuca** (above), one of Rio's loveliest beaches.
- Visiting the lushly landscaped gardens of the **Sitio Burle Marx** (p92).
- Dining on decadent, fresh seafood at **Tia Palmira** (p122) in Barra de Guaratiba.
- Taking the **hang-gliding** (p146) plunge off São Conrado for 10-minutes of airborne bliss –or terror, as the case may be.
- Shopping at the sensory-rich **shoppings** (malls; p163) in Barra da Tijuca.

Neighborhoods – Barra da Tijuca & West of Rio

The Other Beaches of Rio

Although Copacabana and Ipanema are Rio's most famous stretches of sand, there are many lovely beaches in the area, some in spectacular natural settings, each attracting its own particular crowd.

Arpoador (Map pp236-8) This small beach is wedged between Copacabana and Ipanema. There's good surfing here, even at night (when the beach is lit), and there's a giant rock formation jutting out into the ocean. It makes a great spot to watch the sunset or have a makeshift picnic. A lot of people from the Zona Norte come down here on weekends.

Pepino/São Conrado (Map pp226-7) The first major beach you'll reach heading west of Leblon is Praia do Pepino in São Conrado. Pepino is a beautiful beach, and is less crowded than Ipanema. It's also where the hang-gliders hang out when they're not soaring overhead. Along the beach are two big resort hotels, the Hotel InterContinental and the Hotel Nacional. Nestled behind them is Rocinha, Brazil's biggest favela.

Grumari The most isolated and unspoiled beach close to the city, Grumari is quiet during the week and packed on weekends with Cariocas looking to get away from city beaches. It is a beautiful setting, surrounded by mountains and lush vegetation. Four kilometers of this stretch have been set aside as a protected area. Scenes from the movie *Blame It On Rio* were filmed here.

Guaratiba From Grumari, a narrow road climbs over a jungle-covered hillside toward Guaratiba. There's a good view of the Restinga de Marambaia (a vegetation covered sandbank separating the lagoon from the sea), closed off to the public by a naval base. Cariocas enjoy eating a seafood lunch at one of the restaurants in the area.

Prainha This secluded 700m-long beach lies just past Recreio. It's one of the best surfing beaches in Rio, so it's always full of *surfistas* (surfers). Waves come highly recommended here (1m to 3m).

Recreio dos Bandeirantes (Map p239) Although it gets crowded on weekends, the beach is almost deserted during the week. The large rock acts as a natural breakwater, creating a calm bay. The 2km-long stretch of sand remains popular with families.

Vidigal (Map pp236-8) More or less beneath the Sheraton Hotel and the Morro Dois Irmãos, this small 500m-long beach has a mix of hotel patrons and favela dwellers from Dois Irmãos. Security is good here, with the only entrance under surveillance by hotel staff. It's a quiet beach, with few vendors. Unfortunately, the water's often polluted.

The young and hip hang out in front of *barraca* (stall) No 1 – also known as the *barraca do Pepê*, after the famous Carioca hang-gliding champion who died during a competition in Japan in 1991.

The further out you go the more deserted it gets, and the stalls turn into trailers. It's calm on weekdays and crazy on hot summer weekends.

RIO WATER PLANET

☎ 2428 9000; Estrada das Bandeirantes 24000, Recreio dos Bandeirantes; admission US$20; ⏲ 10am-5pm Sat, Sun & holidays
Rio Water Planet claims to be the biggest aquatic park in Latin America. Waterfalls, artificial beaches (a bit surprising in this part of the world) and lazy rafting rivers are part of the attractions, as are **Rio Kart Planet** (an open-air kart track), **Rio Show Planet** (an area for shows), and **Rio Circus Planet**.

SITIO BURLE MARX

☎ 2410 1412; burlemarx@alternex.com.br; Estrada da Barra de Guaratiba 2019, Guaratiba; ⏲ 7am-4pm (by advanced appointment only)
This huge 350,000-sq-meter estate was once the home of Brazil's most famous landscape architect, Roberto Burle Marx. The estate's lush vegetation includes thousands of plant species, some of which are rare varieties from different corners of the globe. A 17th-century **Benedictine chapel** also lies on the estate, along with Burle Marx's original farmhouse and studio, where you can see displays of paintings, furniture and sculptures by the talented designer.

TERRA ENCANTADA Map p239

☎ 2421 9369; www.terra-encantada.com.br in Portuguese; Av Ayrton Senna 2800, Barra da Tijuca; adult/child US$12/4; ⏲ 2-9pm Thu-Sat, noon-9pm Sun
The Enchanted Land is a large amusement park in Barra. It includes Cabhum, a 64m, 100km/h free fall; and Ressaca, a toboggan ride that goes over a waterfall, as well as many other rides.

WET 'N' WILD RIO DE JANEIRO

☎ 2428 9300; Av das Américas 22000, Recreio dos Bandeirantes; admission US$14; ⏲ 10am-5pm Wed-Sun & holidays
Although it sounds more like the title of an adult film, Wet 'n' Wild Rio is a water park similar to Rio Water Planet – although its water slides are a bit more radical.

Walking & Cycling Tours

Walking & Cycling Tours

Rio's tropical climate, its lush, mountainous setting and its glorious location make it an excellent city for power walking, biking or just strolling. We've included a number of options to showcase the city's vibrant blend of old and new, tropical and urban – along with its natural splendor. For those who prefer to take part in an organized walking tour, see p56.

HISTORIC CENTRO

A blend of historic buildings and young skyscrapers, the center of Rio is an excellent place to discover the essence of the city away from its beaches and mountains. Among the hustle and bustle of commerce, you'll find museums, historic bars and theaters, open-air bazaars and the colonial antique-jazz part of town. This tour is best done during the week, when Centro is at its most vibrant.

Walk Facts

Start Praça Floriano (metro Cinelândia).
End Praça Floriano.
Distance 4km.
Duration 3 hours.
Fuel stop Bar Luiz (p130).

Start at the **Praça Floriano 1** (p83), which is where the Cinelândia metro stop is. This main square is the heart of modern Rio. Praça Floriano comes to life after work when the outdoor cafés are filled with beer drinkers, samba musicians and political debate. The neoclassical **Teatro Municipal 2** (p125) overlooking the plaza is one of Rio's finest buildings.

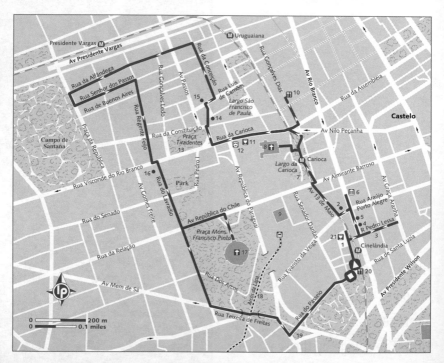

On the east side of Av Rio Branco facing Praça Floriano is the Rua Pedro Lessa, where you can browse the record and CD stalls at the open-air music market called the **Feira de Música 3** (p159). Next to it is the **Centro Cultural Justiça Federal 4** (p80), which often hosts decent exhibitions. The solid **Biblioteca Nacional 5** (p79) is next door, while north on Av Rio Branco is another historic building, which currently hosts the **Museu Nacional de Belas Artes 6** (p82). Take a peek inside if you're interested in seeing some of Rio's best-known 19th-century painters.

Now cross Av Rio Branco and walk briefly back toward Praça Floriano. Take a right on Evaristo da Veiga (in front of the Teatro Municipal) and another right onto the pedestrian-only Av 13 de Maio. Cross a street and you're in the **Largo da Carioca 7**, a bustling area with a small market where vendors sell sunglasses, bootleg CDs, maps, leather goods and a wide array of items you probably don't need. Up on the hill is the recently restored **Convento de Santo Antônio 8** (p81). The original church here was built in 1608, making it one of Rio's oldest.

Historic building, Centro (p78)

Walking & Cycling Tours – Historic Centro

Gazing at the skyline from the convent, you'll notice the **Petrobras building 9** whose boxlike metal chassis seems to cast an ominous shadow over the area.

After coming back down from the convento, continue along Av 13 de Maio, then turn right onto Rua da Carioca and left onto Gonçalves Dias before stopping in the **Confeitaria Colombo 10** (p113) for a dose of caffeine and art nouveau. Head back to Rua da Carioca. Along this street you'll find an array of old shops, a slice of 19th-century Rio. **Bar Luiz 11** (p130) at number 39 makes a fine stop for a bite or a *chope* (draft beer).

At the end of the block you'll pass the **Cinema Iris 12** (p141), which used to be one of Rio's most elegant theaters, and will emerge into the hustle of **Praça Tiradentes 13**. Soak up some of the stately ambience. On opposite sides of the square are the **Teatro João Caetano** (p125) and the **Teatro Carlos Gomez** (p124), and around the corner is the **Centro Cultural Carioca 14** (p80). Stop in here to see what's on musically for the evening. Just across from the theater is the **Real Gabinete Português de Leitura 15** (p82), Rio's loveliest reading room.

Walk up to Rua da Conceiçao and take a left onto Rua da Alfândega. This will take you into the heart of Saara, a longstanding neighborhood bazaar packed with shops, pedestrians and Lebanese restaurants. Walk, shop and snack as far as Campo de Santana. Make a U-turn there and proceed back along Rua Senhor dos Passos. Take a right on Rua Regente Feijó. When this street ends, take a short right and then a left and head down Rua do Lavradio. This street is famous for its antique shops set in the colorful 19th-century buildings. A number of great nightspots, like **Río Scenarium 16** (p137) have sprung up on this street, some set in brick-lined colonial relics. The mix of samba-jazz and antiques makes a fine setting.

When you reach Av República do Chile, take a left and stop in the **Catedral Metropolitana 17** (p86) for a break. There, check out the marvelous stained-glass windows. When you leave, head back to Rua do Lavradio for more antique browsing. When you reach Av Mem de Sá, take a left and follow the road around the curve as you pass beneath the **Arcos de Lapa 18** (p86). This is Rio's big samba center at night, with clubs and old-school bars scattered all over this neighborhood. When you reach the **Largo da Lapa 19**, take a left and walk along Rua do Passeio. You'll have great views of the arches from here. In two more blocks you'll be back to where you started. When you reach Praça Floriano, grab a seat at one of the outdoor tables at **Ateliê Odeon 20** (p130) or **Amarelinho 21** (p130), and cool off with a *chope* or fresh-squeezed *suco* (juice), a fine cap to the walk.

LAGOA TO LEME

It's hard to think of a better setting for a bike ride than the Zona Sul's lovely coastline and its nearby lakeside jewel, **Lagoa Rodrigo de Freitas** (p61). The mountains rising out of the sea and the white-sand beaches facing them are a big part of the allure of the Cidade Maravilhosa, and you'll be rewarded with a number of panoramic views along this journey. Beaches, bay, and Corcovado, Pão de Açúcar (Sugarloaf) and many of Rio's other lush peaks are the backdrop for your ride.

Ride Facts

Start Parque Brigadeiro Faria Lima.
End Parque Brigadeiro Faria Lima.
Distance 26km.
Duration 3 hours.
Fuel stop Lagoa kiosks (p110) or **Bar 12** (p112).

Be sure you bring along some money for snacks and *agua de coco* (coconut water) – both prevalent along the beach – and a meal at the end of your ride. You'll work up an appetite out in the sun.

Most of this journey follows a bike path separate from the traffic on the street. Sundays are the best day to do this ride, as the road bordering the bike path is closed then – giving you more room to connect to your inner Armstrong.

Begin in the **Parque Brigadeiro Faria Lima 1** on the edge of Lagoa. Conveniently, there's a bike rental place right there. You can also rent bikes at a number of other places in town (p194).

Once you're on the bike path, follow it north as it loops around the lake. You'll soon pass the **Ilha Piraquê 2**, one of the island country clubs out on the lake. As you make your way west you'll probably see a few egrets . Continue along the path, curving south and pedaling past some of the **Lagoa kiosks 3** (p128). These become crowded at night with live music and Cariocas enjoying the lakeside dining. After your third turn you'll pass another island, the **Ilha dos Caiçaras 4**. In another 500m, exit onto **Rua Mario Ribeiro 5**, but keep your eyes peeled. It's a major street with a bike lane along the north side of the road. Once on this lane follow it

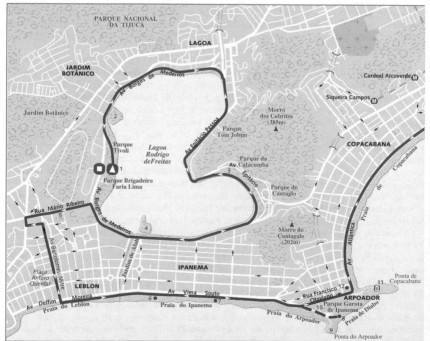

until just beyond Av Bartolomeu Mitre. You'll be riding south down this street, but there's a better crossing one block up. Once you find the crosswalk, head across and stay on the bike path. At Av Bartolomeu Mitre take a right. In a few blocks you'll reach the beach.

From Leblon, start pedaling east along Av Vieiro Souto. As you ride along note how the crowds change along the beach from **Posto 10 6** (Cariocas who've obviously spent a lot of time at the gym) to **Posto 9 7** (a laidback crowd not averse to lighting a joint from time to time). When you reach Arpoador, you can pull off the bike path for your first maté or *agua de coco* from the stand in the **Praça do Arpoador 8**. You'll need to walk your bike here, as it's usually full of pedestrians. Take a seat under a palm tree and enjoy the fine view west, with Dois Irmãos rising over Leblon. The rock outcropping to your left is **Ponta do Arpoador 9**, which offers decent waves. It's a rare day when there aren't at least a dozen surfers jockeying for good breaks. After your rest, get back on the bike path – either pushing your bike through the **Parque Garota de Ipanema 10** (p107), or going back up to Francisco Otaviano, where the bike path continues.

As you continue on the path, you'll pass the **Forte de Copacabana 11** (p62) and will soon have a splendid view of Morro de Leme at the end of the long stretch of sand formed by Copacabana and Leme Beaches. At the beginning of Copacabana you'll see the **posto dos pescadores** (fishermen's place) **12**. If you do this ride early in the morning, it's possible to see the fishermen pulling their nets out of the water. As you continue along the bike path, which is now running parallel with Av Atlântica, be sure to stop for cups of *agua de coco*; there are a lot of stands all along the beach.

Although you'll probably be watching the beach, the mountains and the sea, keep an eye out for the whitewashed **Copacabana Palace 13** (p129); it was Copa's first hotel (1923) back when the beach was still a remote getaway from Centro. In Leme the path ends at the **Morro do Leme 14**, where you'll probably see kids fishing off the rocks. Take a break (there's yet another **drink stand 15** here) before starting the return journey, which follows the same route back. If you haven't eaten by the time you return to Lagoa, grab a meal at one of the **kiosks** (p110).

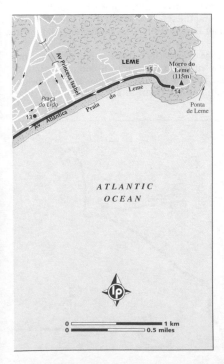

Cyclist, Lagoa Rodrigo de Freitas (p61)

SANTA TERESA

Santa Teresa's colorful colonial buildings, narrow brick-lined streets and sweeping views of downtown are a few of the reasons artists flocked here in the mid '70s (cheap rents in gorgeous old mansions is another). Today the hood is still experiencing a cultural renaissance. You never know what's going to turn up here: old mansions hosting African drumming, bossa-jazz in a

Walk Facts

Start *Bonde* to Largo das Neves (Paulo Matos line).
End Bus 572 from Rua da Lapa to the Zona Sul.
Distance 3.5km.
Duration 2½ hours.
Fuel stop Bar do Mineiro (p121).

bombed-out building overlooking the city or impromptu music jams in the middle of the afternoon (or night). No other neighborhood has quite the energy that Santa Teresa has. All of which means this neighborhood is worth getting to know. Buy your *bonde* (tram) ticket and get thee to Santa Teresa…

…**Largo das Neves 1** (p85), to be specific. This small square is where our saunter begins. It's also the end of the *bonde* line. The first part of our walk will follow the tracks, removing the possibility of getting lost among the winding streets.

Above the small Largo das Neves are the twin spires of **Igreja de Nossa Senhora das Neves 2**, one of many 19th-century churches in the area. On weekend nights, the Largo becomes the set piece for the music-filled cafés and bars, which open onto it.

Start following the tracks. You'll pass through a few curves before reaching an even sharper turn leading to Rua Monte Alegre. If you need a drink, the old-time **Bar do Gomes 3** (p131) is a good place to stop. Across the street is **Brechó Arte 4** (p162), a thrift shop worth a browse.

Keep following the tracks and you'll pass **Centro Cultural Laurinda Santos Lobo 5** (p84). Stop here and take a look at current exhibitions and find out if any concerts are planned. When you reach the end of this street, diverge from the tracks and keep walking straight (down the hill) and you'll reach **Casa de Benjamin Constant 6** (p84). Check out the museum and the lovely gardens. Walk back up the hill, continue following the tracks, and you'll soon reach the **Bar do Mineiro 7** (p121), an old-school *boteco* (open air bar) that's famous throughout Rio for its excellent home cooking.

Continue down the hill and you'll reach **Largo do Guimarães 8** (p85), a popular reference point for Santa Teresa bohemians. If you take a left down Rua Carlos Brandt, you can visit the tiny **Museu do Bonde 9** (p85) for a symphonic journey back to the *bonde's* once glorious day in the sun. After checking out the museum and the tram storage building next door,

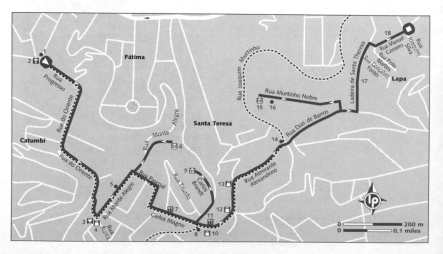

walk back up to Largo dos Guimarães and head up the little staircase to visit another thrift shop, **Brechó Antigamente 10** (p162). Back on the tracks, you'll notice many more restaurants and shops. Pleasant **Porta Quente 11** (p122) serves coffee and light snacks. When you continue, you'll pass **La Vareda 12** (p163) and **Trilhos Urbanos 13** (p163), both good spots to purchase Brazilian handicrafts.

Keep walking down hill. Soon you'll reach **Curvelo 14**, a *bonde* shelter astride the road. Here you'll turn right (leaving the tracks behind, so get your bearings) onto Rua Dias de Barros. Follow this street until you reach a road branching off to the left (Rua Murtinho Nobre). Follow this all the way around and you will reach the **Museu Chácara do Céu 15** (p85) with its small collection of modern art, and the **Parque das Ruinas 16** (p86) next door. Don't miss the splendid views from here. Make your way back to Rua Dias de Barros. It gets tricky here, but if you lose your way, just keep heading downhill and you'll eventually end up in Lapa. Heading downhill from Rua Dias de Barros, veer to the left and follow the old **Ladeira de Santa Teresa 17**, a steep, narrow and winding street lined with colonial buildings. As you head downhill, you'll have two paths leading off to the right. Take the second one, Rua Pinto Martins, which then leads to Rua Manuel Carneiro. This will place you at the top of the **Escadaria Selarón 18** (p87), the beautifully tiled stairs that are a constantly changing installation.

URCA: THE VILLAGE BY THE SEA

One of Rio's most charming neighborhoods is one of its least explored – and safest (this is one place where you won't have any worries with a camera). The peaceful streets are lined with trees, beautiful houses and lush gardens. Out by the bay, fishermen cast just beyond the rocky shoreline as couples lounge on the seawall, Corcovado nicely framing the scene.

Walk Facts

Start Bus 511 or 512 to Rua Marechal Cantuária.
End Praia Vermelha.
Distance 4km.
Duration 3 hours.
Fuel stop Praia Vermelha (p115) or **Bar Urca** (p115).

Our walk begins where Rua Marechal Cantuária meets Av São Sebastião. On your left, you'll see **Cassino da Urca 1**, or at least what remains of the once popular gambling and night spot where Carmen Miranda and Josephine Baker both performed. Veer to the right along Av São Sebastião, noting the splendid Tudor-style **Instituto Cultural Cravo Albim 2** against the back of Morro da Urca. The road goes uphill from here. Follow the road all the way along; you'll pass **Carmen Miranda's former residence 3** at number 131. You'll also pass beneath the wall that separates the military fort from the neighborhood. High up are **mango trees 4**. If you're lucky, a mango will fall into your hands.

When you get to the end of the street, take the steps down to Av João Luis Alves. From here you'll have splendid views of Corcovado, Parque do Flamengo and the Rio-Niterói bridge as you walk along the bay. Stop for a juice or a plate of fresh fish at **Bar Urca 5** (p115). Then stroll down **Rua Otávio Correira 6** to get a glimpse of the charming houses on this side of Rio. Retrace your footsteps and continue along Av João Luis Alves until you reach **Praia da Urca 7** (p65). You have the option of walking across the sand or taking the road around. Stick to the bayside as the road forks. Look for the small **Igreja de Nossa Senhora do Brasil 8**. Peek inside the small church (the chapel is on the first floor; the church is upstairs). Note the small Brazilian flag on the Madonna's cloak on your way out – perhaps it really is true that God is Brazilian after all. Facing the church is the floating **statue of São Pedro no Mar 9**. On June 29, St Peter's feast day, the fishermen make a procession across the bay, scattering flowers across the water.

Tip

Start your walking tour of Urca in the afternoon, around 3pm. When you finish, you can take the cable car up to Pão de Açúcar for sunset over the city. After coming back down, stop in **Praia Vermelha** (p115) for drinks and excellent live music by the sea.

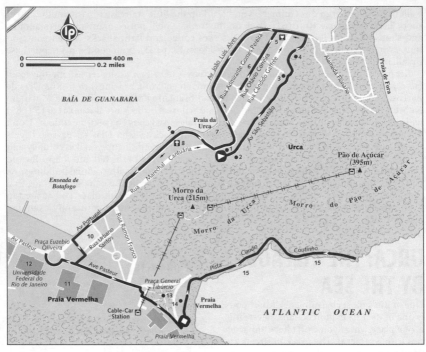

Keep going along the avenue, now called Av Portugal, and you'll reach a bridge. To your left is the **Quadrado da Urca 10**, which is a harbor for the poor fishermen. Dozens of tiny fishing boats bob on the sadly polluted water. Keep going on this street until it ends on Av Pasteur. Urca's most majestic buildings lie along this stretch. Walk up the stairs at **Companhia de Pesquisa de Recursos Minerais 11** (if the lion doesn't scare you off). A little up the road is the neoclassical masterpiece of the **Universidade Federal do Rio de Janeiro 12**. Turn back down Pasteur and walk toward Pão de Açúcar. Just beyond the cable car station is the beautifully laid-out **Praça General Tibúrcio 13**. Keep walking toward the sea and you reach the **statue of Chopin 14**, donated to the city by Rio's Polish community.

The last part of the tour follows the paved **Pista Cláudio Coutinho 15** (p66) out and back. Look for monkeys (tiny micos) and birds, and enjoy the verdant setting, the waves crashing against the rocks below and the panoramic views out to sea.

Eating

Eating

Cariocas are known for their samba, their soccer and their Carnaval, but most visitors still equate eating out in Rio to masticating on rump roast at a beachside diner. While the merits of Rio's many fine *churrascarias* (traditional barbecue restaurants) should not be underestimated, the Cidade Maravilhosa has much more to offer than just *carne* (meat). In fact, the city is in the grip of a culinary renaissance – and has been for some time. Every week eclectic new bistros, sushi bars and restaurants open their doors creating some fierce competition for Rio's many epicureans.

The bounty of the coastline, the lush tropical setting (fresh fruit, anyone?) and the diversity of Rio's large immigrant population add up to some fantastic dining opportunities. Regional cuisines from all over Brazil – Minas Gerais, Bahia and even Amazonia – are well represented, and any night of the week connoisseurs can enjoy traditionally prepared Italian, French, German, Japanese and Syrian cuisine.

In general, Ipanema and Leblon are the Soho of Rio's dining scene. There you'll find a mix of excellent chefs, beautifully set dining rooms and the style mavens that fill them. Centro's restaurants garner as many awards as those found throughout the Zona Sul, while Copacabana has both the hidden and the indiscreet, many of which spill along Av Atlântica overlooking the beach. Other areas have their gems, notably Santa Teresa, where a handful of restaurants, with panoramic views, serve delightful cuisine, and Botafogo with its fine spots tucked away on tree-lined streets.

Opening Hours

Aside from juice bars, cafés and bakeries, few restaurants open for breakfast (those that do start serving around 7am). Cariocas don't typically order a sit-down meal until noon, which is when most restaurants open. Most restaurants in Centro open only during the week and only for lunch – usually from noon until 3pm. Restaurants in the Zona Sul, with its wealth of culinary options, serve larger dinner crowds than lunch ones. Typically, they don't close until midnight – and some serve until three or four in the morning. Cariocas aren't known for rushing off to eat when the sun goes down. Most restaurants don't pack crowds until 9pm or so. On Saturdays and Sundays, lunch is the big meal of the day – Saturday being the traditional day to enjoy *feijoada* (black-bean stew) – and Brazilians can linger for hours over a fine meal.

How Much?

Rio can be light or hard on the wallet, depending on where and what you eat (but mostly on where). Juice bars and *botecos* (small open-air bars) are the cheapest places to get a meal, where you can order a *misto quente* (hot ham and cheese sandwich) and juice or a *comida corriente* (a plate of chicken, steak or fish with sides) for around US$3. Another budget option is the pay-by-weight restaurant. Prevalent throughout the city, these eateries vary in price and quality, but average about US$7 per kilo (a fairly loaded plate will cost US$4). For more ideas, see the Cheap Eats listings in each Neighborhood section.

Mid-range places offer a vast array of dining options, and you can expect to pay between US$6 and US$10 for a main course. *Churrascarias* offer all-you-can-eat dining options – try to fast at least six hours before going. Most charge around US$10-$15, which includes more food than you could possibly imagine (much less *eat*).

To experience the talents of Rio's top chefs, head to Centro by day, where power-lunching executives enjoy masterfully prepared sushi, steak or duck confit in stately environments. By night, Leblon and Ipanema – and a handful of Copacabana – restaurants compete for annual culinary prizes. A main course in any of these locations will cost between US$12 and US$25. Rio's best restaurants stock impressive wine cellars that range far beyond the Argentine, Chilean and Brazilian vintages you'll find at other places.

Booking Tables

Most restaurants accept reservations for both lunch and dinner, so call ahead if you want to avoid the wait. Restaurants that don't accept reservations often have a bar inside where you can have a drink while you wait for a table.

Unfortunately, when you call to make a reservation, the person who answers the phone is not likely to speak English. Concierges are adept at booking seats for you, but if you're game, give a stab at the Portuguese – Brazilians, after all, are known for their patience.

Tipping

Tipping is rare in cafés and juice bars but is always appreciated. In restaurants, 10% is usually included on the bill. When it isn't included – and your waiter will usually tell you if it's not – it's customary to leave 10%. If the service was exceptionally bad or good, adjust accordingly.

Brazilian Dishes

acarajé A specialty of Bahia made from peeled brown beans mashed with salt and onions, and then fried in *dendê* oil. Inside these delicious croquettes is *vatapá*, dried shrimp, pepper and tomato sauce.

angú A kind of cake made with very thin cornflour called *fubá*, mixed with water and salt.

bobó de camarão Manioc paste cooked and flavored with dried shrimp, coconut milk and cashew nuts.

camarão á paulista Unshelled fresh prawns (shrimp) fried in olive oil with lots of garlic and salt.

canja A big soup with chicken broth; often a meal in itself.

carangueijada Crab cooked whole in seasoned water.

carne de sol A tasty salt-cured meat, grilled and served with beans, rice and vegetables.

caruru One of the most popular Brazilian dishes of African origin. Made with boiled okra or other vegetables mixed with grated onion, salt, shrimp, *malagueta* peppers and *dendê* oil. Traditionally, a saltwater fish such as *garoupa* (grouper) is added.

casquinha de carangueijo or siri Stuffed crab, prepared with manioc flour.

cozido Any kind of stew, usually with vegetables (such as potatoes, sweet potatoes, carrots and manioc).

dendê Palm oil; decidedly strong stuff. Many non-Brazilian stomachs can't handle it.

dourado A scrumptious freshwater fish found throughout Brazil.

farofa Otherwise known as cassava, manioc flour is a legacy of the Indians, for whom it has traditionally been an essential dietary ingredient; it remains a Brazilian staple.

feijoada The Carioca answer to cassoulet. See p16.

frango ao molho pardo Chicken pieces stewed with vegetables and covered with a seasoned sauce made from the blood of the bird.

moqueca A kind of sauce or stew, as well as a style of cooking from Bahia, which is properly prepared in a covered clay pot. Fish, shrimp, oyster, crab or a combination of those served with a *moqueca* sauce, which is defined by its heavy use of *dendê* oil and coconut milk, and often contains peppers and onions.

moqueca capixaba A moqueca from Espírito Santo that uses lighter *urucum* oil from the Indians instead of *dendê* oil.

pato no tucupi Roast duck flavored with garlic and cooked in *tucupi* sauce, which is made from the juice of the manioc plant and *jambu*, a local vegetable. A very popular dish in Pará.

peixada Fish cooked in broth with vegetables and eggs.

peixe a delícia Broiled fish usually served in a sauce made with bananas and coconut milk.

petiscos Appetizers.

picanha Thin cut of rump steak.

prato de verão Literally, a 'summer plate,' which is served at many juice stands in Rio. It's basically a fruit salad.

prato feito Literally, a 'made plate,' usually a serving of rice, beans, salad, with chicken, fish or beef.

pirarucu ao forno Pirarucu, the most famous fish from the rivers of Amazônia, baked with lemon and other seasonings.

tacacá An Indian dish of dried shrimp cooked with pepper, *jambu*, manioc and much more.

tutu á mineira A bean paste with toasted bacon and manioc flour, often served with cooked cabbage.

vatapá A seafood dish with a thick sauce made from manioc paste, coconut and *dendê* oil. Perhaps the most famous Brazilian dish of African origin.

xinxim de galinha Pieces of chicken flavored with garlic, salt and lemon. Shrimp and dendê oil are often added.

Eating

Self-Catering

Open-air markets abound in the city. Juicy pineapples, plump mangos and the plethora of other fruits make fine snacks for the beach. Some markets (p157) – like the Feira Hippie on Sundays in Ipanema – feature fresh-cooked food from Brazil's Northeast.

Supermarkets provide another option for self-caterers. Pão de Açúcar and Zona Sul supermarkets are prevalent throughout Ipanema, Leblon and Copacabana. The **Zona Sul** (p109) on Rua Dias Ferreira in Leblon is Rio's best supermarket, with an excellent assortment of imported cheeses, fresh breads and salads, wines and spirits, and deli items. Nearby is an indoor **fruit and vegetable market** (p157) that's open daily. Leblon's **Garcia & Rodrigues** (p106), which is also a restaurant, stocks an enviable selection of French and Italian wines, cheeses and deli items. The patisserie and ice cream counter alone warrant a visit.

Downtown, the gleaming shelves at **Lidador** (p120) keep commuters nicely stocked with smoked meats, chocolates and delicacies before they head off to the suburbs. Lidador also has a small stand in back where you can order a drink, lest the busy streets outdoors unsettle you.

Per-kilo places all have take-away containers, if you simply want to grab something freshly cooked in a hurry, while juice bars also accommodate takeout customers.

One needn't even step off the streets, however, to find a meal. Throughout town, you'll find vendors selling *agua de coco* (coconut water), available in cups or takeout plastic cartons. Look for the ones advertising *'bem gelado'* (well chilled) for ice-cold refreshment on a steamy day.

On the beach, you're never more than a stone's throw from drink stands. Many offer *caipirinhas*, beer and snack food in addition to *agua de coco*, here served straight from the coconut. If you're frolicking in the waves and can't be bothered making the trek up the beach, don't worry. Vendors laden with heavy bags roam the beach till sundown offering beer, soda, maté (a kind of sweetened tea) or *sanduich natural* (a sandwich, featuring ricotta cheese or chicken- or tuna-salad). Others offer *queijo coalho* (hot cheese), which will be cooked on a small stove in front of you and served to you on a stick (with herbs if you prefer). You can also find vendors cooking *churrasco* (roasted meat) – also served on a stick, with or without *farofa* (manioc flour).

IPANEMA & LEBLON

Rio's most decadent dining scene offers a variety of international and Brazilian cuisines in a charming, neighborhood setting. By day its busy cafés and juice bars fill with bronze bodies heading to and from the beach, while at night its tree-lined streets set the stage for open-air dining, forming the backdrop to the city's young and beautiful. Rua Barão da Torre in Ipanema and Rua Dias Ferreira in Leblon are the major restaurant strips in each hood. The newest, hottest spots opening here don't always live up to the hype, but these twin neighborhoods feature plenty of time-tested favorites that do.

ANTIQUARIUS Map pp236-8 *Portuguese*
☎ 2294 1049; Rua Aristídes Espínola 19, Leblon; mains US$25-35; ☾ noon-2am

It's hard to think of a better place to lay down some serious *reais* than five-star Antiquarius. The menu features items like wild boar in red wine sauce and roast rabbit with bean sauce.

Everything is spectacularly prepared, and you can't go wrong no matter what you order. Before you venture into the antique-filled dining room, don't forget to dress the part. Once you're there, be sure to solicit the knowledge of Antiquarius' semi-omniscient sommelier.

ARMAZÉM DO CAFÉ Map pp236-8 *Café*
☎ 2259 0170; Rua Rita Ludolf 87B, Leblon; ☾ 9am-midnight Mon-Thu & Sun, 9am-1am Fri & Sat

Dark wood furnishings and the scent of fresh-ground coffee lend an authenticity to this Leblon coffeehouse. A popular meeting spot in the neighborhood, Armazém fills with chatter throughout the day. It also serves snacks and desserts.

ATAÚLFO Map pp236-8 *Self-Serve*
☎ 2540 0606; Av Ataúlfo de Paiva 630, Leblon; sandwiches US$3, mains US$6-10; ☾ 9am-midnight Mon-Thu & Sun, 9am-2am Fri & Sat

The front of the restaurant features a lunch counter where you can grab a quiche, a tasty sandwich or a juice. In back, the narrow restaurant opens up, and you'll encounter a small but excellent self-serve buffet by day – serving salmon with artichoke and sun-dried tomato tagliatelle among other things. At night Ataúlfo serves à la carte.

ATELIÊ CULINÁRIO

Map pp236-8   *Patisserie & lighter fare*

☎ 2239 2825; Rua Dias Ferreira 45, Leblon; desserts US$3-4; ☾ 6pm-1am Mon-Fri, 1pm-1am Sat & Sun

This small café offers quiches, salads and empanadas, but it's their desserts that draw most people here. Dense cheesecake with guava sauce or moist chocolate mud cake are best enjoyed at the small tables out front, allowing premium views of the people-parade filing past.

B! Map pp236-8   *Café*

☎ 2249 4977; Rua Visconde de Pirajá 572, Ipanema; salads US$4-6; ☾ 9am-midnight Mon-Sat, 1pm-midnight Sun

Located on the 2nd floor of the Ipanema branch of the **Livraria da Travessa bookstore** (p155), this stylish café makes a fine setting for a light lunch after rainy-day browsing. Salads, quiches and chocolaty brownies are served by attentive – and good-looking – servers.

CAFEÍNA Map pp236-8   *Café*

☎ 2521 2194; Rua Farme de Amoedo 43, Ipanema; ☾ 9am-8:30pm Mon & Sun, 8am-11:30pm Tue-Sat

The popular café in the heart of Ipanema has outdoor tables for watching the world stroll by. If you're more intent on what's inside, the decent waffles, desserts, dark coffees and espressos will do just fine. They also have a branch in Copacabana.

CAFÉ SEVERINO Map pp236-8   *Café*

☎ 2239 5294; Rua Dias Ferreira 417, Leblon; ☾ 9am-midnight Mon-Sat, 10am-midnight Sun

In the back of the **Argumento bookshop** (p153), this charming café and bistro serves tasty lighter bites – sandwiches, salads, soups and desserts, as well as ample coffee and tea selections.

CAFFÉ FELICE Map pp236-8   *Sandwiches*

☎ 2522 7749; Rua Gomes Carneiro 30, Ipanema; sandwiches US$5-8; ☾ noon-1am Mon-Thu, noon-3am Fri, 10am-3am Sat, 11:30am-6pm & 7:30pm-midnight Sun

Formerly a cruisy hangout among Ipanema's pretty boys, Caffé Felice today draws mostly straight crowds to its indoor-outdoor eatery. Sandwiches and *sorvete* (ice cream) make a great combo after a steamy day at the beach.

CAPRICCIOSA Map pp236-8   *Pizza*

☎ 2494 2212; Rua Vinícius de Moraes 134, Ipanema; pizzas US$9-13; ☾ 6pm until last customer

At night, Capricciosa's windows create a fishbowl effect. You can watch people passing on the street, they can watch you, and everyone in this trendy space can watch each other. Of course, it's enough for us just to gaze into those lovingly prepared, thin-crust pizzas. Ingredients aren't so much tossed onto the crusts as they are artfully arranged – much like an artist's palette – and include daring combinations like ham, bacon, an egg, artichoke hearts, mushrooms and mozzarella (that's one pizza by the way – the capricciosa).

CARPACCIO & CIA Map pp236-8   *Seafood*

☎ 2511 4094; Rua Prudente de Moraes 1838, Ipanema; carpaccio US$9-13; ☾ 5pm-2am Mon-Thu, 5pm-3am Fri, noon-3am Sat & Sun

Those who like their meat on the rare side – extremely rare – should visit this late-night spot in Ipanema. Offering over 60 varieties of raw, tender slices, Carpaccio & Cia features smoked salmon and octopus for more conservative palates. Its open-air patio is also enjoyed by those who simply want to drink. In addition to beer, sake and *caipirinhas* with a twist (infused violets or berries) are top sellers here.

CASA DA FEIJOADA

Map pp236-8   *Feijoada & regional cuisine*

☎ 2247 2776; Rua Prudente de Moraes 10B, Ipanema; feijoada for 2 US$15; ☾ noon-11:30pm

Admirers of Brazil's historic *feijoada* needn't wait until Saturday to experience the meaty meal. At this 15-year-old institution any day is fine enough to sample the rich, black bean

Eating – Ipanema & Leblon

and salted pork dish. Served with the requisite orange slices, *farofa* (manioc flour) and grated kale (cabbage), all of which blend nicely, especially when paired with a *caipirinha*.

CELEIRO Map pp236-8 *Salads & lighter fare*
☎ 2274 7843; Rua Dias Ferreira 199, Leblon; salads US$6-10; 🕙 10am-5:30pm Mon-Sat

This casual spot on one of Leblon's main restaurant strips packs crowds during lunchtime. Celeiro is mostly famed for its salad bar, though the small eatery serves excellent soups, pastries and quiches. Get there early to avoid the rush.

COLHER DE PAU Map pp236-8 *Patisserie*
☎ 2274 8295; Rua Farme de Amoedo 39, Ipanema; desserts US$2-5; 🕙 10am-8pm

Colher de Pau's cakes and pies are displayed in such a way that their magnetic powers exert a force that would be foolish to resist. Don't worry, indulging in the popular 'Charlotte de Chocolate' will hardly leave you disappointed.

DA SILVA Map pp236-8 *Portuguese*
☎ 2521 1289; Rua Barão da Torre 340, Ipanema; plates US$7-15; 🕙 11:30am-2am

Run by the same family that owns Antiquarius, Da Silva spreads a fine buffet for those who want to sample excellent Portuguese cuisine without all the fussiness. Lamb stew, pork tenderloin and delicate desserts all make regular appearances on the lunchtime self-serve per-kilo buffet – and on the nightly à la carte menu.

DOCE DELÍCIA Map pp236-8 *Brazilian*
☎ 2249 2970; Rua Dias Ferreira 48, Leblon; mains US$6-10; 🕙 noon until last customer

A narrow restaurant featuring bamboo, water and other zenlike elements, Doce Delícia has a small but loyal following who are sold on the restaurant's innovative concept. Here designer eating and customer empowerment join forces as restaurant-goers create their own salads from over 40 ingredients on the menu. Feeling daring? Go for the pumpkin, jerked meat and leeks. The only limits are your imagination, *cara*.

ESPLANADA GRILL
Map pp236-8 *Churrascaria*
☎ 2512 2970; Rua Barão da Torre 600, Ipanema; mains US$14-22; 🕙 noon until last customer

Esplanada's fans vow that they serve the best grilled meats in Rio – not a statement to be taken lightly in a city that takes its meat very seriously. Whatever the case, Esplanada certainly serves some of the most exotic brands of the stuff. New Zealand lamb, Australian kangaroo and French ostrich are among the options favored by the uber-fashionable regulars.

FELLINI Map pp236-8 *Self-Serve*
☎ 2511 3600; Rua General Urquiza 104, Leblon; plates US$8-15; 🕙 11:30am-4pm & 7:30pm-midnight Mon-Sat, 11:30am-6pm & 7:30pm-midnight Sun

If you can't decide what to eat but want something *good* – head to Fellini, where the seemingly endless buffet is sure to overcome even the most indecisive of diners. File past the salads, pastas, grilled fish and shrimp, or skip the buffet table and head straight to the sushi or roast meats counter. The modest dining room attracts a broad mix of people – tourists, neighborhood folk and the beauty crowd included (this is still Leblon, after all).

FRATELLI Map pp236-8 *Italian*
☎ 2259 6699; Av General San Martin 983, Leblon; mains US$9-15; 🕙 6pm-2am Mon-Fri, noon until last customer Sat & Sun

On a quiet street in Leblon, Fratelli's large glass windows frame families and young couples enjoying a fine neighborhood restaurant. It's the food, however, that ought to be on display: creamy linguini with lobster (langosta), polenta with porcini and brie and plump tortellini, all pair nicely with Fratelli's decent wine selections.

GALANI Map pp236-8 *Brazilian Eclectic*
☎ 2525 2532; Av Vieira Souto 460, Ipanema; dishes US$10-16; 🕙 6:30am-10:30pm

Set in the splendor of Ipanema's Caesar Park, Galani has handsome views overlooking the beach and an equally attractive buffet table at lunch. The Saturday *feijoada* here has become something of a local legend. Galani serves a full brunch on Sundays.

GARCIA & RODRIGUES
Map pp236-8 *French restaurant, deli & patisserie*
☎ 3206 4100; Av Ataulfo de Paiva 1251, Leblon; mains US$13-20; 🕙 8am-midnight Mon-Thu & Sun, 8am-1am Fri & Sat

Serving French food with a Brazilian accent (like roast veal a la Pantanal), Garcia & Rodrigues remains popular with Gallic expats in the city. Its two floors provide an elegant dining experience, though you can also sit in the café in front if you simply want a quick bite. Behind the glass counters surrounding the tile floor, you'll find breads and cheeses, a good wine selection, homemade ice cream and handsome desserts.

GAROTA DE IPANEMA
Map pp236-8   *Brazilian*

☎ 2523 3787; Rua Vinícius de Moraes 49, Ipanema; mains US$5-10 ⏰ 10:30am-2:30am

Although the food is standard fare here, the lively open-air dining draws crowds more for its historic past. It was originally called the Bar Veloso back in the day when two scruffy young artists – Tom Jobim and Vinícius de Moraes – frequented the spot. All that changed (and the name of the street, too) after the success of the famous song they wrote here. The first few lines of 'A Garota de Ipanema' ('The Girl from Ipanema') are printed on the wall. Best bet: enjoy appetizers (the *kibes* – meatballs – aren't bad) and a few cold *chopes* after a day on the beach.

GULA GULA Map pp236-8   *Brazilian*
☎ 2259 3084; Rua Aníbal de Mendonça 132, Ipanema; mains US$6-10; ⏰ noon-midnight Sun-Thu, noon-1am Fri & Sat

Founded over 20 years ago, Gula Gula still remains popular in Ipanema – which counts for a lot in a neighborhood ever in search of the new. Quiches and salads are tops at this casual spot, but those in search of heartier fare can opt for grilled meats or other Brazilian dishes. For dessert, the rich chocolate mousse doesn't disappoint. Order it *quente* (hot).

HORTIFRUTI Map pp236-8   *Fruit market*
☎ 2512 6820; Rua Dias Ferreira 57, Leblon; ⏰ 8am-8pm Mon-Sat, 8am-2pm Sun

Leblon's popular indoor market features a wide variety of fruits and vegetables, as well as a small juice bar.

KILOGRAMA Map pp236-8   *Self-Serve*
☎ 2512 8220; Rua Visconde de Pirajá 644, Ipanema; plates US$6-10; ⏰ 11am-11pm

A mix of young and old converge on this excellent lunch buffet during the day. There's a vague art-modern glow to the place, giving it a splash of style – which is a rarity among *a quilo* (self-serve per-kilo) restaurants. Kilograma features lots of fresh fruits and salads, good cheeses, roast meats and sushi. It stays open for dinner as well.

KURT Map pp236-8   *Patisserie*
☎ 2294 0599; Rua General Urquiza 117B, Leblon; pastries US$1.50-3; ⏰ 8am-6pm Mon-Fri, 8am-5pm Sat

Entering a true patisserie should delight all of your senses, and Kurt does just that. The flaky strudels and palm-sized torts with strawberries and kiwi lie illuminated behind the glass counter. The smell of cappuccino hangs in the air as classical music plays overhead. A few round tables then set the stage for the most rewarding sensory experience: tasting these delicate cakes and pastries.

MADAME BUTTERFLY
Map pp236-8   *Japanese*

☎ 2267 4347; Rua Barão da Torre 472, Ipanema; dinner for two US$40-60; ⏰ noon-midnight

Befitting its name, this charming Japanese restaurant plays operas in the background. Madame Butterfly serves beautifully displayed plates of sushi to young couples, one of many such restaurants on this street.

MIL FRUTAS
Map pp236-8   *Ice cream & sandwiches*

☎ 2521 1384; Rua Garcia D'Avila 134A, Ipanema; ice cream US$2-4; ⏰ 10:30am-1am Mon-Fri, 9:30am-1am Sat & Sun

On chic Garcia D'Avila street (next door to Rio's latest Luis Vuitton installment, to be precise), Mil Frutas serves tasty ice cream that showcases fruits from the Amazon and abroad. *Jaca* (jackfruit), lychee and *açaí* are among the several dozen varieties – all of which are best enjoyed on the tiny shade-covered patio out front.

MUSTAFÁ Map pp236-8   *Middle Eastern*
☎ 2540 7299; Av Ataúlfo de Paiva 1174, Leblon; hummus US$2-4; ⏰ noon-8pm Mon-Sat, noon-7pm Sun

It's easy to walk right by the small takeout counter in Leblon, but if you have a craving for fresh pita bread, tabouli, hummus or *kibe*, that would be a serious mistake. In business for over 33 years, Mustafá is a favorite among Leblon residents.

NAM THAI Map pp236-8   *Thai*

☎ 2259 2962; Rua Rainha Guilhermina 95B, Leblon; mains US$7-13; ⏱ 7pm until last customer Tue-Fri, noon until last customer Sat, noon-10pm Sun

The charming colonial interior of Nam Thai matches nicely with the traditional Thai dishes. Favorites are squid salad and spicy shrimp curry with pineapple. No less intoxicating are Nam Thai's tropical drinks, like the *caipivodca de lychee* (lychee vodka *caipirinha*).

NATURALUNA
Map pp236-8   *Health-food store*

☎ 2522 1985; Rua Vinícius de Moraes 74, Ipanema; ⏱ 9am-8pm Mon-Sat, 10am-4pm Sun

In addition to its small selection of health-food products – granola, whole wheat breads and yogurts – the Natural Moon (as it translates) sells tasty *salgados* (bar snacks). The sun-dried tomatoes with ricotta make a quick meal on the run – or on the way to the beach.

OSTERIA DELL'ANGOLO
Map pp236-8   *Italian*

☎ 2259 3148; Rua Paul Redfern 40, Ipanema; mains US$12-17; ⏱ noon-4pm & 6pm until last customer Mon-Fri, 6pm until last customer Sat & Sun

Northern Italian cuisine, something of a rarity in Rio, is served here with consummate skill,

and you'd be hard pressed to find anything that doesn't arrive perfectly prepared to your table. In addition to fresh pastas, seafood and steaks, the risottos are famous. *Risotto nero di sepia* (squid risotto in ink sauce) is one of the best dishes on the menu. President Lula, among other notable visitors, once dined in the elegant but understated Osteria.

PLATAFORMA Map pp236-8   *Churrascaria*

☎ 2274 4022; Rua Adalberto Ferreira 32, Leblon; mains US$10-17; ⏱ noon until last customer

This recently restored *churrascaria* still draws a garrulous mix of politicians, artists and tourists. Dark mellow woods in the dining room match the roast meats traveling from table to table. Also in this complex is the **Bar do Tom** (p133), featuring live bossa nova, and the Plataforma Show downstairs – the over-the-top Carnaval show for tourists.

SATYRICON Map pp236-8   *Seafood*

☎ 2521 0955; Rua Barão da Torre 192, Ipanema; mains US$16-25; ⏱ 6pm-2am Mon, noon-2am Tue-Sat, noon-midnight Sun

Often topping critics' lists of Rio's best restaurants, Satyricon serves pure decadence from its hallowed kitchen. Lovingly prepared fish, oysters and shrimp must be experienced to

Nam Thai (above)

be believed. The menu also features meats, pastas and risottos as well as delicacies like live lobster sashimi. Naturally, a well-dressed crowd – and the occasional international pop star – dines here.

SUSHI LEBLON Map pp236-8 *Japanese*
☎ 2512 7830; Rua Dias Ferreira 256, Leblon; dinner for two US$25-45; ⏱ noon-4pm & 7pm-1:30am Mon-Fri, 1:30pm until last customer Sat & Sun
Leblon's premier sushi destination, the Sushi Leblon boasts creative additions to its award-winning sashimi. Shrimp with foie gras, *namorada* with sea urchin salsa and duck sashimi are all part of the menu. The usual stylish crowd gathers here, and the wait can be exhausting, so steel yourself with a few rounds of sake.

VEGETARIANO SOCIAL CLUB
Map pp236-8 *Vegetarian*
☎ 2540 6499; Rua Conde Bernadotte 26L, Leblon; mains US$5-8; ⏱ noon-5:30pm
Vegetarians interested in sampling Brazil's signature dish should visit this zenlike spot on Saturday when tofu *feijoada* is served. The small menu changes regularly, and features different types of salads, soups and *sucos* (juices), like rose-petal juice or *guaraná* with mint and ginger. The café also serves organic wine.

YEMANJÁ Map pp236-8 *Bahian*
☎ 2247 7004; Rua Visconde de Pirajá 128A, Ipanema; moquecas for 2 US$12-20; ⏱ 6pm-midnight Mon-Thu, noon-midnight Fri & Sat, noon-10pm Sun
Bobó de camarão (shrimp pastries) are an excellent introduction to Bahian cuisine at this traditional spot near Praça General Osorio. Follow with a hearty *moqueca* (seafood stew cooked in coconut milk), and you may find yourself wanting to catch the next bus to Salvador. Waitresses in traditional dress provide excellent service.

ZAZÁ BISTRO TROPICAL
Map pp236-8 *French-Thai*
☎ 2247 9101; Rua Joana Angélica 40, Ipanema; mains US$10; ⏱ 7:30pm-midnight Mon-Wed & Sun, 7:30pm-1:30am Fri & Sat
French-colonial decor and delicately spiced cuisine await those venturing inside this charming converted house in Ipanema. Inventive combinations like pumpkin and chestnut risotto or sesame-battered tuna with wasabi cream match the seductive mood inside. Upstairs, diners lounge on throw pillows, with candles glowing along the walls. If the scene

---

Top Five Ipanema & Leblon Eats

- **Mil Frutas** (p107)
- **Osteria Dell'Angolo** (p108)
- **Sushi Leblon** (p109)
- **Zazá Bistro Tropical** (below)
- **Zuka** (below)

---

doesn't do it for you, take your dinner on the porch out front, enjoying healthy plates – everything here is organic – al fresco.

ZONA SUL SUPERMARKET
Map pp236-8 *Supermarket*
☎ 2259 4699; Rua Dias Ferreira 290, Leblon; ⏱ open 24hr except from midnight Sun to 7am Mon
A Rio institution for 44 years, Zona Sul has branches all over the city. The one in Leblon, however, is the best of the bunch, and you'll find plenty of fresh-baked breads, imported cheeses, olives, French Bourdeax, prosciutto and any other delicacy you can think of. Zona Sul is perfect for late night shopping or assembling a picnic for the beach.

ZUKA Map pp236-8 *Eclectic*
☎ 3205 7154; Rua Dias Ferreira 233, Leblon; ⏱ 7pm-1:30am Mon, noon-4pm & 7pm-1:30am Tue-Fri, 1:30pm-1:30am Sat & Sun
'Is the chef at Zuka a genius?' is what you might overhear after a meal at this trendy spot in Leblon. Judging by the restaurant's continued popularity and the ever-inventive combinations coming from the kitchen, you might answer yes. Or you might not care. After savoring tuna foie gras in thyme or the smoked duck with caramelized pineapple, you'll probably be thinking of something else entirely – like what to order for dessert. Skewers of fruit in sake or chocolate soufflé? This, after all, is the more pressing question.

CHEAP EATS
CHAIKA Map pp236-8 *Fast food*
☎ 2267 3838; Rua Visconde de Pirajá 321, Ipanema; lunch specials US$4; ⏱ 9am-1am
The neon sign overhead is like a beacon for those looking to eat on the cheap. The stand-up bar in front doles out hamburgers, pastries and sodas. The sit-down restaurant in back offers a bigger menu – panini, salads and pancakes – and they'll still bring it to you in a hurry.

L'ASSIETTE

Map pp236-8 — *French bistro*

☎ 2227 1477; Rua Visconde de Pirajá, Ipanema; weekday specials US$3.25; ☙ noon-9pm

This cute bistro just off the beaten path has a small but lovely menu of French specialties, none of which cost more than US$6. If you're really on a dime, try their weekday specials, featuring the plate of the day (stroganoff, grilled chicken etc) served with salad and a drink. Or stick with their popular standards – crepes, smoked salmon on baguettes and salad *niçoise*. Wines are also available by the glass.

NEW NATURAL Map pp236-8 — *Vegetarian*

☎ 2287 0301; Rua Barão da Torre 167, Ipanema; lunch specials US$4; ☙ 11am-6pm Tue-Sun

Featuring an excellent vegetarian lunch buffet, New Natural was the first 'health-food' restaurant in the neighborhood. Fill up on fresh pots of soup, rice, veggies and beans for less than US$5. Other good options include pancake dishes with assorted fillings.

POLIS SUCOS Map pp236-8 — *Juice Bar*

☎ 2247 2518; Rua Maria Quitéria 70, Ipanema; juices US$1.50-3; ☙ 7am-midnight

Got rickets? Scurvy? This juice bar facing the Praça NS de Paz has the antidote. Fresh-squeezed vitamins feature prominently in the 40 or so flavors served at Polis Sucos, and you can pair those tangy beverages with sandwiches (vegetarian, chicken, filet mignon), *pão de queijo* (cheese-filled roll) or a slice of *bolo* (cake). Those who prefer their juices without sugar or ice order it *natural*.

GÁVEA, JARDIM BOTÂNICO & LAGOA

Although Leblon and Ipanema take all the credit for hosting Rio's brightest culinary spots, Lagoa and neighboring areas have plenty to brag about in their own right. With small outdoor restaurants perched along its shore, the lake is the region's centerpiece. During the summer, live music fills the air as diners eat, drink and stroll along the lake. The east side, around Parque do Cantaglo, offers more choices than the west side; a number of restaurants lie scattered in the streets overlooking the lake, as well.

00 (ZERO ZERO)

Map pp236-8 — *Brazilian Eclectic*

☎ 2540 8041; Planetário da Gávea, Av Padre Leonel Franca 240, Gávea; ☙ 8pm until late

Housed in Gávea's planetarium, 00 is a sleek restaurant-lounge that serves Brazilian cuisine with Asian and Mediterranean overtones. Jerked beef and leek tapioca rolls or filet mignon with puree of *arracacha* are best enjoyed on the open-air veranda. After dinner, have a few cocktails and stick around: some of Rio's best DJs spin at parties here (p138).

BOTECO 66 Map pp236-8 — *French*

☎ 2266 0838; Av Alexandre Ferreira 66, Lagoa; mains US$10-18; ☙ noon until last customer Tue-Fri, 6pm until last customer Sat

A small outdoor garden lends a rustic air to this French bistro bordering Jardim Botânico. A couples' favorite, the vibe always remains casual in spite of the elegant selections. Gorgonzola and apricot salads pair nicely with seared tuna or filet mignon here.

GUIMAS Map pp236-8 — *Eclectic*

☎ 2259 7996; José Roberto Macedo Soares 5, Gávea; mains US$10-18; ☙ noon-1am

A classic Carioca *boteco* with a creative flair, Guimas has been going strong for almost 20 years. Trout with leeks or the roast duck with honey and pear rice go nicely with the superfine *caipivodcas* (*caipirinhas* made with vodka instead of *cachaça*). The small but cozy open-air restaurant attracts a more colorful mix of diners as the night progresses.

LAGOA KIOSKS Map pp236-8 — *Various*

Parque Brigadeiro Faria Lima & Parque do Cantaglo, Lagoa; plates US$5-12; ☙ 5pm until last customer Mon-Fri, noon until last customer Sat & Sun

Scattered along the edge of the lake, lie a dozen or so restaurants offering a range of regional and international cuisines. You can dine on sushi, Italian, Lebanese, German and cuisine from Minas Gerais among others. Music happens nightly, making for one of Rio's more seductive open-air scenarios.

MISTURA FINA

Map pp236-8 — *Brazilian Eclectic*

☎ 2537 2844; www.misturafina.com.br in Portuguese; Av Borges de Medeiros 3207, Lagoa; dishes US$8-14; ☙ noon until last customer

This popular Lagoa restaurant serves excellent eclectic cuisine. The roast duck, filet mignon

Kiosk, Lagoa (opposite)

and Saturday *feijoada* are favorites. It's the music and views, however, that make this restaurant such a draw. The upstairs level features shows nightly (p134), while the downstairs veranda offers an impressive vista of the lake.

OLYMPE Map pp236-8 *French*

☎ 2539 4542; Rua Custódio Serrão 62, Lagoa; plates US$13-20; ⏱ 7pm-12:30am Mon-Thu & Sat, noon-4pm & 7pm-12:30am Fri

Chef Claude Troisgros recently reopened his award-winning restaurant under a new name, Olympe, as a homage to his mother. The brilliant French cooking, the casual but stylish interior, and the crowds (casual but stylish) are still the same. Quail, risotto with crayfish, shrimp with Moroccan couscous are among the offerings.

QUADRIFOGLIO Map pp236-8 *Italian*

☎ 2294 1433; Rua JJ Seabra 19, Jardim Botânico; plates US$12-20; ⏱ noon-3:30pm & 7:30pm-midnight Mon-Thu, noon-3:30pm & 7:30pm-1am Fri, 7:30pm-1am Sat, noon-5pm Sun

A charming Italian spot famed for exotic raviolis like its *ravioli de maçã ao creme e semente de papoula* (apple ravioli with cream and poppy seed sauce), Quadrifoglio has been a neighborhood favorite since it opened.

CHEAP EATS
BRASEIRO DA GÁVEA

Map pp236-8 *Brazilian*

☎ 2239 7494; Praça Santos Dumont 116, Gávea; plates US$4-8; ⏱ 11am-1am Mon-Thu & 11am-3am Fri & Sat

This family-style eatery serves up large portions of their popular steak with *farofa*, pot roast or fried chicken. On weekends, the open-air spot fills with the din of conversation and the aroma of fresh *chopes* drifting by. A younger crowd takes over at night and keeps things going early into the morning.

COPACABANA & LEME

Copacabana has many culinary gems, from venerable five-star institutions atop beachfront hotels to charming old bistros dating from the mid-century. In general, you will encounter less experimentation here, but if you're looking for excellent traditional cuisine – both Brazilian and international – you will find plenty of delectable options in Copacabana.

Dozens of restaurants line Av Atlântica. With a constant breeze and the shoreline stretching across the horizon, it's a charming view. Unfortunately, the panorama is much better than the restaurants on this strip – with a few exceptions of course. Things get seedy here at night, and if you're looking for an escort, you're in the right spot. If you're looking for good cuisine, however, look elsewhere. The narrow roads crisscrossing Av NS de Copacabana all the way from Leme to Arpoador contain many fine establishments – and many mediocre ones. Do some exploring, trust your instincts and *bom proveito* (happy eating).

AMIR Map pp234-5 *Middle Eastern*
☎ 2275 5596; Rua Ronald de Carvalho 55C, Copacabana; platters for 2 US$7-12; ⏱ 11am-7pm Mon-Tue & Sat, 11am-11pm Wed-Fri

A cozy air pervades this small, casual restaurant near the beach. As you step inside, you'll notice the meats roasting in the corner, the handsomely dressed waiters in red fezes and embroidered vests, and heavenly aromas wafting from the kitchen. The details aren't only in the setting. Amir's plates are consistently good – hummus, kaftas, falafel and salads – rivaled only by the delectable desserts which change daily.

ARS BRASILIS
Map pp234-5 *Minas Gerais*
☎ 2287 2488; Rua Souza Lima 37, Copacabana; small plates US$2-4; ⏱ 9am-10pm Mon-Fri, 9am-6pm Sat, noon-6pm Sun

At first glance, this colorful handicrafts shop (p156) may not appear to offer much in the way of refreshment, but look closer – those front tables that look like they're for sale are actually part of the restaurant. The portions here are small but flavorful. Among the offerings: *casquinha de siri*, a Minas stew cooked in a small clay pot and covered with *farofa*. *Empadas* (round, flaky pies) are also tasty, and come in three flavors: heart of palm, shrimp or onion.

AZUMI Map pp234-5 *Japanese*
☎ 2541 4294; Rua Ministro Viveiros de Castro 127, Copacabana; plates US$7-14, Copacabana; ⏱ 7pm-midnight Tue-Thu & Sun, 7pm-1am Fri & Sat

Some critics claim Azumi is the bastion of traditional Japanese cuisine in the city. This laid-back sushi bar with a handful of tables certainly has its fans – both from the nisei community and abroad. Azumi's *sushiman* masterfully prepares delectable sushi and sashimi, though tempuras and soups are also excellent. Be sure to ask what's in season.

BAKERS
Map pp234-5 *Bakery & patisserie*
☎ 2256 7000; Rua Santa Clara 86B, Copacabana; Danishes US$1.50; ⏱ 9am-8pm Mon-Fri, 9am-6:30pm Sat, 9am-5pm Sun

The red awning out front gives a hint of the royal displays waiting inside. Behind shiny countertops lie banana Danishes, apple strudel and flaky croissants – all of which are as tasty as they look (we know because we tried them all). Coffee and cappuccinos pair nicely with the baked goods.

BAR 12 Map pp234-5 *Brazilian*
☎ 2543 3805; Av Atlântica 994A; mains US$6-10, Copacabana; ⏱ 11am-midnight

One of the newest additions to Av Atlântica's restaurant scene, Bar 12 serves Brazilian basics to live music during the week. The food isn't spectacular, but the atmosphere is festive and the ocean breeze doesn't hurt. *Feijoada* is a favorite here on Saturdays.

CAFÉ FLEURI
Map pp234-5 *Brazilian Eclectic*
☎ 3873 8881; Le Meridien Hotel, Av Atlântica 1020, Copacabana; mains US$11-20; ⏱ noon-3:30pm & 7pm-midnight Mon-Fri, 12:30-5pm & 7pm-midnight Sat & Sun

Café Fleuri serves excellent cuisine at much more affordable prices than its big brother upstairs (**Le Saint Honoré**, opposite). Amid a dining room with a vaguely country-kitchen air, Fleuri's chefs spread elegant lunch buffets during the week. Specialties vary by the day, with Thursday devoted to Asian cuisine, Friday to Bahian, *feijoada* arriving on Saturday and elegant brunch on Sunday.

CERVANTES Map pp234-5 *Brazilian*
☎ 2275 6147; Av Prado Júnior 335B, Copacabana; sandwiches US$3-6; ⏱ noon-4am Tue-Thu, noon-5am Fri & Sat, noon-3am Sun

A Copacabana institution, Cervantes gathers a strange, colorful crowd late at night. The rest of the time, a mix of young and old, professional and working class, rub elbows over Cervantes' trademark meat-and-pineapple sandwiches. *Filé com queijo e abacaxí* (filet mignon with cheese and pineapple) is unbeatable, and fussy waiters are quick to the tap when your *chope* runneth dry. Around the corner (Rua Barato Ribeiro 7) is Cervantes' stand-up *boteco*, good for getting those excellent bites when you're in a hurry.

Top Five Copacabana Eats

- **Amir** (opposite)
- **Cervantes** (opposite)
- **La Trattoria** (below)
- **Le Saint Honoré** (below)
- **Marius Crustáceos** (p114)

CIPRIANI Map pp234-5 *Italian*

☎ 2545 8747; Copacabana Palace Hotel, Av Atlântica 1702, Copacabana; mains US$25-35; ⏱ 12:30pm-3pm & 7pm-1am Mon-Sat, 12:30pm-4pm & 7pm-1am Sun

On a candlelit patio beside the Palace's pool, Cipriani serves fine northern Italian cuisine to a well-dressed, largely non-Brazilian crowd. The gnocchi, the sirloin with port sauce, and the smoked scallops all meet their mark. For dessert, tiramisu and chocolate mousse are both good options. The dress code is once again in force, so leave your havaianas at home.

CONFEITARIA COLOMBO
Map pp234-5 *Café & lighter fare*

☎ 2247 5994; Av Atlântica Posto 6, Forte de Copacabana; salads US$4-7; ⏱ 10am-8pm

One of the few places in the city where you can sit and watch young soldiers in fatigues filing past a superb view of Copacabana. The recently opened (December 2003) café serves the same rich desserts, salads and coffee you'd find at their landmark building in Centro, only in place of stained glass and 19th-century furnishings you have the **old fort** (p62), with its brick-lined walkways and fine sea views. Admission to the café area of the fort only is US$0.30, or you can peruse the **museum** (p62) for another US$0.70.

DON CAMILLO Map pp234-5 *Italian*

☎ 2225 5126; Av Atlântica 3056; mains US$7-12, Copacabana; ⏱ noon-2am

The wandering street musicians and carnivalesque street parade lends a festive air to this beachfront Italian spot. Pastas are flavorful, and hearty seafood dishes won't disappoint. With many desserts to choose from, you may have a tough time deciding how to finish that meal.

LA TRATTORIA Map pp234-5 *Italian*

☎ 2255 3319; Rua Fernando Mendes 7A, Copacabana; mains US$6-12; ⏱ 11am-1am

Old photos, simple furnishings, hearty dishes and the constant din of conversation have made this trattoria a neighborhood favorite for over 25 years. Shrimp dishes are the Italian fami-

ly's specialty – they've won over many diners with their *espaguete com camarão e óleo tartufado* (spaghetti with shrimp and truffle oil).

LE BLÉ NOIR Map pp234-5 *French Creperie*

☎ 2287 1272; Rua Xavier da Silveira 15A, Copacabana; mains US$8-12; ⏱ 7pm-1am Wed-Thu & Sun, 7pm-2am Fri & Sat

Flickering candles, subdued conversation and tasty crepes make this popular restaurant a real date-pleaser. Le Blé Noir offers over 50 different varieties, and pairs rich ingredients like shrimp and artichoke hearts or brie, honey and toasted almonds. Call ahead for a reservation or enjoy a cocktail on the small patio in front.

LE PRÉ CATALAN Map pp234-5 *French*

☎ 2525 1232; Level E, Hotel Sofitel, Av Atlântica 4240, Copacabana; mains US$25-35; ⏱ 7:30pm-midnight Mon-Sat

Sofitel's star restaurant is set in an art-deco dining room. Award-winning chef Roland Villard prepares French cuisine with a tropical infusion. Grouper in confit tomato sauce, osso buco and the tiramisu mousse are fit for superstars – who do occasionally drop in for a meal.

LE SAINT HONORÉ Map pp234-5 *French*

☎ 3873 8888; 37th fl, Meridien Hotel, Av Atlântica 1020, Copacabana; mains US$22-35; ⏱ 7:30pm-1am Mon-Sat

Amid a lavish dining room overlooking the coast, Le Saint Honoré does its best to dazzle you with culinary pyrotechnics. Chef Dominique Oudin prepares petit slices of heaven – scallops carpaccio, roast caramelized duck – while his sous chef delivers the coup de grace with hot raspberry soufflé. Given the decadent display of food that will arrive at your table, you will have to dress accordingly: jacket and tie are required.

LUCAS Map pp234-5 *German*

☎ 2521 4705; Av Atlântica 3744, Copacabana; mains US$8-13; ⏱ 10am-1am Mon-Thu, 10am-2am Fri & Sat

Classic German cooking with a view of the beach? We're not in Dusseldorf any more, but the *kasslers*, frankfurters and strudel might as well have been made in the old country. Tourists and Cariocas frequent this low-key spot.

MARIUS Map pp234-5 *Churrascaria*

☎ 2542 2393; Av Atlântica 290B, Leme; US$18 per person; ⏱ noon-4pm & 6pm-midnight Mon-Fri, noon-midnight Sat & Sun

In addition to the breathtaking array of delicious meats carried from table to table, this

Leme *churrascaria* features a lavish buffet table. Oysters on the half shell, sushi, grilled vegetables with herbs, all seem almost too lovely to eat. But somehow the garrulous crowd here manages to overcome their aesthetic inhibitions, and gets down to serious eating.

MARIUS CRUSTÁCEOS

Map pp234-5   *Seafood*

☎ 2543 6393; Av Atlântica 290A, Leme; US$30 per person; ☺ noon-4pm & 6pm-midnight Mon-Fri, noon-midnight Sat & Sun

Marius' *churrascaria* was such a success that they decided to open a seafood version of the all-you-can-eat meat place next door. Aquatic decoration and subtle shades of blue here create a 20,000-leagues-under-the-sea-like ambience. Of course, the oceanic theme is only enhanced by all the seafood served here. Waiters file past bearing tuna, salmon, lobster, mussels, scallops – there's more marine life here than in most aquariums. And it's much tastier, too.

SHIRLEY Map pp234-5   *Spanish*

☎ 2275 1398; Rua Gustavo Sampaio 610, Leme; mains US$9-18; ☺ 11am-12:30am

The aroma of succulent paella hangs in the air as waiters hurry to and from the kitchen, bearing platefuls of fresh seafood. Some critics say Shirley isn't what it used to be, but crowds still pack this simple Leme restaurant on weekends (making reservations advisable). In addition to paella, the mussel vinaigrette appetizer or the octopus and squid in ink are also recommended. One dish easily serves two.

SIRI MOLE & CIA

Map pp234-5   *Brazilian seafood*

☎ 2267 0894; Rua Francisco Otaviano 50, Copacabana; mains US$10-17; ☺ 7pm until last customer Mon, noon until last customer Tue-Sun

Understated elegance is the key to Siri Mole & Cia's longstanding success – both in ambience and in the perfectly prepared seafood. Among the favorites – *moqueca de siri mole* (spicy, soft-shell crab stew), *acarajé* (mussels in broth) and the grilled fish.

CHEAP EATS

CARRETÃO Map pp234-5   *Churrascaria*

☎ 2542 2148; Rua Ronald de Carvalho 55, Leme; all-you-can-eat US$8; ☺ 11:30am-midnight

It's all about the meat at this decent but inexpensive *churrascaria* in Leme. With several

branches throughout the city, including an Ipanema **Carretão** (☎ 2267 3965; Rua Visconde de Pirajá 112), this chain serves up consistently good roast meats – and heaps of it. The salad bar isn't as substantial as one you'd find at, say, Marius, but you can also order sides (French fries, cooked vegetables) off the menu at no added charge.

LOPE'S CONFEITERIA Map pp234-5   *Brazilian*

Av NS de Copacabana 1334, Copacabana; lunch plates US$3-4; ☺ 7am-midnight

Lope's is like a vision of 1950s Rio – chicken roasting on the sidewalk out front, aged black-and-white photos along the walls, simple tables scattered around the large elliptical lunch counter. A noisy lunch crowd still fills the chairs, with no-nonsense service hurrying them along; and the food hasn't changed much since then – portions are large, grease is plentiful and the dessert shop lies just next door.

SERAFINA Map pp234-5   *Italian*

☎ 2256 5565; Rua Figueiredo de Magalhães 28, Copacabana; mains US$4-7; ☺ 8am-11pm Tue-Thu, 8am-1am Fri & Sat, 8am-9pm Sun

A few paintings adorn the walls of this cheerful eatery just off the beach. Here the decor matches the cooking: simple but successful. Grilled fish, risottos and pastas all cost under US$8. The US$2 breakfast is one of Serafina's best deals: bread, fruit, ham, an egg, juice and coffee.

TEMPERARTE Map pp234-5   *Self-Serve*

☎ 2267 1149; Av NS de Copacabana 1250, Copacabana; plates US$4-8; ☺ 11am-10:30pm Mon-Sat, 11am-5pm Sun

One of the neighborhood's best pay-by-weight restaurants, the casual Temperarte has a good selection of salads, roast meats, vegetables and sushi, as well as ample dessert offerings. Closer to Leme, a second **Temperarte** (Map pp234-5; Av NS de Copacabana 266) opens for lunch only.

YONZA Map pp234-5   *creperie*

☎ 2521 4248; Rua Miguel Lemos 21B, Copacabana; crepes US$3-5; ☺ 10am-midnight Tue-Fri, 6pm-midnight Sat & Sun

Surfboards and animated Japanese superhero posters create the ambience at this creperie on an otherwise empty stretch of Copacabana. A young crowd flocks here at night to fill up on hearty platefuls of filling crepes. Best not to get too experimental here: the simple *queijo e tomate* (cheese and tomato) does just fine.

BOTAFOGO & URCA

Botafogo has only a sparse selection of restaurants, and Urca, which is still untouched by commercial development, has even fewer. The lack of restaurant strips in either neighborhood still keeps many visitors – and Cariocas – from exploring the area. This of course means that diners looking for something off the beaten path shouldn't overlook these neighborhoods. Some splendid offerings await – great views, live music, or simply that inexplicable allure of finding that splendid but largely undiscovered place.

ADEGA DO VALENTIM
Map pp232-3   *Portuguese*
☎ 2541 1166; Rua da Passagem 178, Botafogo; mains US$8-14; ☿ noon-1am

Bacalhau (cod) is the specialty at this old-fashioned Portuguese restaurant, and it offers over a dozen different ways of preparation. Jocular old waiters also serve plenty of other favorites: baked rabbit, roast suckling pig, octopus, the list goes on...

BAR URCA Map pp232-3   *Brazilian seafood*
☎ 2295 8744; Rua Cândido Gaffré 205, Urca; lunch specials US$3-5; ☿ 11am-5pm

This upstairs spot has a nice view of the bay along with a fresh sea breeze to cool things off. The food is a straightforward affair: *bobo de camarão* (shrimp and coconut stew), grilled fish and squid aren't winning any culinary awards, but they're reliably decent.

BOM DIA MARIA Map pp232-3   *Amazonian*
☎ 2275 6971; Rua Elvira Machado 10, Botafogo; mains US$7-11; ☿ noon-4pm Tue, noon-4pm & 7pm-midnight Thu-Sat, noon-6pm Sun

In an old mansion on a fairly hidden street, Bom Dia Maria (named after one of the owners) serves delights from Amazonia: *piraracu, tucupi, maniçoba* – delicacies that probably don't mean a damn to you unless you hail from Belém. All the same, discover these culinary riches. You'll find wondrously spiced fish, roast duck, intoxicating stews – and intoxicating *caipirinhas* to accompany them (infused with Amazonian fruits like *cupuaçu* and *murici*, naturally).

CARÊME BISTRO Map pp232-3   *French*
☎ 2537 2274; Rua Visconde de Caravelas 113, Botafogo; mains US$15-25; ☿ 8pm until last customer Tue-Sat

This French bistro does everything right to keep its small fan-base coming back. In an intimate but unpretentious space, attentive waiters bring plates of marinated snapper, braised rabbit, and apple and nut risotto (among other vegetarian offerings). Don't neglect the small but excellent wine list.

LIVRARIA PREFÁCIO
Map pp232-3   *Café & Bistro*
☎ 2527 5699; Rua Voluntarios da Pátria 39, Botafogo; ☿ 10am-10pm Mon-Fri, 2-10pm Sat & Sun

In the back of the small arts-oriented bookshop **Livraria Prefácio** (p157), this café seems reminiscent of something out of an Umberto Eco novel – exposed brick walls with candles throwing shadows across them as the hushed conversation of revolutionaries – or up and coming samba bands – transpires around the small corner tables. The café hosts an occasional poetry reading or record-release party.

PAX Map pp232-3   *Brazilian Eclectic*
☎ 2550 9713; 7th fl, Praia de Botafogo 400, Botafogo; mains US$7-12; ☿ noon-8:30pm

Located on the 7th floor of Botafogo Praia Shopping, Pax has spectacular views of Pão de Açúcar, with the curved Botafogo marina in the foreground. Families and shoppers converge here during the day, dining on the good selection of steaks, pastas and grilled fish. Try the creamy pumpkin gnocchi with brie or the Tropical, grilled salmon in mango and mustard sauce.

PIZZA PARK Map pp232-3   *Pizza*
☎ 2537 2602; Rua Voluntarios da Pátria 446, Botafogo; pizzas US$7-14; ☿ 10am-1am

A lively – sometimes exuberant – crowd gathers at this popular spot until late into the evening most nights. Pizza Park's thin-crust pizzas are just as popular as its ice-cold beer, and make a beautiful couple on a steamy summer night.

PRAIA VERMELHA Map pp232-3   *Brazilian*
☎ 2275 7245; Praça General Tibúrcio, Urca; mains US$5-10; ☿ 11:30am-midnight

Perched over the beach of the same name, Praia Vermelha has gorgeous views of the coast, with Pão de Açúcar looming overhead. By night, live *forró* (popular dance music) and *chorinho* (fast-paced instrumental music) musicians play from 6pm onward, making for one of the finest settings in the Zona Sul. The food, however, is less than spectacular. Pizzas from the wood-burning oven are the best bet, and the lunch buffet isn't bad if you're around during the day.

YORUBÁ Map pp232-3 *Bahian*
☎ 2541 9387; Rua Arnaldo Quintela 94, Botafogo; mains US$10-20; ⏰ 7-11pm Wed-Fri, 2-10pm Sat, noon-6pm Sun

Yorubá looks as if it's always ready for the arrival of an Orixá. Leaves lie scattered across the floor as candles flicker on the walls. Young waiters in red aprons stand at attention while something mystical transpires in the kitchen. And if Iemanjá or Oxúm were to pay a surprise visit, it's unlikely they'd be disappointed. Plates here are heavenly: plump shrimp and rich coconut milk blend to perfection in *babão de camarão*, and the *moqueca* is outstanding. As a final offering: don't pass up *queijo quebras* (condensed milk and coconut sweets).

CHEAP EATS

GAROTA DA URCA Map pp232-3 *Brazilian*
☎ 2541 8585; Rua João Luís Alves 56, Urca; ⏰ 11am until last customer

Overlooking the small Praia da Urca, this neighborhood restaurant serves standard Brazilian fare at decent prices. The weekday lunch specials feature plates of fish or chicken for US$3. Not a bad venture given the nice views out over the bay from the open-air veranda. By night, a more garrulous crowd meets here for steak and *chope*.

ZIN Map pp232-3 *Brazilian*
☎ 2559 6430; 8th fl, Praia de Botafogo 400, Botafogo; mains US$7-12; ⏰ noon-8:30pm

Boasting the same sweeping views as Pax, Zin also has an outdoor veranda – perfect for breezy views in the summertime. Zin caters to shoppers passing through in a hurry, and offers them tasty Brazilian bites like roast meats, shrimp dishes and a range of dessert offerings.

FLAMENGO

One of Rio's oldest neighborhoods, Flamengo has its share of historic restaurants scattered among its tree-lined streets. Flamengo's ongoing gentrification, on the other hand, ensures that new restaurants are constantly being added to the mix. Rua Marquês de Abrantes is one of the best streets to wander to see old and new vying for attention. On weekend nights, the sidewalks grow crowded with people eating, drinking and flirting, all of which Cariocas do quite well.

ALHO E ÓLEO Map pp232-3 *Brazilian Eclectic*
☎ 2558 3345; Rua Buarque de Macedo 13, Flamengo; plates US$13-20; ⏰ noon until last customer

Impeccable service, a stately air and innovative dishes make Alho e Óleo a top choice

Yorubá (above)

for lunching execs trying to cut a deal. In the evening, older couples hold court as the chef churns out lobster in tangerine sauce or duck tortellini with fresh mushrooms.

CHURRASCARIA MAJÓRICA
Map pp232-3   *Churrascaria*

☎ 2285 6789; Rua Senador Vergueiro 11, Flamengo; ☽ noon-midnight Tue-Thu, noon-1am Fri & Sat

A true gaucho would chuckle at the kitschy cowboy accoutrements that cover the inside of this restaurant. He'd shut his trap, however, once his plate of steak arrived. Meat is very serious business at Majórica, and if you're looking for an authentic *churrascaria* experience, look no further.

LAMAS
Map pp232-3   *Brazilian*

☎ 2556 0799; Rua Marquês de Abrantes 18A, Flamengo; mains US$8-14; ☽ 8am-2:30am Sun-Thu, 8am-4am Fri & Sat

This classic Brazilian restaurant opened here in 1874, and it has fans from all over the city. In spite of the mileage, dishes here hold up well, and those omniscient waiters you see in starched white coats will tell you what's hot in the kitchen. You can't go wrong with grilled *linguiça* (sausage) or filet mignon with garlic.

PORCÃO RIO'S
Map pp232-3   *Churrascaria*

☎ 2554 8535; Av Infante Dom Henrique, Flamengo; all you can eat US$15; ☽ 11:30am-midnight Mon-Thu & Sun, 11:30am-1am Fri & Sat

Set in the Parque do Flamengo with a stunning view of Pão de Açúcar, Porcão Rio's has been gradually moving up the charts in the *churrascaria* ratings. Some claim it's the best in the city; others are content just to go for the view. Whatever the case, you're in for an eating extravaganza. Call a few days in advance to book that table by the window.

SENAC BISTRO
Map pp232-3   *Brazilian Eclectic*

☎ 3138 1540; Rua Marquês de Abrantes 99, Flamengo; mains US$7-12; ☽ 11:30am-4pm Sun-Thu, 11:30am-4pm & 7pm-midnight Fri & Sat

On the bottom floor of an old mansion built 100 or so years ago, Senac serves tasty plates of seared tuna, shrimp *moqueca* and other Brazilian specialties. In spite of the splendid exterior, the decor inside is a bit lacking. The chocolate cake, however, makes up for any ambience issues. It comes warm and oozing decadence.

Top Five Botafogo, Urca & Flamengo Eats
- **Belmonte** (below)
- **Bom Dia Maria** (p115)
- **Porcão Rio's** (p117)
- **Praia Vermelha** (p115)
- **Yorubá** (opposite)

CHEAP EATS

BELMONTE
Map pp232-3   *Brazilian*

☎ 2552 3349; Praia do Flamengo 300, Flamengo; mains US$4-8; ☽ 7am until last customer

One of the classic *botecos* in Rio, Belmonte is a vision of Rio from the '50s. Globe lights hang overhead as a few patrons steel their nerves with *cachaça* (or Pepsi) from the narrow bar. Meanwhile, unhurried waiters make their way across the intricate tile floors, carrying plates of trout or steak sandwiches. And history repeats itself.

TACACÁ DO NORTE
Map pp232-3   *Amazonian*

☎ 2205 7545; Rua Barão do Flamengo 35R, Flamengo; tacacá US$2.50; ☽ 9am-10pm Mon-Sat 9am-7pm Sun

In the Amazonian state of Pará, most people order their *tacacá* late in the afternoon from their favorite street vendor. The dish is usually served from a gourd bowl. In Rio, you don't have to wait until the sun is setting to get your *tacacá*. The fragrant soup of manioc paste, jambu leaves and fresh and dried shrimp isn't for everyone. But then again, neither is the Amazon. For the faint of heart, this simple lunch counter also offers fruit juices and a handful of daily specials like *pirarucu* (a kind of fish), from Amazonia.

CATETE & GLÓRIA

As the twin rulers of Rio's budget-hotel kingdom, Glória and Catete offer plenty of inexpensive restaurants to match. A stroll down Rua Catete will lead past half a dozen lunch counters mostly serving the same uninspiring brand of lunch special. Those on a tight budget can still eat well here, while those looking for something fancy usually skip the area – but not always.

AMAZÓNIA
Map pp232-3   *Brazilian*

☎ 2557 4569; Upstairs, Rua do Catete 234, Catete; mains US$7-12; ☽ 11am-midnight

Don't be fooled by the name. The only thing Amazonian about this place is the size of the

Eating – Catete & Glória

portions. Traditional Brazilian cuisine, however, comes in many forms at this simple restaurant: try the juicy steak, tasty grilled chicken with creamed corn sauce or *feijão manteiga* (butter-simmered beans).

BISTRO JARDINS Map pp232-3 *Café*
☎ 2558 2673; Parque do Catete, Rua do Catete 153, Catete; cappuccino US$1.25; ☽ 9:30am-6pm
Behind the Museu da Republica, the lovely Catete gardens unfold – a verdant respite from the chaotic streets. The Bistro serves lunch, but it's the ambience that's noteworthy here, not the cuisine. Stick to cappuccinos, desserts and quiches, and you'll walk away charmed.

CASA DA SUÍÇA Map pp228-30 *Swiss*
☎ 2552 5182; Rua Cândido Mendes 157, Glória; plates US$10-20; ☽ noon-3pm & 7pm-midnight Mon-Fri, 7pm-1am Sat, noon-4pm & 7-11pm Sun
Tucked away on a quiet street in Glória lies a slice of Switzerland in the tropics. Featuring *flambés*, fondues and an ever-changing menu, the Casa da Suíça creates an almost tangible aura of sensuality – perhaps owing to all those open fires flaring in the intimate space. It's not a bad place to propose, if you've just met the man or woman of your dreams.

CHEAP EATS

CATETE GRILL Map pp232-3 *Self-Serve*
☎ 2285 3442; Rua do Catete 239, Catete; plates US$4-8; ☽ 11am-midnight Mon-Sat, 11am-11pm Sun
One of the newest restaurants in Catete, the Catete Grill has won over the neighborhood with its excellent buffet – served all day. It also offers ice creams – *a quilo* (per kilo), of course.

ESTAÇÃO REPÚBLICA
Map pp232-3 *Self-Serve*
☎ 2225 2650; Rua do Catete 104, Catete; plates US$4-8; ☽ 11am-midnight Mon-Sat, 11am-11pm Sun
In an aging mansion fronted by red awnings, Estaçáo's buffet table is a neighborhood in-

stitution. Featuring an extensive selection of salads, meats, pastas and vegetables, it's easy to indulge without breaking the bank. Sundays are family affairs here.

TABERNA DA GLÓRIA
Map pp228-30 *Brazilian*
☎ 2265 7835; Rua do Russel 32A, Glória; mains US$5-10; ☽ 11:30am-1am Mon-Thu & Sun, 11:30am-2am Fri & Sat
On a small plaza in the heart of Glória, this large outdoor eatery serves decent Brazilian staples, and in abundance – most dishes here serve two. The *feijoada* on Saturday still draws crowds, and if you're not up for a big meal, appetizers and ice-cold *chope* are a good way to enjoy the open-air ambience.

CENTRO & CINELÂNDIA

Catering to Rio's workday crowds, Centro offers a wide variety of restaurants, from divy diners to haute cuisine, sushi bars and French bistros to juice bars and *churrascarias*. With a few exceptions, most restaurants open only for lunch during the week. Many pedestrian-only areas throughout Centro (like Rua do Rosario) are full of restaurants, some spilling onto the sidewalk, others hidden on upstairs floors, all of which make restaurant-hunting something of an art. Several areas worth exploring are Travessa do Comércio just after work, when the restaurants and cafés fill with chatter. Another early-evening gathering spot is Av Marechal Floriano, full of snack bars specializing in fried sardines and beer. Cinelândia, just behind the Praça Floriano, features a number of open-air cafés and restaurants. Not many of these serve anything of note, and most Cariocas stop here just for the ice-cold *chopes* and a few appetizers before heading elsewhere.

ATELIÊ ODEON Map pp228-30 *Bistro*
☎ 2240 0746; Praça Floriano, Cinelândia; mains US$6-10; ☽ noon-10pm Mon-Fri
Next to the art-house cinema of the same name, the new Ateliê Odeon serves up decent Brazilian fare to a festive crowd on its open-air terrace. Ateliê opens onto the Praça Floriano, which is a lively gathering spot weekday evenings. On the weekends, Ateliê stays opens around film screenings next door.

ATRIUM Map pp228-30 *Bistro*
☎ 2220 0193; Praça XV de Novembro 48 – Paço Imperial, Centro; mains US$10-20; ⏱ 11:30am-3:30pm Mon-Fri

A stately dining room in the Paço Imperial, Atrium serves power-lunching business execs and those simply wanting a taste of decadence – during a weekday lunch period, of course. Lamb with rosemary and trout with orange sauce would have brought a smile to Dom Pedro I (a Portuguese ruler not unknown for his magnificent appetite).

BAR DAS ARTES Map pp228-30 *Bistro*
☎ 2215 5795; Praça XV de Novembro 48, Centro; sandwiches US$3-4; ⏱ 9am-8pm Mon-Fri, 9am-2pm Sat

Inside this book and record store in the Paço Imperial, bossa nova plays overhead as customers browse through old books of Rio. Meanwhile diners at the tables in front enjoy quiches, salads and lighter fare. Several other restaurants lie in this complex.

BAR LUIZ Map pp228-30 *German*
☎ 2262 6900; Rua da Carioca 39, Centro; mains US$6-10; ⏱ 11am-11:30pm Mon-Sat

Bar Luiz first opened in 1887, making it one of the city's oldest *cervejarias* (pubs). A festive air fills the old saloon as diners get their fill of traditional German cooking (potato salad and smoked meats), along with ice-cold drafts – including dark beer – on tap.

CAFÉ DO ATELIÊ Map pp228-30 *Bistro*
☎ 2221 2133; Rua do Lavradio 34, Centro; dishes US$3-7; ⏱ 11am until last customer

Set in a historic building (Countess Belmonte once lived here), Café do Ateliê with its stone walls makes for one of the more unusual environments in which to enjoy a meal. In contrast to the solid architecture surrounding the place, the café serves light repasts: sandwiches, quiches, salads, muffins and other dessert items. On the weekend, the café hosts live music (p133).

CAFÉ DO RODRIGUES
Map pp228-30 *Bistro & Café*
☎ 3231 8015; Travessa de Ouvidor 17, Centro; lunch US$3-6; ⏱ 9am-8pm Mon-Fri, 10am-1pm Sat

On a narrow alleyway inside the charming Centro branch of the **Livraria da Travessa bookstore** (p161), Café do Rodrigues is a suitable setting for philosophical conversation when the world – or the humidity – has you down. Browse for books, then peruse your finds over a *torta do palmito* (heart of palm quiche), a hearty soup or a flavorful salad.

Cais do Oriente (p120)

Top Five Centro & Cinelândia Eats

- **Ateliê Odeon** (p118)
- **Cais do Oriente** (below)
- **Cedra do Líbano** (opposite)
- **Confeitaria Colombo** (below))
- **Le Champs Elysées** (opposite)

CAIS DO ORIENTE Map pp228-30   *Eclectic*
☎ 2203 0178; Rua Visconde de Itaboraí 8, Centro; mains US$8-14; ☯ noon-4pm Mon, noon-midnight Tue-Sat
Brick walls lined with tapestries stretch high to the ceiling in this almost cinematic 1870s mansion. Set on a brick-lined street hidden from the masses, Cais do Oriente blends west with east in dishes like filet steak and sesame tuna. On Friday and Saturday nights, live bands perform in the restaurant (US$10 cover; see p133).

CONFEITARIA COLOMBO
Map pp228-30   *Brazilian & patisserie*
☎ 2232 2300; Rua Gonçalves Dias 34, Centro; desserts US$2-4; ☯ 8am-8pm Mon-Fri, 10am-5pm Sat
Stained glass windows, brocaded mirrors and marble countertops create one of the most lavish settings for coffee or a meal. Dating from the late 1800s, the art-nouveau Confeitaria Colombo serves desserts equally decadent. The restaurant overhead serves traditional Brazilian cuisine for those wanting to soak up the splendor.

DE MIRANDA CAFÉ
Map pp228-30   *Brazilian Eclectic*
☎ 2262 3552; Av Beira Mar 406C, Centro; mains US$4-6; ☯ 11:30am-8pm
A few small paintings and a fresh breeze through the open windows add to the charm of this small restaurant just off the beaten path. De Miranda Café features a simple menu of Brazilian and international dishes, any of which plainly showcase the talents of the young chef. Try chicken with fruit compote and roasted potatoes or the salmon carpaccio.

EÇA Map pp228-30   *French Contemporary*
☎ 2524 2399; Downstairs, Av Rio Branco 128, Centro; mains US$14-22; noon-4pm Mon-Fri
The well-dressed cut deals over beautifully presented dishes at this classic of French eclectic cuisine. Among the offerings, breast of duck with lime confit has earned Eça its admirers as has the fine chocolate soufflé for dessert. Our only complaint: eating at Eça, with its polished

walls and artful lighting, is not unlike eating inside a museum – which is, perhaps, just the point, given chef Frédéric De Maeyer's artful combinations.

LE CHAMPS ELYSÉES Map pp228-30   *French*
☎ 2220 4713; 12th fl, Av Presidente Antônio Carlos 58, Centro; mains US$12-20; ☯ 11am-4:30pm Mon-Fri
On the top floor of the French consulate, Gallic chefs reinvent themselves week after week to give diners a royal experience to add to a fine view over the city. Grilled lobster, Cornish game hen and bouillabaisse taste as though they were prepared for a Louis. Swords flash when champagne is ordered – the fastest way of freeing the cork, the chef will explain.

LIDADOR Map pp228-30   *Liquor store & deli*
☎ 2533 4988; Rua da Assembléia 65, Centro; ☯ 9am-8pm Mon-Fri
Gleaming bottles stretch high to the ceiling of this well-stocked liquor cabinet. Founded in 1924, Lidador also sells a range of smoked meats, chocolates and imported goods. A tiny area in the back serves as an informal pub.

MIAKO Map pp228-30   *Japanese*
☎ 2222 2397; Upstairs, Rua do Ouvidor 45, Centro; sushi for 2 US$12-24; ☯ 11:30am-3:30 Mon-Thu, 11:30am-3:30pm & 6-11pm Fri
A bastion of tradition, Miako for years was the only Japanese restaurant in Centro. Today its *sushiman* prepares sashimi and sushi that's no less exquisite than it was at its founding. Tasty, light and healthy, meals will leave you walking away from this elegant sushi bar rejuvenated.

RANCHO INN Map pp228-30   *French*
☎ 2263 5197; 2nd fl, Rua do Rosário 74, Centro; mains US$5-8; ☯ 11:30am-3:30pm Mon-Fri
Exposed brick and tall windows lend a vaguely Parisian air to this charming lunchtime spot. In addition to offerings like caprese raviolini and snapper with basil and almonds, the salads and quiches are *muito gostoso*.

RESTAURANTE ALBAMAR
Map pp228-30   *Seafood*
☎ 2240 8378; Praça Marechal Âncora 186, Centro; mains US$10-20; ☯ 11:30am-6pm Tue-Sun
The green gazebo structure perched over the water offers excellent views of the Baía de Guanabara and Niterói. The seafood has its fans, but it's not nearly as outstanding as the view. The *peixe brasileira* (fish in coconut milk) is one of the most popular dishes.

CHEAP EATS

CASA CAVÊ Map pp228-30 *Patisserie*
☎ 2222 2358; Rua Sete de Setembro 137, Centro;
mains US$7-12; ✆ 9am-7pm Mon-Fri, 9am-1pm Sat
A simple but historic coffeehouse (circa 1860),
the Casa Cavê has a few stand-up tables and a
long counter full of lovely desserts. Piping hot
coffee is served by kindhearted waitstaff.

CEDRO DO LÍBANO Map pp228-30 *Lebanese*
☎ 2224 0163; Rua Senhor dos Passos 231, Centro;
mains US$4-8; ✆ 11am-5pm
White plastic chairs and tables covered by
white tablecloths might make you feel like you
stumbled into someone's wedding reception
at this dining spot in the heart of Saara. But
in fact, the white decorating this 70-year-old
Lebanese institution has more to do with the
purity of the Lebanese cooking: kibes, kaftas,
lamb – tender portions of perfection.

VIA SETE Map pp228-30 *Sandwiches*
☎ 2221 8020; Rua Sete de Setembro 43, Centro;
wraps US$3-4; ✆ 10am-8pm Mon-Fri
A wooden patio fronts Via Sete, making a fine
spot to enjoy their tasty wraps and sandwiches
while watching Cariocas hurry about their day.
Brownies and *frozens* (fruit shakes) finish off
the proceedings nicely.

SANTA TERESA & LAPA

As one of the most charming neighborhoods of Rio, Santa Teresa, not surprisingly,
has a range of attractive dining spots. Great
views, historic ambience and live music are
a few of the ingredients that make the
neighborhood's regional and international
restaurants such an attraction. The biggest
swath of restaurants stretch on either side
of Largo dos Guimarães. Although Lapa is
known more for its samba than its cuisine, a
handful of restaurants lay scattered in the
area, many serving to the young crowds
heading to the bars.

APRAZÍVEL Map p231 *Brazilian*
☎ 3852 4935; Rua Aprazível 62, Santa Teresa; mains
US$10-16; ✆ 8pm until last customer Thu, noon-mid-
night Fri & Sat, 1-6pm Sun
Hidden on a windy road high up in Santa Teresa, Aprazível offers beautiful views and a lush
garden setting. Brazilian fare with a twist showcases plates of succulent quail and salmon

with mango chutney. Wednesday nights are
dedicated to live *chorinho* (US$5 cover).

BAR BRASIL Map pp228-30 *German*
☎ 2509 5943; Av Mem de Sá 90, Lapa; mains US$6-12;
✆ 11:30am-11pm Mon-Fri, 11:30am-4pm Sat
According to legend, this German restaurant
went by the name Bar Adolf until WWII. Although the name has been subtly Brazilianized,
the cuisine is still prepared in the same tradition
as it was back before the war. Sauerkraut, wursts,
lentils and an ever-flowing tap quenches the appetites of the sometimes rowdy Lapa crowd.

BAR DO MINEIRO Map p231 *Minas Gerais*
☎ 2221 9227; Rua Paschoal Carlos Magno 99, Santa
Teresa; mains US$6-10; ✆ 11am-2am Tue-Thu, 11am-
4am Fri & Sat, 11am-8pm Sun
Photographs of old Rio cover the walls of this
old-school *boteco* in the heart of Santa Teresa. Lively crowds have been filling this spot
for years to enjoy traditional Minas dishes.
Feijoada is tops on Saturdays. Other good
anytime dishes include *carne seca* (dried meat
with spices) and *lingüiça* (pork sausage). Strong
caipirinhas will help get you in the mood.

MIKE'S HAUS Map p231 *German*
☎ 2509 5248; Rua Almirante Alexandrino 1458A, Santa
Teresa; mains US$8-14; ✆ 11:30am-midnight Mon-Sat
Mike's Haus has German pub atmosphere with
traditional cooking and cold glasses of imported Weizenbier. Although plates are small
here, the place remains a popular gathering
spot for expats and Cariocas on weekends.

NOVA CAPELA Map pp228-30 *Portuguese*
☎ 2252 6228; Av Mem de Sá 96, Lapa; mains US$6-12;
✆ 11am until last customer
Like Bar Brasil next door, Nova Capela dates from
the beginning of the 20th century. It stays open
late into the evening, and fills with a noisy mix
of artists, musicians and party-kids. Legendarily
bad-tempered waiters (no surprise given what
they have to work with) serve up big plates of
traditional Portuguese cuisine. The *cabrito* (goat)
is among the best you'll encounter in Rio.

BAR DO ERNESTO Map pp228-30 *Brazilian*
☎ 2221 4116; Largo da Lapa 41, Lapa; mains US$6-12;
✆ 11:30am-midnight Mon-Sat
For years Ernesto has been a popular spot for
the patrons and musicians who come here
after a concert next door at **Sala Cecília Meireles**
(p124). The menu features fine Brazilian fare as
well as pastas, pizzas and rich desserts.

SOBRENATURAL Map p231 *Seafood*

☎ 2224 1003; Rua Almirante Alexandrino 432, Santa Teresa; mains US$5-10; 🕙 11:30am-midnight Mon-Sat

The exposed brick and old hardwood ceiling set the stage for feasting on the *frutas do mar* (seafood). Lines gather on weekends for the grilled fish and *moqueca*. During the week, stop by for the US$3 to US$4 lunchtime specials.

CHEAP EATS

NEGA TERESA Map p231 *Bahian*

☎ 2245 4034; Rua Almirante Alexandrino 1458, Santa Teresa; dishes US$2-4; 🕙 5-10pm Thu-Sun

Nega has quite a following in Santa Teresa. She's also won a few fans from more distant neighborhoods. They all come to sample the home-cooked Bahian specialties like *acarajé* (spicy shrimp-filled croquettes) that are served from a stand in front of **Favela Hype** (p163) – next door to **Mike's Haus** (p121).

PORTA QUENTE Map p231 *Pizza*

☎ 2232 6298; Rua Almirante Alexandrino 470, Santa Teresa; pizzas US$4-8; 🕙 noon-midnight Mon-Sat

A new addition to the Santa Teresa scene, Porta Quente serves good, thin-crust pizzas, salads and lighter fare. The small, charming café sometimes features live music on the weekends.

BARRA DA TIJUCA & GREATER RIO

Other parts of Rio offer some of the city's more rustic dining experiences. Outside the city limits one can find open-air spots overlooking the coast – beautiful views complemented by fresh seafood.

BARREADO Map p239 *Seafood*

☎ 2442 2023; Estrada dos Bandeirantes 21295, Vargem Grande; lunch for two US$25-40; 🕙 noon-midnight Tue-Sat, noon-8pm Sun

In a lush setting west of Barra, this rustic spot serves fresh Brazilian seafood with a wildly

eclectic twist. Pumpkin flavoring is the chef's current favorite, and he's not afraid to forge daring combinations like lobster and mango served inside a whole pumpkin mixed with cream. For those who'd rather save the pumpkins for Halloween, *vatapá* (a Bahian seafood dish made with manioc paste, coconut milk and *dendê* oil) and roast meats are also a favorite.

BIRA *Seafood*

☎ 2410 8304; Estrada da Vendinha 68A, Barra de Guaratiba; plates US$13-20; 🕙 noon-midnight Mon-Sat

Splendid views of Marambaia bay await diners who make the trek to Bira, about 45 minutes outside the city. On a breezy, wooden deck, diners can partake in the flavorfully rich seafood emerging from the kitchen. *Moquecas*, sea bass, shrimp, crabmeat pastries – all prepared with doting tenderness.

MUSEU DO AÇUDE

Map p239 *Brunch*

☎ 2492 2119; Estrada do Açude 764, Tijuca Forest; 🕙 12:30pm-4pm last Sun of the month

On the last Saturday of the month, the museum hosts a gastronomic festival, with brunch in a lovely mansion in the Tijuca forest. There's often live music, adding to the charm of the natural setting. If you happen to be around, don't miss it.

TIA PALMIRA *Seafood*

☎ 2410 8169; Caminho do Souza 18, Barra de Guaratiba; prix-fixe lunch US$17; 🕙 11:30am-5pm Tue-Fri, 11:30am-6pm Sat & Sun

On weekends, Cariocas feast on seafood at this simple open-air eatery overlooking the coast. A venerable destination for 40 years, Tia Palmira keeps its fans coming back for its exquisite seafood *rodizio* (all-you-can-eat barbecue dinner). Plate after plate of *vatapá*, crabmeat, grilled fish, shrimp pastries and other fruits of the sea come to your table until you can eat no more.

Entertainment

Entertainment

The city that throws the world's largest party, Carnaval, doesn't go into hibernation after Ash Wednesday. Rio's vibrant music and arts scene spans the entire year with hundreds of entertainment options. Cariocas are a diverse bunch, so there's something to suit every mood and budget: classical music and opera, art-house cinema, laidback jazz and *chorinho* spots, open-air bars, over-the-top samba clubs, and throbbing nightclubs – gay and straight.

For the latest on what's on in the city, pick up the Veja Rio insert in *Veja* magazine. It comes out each Sunday and can be found at newsstands and shops throughout the city. Thursday and Friday editions of *O Globo* and *Jornal do Brasil* also have excellent entertainment sections.

Tickets & Reservations

TICKETMASTER
☎ 0300 789 6846; www.ticketmaster.com.br in Portuguese; ⏲ 9am-8pm Mon-Sat
Although this international company is growing in Brazil, at present the only venues connected to Ticketmaster are Claro Hall in Barra da Tijuca and the Teatro Municipal in Centro. Tickets can be purchased over the phone or online for shows at either of these locations.

TICKETRONICS
☎ 0300 789 3350; www.ticketronics.com.br in Portuguese; Modern Sound, Rua Barata Ribeiro 502, Copacabana; ⏲ 9am-9pm Mon-Fri, 9am-8pm Sat
Tickets for a wide range of shows, concerts and dance performances can be purchased through Ticketronics either over the phone or through a distributor like Modern Sound. Check the website for show listings.

PERFORMING ARTS

Rio has many theaters and halls that stage plays, musicals, concerts and live performances. Riotur's quarterly *Rio Guide* lists entertainment events. Pick one up at any office of Riotur (p206). If you speak a bit of Portuguese, you can also find up-to-the-minute arts and entertainment listings online through Terra Guides (http://cidades.terra.com.br/rio).

ARTE SESC CULTURAL CENTER Map pp232-3
☎ 3138 1020; Rua Marquês de Abrantes 99, Flamengo
Housed in one of Flamengo's lovely old mansions, Arte Sesc has occasional classical recitals throughout the year. They also host panel discussions on various art and cultural topics.

ESPAÇO BNDES Map pp228-30
☎ 2277 7757; Av República do Chile 100, Centro
Weekly concerts are held at this Centro venue throughout the year. Featuring a mix of popular and classical music, BNDES in the past has featured musicians exploring symphonic pop, as well as other experimental groups playing 'samba-jazz.'

SALA CECÍLIA MEIRELES Map pp228-30
☎ 2224 3913; Largo da Lapa 47, Lapa
Lapa's splendid early-20th-century gem hosts orchestral concerts throughout the year.

TEATRO CARLOS GOMES Map pp228-30
☎ 2232 8701; Rua Pedro I, 22, Centro
Facing the Praça Tiradentes, the large Teatro Gomes stages avant-garde dance shows and experimental theater. The theater seats 600; tickets for events here can be purchased through Ticketronics.

TEATRO DO CENTRO CULTURAL BANCO DO BRASIL Map pp228-30
☎ 3808 2000; Rua Primeiro de Março 66, Centro
In addition to its exhibitions, this large cultural center downtown has two stages and a cinema. Film, dance and musical events are usually coordinated with current exhibits: the recent African Art exhibit, for instance, featured musicians from Cameroon and recent films from the African Diaspora.

TEATRO DO CENTRO CULTURAL JUSTIÇA FEDERAL Map pp228-30
☎ 2510 8846; Av Rio Branco 241, Centro
Samba singers, classical and Música Popular Brasileiro (MPB) groups are all starting to make appearances at this stately cultural center across from the Praça Floriano. Shows typically occur on Tuesdays at 12:30pm and 6:30pm.

TEATRO JOÃO CAETANO Map pp228-30
☎ 2221 0305, 2221 1223; Praça Tiradentes, Centro
Another historical theater fronting Praça Tiradentes, Teatro João Caetano hosts national ballet, popular plays and musicals.

TEATRO LAURA ALVIM Map pp236-8
☎ 2267 1647; Av Viera Souto 176, Ipanema
Across from the beach in Ipanema, this small center stages plays and hosts classical and other live-music styles. It also has art openings and a cinema. Stop in to see what's on.

TEATRO MUNICIPAL Map pp228-30
☎ 2299 1711; Praça Floriano, Cinelândia
This gorgeous art nouveau theater provides the setting for Rio's best opera, ballet and symphonic concerts. Tickets are available at the box office or at **Ticketronics** (opposite). The Municipal seats 2400, and sight lines are generally quite good.

DRINKING
Rio's drinking spots vary from neighborhood to neighborhood. Leblon and Ipanema offer flashy night spots as well as 1950s-era watering holes. A youthful bar scene draws weekday revelers to Gávea, while a more sedate crowd enjoys Lagoa's scenic spots. Copacabana has a mix of brash, open-air spots lining Av Atlântica and has panoramic bars atop the beachside hotels. Botafogo is known for its neighborhood bars, while Centro's narrow pedestrian streets draw drinkers only during weekday cocktail hours. Amid its colorful buildings, a mix of old and new clutters the streets of Santa Teresa. Further afield, Barra da Tijuca is home to large entertainment complexes with bars, discos and restaurants all in one shopping-mall-like structure.

IPANEMA & LEBLON
ACADEMIA DA CACHAÇA pp236-8
☎ 2239 1542; Rua Conde de Bernadotte 26G, Leblon; ☾ noon-2am Mon-Sat, noon-1am Sun
Although *cachaça* has a bad reputation in some parts, here the fiery liquor is given the respect it nearly deserves. This pleasant indoor-outdoor spot serves over 500 varieties, and you can order it straight, with honey and lime or disguised in a fruity *caipirinha*. For a treat (and/or a bad hangover), try the passionfruit *caipirinha*.

BAR 121 Map pp236-8
☎ 2274 1122; Av Niemeyer 121, Vidigal; ☾ 5pm-1am
With sweeping views of the beaches of Leblon and Ipanema, Bar 121 is a lovely spot to take in the sunset. The dexterous bartender creates tasty drink combinations that are enjoyed by an upscale crowd as the weekend nears. Live bossa nova and MPB bands (9pm Thu, 10pm Fri & Sat) draw a mix of Brazilians and tourists.

BAR BOFETADA Map pp236-8
☎ 2227 1676; Rua Farme de Amoedo 87, Ipanema; ☾ 8am until last customer
A buff and predominantly gay crowd gathers at this lively Ipanema spot for cold drinks after a day at the beach. It has two floors and a few

---

Saved by Salgados (& Other Snacks)
If you're heading home from the beach, but can't be bothered with a sit-down meal, go Carioca and grab a few bites (and *chope*) at the *boteco*. Bars in Brazil offer a wide variety of snacks and appetizers. Here are some items you are most likely to find.

batida A strong mixed drink made with *cachaça* (a rumlike cane liquor) and fruit juice, usually passionfruit or lime.
bolinhos de bacalhau Deep-fried codfish balls, usually served with sauce.
bolinhos de queijo Crispy deep-fried cheese balls.
caipirinha The national drink of Brazil; a strong mixed drink made with limes, sugar and *cachaça*.
chope Light pilsner draft beer.
coxinha Pear-shaped cornmeal balls filled with fried chicken. They are eaten as a snack, but a few of these will fill most people up fast.
misto quente A hot ham-and-cheese sandwich.
pão de queijo A slightly gooey cheese bread, baked into bite-sized biscuits; they're so popular in Brazil that a whole franchise was launched on their success (naturally named Pão de Queijo).
paste A crispy pastry filled with cheese or meat.
salgado Any savory pastry filled with cheese or meat; types include *pastels, coxinhas, bolinhos de queijo* and *bacalhau*. Most bars offer a variety of *salgados*. Sometimes they are on the menu under *tira-gostos* (appetizers).

outside tables, which get packed during the summer. You can catch live music – *chorinho* or bossa nova – from time to time.

BAR BRACARENSE Map pp236-8
☎ 2294 7494; Rua José Linhares 85B, Leblon; ⏱ 7am-1am Mon-Fri, 9am-8pm Sat

A classic Carioca watering hole, Bar Bracarense is famous for its simple, unpretentious ambience and its heavenly *salgados*. A steady stream of neighborhood regulars enjoy over 20 varieties of the snacks (try the *aipim com camarão* – cassava with shrimp) to the accompaniment of icy-cold *chope*.

BAR D'HOTEL Map pp236-8
☎ 2540 4990; 2nd fl, Marina All Suites, Av Delfim Moreira 696, Leblon; ⏱ 7am-1am Sun-Thu, 7am-2am Fri & Sat

The waves crashing on the shore are just part of the background of this texture-rich bar overlooking Ipanema Beach. The narrow bar is like a magnet for the style set, who gather in the intimate space to enjoy tropical drinks to the backdrop of sea and ambient electronic music.

CANECO 70 Map pp236-8
☎ 2294 1180; Av Delfim Moreira 1026, Leblon; ⏱ 11am-4am

Facing the beach, the large open-air Caneco 70 is one of Leblon's most traditional after-

beach hangouts. The fresh breeze, well-chilled drafts and hum of conversation make a nice prelude to the evening (or the morning, as the case may be).

CLIPPER Map pp236-8
☎ 2259 0148; Rua Carlos Góis 263A, Leblon; ⏱ 8am-1am

In business for over 60 years, Clipper is a simple neighborhood *botequim* (bar with table service) popular with a broad range of Cariocas – old bohemians, young professionals, burned-out socialites and an occasional pro-footballer. At night an almost celebratory air pervades the place as crowds pack this indoor-outdoor spot.

COBAL Map pp236-8
☎ 2239 1549; Rua Gilberto Cardoso, Leblon; ⏱ closed Monday

Leblon's flower and produce market features a number of open-air bars and restaurants. A vibrant, youthful air pervades this place, and it's a major meeting spot in the summer.

DEVASSA Map pp236-8
☎ 2540 6087; Rua General San Martin 1241, Leblon; ⏱ 5pm until last customer Mon-Fri, noon until last customer Sat & Sun

Serving perhaps Rio's best beer, Devassa makes its own creamy brews (in Vargem Grande, a large suburb west of Barra da Tijuca),

Banda de Ipanema (p27)

before offering them up to thirsty, festive crowds at its two-floor *chopperia*. The mulatta – a mix of dark and light beer with a shot of coffee – is a favorite. An occasional MPB band adds to the din on the upstairs level.

EMPÓRIO Map pp236-8

☎ 2267 7992; Rua Maria Quitéria 37, Ipanema; ☾ noon-2am

A young mix of Cariocas and gringos stir things up over cheap cocktails at this battered old favorite in Ipanema. A porch in front overlooks the street – a fine spot to stake out when the air gets too thick with cigarette smoke or bad '80s music hammering out of the jukebox.

FLOR DO LEBLON Map pp236-8

☎ 2294 2849; Rua Dias Ferreira 521A, Leblon; ☾ 10am-2am

To get an idea of how a Carioca neighborhood comes together, visit Flor do Leblon. It may not seem like much: it's just a storefront with a few tables scattered along the sidewalk, but as the day wanes this watering hole draws a garrulous bunch, there to enjoy the abundantly flowing beer, meats grilling out front, an impromptu music jam or two, and the satisfying camaraderie among neighbors.

GAROTA DE IPANEMA Map pp236-8

☎ 2523 3787; Rua Vinícius de Moraes 49, Ipanema; ☾ 10:30am-2:30am

History and draft beer blend smoothly at this historic (but a bit touristy) open-air spot in Ipanema. See p107.

IRISH PUB Map pp236-8

☎ 2227 6173; Rua Jangadeiros 14A, Ipanema; ☾ 7pm until last customer

Less of a pickup scene than Shenanigan's, the Irish Pub is full of visitors who've traveled a long way to get their hands on that pint of Guinness. Most nights, a sedate, orderly crowd runs the show, though patrons are known to occasionally burst into song (during English football matches for instance).

JOBI Map pp236-8

☎ 2274 0547; Av Ataulfo de Paiva 1166, Leblon; ☾ 9am until last customer

A favorite since 1956, Jobi has served a lot of beer in its day, and its popularity hasn't waned. The unadorned *botequim* still serves plenty of it – icy-cold beer best enjoyed at one of the sidewalk tables. If hunger beckons, try the tasty bean soup or jerked meat.

LORD JIM PUB Map pp236-8

☎ 2259 3047; Rua Paul Redfern 63, Ipanema; ☾ 6pm-2am Mon-Thu, 6pm-3am Fri, 1pm-3am Sat & Sun

Something of a novelty for Cariocas, Lord Jim is one of several English-style pubs scattered about the Zona Sul. Darts, English-speaking waiters and all the requisite expat beers – Guinness, Harps, Bass, Foster's etc – are on hand to complete the ambience. They also host quiz nights on Wednesdays.

SHENANIGAN'S Map pp236-8

☎ 2267 5860; Rua Visconde de Pirajá 112A, Ipanema; ☾ 6pm-3am Mon-Fri, 2pm-3am Sat, 2pm-2am Sun

Overlooking the Praça General Osorio, Shenanigan's is a fairly recent addition to Ipanema's growing pub scene. And it's no small success: through the smoke hanging overhead, the beautiful waitstaff shuttles between tables *packed* full of Cariocas and sunburnt gringos. The exposed brick walls, pool table and mix of spoken languages all contribute to the dark and pubby ambience Shenanigan's aims for.

GÁVEA, JARDIM BOTANICO & LAGOA

BAR LAGOA Map pp236-8

☎ 2523 1135; Av Epitácio Pessoa 1674, Lagoa; ☾ 6pm-2am Mon, noon-2am Tue-Sun

With a view of the lake, Bar Lagoa is one of the neighborhood's classic haunts. Founded in 1935, this open-air spot hasn't changed much since then: the bar still has surly waiters serving the excellent beer to the ever-crowded tables; and in spite of its years, a youthful air pervades the old bar.

CAROLINE CAFÉ Map pp236-8

☎ 2540 0705; Rua JJ Seabra 10, Jardim Botânico; ☾ 6pm-3am Sun-Thu, 6pm-4am Fri, 7pm-4am Sat

A mix of couples and groups of friends out for the night (pre- or post-clubs) fill Caroline Café most nights of the week. The sexy young crowd filling the tables inside and out makes this place a bit sceney at times.

COZUMEL Map pp236-8

☎ 2294 2915; Av Lineu de Paula Machado 696, Jardim Botânico; ☾ 8pm until last customer

Frozen margaritas and *caipirinhas* are consumed by the gallon at this Mexican nightspot in Jardim Botânico. Popular with a young, easily intoxicated crowd, Cozumel helps the rowdiness along with regular parties like its Segunda Loca (Crazy Monday), which involves free beer and margaritas until midnight – once you pay the US$7 (women) and US$14 (men) cover.

HIPÓDROMO UP Map pp236-8
☎ 2274 9720; Praça Santos Dumont 108, Gávea;
⏱ 8am-3am
In an area more commonly referred to as Baixo Gávea, Hipódromo is one of several bars in the area responsible for the local residents' chronic lack of sleep. A young college-age crowd celebrates here most nights, although there's a range of Cariocas thrown into the mix. Currently Monday night is the favorite.

LAGOA KIOSKS Map pp236-8
Parque Brigadeiro Faria Lima & Parque do Cantaglo, Lagoa; ⏱ 5pm until last customer Mon-Fri, noon until last customer Sat & Sun
The restaurants along the edge of Lagoa Rodrigo de Freitas make a fantastic setting for a drink or two in the evening. Many feature live music every night. See p110 for more information.

SITIO LOUNGE Map pp236-8
☎ 2274 2226; Rua Marquês de São Vicente 10, Gávea;
⏱ 8pm-2am Tue-Thu, 8pm-3am Fri & Sat
Blazing the trail in Gávea's fledgling lounge scene, Sitio is a sleek space that toes the line between pretension and style. The cocktails, ambient sounds (mixed by a changing crew of House and drum 'n' bass hands) and attractive staff draw a broad mix to the neighborhood.

COPACABANA & LEME
ALLEGRO BISTRO MUSICAL Map pp234-5
☎ 2548 5005; www.modernsound.com.br; Modern Sound records, Rua Barata Ribeiro 502, Copacabana; admission free; ⏱ 9am-9pm Mon-Fri, 9am-8pm Sat
This small café and drinking spot in Copacabana features live music most days. See p132 for more details.

Allegro Bistro Musical (above)

CERVANTES Map pp234-5

☎ 2275 6147; Av Prado Júnior 335B, Copacabana;
🕒 noon-4am Tue-Thu, noon-5am Fri & Sat, noon-3am Sun

This Copacabana institution is as renowned for its meaty sandwiches as it is for the characters that eat them – at least at four in the morning. Not surprisingly, Cervantes also has excellent *chope*, making it a reliable haunt after the bars give you the boot. See also p112.

COPACABANA PALACE POOLSIDE BAR Map pp234-5

☎ 2548 7070; Copacabana Palace Hotel, Av Atlântica 1702, Copacabana; 🕒 noon-11pm

Even if you can't swing the US$300-a-night rooms, you can still soak up some of the decadence that the Palace delivers in spades. The poolside bar offers dozens of sumptuous libations on a lovely outdoor terrace, a setting suitable for young duchesses and weary travelers alike.

COPACABANA PIANO BAR Map pp234-5

☎ 2548 7070; Copacabana Palace Hotel, Av Atlântica 1702, Copacabana; 🕒 4pm-midnight

The lavish Piano Bar makes a fine setting for connecting with the Palace's once splendid past. Live piano accompaniment and a good selection of rare spirits are on hand to help along the way.

HORSE'S NECK Map pp234-5

☎ 2525 1232; Sofitel Rio Palace, Av Atlântica 4240, Copacabana; 🕒 5pm-1am

This British-style pub with its sober dark-wood interior has the unintended effect of making guests talk more quietly – which may not be a bad thing given the noise level in some bars. Perfect for a scotch and sedate conversation, the Horse's Neck also features a balcony overlooking the ocean.

SINDICATO DO CHOPP Map pp234-5

☎ 2523 4644; Av Atlântica 3806, Copacabana;
🕒 11am-3am

A Copacabana institution, this open-air bar looks out on the wide avenue with the beach in the background. Owing to its breezy location, it attracts a wide mix of people, all playing a part in Copa's inimitable street theater. The food isn't so hot here, but the beers are icy cold and the ocean is, well, right there. A second **Sindicato do Chopp** (Av Atlântica 514) in Leme also overlooks the beach.

SKYLAB BAR Map pp234-5

☎ 2525 1500; 30th fl, Rio Othon Palace, Av Atlântica 3264, Copacabana; 🕒 7pm-midnight

It's all about the view at this bar in the Rio Othon Palace. From 30 floors up, the coastline unfolds, allowing a glimpse of the Cidade Maravilhosa at its most striking.

SOBRE AS ONDAS Map pp234-5

☎ 2522 1296; Av Atlântica 3432, Copacabana;
🕒 6pm until last customer

A mix of Cariocas and tourists – mostly the latter – gather at this upscale spot for cocktails, and listen to live music nightly. Although it can get a bit crammed, the space offers lovely views and right-on acoustics.

BOTAFOGO & URCA

BIG BEN Map pp232-3

☎ 2538 1596; www.bigben.com.br in Portuguese; Rua Muniz Barreto 374, Botafogo; admission US$3-6; 🕒 6pm-1:30am Mon-Fri, 9pm-2:30am

Decked out to resemble an English pub, Big Ben is one of Botafogo's popular neighborhood spots. It features bar games, live music throughout the week (MPB) and an occasional night of karaoke or open dart-throwing (no charge). Check the website or stop in to see what's new.

COBAL DO HUMAITÁ Map pp232-3

Rua Voluntários da Pátria 466, Botafogo

The Cobal is a large farmers' market on the western edge of Botafogo. In addition to fresh fruits and vegetables – one of the city's selections – a number of restaurants and cafés are here. When the sun goes down, Cobal transforms into a nightspot, complete with live music and al fresco dining and drinking, all within view of **Cristo Redentor** (p76).

GAROTA DA URCA Map pp232-3

☎ 2541 8585; Rua João Luís Alves 56, Urca; 🕒 11am until last customer

A neighborhood crowd gathers at this low-key spot in the evening over *chope* and *salgados*. See p116.

PRAIA VERMELHA Map pp232-3

☎ 2275 7245; Praça General Tibúrcio, Urca; mains US$5-10; 🕒 11:30am-midnight

This simple eatery transforms into a lush setting for live music nightly. See p115 for more details.

FLAMENGO

BELMONTE Map pp232-3

☎ 2552 3349; Praia do Flamengo 300, Flamengo; mains US$4-8; ⊗ 7am until last customer

One of Flamengo's ultraclassic *botecos*, Belmonte serves up well chilled *chope* until late into the night. See p117 for more details.

CENTRO & CINELÂNDIA

AMARELINHO Map pp228-30

☎ 2240 8434; Praça Floriano 55, Cinelândia; ⊗ 11am until last customer

Easy to spot by its bright yellow (*amarelo*) awning, Amarelinho has a splendid setting on the Praça Floriano. Yellow-vested waiters serve an abundance of *chope* here, wandering among the crowded tables, with the **Teatro Municipal** (p125) in the background. Amarelinho is a popular lunch spot – though the food's not so hot – but packs even bigger crowds for that oh-so-refreshing after-work brew.

ARCO DO TELES Map pp228-30

☎ 2242 9589; Travessa do Comércio 2, Centro; ⊗ noon-10pm Mon-Thu, 7am-2am Fri

Hidden in a narrow lane leading off Praça XV, the Arco do Teles is one of several charming open-air bars on the colonial Travessa do

Comércio. The scenic lane is a popular meeting spot and a festive air arrives at workday's end as Cariocas fill the tables spilling onto the street. Other nearby spots serving up the same brand of refreshment – *chope, bem gelado* (ice-cold draft) – include **Dito E Feito** (☎ 2509 1407; Travessa do Comércio 7; ⊗ 11:30am-3:30pm & 6pm until last customer Mon-Fri) and **Arco Imperial** (☎ 2507 9477; Travessa do Comércio 13; ⊗ 11am until last customer Mon-Fri).

ATELIÊ ODEON Map pp228-30

☎ 2240 0746; Praça Floriano, Cinelândia; mains US$6-10; ⊗ noon-10pm Mon-Fri

A lunch and after-work crowd gather at this lovely open-air spot on the edge of Praça Floriano. See p118 for more details.

BAR LUIZ Map pp228-30

☎ 2262 6900; Rua da Carioca 39, Centro; mains US$6-10; ⊗ 11am-11:30pm Mon-Sat

Well over 100 years old, this old saloon and dining spot serves some of the city's best brew. See p119 for more details.

BECO DA SARDINHA Map pp228-30

Largo da Santa Rita, Centro; ⊗ 5-10pm Fri

See Centro's quirkier side at this longstanding Friday-night favorite. After work, crowds fill the tables of this open-air spot as bar owners

Belmonte (above)

serve fried sardines – with beer of course – continuing a tradition begun in the 1960s.

CHOPP DA LAPA Map pp228-30
☎ 2224 9358; Av Mem de Sá 17, Lapa; 🕑 6pm until last customer Tue-Thu, 11am until last customer Sat & Sun

Just past the Passeio Público, this classic bar has outside seating with an excellent view of the **Arcos do Lapa** (p86). It attracts a diverse bunch – old artists, shop owners, musicians, prostitutes and the odd ones you can't pin down – and the crowd tends to get more colorful as the night progresses. Note well: the food isn't so hot here, so stick to the drinks.

ESCH CAFÉ Map pp228-30
☎ 2507 5866; Rua do Rosário 107, Centro; 🕑 noon-10pm Mon-Fri

The smoky twin of the Leblon **Esch Café** (☎ 2512 5651; Rua Dias Ferreira 78, Leblon; 🕑 noon until last customer), Esch Café offers the same selection of Cuban cigars from its humidor. Its dark wood interior features stuffed leather chairs, a decent food and cocktail menu, and jazz throughout the week, usually Tuesday to Thursday from 7pm to 9pm.

SANTA TERESA & LAPA

ADEGA FLOR DE COIMBRA Map pp228-30
☎ 2224 4582; Rua Teotônio Regadas 34, Lapa; 🕑 noon until last customer

In the same building that was once the home of Brazilian painter Cândido Portinari, the Adega Flor de Coimbra has been a bohemian haunt since it opened in 1938. Back in its early days leftists, artists and intellectuals drank copiously at the slim old bar looking out on Lapa. Today, it draws a mix of similar types, who drink wine – but also sangria – which washes down nicely with the bolinhos de bacalhau (codfish croquettes) or Portuguese feijoada.

BAR DO GOMES Map p231
Rua Áurea 26, Santa Teresa; 🕑 11am until last customer Tue-Sun

Part grocer, part bar, this hole-in-the-wall drinking establishment features a few stand-up tables and a counter. It doesn't look like much, and the neighborhood regulars would probably say it isn't – between sips of their beers – which is part of its charm. Gomes gets packed on weekends, with people spilling out onto the sidewalks.

BAR DO MINEIRO Map p231
☎ 2221 9227; Rua Paschoal Carlos Magno 99, Santa Teresa; 🕑 11am-2am Tue-Thu, 11am-4am Fri & Sat, 11am-8pm Sun

Famous for its Minas Gerais cuisine, Bar do Mineiro is one of Santa Teresa's most traditional botecos – and an excellent place for a drink no matter what the hour. See p121 for more details.

CAFÉ NEVES Map p231
☎ 2221 4863; Largo das Neves 11, Santa Teresa; 🕑 6pm until last customer Tue-Sat

Small but charming, Café Neves is one of Santa Teresa's gems. It faces out onto Largo das Neves, with the occasional tram rattling by in the early evening. The open-sided bar draws a vibrant mix as the weekend nears, and there's nearly always live music somewhere on hand.

COSMOPOLITA Map pp228-30
☎ 2224 7820; Travessa da Mosqueira 4, Lapa; 🕑 11am until last customer Mon-Thu, 11am-5am Fri & Sat

Behind the stained-glass doors of this 1906 saloon, patrons gather about the long bar as the street scene unfolds outside. Cosmopolita is a fine setting in which to daydream over a few cocktails or wait for the sunrise.

GOIA BEIRA Map p231
☎ 2232 5751; Largo das Neves 13, Santa Teresa; 🕑 6pm until last customer Tue-Sat

Another handsome bar on Largo das Neves, Goia Beira is a small, intimate spot serving a range of tasty cachaças. The open-air scene gets lively on weekends, with an occasional band playing out on the square.

MIKE'S HAUS Map p231
☎ 2509 5248; Rua Almirante Alexandrino 1458A, Santa Teresa; 🕑 11:30am-midnight Mon-Sat

This German-style pub attracts a mix of expats and Cariocas weekend nights. It's a bit off the beaten path, so plan on sticking around a while before moving on. See p121 for more details.

SIMPLESMENTE Map p231
☎ 2508 6007; Rua Paschoal Carlos Magno 115, Santa Teresa; 🕑 7pm-3am Mon-Sat

One of Santa Teresa's longstanding favorites, Simplesmente is just that – a simple place without much decor – where the ambience is provided by the patrons rather than the furniture. A young, boho neighborhood crowd keeps things going until late – especially on weekends.

MUSIC & DANCE

Summarizing Rio's contemporary music scene is quite simple: Rio has one of the best music scenes on the planet. Encapsulating the diversity of its musical offerings, on the other hand, is rather difficult in a city with so much to offer. Samba, jazz, bossa nova, MPB (Musica Popular Brasileiro), rock, hip-hop, reggae, electronic music and the many fusions among them are a big part of the picture. Brazil's many regional styles – *forró*, *chorinho*, *pagode* – are no less a contributor.

Rio's burgeoning and ever-evolving scene showcases its quality in equally diverse settings. Venues range from mega-modern concert halls seating thousands to intimate samba clubs in edgy neighborhoods. Antiquated colonial mansions, outdoor parks overlooking the city, old-school bars, crumbling buildings on the edge of towns and hyper-modern lounges facing the ocean are all part of the mix.

JAZZ, CHORINHO & OTHER REGIONAL STYLES

Although straight-up bossa nova isn't much in fashion today in Rio, there are plenty of places to hear other styles from Brazil's rich musical heritage. Informal, laidback settings like the ones that follow showcase some of the city's best talents. Those looking to dance should check out Samba Clubs (p134). For more information on Brazilian music, see p33.

ALLEGRO BISTRO MUSICAL Map pp234–5

☎ 2548 5005; www.modernsound.com.br; Modern Sound, Rua Barata Ribeiro 502, Copacabana; admission free; ◷ 9am-9pm Mon-Fri, 9am-8pm Sat

This small café in Copacabana's excellent music store **Modern Sound** (p157) features live music most nights of the week. Jazz and MPB groups play to a mix of Cariocas, predominantly aged 30 and up. Most groups play from 5pm to 9pm, though Allegro has lunchtime venues periodically (1pm to 5pm). The more popular groups attract a large audience, with people spilling out into the store. Reservations are available if you want to be sure to snag that table by the piano.

BAR DO ERNESTO Map pp228–30

☎ 2509 6455; Largo da Lapa 41, Lapa; admission US$3.50

This simple *boteco* beside the Sala Cecília Meireles attracts a lively mixed crowd to its *roda de samba* on Friday nights. The action usually gets going around 11:30pm.

Bip Bip (opposite)

Hip-Hop Carioca *Tom Phillips*

US rappers Snoop Dogg and Jah Rule caused uproar when they came to perform in Rio recently. 'Their music represents a cultural litterbin,' roared one Carioca politician, furious that homegrown hip-hop talent was being sidelined in favor of the Yankee rappers. Whatever your views on the dawg father and chums, it is hard to ignore Rio's talented new wave of hip-hoppers. Foremost among them is Marcelo D2 (of Planet Hemp), with his mix of samba/rap. The Madureira-raised rapper's last album – *A Procura da Batida Perfeita* (Looking for the Perfect Beat) – was produced by the Beastie Boys' Mario Caldato Jr no less. Then there's MV Bill – the self-styled 'messenger of the truth' – whose controversial brand of *traficante* (drug dealing) philosophy has landed the Cidade de Deus rapper in hot water with the authorities more than once.

Further from the limelight hundreds of groups are springing from the communities of Rio de Janeiro's periphery, performing their brand of hip-hop (pronounced hippie-hoppie) *consciente*. Weekly hip-hop jams take place in Humaitá at **Humaitá pra Peixe** (☎ 2266 0896; Espaço Cultural Sérgio Porto, Rua Humaitá 163) and in Botafogo at **Let's Hop** (☎ 2266 1014; Casa da Matriz, Rua Henrique de Novaes 107, Botafogo). On Saturdays 'Batalha do Real' takes the stage, hosting its weekly open-mike competition in Lapa at **Carioca da Gema** (p135).

BAR DO TOM Map pp236-8
☎ 2274 4022; Churrascaria Plataforma, Rua Adalberto Ferreira 32, Leblon; admission US$10; 🕒 10:30pm Fri & Sat

A mix of Cariocas and tourists – but mostly tourists – fill this downstairs space at Plataforma in Leblon. The 350-seat bar has excellent acoustics and hosts a range of top musicians performing MPB, bossa nova, tango and jazz.

BIP BIP Map pp234-5
☎ 2267 9696; Rua Almirante Gonçalves 50, Copacabana; admission free; 🕒 10pm-1am Mon, 9:30pm-midnight Tue, 8-11pm Sun

A storefront with a few battered tables, some yellowing photographs hanging on the walls and a cooler full of unopened beer bottles is about all the ambience that Bip Bip has to offer. As the evening progresses, however, the tree-lined neighborhood becomes the setting as music and revelers spill out onto the sidewalk. For years, Bip Bip has been the underground favorite of musicians passing through town, and you never know who's going to show up at the impromptu jam sessions. Sundays are samba night. Monday and Tuesday nights are devoted to *chorinho*.

CAFÉ DO ATELIÊ Map pp228-30
☎ 2221 2133; Rua do Lavradio 34, Centro; 🕒 11am until last customer

During the week, the Café do Ateliê remains a low-key spot for light bites, but when the weekend arrives, so do the musicians. Thursdays and Fridays, the happy hour starts around 5pm, with jazz starting shortly after. On Saturday, things don't get started until around 7pm.

The historic building makes a fine setting for a drink or a meal, whenever you stop in. See p119 for more details.

CAFÉ TEATRO RIVAL Map pp228-30
☎ 2240 4469; www.rivalbr.com.br in Portuguese; Rua Álvaro Alvim 33, Cinelândia; admission US$5-15

Near Praça Floriano, this 450-seat hall has become a popular spot for some of the city's up and coming groups as well as veteran musicians. Four or five nights a week, Teatro Rival hosts MPB, *pagode*, samba, *chorinho* and *forró* groups. Tickets for events here can be purchased through **Ticketronics** (p124).

CAIS DO ORIENTE Map pp228-30
☎ 2233 2531; Rua Visconde de Itaboraí 8, Centro; cover US$12

On the 2nd floor of this 1870s mansion in Centro, excellent jazz, bossa nova and MPB groups perform throughout the year. Most shows happen on Friday or Saturday nights; call or stop in to see what's on. Most shows starts around 10pm. See also, p120.

CLAN CAFÉ Map pp232-3
☎ 2558 2322; Rua Cosme Velho 564, Cosme Velho; admission free; 🕒 6pm-1am Tue & Wed, 6pm-1:30am Thu & Fri, 1pm-2am Sat

Set against the hillside of Corcovado, the fairly unmarked door of Clan Café opens to reveal a large open-air patio covered with abundant greenery. Slow-paced waiters shuffle between the many tables as talented musicians fill the air with sound. Tuesdays belong to *chorinho*, while MPB rules on Wednesday, and jazz on Saturday. The music starts around 9pm.

Entertainment – Music & Dance

ESCH CAFÉ Map pp236-8

☎ 2512 5651; Rua Dias Ferreira 78, Leblon; ☿ noon until last customer

Billing itself as the House of Havana, Esch offers a blend of Cuban cigars and jazz. The dark wood interior combined with the well-dressed over-30 crowd will probably make you feel like you're stepping into a Johnnie Walker photo shoot. Groups perform throughout the week – weekdays around 7pm, weekends around 2pm.

MERCADO MODERNO Map pp228-30

☎ 2508 6083; Rua do Lavradio 130, Centro; admission US$4-5; ☿ 9:30pm-2am Fri & Sat

The brick walls and the modern furnishings (including a chair designed by Le Corbusier) form the backdrop to weekend bossa-jazz, that sultry fusion filtering out of bars up and down Rua do Lavradio. The intimate space attracts a small but attentive audience – couples, musicians and their friends. For more information on the store, see p161.

MISTURA FINA Map pp236-8

☎ 2537 2844; www.misturafina.com.br in Portuguese; Av Borges de Medeiros 3207, Lagoa; shows US$5-10; ☿ noon until last customer

Both a restaurant (p110) and a concert space, Mistura Fina attracts a wide mix of people to dine and take in the music. The piano bar plays for the restaurant downstairs, while jazz, MPB and samba are staged upstairs. With a view of Lagoa, the outdoor veranda becomes particularly lively during happy hour. For the latest show schedules check out the website.

PARQUE DAS RUINAS Map p231

☎ 2252 1039; Rua Murtinho Nobre 169, Santa Teresa; admission free

This scenic park overlooking downtown has live jazz concerts throughout the year. Music ranges from jazz to Brazilian regional. Schedules change regularly, but they often host events on Sunday afternoons.

SEVERYNA Map pp232-3

☎ 2556 1296; Rua Ipiranga 54, Laranjeiras; admission free; ☿ 11:30am-2am

At night this broad, simple dining hall (circa 1950) forms the backdrop to Northeastern rhythms. Large percussive groups perform *xote*, *forró* and *chorinho*, among other styles, to a sometimes packed house. Shows begin at 8:30pm.

TOCA DO VINÍCIUS Map pp236-8

☎ 2247 5227; www.tocadovinicius.com.br; Rua Vinícius de Moraes 129; ☿ 9am-9pm Mon-Fri, 10am-5pm Sun

This small CD and record shop hosts live *choro*, samba and bossa nova throughout the year. During summer, Toca stages several shows a week in its intimate space. Most shows start around 7pm. Stop by to see what's on.

TWENTY POUND BLUES BAR Map pp228-30

☎ 2292 5709; Rua Mem de Sá 82, Lapa; admission US$3-7

Generally speaking, Cariocas are about as familiar with the Mississippi slide as they are with bobsledding. Although the Twenty Pound Blues Bar seems to do everything right – from its upstairs location overlooking a busy Lapa street corner to its decent blues acts performing here – it has yet to catch on in Rio.

VINÍCIUS PIANO BAR Map pp232-3

☎ 2523 4757; Rua Prudente de Moraes 34, Ipanema; admission US$5-15

Billing itself as the 'temple of bossa nova,' Vinícius Piano Bar has been an icon in the neighborhood since 1989. The indoor-outdoor tables make a fine setting to listen to decent bossa nova – although it's mostly tourists filling those seats since bossa nova isn't very popular anymore among Cariocas.

ZEPPELIN BAR Map pp236-8

☎ 2274 1549; Estrada do Vidigal 471, Leblon; ☿ 8pm-2:30am Fri & Sat

Although Zeppelin Bar opens only on weekends, it's worth a trip for the lovely ocean views from the bar's vantage point on Pedra Dois Irmãos. Bands, which play *chorinho*, samba or MPB, go on at 10:30pm. To get there by taxi (recommended), have the driver drop you off at the Sheraton and then follow signs to the bar (you'll walk up the stairs and across the street).

SAMBA CLUBS

Gafieiras, or dancehalls, are rising from the ashes of a once bombed-out neighborhood and reinvigorating it with an air of youth, samba and an artistic edge. The neighborhood in question is Lapa, and after years and years of neglect it is returning to its roots as center stage of Rio's nightlife. In the '20s and '30s, Lapa was a major destination for the bohemian members of society who were attracted to its decadent array of cabaret joints, brothels and *gafieiras*. Today, the neighborhood's crumbling buildings hide beautifully restored interiors leading into rooms with broad dance floors. On top of the long stages a crowd of musicians weave together the seductive rhythms of samba as dancers move gracefully around the room. Although not all the spots mentioned below are in Lapa – and not all of them can be technically classed as *gafieiras* either – they all reconnect with Rio's era of fallen splendor while also providing a splendid contemporary setting.

ASA BRANCA Map pp228-30

☎ 2224 2342; Av Mem de Sá 17, Lapa; admission US$2-6; ⊗ 10pm-2am Wed-Sat

Near the Arcos do Lapa, Asa Branca traditionally attracts an older crowd, who pack its large smoky dance floor. Asa Branca doesn't get going until midnight.

BALL ROOM Map pp232-3

☎ 2537 7600; Rua Humaitá 110, Botafogo; admission US$4-8

One of Botafogo's classic nightspots, Ball Room hosts various parties throughout the week. Orquestra Imperial gets the large dance floor going one night a week – currently Monday nights. The talented musicians play a brand of old-school samba with a modern-infused sound. Catch them if you can.

CARIOCA DA GEMA Map pp228-30

☎ 2221 0043; Av Mem de Sá 79, Lapa; admission US$3-5; ⊗ 8:30pm-1am Tue-Thu, 8:30pm-2am Fri & Sat

This small, colorful club on a busy Lapa street hosts popular parties throughout the week. Samba nights are Fridays and Saturdays. Other nights, the easy-going crowd meets for rapid-fire *choro* or MPB.

CASA DE MÃE JOANA Map pp228-30

☎ 2224 4071; Av Gomes Freire 547, Lapa; admission US$4-6; ⊗ 8pm-2am Thu, 7pm-2am Fri & Sat

At the Casa de Mãe Joana a lion stands guard over the dance floor. A small fountain flows

Samba da Mesa *Carmen Michael*

On Friday nights, Rio's samba community congregates in front of the faded colonial facades of Rua do Mercado under a canopy of *oiti* trees to play *samba da mesa*. On the worn cobblestones, a long table stands altar-like. Around it the musicians sit and the crowd gyrates, paying homage to their favorite religion. *Samba da mesa* in Rio today is a grassroots movement of musicians and appreciators passionately committed to keeping their music on the street and in an improvised form.

It typically involves a table, at least one *cavaquino* player, an assortment of *tambores* and any number of makeshift instruments like coke cans, knives and forks that will make a rattle. The standard of the music can be outstanding, and it is not uncommon to catch sight of a samba bamba (big-name samba performer) keeping the beat for the group or belting out one of their tunes. Depending on which bohemians have blown through for the night, you might even catch a duel, where two singers will pit their wits against each other in a battle of rhymes. It is a challenge of the intellect, and the topics include everything from love to poverty to the opponent's mother. Even if you speak some Portuguese, you probably won't understand the slang and local references, but the delight of the crowd is infectious.

Street samba has taken a battering from the commercialization of music and space, the rising popularity of funk in the favelas and the police clampdown on 'noise pollution' in public spaces. However, for those still interested in a little piece of bohemian Rio, there are several established places that support free improvised street music. On Friday nights, Rua do Mercado and Travessa do Comércio (p130) near Praça Quinze in Centro attract the younger radical chic set. On Sunday and Tuesday nights, a tiny bar in Copacabana, Bip Bip (p133), caters for hard-core sambistas (Copacabana South). And on Sunday afternoons the firmly working-class Cacique de Raimos (buses from Praça Tiradentes) has street music. If you have the fortune to be in Rio on 2 December, Dia de Samba, then you can join the samba train with the rest of Rio's samba community bound for Otavio Cross. The musicians disembark in the dusty back streets of this working-class suburb, which is transformed every year into a labyrinth of makeshift bars and stages that play a 24-hour marathon of *samba da mesa*.

Finding impromptu street gatherings in Rio at other times is more elusive and can sometimes resemble the mad scramble trying to find an illegal rave in the Western world. But it's an unforgettable experience if you find it. There are few fixed places for these parties, and when you find one, return the next week and it will be gone. The *barrio* of Lapa, in particular Rua Joaquim Silva, generally has something going on, but if not, keep your ears open for the unmistakable sound of the samba bateria – follow that sound and you will find a party. Pay heed to the local etiquette: ensure you do not talk over the music, use cameras with a flash or sit down unless you are a contributing musician.

from his mouth as dancers find the groove that will carry them through the evening – not a difficult prospect given the high quality of samba produced at this hidden spot in Lapa. Thursdays are 'classic samba' nights, Friday nights present 'samba with attitude.'

CASA ROSA Map pp232-3

☎ 9363 4645; Rua Alice 550, Laranjeiras; admission US$3-7; ☷ 11pm-5am Fri & Sat, 7pm-2am Sun

In the first decades of the 20th century, Casa Rosa was one of the city's most famous brothels. Today the Pink House is one of Rio's best nightspots. It has a large outdoor patio between several dance floors, where different bands play throughout the night. There's also a thrift shop here – open until about 3am. The rest of the party keeps going until dawn. Saturdays are the best night to go, though Casa Rosa's new Sunday *roda de samba* party also draws its fans – a good mix of Cariocas.

CASARÃO CULTURAL DOS ARCOS Map pp228-30

☎ 2552 8910; Av Mem de Sá 23, Lapa; admission US$4-6; ☷ 10pm-2am Wed-Thu, 11pm-4am Fri

A creatively decked out place made up of old costumes on the walls, antique refrigerators and a red telephone booth, the Casarão gathers young and seriously dance-focused crowds to its jam sessions. Friday nights are the most popular. On Saturdays the center presents a varied program – theater, poetry readings or other bands.

CENTRO CULTURAL CARIOCA Map pp228-30

☎ 2242 9642; www.centroculturalcarioca.com in Portuguese; Rua do Teatro 37, Centro; ☷ noon-8pm Tue-Sun

This restored theater on Praça Tiradentes books top samba groups throughout the year. In this historic setting (p80), listen and dance to live music. Groups perform daily except Sunday. To find out who's playing, check the website. The center also hosts ongoing exhibitions and gives dance lessons. See p149 for more details.

DAMA DA NOITE Map pp228-30

☎ 2221 2072; www.damadanoite.com.br in Portuguese; Av Gomes Freire 773, Lapa; admission US$4-7; ☷ 9pm-2am Tue-Fri, 11pm-3am Sat

This 1907 mansion hosts excellent samba shows during the week. In addition to the stage and dance floor, an outdoor patio, several bars and a creperie (not to be missed) lie scattered about the old building. Check Dama's website for show listings or to reserve a table (recommended).

DEMOCRATICUS Map pp228-30

☎ 9864 1603; Rua do Riachuelo 91, Lapa; admission US$3-5; ☷ 9:30pm-2am Wed, 10pm-2:30am Sat

Murals line the foyer walls of this 1867 mansion. The rhythms filter down from above. Follow the sound up the marble staircase and out onto a large hall filled with tables, an enormous dance floor, and a long stage covered with musicians. In spite of the high ceilings and vast interior, Anjos da Lua, the group that

Baile Funks *Tom Phillips*

It's long past midnight and the streets in the Zona Norte community of Cidade Alta are filling. The local sports hall is crammed with local youths – there for the community's weekly 'baile.' On stage the DJ hammers out a blend of Rio's bass-heavy funk music, around him a troupe of dancers wiggling simultaneously through impossibly complex moves. Security men from the neighborhood's resident drug gang – the Comando Vermelho – hover around the dance floor, in case of trouble.

Bailes (literally a 'dance' or 'ball') sprung out of the Carioca favelas during the 1970s, and since then their popularity has rocketed. Some 100,000 people attend parties like this each weekend in and around the city, in nightclubs, sports centers and on street corners.

The *baile*'s increasing profile has been accompanied by controversy. Many criticize the music's sexually explicit lyrics, which some say encourage under-age sex and violence against women.

The movement's infamy is compounded by its ties to the drugs trade – many of the parties are funded by Rio's *traficantes*, keen to ingratiate themselves with locals. In December one party ended in tragedy when an event promoted by funk pioneer DJ Malboro was the scene of a five-hour shoot-out between rival drug gangs and eight died.

These days the music is undeniably part of the mainstream, with the city's wealthy 'playboyzada' dancing alongside people from the favela. Rio's politicians are even trying to regulate the parties for the first time. Tour guides have begun to include the *bailes* on their itineraries. Most tours visit the Castelo das Pedras venue, which holds some 10,000 people.

plays here on Wednesday, easily fills the space with music. A wide mix of Cariocas gather here to dance, revel in the music and soak up the splendor of the samba-infused setting.

ELITE pp228-30

☎ 2232 3217; Rua Frei Caneca 4, Centro; ⏰ 9pm onward, Tue & Thu-Sun

In a beautiful but crumbling colonial building near Campo de Santana, Elite is a long-time favorite of the young and old samba crowd, who come to dance to *pagode* and *forró* (as well as samba) in this classic *gafieira* (dance hall). Given the excellent bands that play here and the club's old-city charm, it's not surprising that Elite has one of the more popular dance floors on weekend nights.

ESTUDANTINA CAFÉ Map pp228-30

☎ 2507 8067; Praça Tiradentes 79, Centro; admission US$3-5; ⏰ 11pm-3:30am Thu-Sat

Overlooking the Praça Tiradentes, this old dance hall packs large crowds on the weekend to enjoy excellent samba bands. The open-air veranda provides a nice spot to cool off if you've danced yourself into a sweat.

RÍO SCENARIUM Map pp228-30

☎ 3852 5516; Rua do Lavradio 20, Lapa; admission US$5-6; ⏰ 6:30pm-2am Tue-Thu, 6:30pm-3am Fri & Sat

Perhaps Rio's loveliest nightspot, Río Scenarium has three floors, each lavishly decorated with antiques. Balconies overlook the stage on the 1st floor, with dancers keeping time to the jazz-infused samba, *chorinho* or *pagode* filling the air. The endless rooms in Río Scenarium make for fine exploration if you need to walk off some of those *caipirinhas*.

SACRILÉGIO Map pp228-30

☎ 2222 7345; Av Mem de Sá 81, Lapa; ⏰ 8:30pm-1am Tue-Thu, 8:30pm-2am Fri & Sat

Next door to **Carioca da Gema** (p135), Sacrilégio is another charming spot for catching live bands in an intimate setting. The outdoor garden makes a fine spot for imbibing a few cold *chopes* while the music filters through the windows.

ROCK & MPB

In addition to small bars and clubs, Rio has a few large concert halls that attract Brazilian stars like Gilberto Gil and Milton Nascimento, as well as well-known international bands stopping off in Rio on world tours. Citywide music festivals include October's

Casa Rosa (opposite)

Rio Jazz Festival (p11) and January's Rock in Rio Festival. In addition to the venues below, during the summer (December to February) concerts take place on the beaches of Ipanema, Copacabana, Botafogo, Barra da Tijuca and on the Marina de Glória.

ARMAZEM DO RIO Map pp228-30

☎ 2213 0826; Av Rodrigues Alves s/n, Armazem no 5, Cais do Porto

Just north of Centro on the docks of Rio, the Armazem hosts concerts, parties and cultural events throughout the year. You can find listings for upcoming events in *Veja Rio*.

CANECÃO Map pp232-3

☎ 2543 1241; www.canecao.com.br in Portuguese; Av Venceslau Brás 215, Botafogo

Near the **Rio Sul Shopping** (p158), Canecão holds big-venue music concerts – rock, MPB, hip-hop – throughout the year. Tickets are available for purchase online – as well as over the phone – but you'll need some Portuguese to navigate the site.

CLARO HALL Map p239

☎ 2430 0700; Av Ayrton Senna 3000, Barra da Tijuca

Rio's largest concert house hosts big name performers from Rio and abroad. In addition to music shows, Claro Hall hosts ballets, operas and an occasional circus. The Hall, which seats around 6000 is in the **Via Parque Shopping Center** (p164) in Barra.

NIGHTCLUBS

Rio's vibrant dance scene isn't limited to its samba clubs. Here DJs spin a wide variety of beats – from house and hip-hop to more uniquely Brazilian combinations like electro-samba and bossa-jazz. In addition to Brazilian DJs spinning on the circuit, Rio attracts a handful of vinyl gurus from New York, Los Angeles and London to spin at bigger affairs. Flyers advertising dance parties and raves (pronounced *hah*-vees) can be found in some of the boutiques in Ipanema and Leblon, and in the surf shops in **Galeria River** (p156), by Praia Arpoador. Most clubs give a discount if you've got a flyer.

00 (ZERO ZERO) Map pp236-8

☎ 2540 8041; Planetário da Gávea, Av Padre Leonel Franca 240, Gávea; admission US$5-10; ☾ 10pm-4am Fri & Sat, 7pm-2am Sun

Housed in Gávea's planetarium, 00 is a restaurant by day, sleek lounge by night. A mix of Cariocas join the fray here, though they mostly tend to be a fashion literate, Zona Sul crowd. Playground, 00's Sunday party, has quite a following among house fans – gay and straight. In addition to rotating parties, the club also hosts CD-release parties.

BEAT ACELERADO Map pp232-3

Galeria do Centro Comercial Laranjeiras, Rua das Laranjeiras 336, Laranjeiras; admission US$3-5; ☾ 11pm-5am Fri & Sat

The youthful Beat Acelerado is the latest addition to Laranjeiras' growing nightlife scene. It features a lounge, small bar area and dance floor, with ambient films playing in the background. DJs go through a range of styles over the course of the night. Adding to its mystique, Beat Acelerado isn't easy to find. It's hidden in the back of a shopping center off Rua Laranjeiras (walk through the parking lot to the building in back, then walk through the building following signs for Cine Buarque).

BLUE ANGEL Map pp234-5

☎ 2513 2501; Rua Júlio de Castilhos 15B, Copacabana; admission US$2-4; ☾ 10pm-2am Wed-Sat

At night the blue light comes on and Rio's freethinkers converge. A mixed crowd arrives during the week, while weekends belong to the boys, indicated in part by the small shrine to Marlene Dietrich above the bathrooms – the line full of eager G-boys is another. It's a cozy bar, and on weekends there's not much room for dancing – although you'll probably want to (the DJs spin a good mix).

BUNKER 94 Map pp234-5

☎ 2521 0367; Rua Raul Pompéia 94, Copacabana; ☾ 11:30pm-3am Thu-Sun

Featuring big parties throughout the week, Bunker 94 is one of Copacabana's big draws. Its three rooms feature different music in each, and you'll find an eclectic mix of Cariocas and tourists against the backdrop of hip-hop, acid jazz, rock, trance and deep house – among other selections. Weekends get crowded – come early and stake out a spot before the masses converge (around 1am).

CASA DA MATRIZ Map pp232-3

☎ 2266 1014; www.casadamatriz.com.br; Rua Henrique de Novaes 107, Botafogo; ☾ 11:30pm-5am Mon & Thu-Sat

Artwork lines the walls of this avant-garde space in Botafogo. With numerous little rooms to explore – lounge, screening room, dance floors – this old two-story mansion embodies the most creative side of the Carioca spirit. Check the website for party listings – click 'festas.'

CINE ÍRIS Map pp228-30

☎ 2262 1729; Rua da Carioca 49, Centro; admission US$5-12; ☾ 10:30pm-6am every other Sat

This enormous space serves as a porn theater most days, but every other Saturday *Loud* comes to Cine Íris, bringing with it revelers from all over the city. Iris has three cinematic dance floors and a lovely rooftop terrace with views over the city.

CLUB SIX Map pp228-30

☎ 2510 3230; Rua das Marrecas 38, Lapa; men/women US$15/10; ☾ 11pm-6am Fri & Sat

Near the Arcos do Lapa, Club Six is perhaps Rio's only nightclub built to resemble a castle. Three dance floors, five bars and a number of lounge spots lie scattered about the building, with DJs spinning house, hip-hop, trance and MPB till daybreak.

CUBE Map pp234-5

☎ 9802 9020; Rua Francisco Otaviano 20, Arpoador; admission US$5-8; ☾ 9pm-3am Thu-Sat

In a shopping complex on the border between Copacabana and Ipanema, the Cube hosts weekend parties of changing themes. It features a number of loungey rooms for quick

Entertainment – Nightclubs

retreats when the drum 'n' bass gets to be a bit much. Some nights feature live music – *chorinho*, samba and bossa nova – followed by DJs, so check listings to see what's on.

DAMA DE FERRO Map pp236-8

☎ 2247 2330; Rua Vinícius de Moraes 288, Ipanema; admission US$4-8; ⊗ 11pm-3am Fri-Sun

A mix of buff Ipanema boys and older neighborhood queens check each other out in the downstairs lounge before moving it upstairs to the dance floor. DJs spin house most nights.

EL TURF Map pp236-8

☎ 2274 1444; Praça Santos Dumont 31, Gávea; admission US$8-15; ⊗ 11pm-4am Tue-Sat

Near the Joquei Clube in Gávea, El Turf attracts a mixed crowd at its parties. Depending on the night, DJs spin house, drum 'n' bass or hip-hop over the dance-prone crowd.

Samba Schools & Shows

Starting in August and September most big samba schools, in preparation for Carnaval, open their rehearsals to the public. A samba school *(escola de samba)* is a professional troupe that performs in the samba parade during Carnaval. These are large dance parties, not specific lessons in samba, although you may learn to samba at some of them. They typically charge between US$2 and US$5 at the door. And you'll be able to buy drinks there. Many samba schools are in the favelas, so use common sense when going.

You can set up a visit to one or more samba schools through a travel agent, or you can go on a tour (p55). It's always best to call to confirm if there is going to be rehearsal. Following is a listing of the samba schools, rehearsal days and contact information – the best ones for tourists are generally Salgueiro and Mangueira.

Beja-Flor (☎ 2791 2866; www.beija-flor.com.br; Praçinha Wallace Paes Leme 1025, Nilópolis) Rehearsals begin in September and are held every Thursday at 9pm.

Caprichosos de Pilares (☎ 2592 5620; Rua Faleiros 1, Pilares) Rehearsals begin in August and are held every Saturday at 11pm.

Grande Rio (☎ 2775 8422; www.granderio.org.br; Rua Almirante Barroso 5-6, Duque de Caixas) Rehearsals begin in July and are held every Friday at 10pm.

Imperatriz Leopoldinense (☎ 2560 8037; www.imperatrizleopoldinense.com.br; Rua Professor Lacê 235, Ramos) Rehearsals begin in August and are held every Saturday at 10pm.

Mangueira (☎ 2567 4637; www.mangueira.com.br; Rua Visconde de Niterói 1072, Mangueira) Rehearsals begin in August and are held every Saturday at 10pm. This is one of the better samba schools for tourists to visit, but it gets packed close to Carnaval.

Mocidade Independente de Padre Miguel (☎ 3332 5823; www.mocidadeindependente.com.br; Rua Coronel Tamarindo 38, Padre Miguel) Rehearsals begin in August and are held every Saturday at 10pm.

Paraíso do Tuiuti (Map pp240-1; ☎ 3860 6298; Campo de São Cristóvão 33, São Cristóvão) Rehearsals begin in September and are held Friday at 10pm.

Porta da Pedra (☎ 2605 2984; www.portodapedra.com.br; Rua João Silva 84, São Gonçalo) Rehearsals begin in September and are held every Friday at 10pm.

Portela (☎ 2489 6440; www.gresportela.com.br; Rua Clara Nunes 81, Madureira) Rehearsals begin in August and are held every Friday at 10pm.

Salgueiro (☎ 2238 5564; www.salgueiro.com.br; Rua Silva Teles 104, Andaraí) Rehearsals begin in August and are held every Saturday at 10pm. This is another good choice for tourists.

Tradição (Estrada Intendente Magalhães 160, Campinho) Rehearsals begin in August and are held every Friday at 8pm.

União da Ilha do Governador (☎ 3396 4951; Estrada do Galeão 322, Ilha do Governador) Rehearsals begin in August and are held every Saturday at 10pm.

Unidos da Tijuca (☎ 2516 4053; www.unidosdatijuca.com.br; Clube dos Portuários, Rua Francisco Bicalho 47, Cidade Nova) Rehearsals begin in September and are held every Saturday at 10pm.

Viradouro (☎ 2628 7840; www.viradouro.com.br; Av do Contorno 16, Barreto, Niterói) Rehearsals begin in September and are held every Saturday at 10pm.

FUNDIÇÃO PROGRESSO Map pp228-30

☎ 2220 5070; Rua dos Arcos 24, Lapa; admission US$5-8; ⏰ 11pm-4am Sat

An old factory with a battered façade hides one of Lapa's best Saturday-night parties. Both gay and straight find their groove at this vibrant nonstop *festa*. The Foundation is also one of Lapa's premier arts institutions.

HELP Map pp228-30

☎ 2522 1296; Av Atlântica 3432, Copacabana; admission US$10; ⏰ 11pm-4am Wed-Sat

Billing itself as the biggest disco in Latin America, this club plays standard pop and rock and as the evening wears on into morning, the DJs play Brazilian standards. The club attracts a mix of young male tourists and Brazilian prostitutes, lending it a pretty seedy vibe. Muggings are fairly commonplace outside the club.

HIDEAWAY Map pp232-3

☎ 2285 0921; Rua das Laranjeiras 308; admission US$5-10; ⏰ 8pm-2am Tue-Sun

Another recently inaugurated Laranjeiras nightspot, Hideaway is both a pizzeria and a lounge. In spite of the volume-drunk DJ, the intimate space doesn't offer much room for dancing. Most of the lovely people gathered here seem content just to steal glances at one another.

LA GIRL Map pp234-5

☎ 2247 8342; Rua Raul Pompéia 102, Copacabana; admission US$3-5; ⏰ 11pm-2am Tue-Sun

Rio's first – and only – girl bar, La Girl is an upstairs bar that attracts a mix of lesbians, both stylish and over-it. Run by the same owner as **Le Boy** (below), La Girl is a simple stylish place without pretensions.

LE BOY Map pp234-5

☎ 2513 4993; Rua Raul Pompéia 102, Copacabana; admission US$3-5; ⏰ 11pm-4am Tue-Sun

Trannies and pretty boys gather at this festive Copacabana dance club for dancing, drinking and perhaps just a bit of debauchery. A house-throbbing dance floor sprinkled with go-go boys, and the Dark Room (the destination of choice after 3am), give this party space an air of unencumbered freedom.

MELT Map pp236-8

☎ 2512 1662; Rua Rita Ludolf 47A, Leblon; admission US$5-10; ⏰ 10pm-3am Mon-Fri, 9pm-3am Sat & Sun

The sinewy Melt club is one of those places that couldn't possibly be anywhere but Leb-lon. Models and their well-dressed admirers lie draped about the candlelit lounge, while even lovelier waitstaff glide between the tables delivering peach or guava-colored elixirs. Upstairs, DJs break beats over the dance floor, occasionally accompanied by a few percussionists.

NAUTILLUS Map pp236-8

Rua do Catete 124, Catete; admission US$3-5; ⏰ 11pm-4am Fri & Sat

Friday is the night to go if you want to head to this dance spot in nightlife-starved Catete. Seriously young club kids converge here, with resident house DJs sometimes sharing the spotlight with out-of-town guests. Nautillus is all about the music.

CINEMA & FILM

Rio de Janeiro is one of Latin America's most important film centers. The market here is remarkably open to foreign and independent films, documentaries and avant-garde cinema. This isn't to say that mainstream Hollywood films are in short supply in Rio's cinemas. The latest Hollywood blockbusters get ample screening space here – particularly in the shopping centers throughout town. In the cultural centers, museums and old one-screen theaters, you'll find substantially more diverse offerings. Most American, European and independent films are shown in the original language with Portuguese subtitles. Family movies and cartoons are usually dubbed. On weekends, theaters get crowded, so buy your ticket early. Most movies charge US$3 to US$5 per ticket. For extensive listings and times pick up a copy of *O Globo*, *Jornal do Brasil* or *Veja Rio*.

CASA DA CULTURA
LAURA ALVIM Map pp236-8

☎ 2267 1647; Av Vieira Souto 176, Ipanema

Facing the beach, the charming Laura Alvim cultural center screens foreign (of the non-Hollywood variety) and independent flicks. Its small screening room seats 72.

CASA FRANÇA BRASIL Map pp228-30

☎ 2253 5366; Rua Visconde de Itaboraí, Centro

Housed in the **Casa França Brasil** (p79), the small 53-seat theater shows French films and an occasional independent classic.

CINE ÍRIS Map pp228-30

☎ 2262 1729; Rua da Carioca 54, Centro

For those who haven't seen enough flesh on Rio's beaches, Cine Íris screens films of the hard-core pornographic variety. The dilapidated film palace screens the, uh, selections, from noon until late most days. Every other Saturday night, the seedier elements disappear as club kids take over to host the now famous party *Loud*.

CINEMARK BOTAFOGO Map pp232-3

☎ 2237 9484; Botafogo Praia Shopping, Praia de Botafogo 400, Botafogo

On the 7th floor of the **Botafogo Praia Shopping** (p157), the Cinemark offers comfy seating and decent sound (sometimes the volume's a little cranked). American fodder and big-budget Brazilian films are shown regularly.

ESPAÇO LEBLON Map pp236-8

☎ 2511 8857; store 101, Rua Conde Bernadotte 26, Leblon

A one-screen theater in Leblon, Espaço shows foreign and independent films. In the same complex, there are a number of restaurants and cafés, making a perfect prelude to the cinema.

ESPAÇO MUSEU DA REPÚBLICA Map pp232-3

☎ 3826 7984; Museu da República, Rua do Catete 153, Catete

The screening room in the dramatic **Museu da República** (p77) shows films you aren't likely to encounter elsewhere. The focus is world cinema – both contemporary and classic films.

ESPAÇO UNIBANCO DE CINEMA Map pp232-3

☎ 3221 9221; Rua Voluntários da Pátria 35, Botafogo

This two-screen cinema in Botafogo shows a range of films – Brazilian, foreign, independent and the occasional Hollywood film. It has a lovely café inside, as well as a used record and book shop with a number of works focusing on the film arts.

ESTAÇÃO IPANEMA Map pp236-8

☎ 2540 6445; Rua Visconde de Pirajá 605, Ipanema

On the 1st floor of a small shopping complex in Ipanema, Estação Ipanema screens popular contemporary films from Brazil and abroad. Its single theater seats 140.

Espaço Museu da República (this page)

ESTAÇÃO PAÇO Map pp228-30

☎ 2529 4829; Paço Imperial, Praça XV 48, Centro

This small one-room screening room (seats 64) in the Paço Imperial doesn't offer much in the way of state-of-the-art cinema. However, the excellent selection of foreign and independent films shown here make up for its technological shortcomings.

ODEON BR Map pp228-30

☎ 2262 5089; Praça Mahatma Gandhi 5, Cinelândia

Rio's landmark cinema is a remnant of the once flourishing movie house scene that gave rise to the name of this neighborhood – Cinelândia. The restored 1920s film palace shows independent films, documentaries and foreign films. It often hosts the gala for prominent film festivals. Next door, **Café do Ateliê** opens before and after screenings on the weekends.

PALÁCIO Map pp228-30

☎ 3221 9292; Rua do Passeio 40, Cinelândia

The two-screen Palácio shows first-run Hollywood films in an aging building across the street from Praça Mahatma Gandhi.

RIO SUL Map pp232-3

☎ 3221 9292, Rio Sul Shopping, Rua Lauro Müller 116, Botafogo

Inside the **Rio Sul Shopping** (p158) is a four-screen theater showcasing the latest Hollywood hits (and misses). Before and after screenings, the restaurants and food court near the theater provide a popular meeting spot.

SÃO LUIZ Map pp232-3

☎ 3221 9292; Rua do Catete 307, Catete

Catete's new cinema has three screens playing a mix of contemporary Hollywood and Brazilian releases. A bookstore and café adjoin the theater.

TEATRO LEBLON Map pp236-8

☎ 3221 9292; Av Ataulfo de Paiva 391, Leblon

Leblon's popular theater has two screens showing the latest Hollywood releases.

UCI – NEW YORK CITY CENTER Map p239

☎ 2432 4840; New York City Center, Av das Americas 5000, Barra da Tijuca; 🕑 1-10pm Mon-Fri , 11am-midnight Sat & Sun

Brazil's largest megaplex features 18 different screening rooms, complete with large, comfortable chairs and stadium seating. Films are screened constantly (every 10 minutes on weekends).

FILM FESTIVALS
RIO DE JANEIRO INTERNATIONAL FILM FESTIVAL

www.festivaldorio.com.br

The festival is one of the biggest in Latin America. Over 200 films from the world over are shown at some 35 theaters in Rio. Often they hold open-air screenings on Copacabana Beach. The festival runs for 15 days from the last week of September to the first week of October. For films and locations, check the website (in English and Portuguese).

HORSERACING
JOCKEY CLUB Map pp236-8

☎ 2512 9988; www.jcb.com.br in Portuguese; 1003 Jardim Botânico, Gávea; 🕑 6:15-11pm Mon, 4-11pm Fri, 2-8pm Sat & Sun

One of the country's loveliest racetracks, with a great view of the mountains and Corcovado, the Jóquei Clube seats 35,000 and lies on the Gávea side of the Lagoa Rodrigo de Freitas opposite Praça Santos Dumont. It's rarely crowded, and the local race fans are part of the attraction – it's a different slice of Rio life.

Tourists are welcome in the members' enclosure, which has a bar overlooking the track. Races are held on Monday, Friday, Saturday and Sunday. The big annual event is the Brazilian Grand Prix (the first Sunday in August).

Sports, Health & Fitness

Sports, Health & Fitness

Given the mountains, the beaches and the lush forests at their doorstep, it's not surprising that Cariocas are an active bunch. The coastline brings an array of options: jogging, hiking, walking and cycling allows Cariocas to take in the splendid scenery while getting in some cardio. Once you step onto the sand, there are a number of ways you can amuse yourself while taking some sun: volleyball, soccer and *frescobol* are all quite popular, as is surfing. For those who need a break from the sun but not the sea, there's some scenic scuba diving spots. The mountains also beckon. You can hang glide off them or rock climb up them. Lovely hiking trails through Atlantic rain forest lie just outside the city, and for those who'd rather take their sport sitting down, there's always Maracanã, the world's largest soccer arena.

Top Five Ways to Spend a Sun-Drenched Afternoon

- Go hang gliding off **Pedra Bonita** (p146).
- Take a **samba class** (p139).
- Go rock-climbing with the **CEC** (opposite).
- Cycle the **bike path** (p145) from Leblon to Leme or Parque do Flamengo.
- Hone your volleyball game with **Pelé** (p149).

WATCHING SPORTS

MARACANÃ FOOTBALL STADIUM Map pp240-1

☎ 2568 9962; Av Maracanã, São Cristóvão; admission US$3-10; metro Maracanã, any bus marked 'Maracanã' (from the Zona Sul, Nos 434, 455 or 464; from Praça XV in Centro, Nos 238 or 239)

Nearly every Brazilian boy – and some of the girls, judging by the stellar performance of the women's national team – dreams of playing in Maracanã, Rio's enormous shrine to soccer. Matches here rate among the most exciting in the world, and the behavior of the fans is no less colorful. The devoted pound huge samba drums as their team takes the field, and if things are going badly – or very well – fans are sometimes driven to sheer madness. Some detonate smoke bombs in team colors, while others launch beer bottles, cups full of urine or dead chickens into the seats below. Enormous flags spread across large sections of the bleachers as people dance in the aisles (known to inspire a goal or two).

Games take place year round and can happen any day of the week. Rio's big four clubs are Flamengo, Fluminense, Vasco da Gama and Botafogo. Although many buses run to the stadium, the metro is safer and less crowded on game days. The safest seats in the stadium are on the lower level *cadeira*, where the overhead covering protects you from descending objects. The ticket price is US$5 for most games. After the game, avoid the crowded buses, and go by metro or taxi. For more information on the stadium, see p88.

Rio's Other Stadiums *Tom Phillips*

The Maracanã is rarely more than a quarter full these days. The following are alternative ways to sample Rio's world-famous *arquibancadas* (terraces).

Estádio São Januário (Rua General Almério de Moura 131, São Cristóvão) Don't be put off by the fact that dictator-cum-president Getúlio Vargas used to hold his rallies here in the 1940s. Vasco da Gama's lively stadium in the Zona Norte has undergone some renovation since a stand collapsed here during a game in 2000.

Estádio de Caio Martins (Rua Presidente Backer, Niterói) This small 12,000 capacity ground in the nearby city of Niterói is currently home to the newly promoted Botafogo.

Estádio Edson Passos (Rua Cosmorama 200, Edson Passos) América's pint-sized stadium has a capacity of 6000, which is expected to grow to 32,000 in the near future.

OUTDOOR ACTIVITIES

Climb, hike, surf or hang glide your way across Rio's verdant land- and seascapes. For those seeking more than just a taste of the outdoors, take a class and become an expert in your sport of choice. See Courses (p198) for more details.

Capoeira

The only surviving martial art native to the new world, *capoeira* was invented by Afro-Brazilian slaves about 400 years ago. In its original form, the grappling martial art developed as a means of self-defense against the slave owners. Once their fighting art was discovered, it was quickly banned and *capoeira* went underground. The slaves, however, continued to hone their fighting skills; they merely took it out of sight – first to practice secretly in the forest. Later the sport was disguised as a kind of dance, allowing them to practice in the open, which is the form that exists today.

Capoeira, which is referred to as a *jogo* (game), is accompanied by hand-clapping and the plucking of the *berimbau*, a long single-stringed instrument. Initially it was used to warn fighters of the boss' approach; today the music guides the rhythm of the game. Fast tempos dictate the players exchange fast, powerful kicks and blows, while slower tempos bring the pace down to a quasi dance. The *berimbau* is accompanied by the *atabaque*, a floor drum, and a *pandeiro*, a Brazilian tambourine.

The movements combine elements of fighting and dancing, and are executed (at least by the highly skilled) as fluid and circular, playful and respectful, at the same time. *Capoeira's* popularity has spread far beyond Brazil's borders (there's even a *capoeira* club in Serbia). You can see musicians and spectators arranged in the *roda de capoeira* (*capoeira* circle) at the weekly **Feira Nordestina** (p88) in São Cristóvão. Unfortunately, there aren't any special *capoeira* clubs for visitors. Most gyms, however, offer classes (p150).

CLIMBING

Rio de Janeiro is the center of rock climbing in Brazil, with 350 documented climbs within 40 minutes of the city center. Climbing in Rio is best during the cooler months of the year (April to October); during the summer, the tropical sun heats up the rock to ovenlike temperatures and turns the forests into saunas. People climb during the summer, but usually only in the early morning or late afternoon when it's not so hot.

A number of agencies offer climbing and hiking tours (p54) Rio also has several well-organized climbing clubs, which have weekly meetings to discuss outings for the week. The clubs, which welcome outsiders, also have something of a social component for those interested in mingling with Cariocas.

CENTRO EXCURSIONISTA
BRASILEIRA Map pp228-30

☎ 2252 9844; www.ceb.org.br in Portuguese; 8th fl, Av Almirante Barroso 2, Centro; ☾ meetings 7pm Thu, office hours 2-6pm Mon-Fri

Founded in 1919, CEB sponsors day hikes and weekend treks (with camping). They also arrange trips further out – such as two-week hikes across Ushuaia in Southern Argentina. The club plans its activities at its weekly meeting, a good spot to have a chat with the laidback enthusiasts. Its office is open during the week for people who want to stop in, say hello and take a look at the bulletin board, which lists upcoming excursions – as does the website.

CENTRO EXCURSIONISTA
RIO DE JANEIRO Map pp228-30

☎ 2220 3548; www.cerj.org.br in Portuguese; Room 805, Av Rio Branco 277, Centro; ☾ meetings 8pm Thu

CERJ offers a wide range of activities, ranging from hikes to technical climbs, and also host mountaineering courses. Stop by a meeting to see what's on for the week.

CLUBE EXCURSIONISTA
CARIOCA Map pp234-5

☎ 2255 1348; www.carioca.org.br in Portuguese; No 206, Rua Hilário de Gouveia 71, Copacabana; ☾ meetings 8:30pm Thu

Although CEC is 50 years old, it's still going strong. Typically CEC arranges hikes and technical climbs, although from time to time they go rappelling and rafting. The club is also involved in preservation and education efforts, and give five-week courses on basic mountaineering.

CYCLING

Rio has over 74km of bike paths around the city, making it an excellent way to get some exercise. There are bike paths around **Lagoa Rodrigo de Freitas** (p61), along Barra da Tijuca and on the oceanfront from Leblon to Leme. This last path goes all the way to Flamengo and into the center. In the Tijuca forest, a 6km bikeway runs from Cascatinha to Açude. If you don't mind mixing it with the traffic, a bike is an excellent way to discover the city. On Sundays the road along the beaches – from Leblon to Leme – is closed, as is the road through **Parque do Flamengo** (p75). See the Directory (p194) for details on where to hire bikes.

DIVING

CALYPSO Map pp228-30
☎ 2542 8718, 9939 5997; www.calypsobrasil.com.br
in Portuguese; No 502, Rua México 111, Centro
Calypso offers courses (up to Dive Master)
in waters near Rio. The company also offers
excellent excursions for certified divers to
Arraial do Cabo and Angra dos Reis, among
other spots. Those looking to do diving further
afield should consider one of Calypso's afford-
ably priced excursions to Fernando Noronha,
a lovely island in the Northeast.

DIVE POINT Map pp236-8
☎ 2239 5105; www.divepoint.com.br in Portuguese;
Shop 4, Av Ataulfo de Paiva 1174, Leblon
Scuba divers can rent equipment from Dive
Point or take classes from them. It also has
diving courses and dive tours around Rio's
main beaches and Ilha Cagarras (the island in
front of Ipanema), as well as Rio State's premier
dive spots in Angra dos Reis, Búzios.

FISHING

MARLIN YACHT CHARTERS Map pp228-30
☎ 2225 7434; loja A1, Marina de Glória, Av Infante
Dom Henrique, Glória
Those who have their own equipment should
look into hiring a boat. The Marina de Glória

Arpoador Beach (p92)

has a number of outfits, although Marlin Yacht
Charters often has the largest fleet.

UNIVERSIDADE DA PESCA Map pp228-30
☎ 2240 8117, 9949 2363; www.upesca.com.br in
Portuguese; No 502, Rua México 111, Centro
Universidade da Pesca offers a wide range of
fishing tours – from day trips around Baía de
Guanabara and Ilha Cagarras to week-long adventures in the Amazon. Trips include professional instructors and multilingual guides.

GOLF

GÁVEA GOLF & COUNTRY CLUB Map pp226-7
☎ 3322 4141; gaveagol@unisys.com.br; Estrada da
Gávea 800, São Conrado; ⏱ 7am-sunset Mon-Fri
Gávea Golf Club is the most central golf course
in Rio. It has an 18-hole golf course close to
the city. Greens fees are about US$75 a round,
plus club rental of US$25 and caddie hire for
US$25. On weekends, you have to be invited
by a member to play here.

GOLDEN GREEN Map p239
☎ 2434 0696; Av Canal de Marapendi 2901, Barra da
Tijuca; ⏱ 7am-10pm
Near Barra beach opposite Posto 7, this golf
clinic features six par-three holes. The greens
fee is US$20 during the week and US$26 on
the weekend. Club rental costs US$13, and
renting a cart is an extra US$7.

ITANHANGÁ GOLF CLUB Map p239
☎ 2494 2507; Estrada da Barra da Tijuca 2005, Barra
da Tijuca; ⏱ 7am-sunset
Located in Barra, Itanhangá features a field of
27 holes. Prices are similar to those at Gávea,
and you'll also need an invite to play here on
the weekend.

HANG GLIDING, PARA GLIDING & ULTRALIGHT

If you weigh less than 100kg (about 220lb)
and have US$80 to spend, you can do the
fantastic hang glide off 510m Pedra Bonita –
one of the giant granite slabs that tower
above Rio – onto Pepino Beach in São
Conrado. No experience is necessary. We're
told that the winds are very safe here and
the pilots know what they are doing. Guest
riders are secured in a kind of pouch attached to the hang glider.

Flights depend on weather and wind conditions. During summer you can usually fly on all but three or four days a month, and conditions during winter are even better. If you fly early in the day, you have more flexibility to accommodate weather delays. The cheapest, but probably not the safest, way to arrange a flight is to go to the far end of Pepino Beach on Av Prefeito Mendes de Moraes, where the flyboys hang out at the Vôo Livre (hang gliding) club (below). During the week, you might get a flight for around US$60. Travel agents can book tandem flights, but they add their own fee. To cut out the middlemen, call direct.

ASSOCIAÇÃO BRASILEIRO DE VÔO LIVRE

☎ 3322 0266; www.abvl.com.br in Portuguese; Av Prefeito Mendes de Moraes, São Conrado

If you've had a taste of hang gliding, and you think you've found your calling, the Associação Brasileiro de Vôo Livre (Brazilian Association of Hang Gliding) offers classes in the sport.

JUST FLY

☎ 2268 0565, 9985 7540; www.justfly.com.br

Paulo Celani is a highly experienced tandem flyer with over 6000 flights to his credit. His fee includes picking you up and dropping you off at your hotel.

SUPERFLY

☎ 3322 2286, 9982 5703; Casa 2, Estrada das Canoas 1476, São Conrado

Founder Ruy Marra has more than 23 years of experience flying and is an excellent tandem glider pilot. Regarded as one of the best in Rio, Ruy is also the person to see if you want to para glide (gliding with a special parachute).

TANDEM FLY

☎ 2422 6371, 2422 0941; www.riotandemfly.com.br

Three experienced pilots run this flight outfit, and they'll arrange pick up and drop off at your hotel. They also give lessons for those wanting to learn how to fly solo.

CLUBE ESPORTIVO ULTRALEVES

☎ 2441 1880; Av Embaixador Abelardo Bueno 671, Jacarepaguá; ☼ 8am-sunset Tue-Sun

Ultra-leve (ultra light) flights are more comfortable than hang gliders, but you have to listen to the motor. The trips leave from the Aeroclube do Jacarepaguá. The club has some long-range ultra lights that can stay up for more than two hours. Fifteen-minute flights cost around US$30. They also offer courses.

HIKING

Rio is good for hiking and offers some outstanding nature walks. Visitors can hike one of the many trails through **Floresta da Tijuca** (p56) or head to one of the three national parks within a few hours of the city.

In recent years, there's been a boom in organized hikes around the city, including hikes through wilderness areas around Corcovado, Morro da Urca and Pão de Açúcar and of course Tijuca. It's advisable to go with a guide for a number of obvious reasons, getting lost and getting robbed being at the top of the list. Group outings can also be a great way to meet Cariocas. For more information on hiking outfits, turn to p54.

PADDLE BOATING

Although most Cariocas laugh at the idea of paddling a big swan boat out across Parque do Cantaglo's **Lagoa Rodrigo de Freitas** (p61), many of them have done it. Located on the east shore of the lake near the kiosks, boats are available on the weekends (US$8 per half hour). During the summer, you can rent boats until late at night on weekends – and it's always an admirable goal to paddle toward the Christmas tree across the way if you're around in December.

SURFING

When the surf is good, it gets crowded. Arpoador, between Copacabana and Ipanema, draws a large flock surfers, though there are much better breaks farther out in Barra, Grumari, Joá and Prainha – by far the best surf spot in Rio. Itacoatiari across the bay also has good breaks. For more information on these beaches, see (p92).

If you don't have a board, you can rent one in Arpoador at **Galeria River** (p156), a commercial center full of surf shops.

ESCOLINHA DE SURF BARRA DA TIJUCA

☎ 3209 0302; 1st kiosk after Posto 5, Av Sernambetiba, Praia da Barra da Tijuca

This surfing school is run by a Brazilian ex-champion and former professional surfer.

Young surfers aged five and up are supervised by a team of lifeguards. It's open every day.

ESCOLINHA DE SURF PAULO DOLABELLA Map pp236-8

☎ 2490 4077, 2259 2320; Ipanema Beach in front of Rua Maria Quitéria

Although you'll have to ask around to find him, Paulo gives private lessons to those looking to learn. In the past, those who have taken lessons from him have said that Arpoador is a good place to learn. Lessons typically cost US$7 per hour; or sign up for a month for US$40.

TENNIS

Although the humidity in the summer can make games rather unpleasant, if you fancy a match, you can book a court at the **Intercontinental** (Map pp226-7; ☎ 3323 2200; Av Preifeito Mendes de Moraes 222, São Conrado) or **Sheraton** (Map pp236-8; ☎ 2274 1122; www.sheraton-rio.com; Av Niemeyer 121, Vidigal). Courts are available to nonguests for around US$10 an hour during the day, a bit more at night.

In Barra you can play at the **Rio Sport Center** (☎ 3325 6644, Av Ayrton Senna 2541, Barra da Tijuca), opposite the Terra Encantada amusement park.

VOLLEYBALL & OTHER BEACH SPORTS

Volleyball is Brazil's second most popular sport (after soccer). A natural activity for the beach, it's also a popular spectator sport on TV. A local variation of volleyball you'll see on Rio's beaches is *futevôlei*: volleyball played without using hands. It's quite fun to watch, but frustratingly difficult to play.

Peteca is a cross between volleyball and badminton. It's played with a *peteca*, an object similar to, but larger than, a shuttlecock – you'll see them being hawked on the beach. *Peteca* is a favorite with older Cariocas who are too slow for volleyball.

Usually played on the firm sand at the shoreline, *frescobol* involves two players, each with a wooden racquet, hitting a small rubber ball back and forth as hard as possible. Cariocas make it look easy.

Arpoador Beach (p92)

ESCOLINHA DE VÔLEI Map pp236-8

☎ 9702 5794; www.voleinapraia.com.br in Portuguese; near Garcia D'Ávila on Ipanema Beach

Those interested in improving their game – or just meeting some Cariocas – should pay a visit to Pelé. Pelé, who speaks English, has been giving one-hour volleyball classes for 10 years. Lessons are in the morning (from about 8 to 11am) and in the afternoon (5 to 7pm). He charges around US$17 for the month and you can come as often as you like. Look for his large Brazilian flag on the beach near Garcia D'Ávila. Pelé's students are a mix of Carioca and expats, who then meet for games after honing the fundamentals.

WALKING & JOGGING

There are some good walking and jogging paths in the Zona Sul. If you're staying in the Catete/Flamengo area, **Parque do Flamengo** (p75) has plenty of space and lots of workout stations. Around **Lagoa Rodrigo de Freitas** (p61) a 7.5km track provides a path for cyclists, joggers and power-walkers (and saunterers). At the Parque do Cantaglo there, you can rent bicycles, tricycles or quadricycles. Along the seaside, from Leme to Barra da Tijuca, there's a bike path and footpath. On Sunday the road is closed to traffic and fills with cyclists, joggers, rollerbladers and strollers.

Closed to bicycles but open to walkers and joggers is the Pista Cláudio Coutinho, between the mountains and the sea at Praia Vermelha in Urca. It's open from 7am until 6pm daily and is very secure because of the army post nearby. People in bathing suits aren't allowed in (unless they're running). It's a nice place to be around sunset.

HEALTH & FITNESS
DANCING

Given samba's resurgence throughout the city, it's not surprising there are a number of places where you can learn the moves. Truth be told, Cariocas are just as interested in learning dance styles that aren't native to Brazil. (Salsa, anyone?) Regardless, a dance class is a good way to meet other people while getting those two left feet to step in time.

CASA DE DANÇA
CARLINHOS DE JESUS Map pp232-3

☎ 2541 6186; www.carlinhosdejesus.com.br; Rua Álvaro Ramos 11, Botafogo

At this respected dance academy in Botafogo, Carlinhos and his instructors give classes daily, mostly in the evenings from about 7pm to 10pm. The offerings include samba, *forró*, salsa and hip-hop – geared for a variety of levels. On Friday nights the academy often hosts open dance parties for students and guests. One of Botafogo's colorful **Bloco parties** (p27) begins from here around Carnaval.

CENTRO CULTURAL
CARIOCA Map pp228-30

☎ 2252 6468; www.centroculturalcarioca.com in Portuguese; Rua Sete de Setembro, Centro; ☉ 11am-8pm Mon-Fri

The cultural center is an excellent place to take classes. Most classes meet twice a week and cost from US$25 to 35 for a six-week course. The large dance hall hosts parties on Friday when samba bands perform. Sundays are often dedicated to tango. For more information, check out the website or stop in.

ESTUDANTINA CAFÉ Map pp228-30

☎ 2242 5062; www.estudantina.com.br; Praça Tiradentes 79, Centro

Although they don't offer the range of classes that other studios do, Estudantina receives favorable reviews for its instructors. A broad mix of skilled and unskilled meet for Tuesday- and Friday-night classes at this cultural center and samba club. Excellent parties, by the way, are thrown here on weekends. See p137.

NÚCLEO DE DANÇA Map pp228-30

☎ 2221 1011; Rua da Carioca 14, Centro

A large upstairs spot on the edge of Lapa, Núcleo de Dança gives classes on *forró*, tango, salsa and samba. Instructor Marcia Pinheiro is flexible, and you can usually drop in and join a class. Most are held during the day – around noon – so stop in to see what's on.

SOCIAL DANCE Map pp228-30

☎ 2220 6020; Rua do Ouvidor 12, Centro

Specializing in tango, Social Dance offers beginner and intermediate classes twice a week in their historic location near Travessa do Comércio. Classes run from 6 to 8pm Tuesday and Thursday, and cost US$20 a month. On Friday nights they often throw open dance parties for students and guests.

GYMS

Many hotels in Rio feature small workout centers with perhaps an adjoining sauna, but for those looking for a more intensive workout – or a more social atmosphere – the following gyms are recommended.

ACADEMIA PEDRO AQUINO Map pp234-5

☎ 2541 2384; 2nd fl, Ministro Viveiros de Castro 157, Copacabana; per month US$20; ⏰ 6am-10pm Mon-Fri, 9am-2pm Sat

In addition to step, cycling and kick-boxing, this small gym gives classes in *capoeira*. They usually offer one to three classes per day during the week.

BODY TECH Map pp236-8

☎ 2287 8038; Rua Gomes Carneiro 90, Ipanema; per day/month US$30/100; ⏰ 6am-11pm Mon-Fri, 9am-noon Sat, 9am-2pm Sun

Body Tech has gyms all over the Zona Sul, and they offer a full range of services: swimming pool, free weights and cardio machines as well as classes such as dance, gymnastics and spinning. Other locations include **Copacabana** (Map pp234-5; NS Copacabana 801) and **Ipanema** (Map pp236-8; Barão de Torre 577).

Shopping

Shopping

The city that prides itself on aesthetics naturally has a large selection of shopping options to satisfy consumer appetites. Cariocas are a diverse bunch, but the urge to buy seems to be a gene shared by all. How else could one explain the shopping phenomenon that happens on weekends: the malls are packed – as are the boutiques, the bookstores, the record shops, the antique markets and anywhere else that has objects for sale.

But shopping for Cariocas isn't strictly a practical pursuit. For most, it's an excuse to get together with friends, fulfill a few social obligations and perhaps stumble across one or two (or six!) irresistible finds in the process.

In Centro, bargain hunters crowd the narrow pedestrian streets around Saara (p79), the Middle Eastern neighborhood, where anything and everything is for sale (you only need know where to look). Centro also has elegant bookstores, music shops and a large antique market. Most people, however, think of the Zona Sul when the word shopping pops up. Leblon and Ipanema have scores of boutiques, chain stores and shopping centers all woven into the tree-lined landscape. This is the first place most people visit when seeking top Brazilian and international designers. The twin neighborhoods cater to a wide mix of shoppers – young and old, edgy and conservative. Copacabana also has many shops that cater to a diverse crowd, though these tend to be more crowded during the week. Lapa and Santa Teresa have a mix of thrift shops, used-book shops and record shops and a few handicraft shops serving the boho neighborhood. *Shoppings* (malls), are popular in Rio, and feature abundant entertainment options beyond designer stores. Eclectic restaurants with panoramic views and movie theaters come standard at most. Barra is the kingdom of shopping malls, each offering something slightly different than the one next door – one even services its 4.8km of stores with a monorail. Wherever you are in Rio, you're probably not far from an open-air market. Fruit and vegetables dominate, but you'll also find markets selling used CDs and records, furniture, clothing, antiques – there's even a market for stamp collectors.

Opening Hours

Most stores in Centro open from 9am to 6pm Monday to Friday. A few open on Saturday, usually from 9am to 1pm. In the Zona Sul, stores typically open from 10am to 6pm Monday through Friday, though some stay open until 8pm or 9pm. On Saturday, the hours run from 10am to 2pm. Only a few of the big shopping malls open on Sunday – from about 3pm to 8pm.

Consumer Taxes

Most stores list their prices with the tax already included. What you see on the price tag is what you'll pay.

Bargaining

Bargaining is uncommon in Rio shops, but if you buy on the street or at markets it's a different story. Bargain as much as you can, but don't be surprised if the seller won't meet you half way. Some vendors will let you walk away if you don't meet their asking price.

Top Five Shopping Strips

- **Av Ataulfo de Paiva, Leblon** Boutiques selling haute couture sprinkled among cafés, bookshops and restaurants.
- **Av NS de Copacabana, Copacabana** Packed during the week, this strip is lined with shops selling everything from chocolates to soccer balls, with plenty of street vendors hawking their wares along the sidewalks.
- **Rua do Lavradio, Lapa** Rows of antique stores, mixed with hypermodern furniture shops, along with a few cafés and bars – sometimes inside the store.
- **Rua Visconde de Pirajá, Ipanema** Ipanema's vibrant shopping strip has boutiques, shopping centers and scores of dining and coffee-sipping options.
- **Senhor dos Passos, Centro** One of the main streets coursing through the Middle Eastern bazaar-like Saara, with clothing and curio shops spilling onto the street.

IPANEMA & LEBLON

AMSTERDAM SAUER

Map pp236-8   *Jewelry & Accessories*

☎ 2512 1132; www.amsterdamsauer.com; Rua Garcia D'Ávila 105; ☯ 9:30am-2:30pm Mon-Fri, 10am-2pm Sat

Although well known for their impressive collection of precious stones, Amsterdam Sauer also sells watches, pens, wallets and other accessories in addition to their finely crafted jewelry. Visitors can also check out their museum (p59).

ANTONIO BERNARDO

Map pp236-8   *Jewelry*

☎ 2512 7204; Rua Garcia D'Ávila 121, Ipanema; ☯ 10-8pm Mon-Fri

Designer-goldsmith Antonio Bernardo has garnered attention for his lovely bracelets, earrings and necklaces. He has several boutiques in Rio, including one in **Forum de Ipanema** (p154).

ARGUMENTO Map pp236-8   *Books*

☎ 2239 5294; Rua Dias Ferreira 417, Leblon; ☯ 9am-12:30am

One of Leblon's fine neighborhood bookstores, Argumento stocks a small but decent selection of foreign-language books and magazines. The charming café in back is a perfect place to disappear with a book – or a new friend.

ARTE E PALADAR Map pp236-8   *Deli*

☎ 2512 1352; Cobal de Leblon, Rua Gilberto Cardoso, Leblon; ☯ 8am-6pm Mon-Sat, 8am-1pm Sun

In Leblon's lovely **farmers' market** (p157), Arte e Paladar sells an irresistible selection of Italian pastries, Dutch goat cheeses, salmon dishes and French pâtés.

BOCA DO SAPO

Map pp236-8   *Books & Music*

☎ 2287 5207; Rua Visconde de Pirajá 12D, Ipanema; ☯ 10am-8pm Mon-Fri, 10am-7pm Sat, 1-7pm Sun

This charming used-book and record shop is a good place to browse on a rainy day – or when the sun gets to be too much. Indie rock, MPB, samba and funk are well represented in the music department.

CHEZ BONBON Map pp236-8   *Chocolates*

☎ 2521 4243; Rua Visconde de Pirajá 414, Ipanema; ☯ 9am-7pm Mon-Fri, 10am-2pm Sat

This small chocolate shop tucked away in a small gallery of shops sells decadent truffles and solid chocolates. It's a popular stopping point between shops…for obvious reasons.

Top Five Spots to Expand Your Music Collection

- **Bolacheiro** (p162) An underground favorite among local DJs, Bolacheiro has new and used records and CDs, as well as a tattoo parlor in back.
- **Feira de Música** (p159) During the week browse through bins of records and CDs at this open-air market in Centro.
- **Modern Sound** (p157) One of Brazil's largest music stores stocks an impressive selection, with lots of staff recommendations, top Rio artists and imports. Live music shows are staged here daily.
- **Toca do Vinícius** (p155) Bossa nova's smooth grooves live on in this shop dedicated to old and new artists of the genre. Upstairs, Vinícius' fans can get a glimpse of his life's work in the small museum dedicated to him.
- **Top Sound** (p157) The excellent selection of used CDs here makes stopping in a must.

CONTEMPORÂNEO

Map pp236-8   *Clothing & Accessories*

☎ 2287 6204; Rua Visconde de Pirajá 437, Ipanema; ☯ 9am-8pm Mon-Sat

A glowing boutique reminiscent of something you'd find in Soho – better yet Nolita (the fashionistas' neighborhood of choice in New York). See the work of Brazil's best up-and-coming designers here. The space also hosts parties from time to time.

DANTES

Map pp236-8   *Books*

☎ 2511 3480; Rua Dias Ferreira 45B, Leblon; ☯ 10am-10pm Mon-Thu, 10am-midnight Fri & Sat, 2-8pm Sun

The smell of pipe tobacco hangs in the air of this handsome bookshop in Leblon. Dark wood shelves, used books – in foreign languages, as well – and a well-spoken shopkeeper heighten the professorial air. Dantes is also a publishing house.

EMPÓRIO BRASIL

Map pp236-8   *Brazilian Handicrafts*

☎ 2512 3365; Rua Visconde de Pirajá 598, Ipanema; ☯ 10am-6pm Mon-Fri, 10am-4pm Sat

Hidden in the back of a small shopping center, Empório Brasil sells some of Rio's loveliest objets d'art. Works here showcase the talents and fibers of the country – jewelry, vases, instruments, baskets and an ever-changing array of works produced by Brazilian artists and artisans.

ESCADA Map pp236-8 *Antiques*
☎ 2274 9398; Av General San Martin 1219, Leblon; ☺ 5-10pm Mon-Sat

One step inside this rambling antique shop, and you'll just know there's some treasure hidden within. The only problem is that it may not fit in your suitcase. Chandeliers, papier-mâché sculptures, along with antique rings, rugs, little statues and countless other objects litter the interior of this store. Peer beneath the dust and you might find a gem.

ESCH CAFÉ Map pp236-8 *Cigars*
☎ 2512 5651; Rua Dias Ferreira 78, Leblon; ☺ noon until last customer

This **restaurant-bar** (p134) is also the 'house of the Havana,' which means if you have a taste for the Cubans, this is your place. The humidor is stocked with a decent selection, which you can enjoy there over a glass of port, or a few blocks away on the beach (over a sunset).

FORUM DE IPANEMA
Map pp236-8 *Shopping Center*
Rua Visconde de Pirajá 351, Ipanema; ☺ 10am-8pm Mon-Sat

One of Ipanema's best collections of boutiques lies inside this shopping center near Praça NS de Paz. Look for footwear by Via Milano; stylish men's and women's wear by Yes, Brazil; and sexy bikinis carried by Bum Bum and Salinas (both sell men's swim trunks as well). There are also dozens of other designer shops in the complex.

GALERIA IPANEMA SECRETA
Map pp236-8 *Shopping Center*
Rua Visconde de Pirajá 371, Ipanema; ☺ 10am-8pm Mon-Sat

This collection of boutiques on the 2nd floor of this shopping gallery may be a secret, but not to anyone in Ipanema. You can find a number of youthful designers on display here. Look for ones like Constança Basto, whose shoes are highly prized by Ipanema's belles.

GILSON MARTINS Map pp236-8 *Accessories*
☎ 2227 6178; Rua Visconde de Pirajá 462, Ipanema; ☺ 10am-8pm Mon-Fri, 10am-4pm Sat

Designer Gilson Martins turns the Brazilian flag into a fashion statement in his flagship store in Ipanema. In addition to glossy handbags, wallets and other accessories, the shop sports a gallery in back with ongoing exhibitions – usually dealing with outsider fashion.

H STERN Map pp236-8 *Jewelry & Accessories*
☎ 2259 7442; hstern@hstern.com.br; Rua Garcia D'Ávila 113; ☺ 8:30am-6:30pm Mon-Fri, 8:30am-2pm Sat

The headquarters of the famous jeweler, H Stern has an array of finely crafted jewelry, watches and other accessories for sale. You can also take a tour of their **gem museum** (p59).

IPANEMA 2000
Map pp236-8 *Shopping Center*
Rua Visconde de Pirajá 547, Ipanema; ☺ 10am-8pm Mon-Fri

Another one of Ipanema's good collections of boutiques, Ipanema 2000 draws crowds of fashion-conscious shoppers in search of something new for the after-office soirée – or the upcoming trip to Búzios. Stores like the brightly decorated Fabia Raquel shop offer something a little different – interesting designs with beadwork. There's also a money-exchange booth on the 1st floor.

IPANEMA.COM
Map pp236-8 *Clothing & Accessories*
☎ 2227 1288; Rua Prudente de Moraes 237c, Ipanema; ☺ 10am-7pm Mon-Fri, 10am-4pm

Featuring local and international designers, Ipanema.com focuses on men's fashion – though it also has women's wear. A good spot if you need a new look in a hurry – ie for the night out.

LETRAS E EXPRESSÕES
Map pp236-8 *Books & Music*
☎ 2521 6110; Rua Visconde de Pirajá 276, Ipanema; ☺ 8am-midnight

One of Ipanema's growing assortment of bookshops, Letras e Expressões carries a decent selection of foreign-language books – from architectural tomes to fiction and travel books (Lonely Planet titles notwithstanding). It also has a variety of English-language magazines and an internet café (Café Ubaldo), which is nice for sipping cappuccino and sending envy-worthy letters back home.

LETRAS E EXPRESSÕES
Map pp236-8 *Books & Music*
☎ 2511 5085; Av Ataulfo Paiva 1292, Leblon; ☺ 24hr

The bookstore to turn to when you just have to get that biography of Chico Buarque at four in the morning. The aisles are often crowded with people reading (and occasionally buying) the many magazines lining the shelves. It stocks Rio's largest selection of foreign-language mags and has the usual assortment of books.

Shopping – Ipanema & Leblon

LIMITS Map pp236-8 *Clothing & Accessories*
☎ 2227 2870; Rua Maria Quitéria 91, Ipanema;
🕙 9am-8pm Mon-Fri, 9am-5pm Sat

A young, good-looking group converges on this boutique, drawn no doubt by the ice-cream parlor and lounge. For those who weary of browsing the tops and skirts, jeans and colorful tees, Limits offers pinball, which later becomes a set piece to their happy hour with DJs.

LIVRARIA DA TRAVESSA
Map pp236-8 *Books & Music*
☎ 2249 4977; Rua Visconde de Pirajá 572, Ipanema;
🕙 9am-midnight Mon-Sat, 1pm-midnight Sun

One of a growing chain of bookstores around the city, Livraria da Travessa has a small selection of foreign-language books and periodicals. Upstairs it has a good music collection – most of which you can listen to by scanning the discs under the headphone stations. A stone's throw away, **B!** (p105) serves tasty salads, quiches and desserts.

MIXED Map pp236-8 *Clothing & Accessories*
☎ 2259 9544; www.mixed.com.br in Portuguese; Rua Visconde de Pirajá 476, Ipanema; 🕙 10am-8pm Mon-Fri

One of Rio's premier boutiques, Mixed actually originated in São Paolo. Ipanemans, however, love it as their own. The shoes and platforms, blouses and pants sold here aim to capture the essence of Carioca sensuality. And they do quite well, as a matter of fact.

MUSICALE Map pp236-8 *Music*
☎ 2540 5237; Rua Visconde de Pirajá 483, Ipanema;
🕙 10am-7pm

This small music shop has narrow aisles, but you'll come across some real finds if you brave the elbow jousting at Musicale. Used and new CDs are somewhat organized by category, and you can listen to any used CD at one of the decks up front.

NO MEIO DO CAMINHO
Map pp236-8 *Art & Home Furnishings*
☎ 2294 1330; Av General San Martin 1247, Leblon;
🕙 10am-7pm Mon-Fri, 10am-2pm Sat

Showcasing the work of talented Brazilian artisans, No Meio do Caminho has two floors full of pottery, vases, ceramics and woodwork. Decorative items here are more akin to art pieces – and are priced accordingly. No Meio do Caminho will ship anywhere.

PHILIPPE MARTIN
Map pp236-8 *Clothing & Accessories*
☎ 2512 9163; Rua Visconde de Pirajá 529A;
🕙 10am-8pm Mon-Fri

One of Brazil's more popular designers, Philippe Martin is known for stylish but casual wear. The shop here sells a wide range of men's and women's clothing, pushing styles somewhat ahead of the rest.

RIO DESIGN CENTER
Map p239 *Home Furnishings*
☎ 2274 8797; Av Ataulfo de Paiva 270, Leblon;
🕙 10am-6pm Mon-Sat

The polished black building that looms over the street houses four floors of galleries and stores, all dedicated to home decor. The 3rd floor contains an assortment of antiques.

SPECIAL BIKE
Map pp236-8 *Bicycles & Accessories*
☎ 2521 2686; www.specialbike.com.br; Rua Visconde de Pirajá 135B, Ipanema; 🕙 9am-7pm Mon-Fri, 9am-2pm Sat

Although the name doesn't make much of an impression on English-speakers, the bikes at **Special Bike** (p194) aren't bad. Mountain bikes, road bikes, helmets and lots of parts and accessories comprise the offerings here. Special Bike also rents what it sells – US$5 per hour; US$15 per day.

TOCA DO VINÍCIUS Map pp236-8 *Music*
☎ 2247 5227; www.tocadovinicus.com.br; Rua Vinícius de Moraes 129, Ipanema; 🕙 9am-9pm Mon-Fri, 10am-5pm Sun

Bossa nova fans shouldn't miss this store. In addition to its ample CD selection of contemporary and old performers, Toca do Vinícius sells music scores and composition books. Upstairs a **tiny museum** (p59) displays memorabilia of the great songwriter and poet. Occasional concerts in the afternoon fill this neighborhood with smooth bossa sounds.

VALE DAS BONECAS
Map pp236-8 *Clothing & Accessories*
☎ 2523 1794; Rua Farme de Amoedo 75C, Ipanema;
🕙 10am-8pm Mon-Fri, 10am-2:30pm Sat

Youthful street fashion is the focal point at this small Ipanema boutique. Local designers play with color and material here – not always successfully. But if you're looking for something a little edgy, the Valley of the Dolls (*Vale das Bonecas*) is a fine destination.

Clothing Sizes

Measurements approximate only, try before you buy

Women's Clothing

Aus/UK	8	10	12	14	16	18
Europe	36	38	40	42	44	46
Japan	5	7	9	11	13	15
USA	6	8	10	12	14	16

Women's Shoes

Aus/USA	5	6	7	8	9	10
Europe	35	36	37	38	39	40
France only	35	36	38	39	40	42
Japan	22	23	24	25	26	27
UK	3½	4½	5½	6½	7½	8½

Men's Clothing

Aus	92	96	100	104	108	112
Europe	46	48	50	52	54	56
Japan	S		M	M		L
UK/USA	35	36	37	38	39	40

Men's Shirts (Collar Sizes)

Aus/Japan	38	39	40	41	42	43
Europe	38	39	40	41	42	43
UK/USA	15	15½	16	16½	17	17½

Men's Shoes

Aus/UK	7	8	9	10	11	12
Europe	41	42	43	44½	46	47
Japan	26	27	27½	28	29	30
USA	7½	8½	9½	10½	11½	12½

WÖLLNER OUTDOOR

Map pp236-8   *Clothing & Accessories*

☎ 2512 6531; Rua Visconde de Pirajá 511, Ipanema;
◷ 10am-9pm Mon-Fri

The great outdoors, and the shirt and shorts you'll need to enjoy it, seems to be the mantra of Wöllner. Men's and women's clothes feature rugged styles, nicely cut – though not always so interesting. Once you've browsed the selections, grab a *cafezinho* and a window seat in their café and watch the day go by.

GÁVEA, JARDIM BOTÂNICO & LAGOA

O SOL
Map pp236-8   *Brazilian Handicrafts*

☎ 2294 5099; Rua Corcovado 213, Jardim Botânico;
◷ 9am-6pm Mon-Fri, 9am-1pm Sat

O Sol is run by Leste-Um, a nonprofit social-welfare organization. This delightful store displays the works of regional artists and sells Brazilian folk art in clay, wood and porcelain. They also sell baskets and woven rugs.

COPACABANA & LEME

ARS BRASILIS

Map pp234-5   *Brazilian Handicrafts*

☎ 2287 2488; Rua Souza Lima 37, Copacabana;
◷ 9am-10pm Mon-Fri, 9am-6pm Sat, noon-6pm Sun

Ars Brasilis sells colorful handicrafts from Minas Gerais and the Northeast. Woodcarvings, candlesticks, small figurines (including a rather graphic pose of a man and a wolf) and furniture comprise the offerings. The friendly shopkeepers also cook up tasty small plates of Minas Gerais cuisine (p112).

FAST CELL Map pp234-5   *Cell Phones*

☎ 2548 1008, 9609 5450; www.fastcell.com.br; No 919, Rua Santa Clara 50, Copacabana; ◷ 9am-8pm Mon-Fri, 10am-7pm Sat & Sun

If you forgot your cellular and can't live without it, Fast Cell can get you reconnected quickly. English-speaking manager Felipe Gilaberte will even drop the phone off at your hotel or apartment. Prices vary, but calls to the USA or Europe cost around US$1 per minute.

FERUCCIO E MASSIMO

Map pp234-5   *Magazines & Newspapers*

☎ 2275 4547; Av NS de Copacabana 95, Copacabana;
◷ 7am-10pm Mon-Fri, 7am-11pm Sat, 7am-8pm Sun

A wide range of magazines and newspapers – including foreign presses – are sold at this small neighborhood shop near Av Princessa Isabel. You can also find film here, and drop it off for development.

GALERIA RIVER

Map pp234-5   *Shopping Center*

Rua Francisco Otaviano 67, Arpoador; ◷ 10am-6pm Mon-Sat

Surf shops, skateboard and rollerblade outlets, and dozens of shops selling beachwear and fashions for young nubile things fill this shopping gallery in Arpoador. Shorts, bikinis, swim trunks, party attire and gear for outdoor adventure are in abundance. The shops here – like Ocean Surf Shop – are a good place to inquire about board rentals – which run about US$10 per day. Those interested in rock climbing and trekking should stop by the **Casa do Montanhista**. It also has information about courses.

KOPENHAGEN Map pp234-5   *Chocolates*

☎ 2521 5949; Av NS de Copacabana 583, Copacabana;
◷ 9am-8pm Mon-Fri, 10am-7pm Sat & Sun

For 75 years Kopenhagen has been supplying Rio with bon bons, truffles and dark chocolate bars. This small shop makes a worthwhile stop for a treat, or if you need to bring a few sweet presents back home.

MODERN SOUND Map pp234-5 *Music*
☎ 2548 5005; www.modernsound.com.br; Rua Barata Ribeiro 502, Copacabana; ⊙ 9am-9pm Mon-Fri, 9am-8pm Sat

One of Brazil's largest music stores, Modern Sound makes a fine setting for browsing through the many shelves of samba, electronica, hip-hop, imports, classical and dozens of other well-represented categories. The small **café** (p132) in the store features live jazz daily.

MUNDO VERDE
Map pp234-5 *Health-Food Store*
☎ 2257 3183; www.mundoverde.com.br in Portuguese; Av NS de Copacabana 630, Copacabana; ⊙ 9am-6pm Mon-Fri, 9am-2pm Sat

Brazil's largest health-food retailer, Mundo Verde sells organic products (including *salgados* and other snacks here), jams made from Amazonian fruits and other assorted goods. The sun-care products are usually cheaper here than in pharmacies – and much better for your skin.

TOP SOUND Map pp234-5 *Music*
☎ 2267 9607; Av NS de Copacabana 1103C, Copacabana; ⊙ 10am-8pm Mon-Sat

One of Rio's top used-CD stores, Top Sound doesn't have racks and racks of CDs like Modern Sound, but what they do have is usually quite good. Like the neighborhood that surrounds the store, a diverse bunch shop here – club kids, old samba softies, expats trapped in the '80s – which is reflected in the range of offerings for sale. Top Sound also buys and trades CDs.

BOTAFOGO & URCA

ARTÍNDIA Map pp232-3 *Brazilian Handicrafts*
☎ 2286 8899; Museu do Índio, Rua das Palmeiras 55, Botafogo; ⊙ 9:30am-5:30pm Tue-Fri, 1-5pm Sat & Sun

Inside the grounds of the **Museu do Índio** (p65), Artíndia sells a variety of indigenous handicrafts – masks, musical instruments, toys, pots, baskets and weapons. Regional artists, mostly from northern tribes, craft objects using native materials like straw, clay, wood and feathers.

BOTAFOGO PRAIA SHOPPING
Map pp232-3 *Shopping Center*
☎ 2559 9880; Praia de Botafogo 400, Botafogo; ⊙ 10am-10pm Mon-Sat, 3-10pm Sun

Botafogo's large shopping center has dozens of stores, featuring Brazilian and international designers to suit every style – and clothe every part of the body. The 3rd floor's the best – for top designers check stores like Philippe Martins, Giselle Martins, Osklen, Equatore and more whimsical shops like d-xis. The mall also has a cinema and several top-floor restaurants, such as **Pax** (p115) and **Zin** (p116) with panoramic views.

LIVRARIA PREFÁCIO
Map pp232-3 *Books & Music*
☎ 2527 5699; Rua Voluntarios da Pátria 39, Botafogo; ⊙ 10am-10pm Mon-Fri, 2-10pm Sat & Sun

This charming bookshop stocks a small selection of foreign titles as well as music selections. And perusers need not go hungry or thirsty while they browse for titles. A slender bar in front delivers refreshing glasses of *chope*, while seating in the upstairs and the **café** (p115) in

Shopping – Botafogo & Urca

Farmers' Markets

The *feiras* (produce markets) that pop up in different locations throughout the week are the best places to shop for fruit and vegetables. For an authentic slice of home-grown Carioca commerce, nothing beats wandering through and taking in the action.

- **Cobal de Humaitá** (Map pp232-3; ☎ 2266 1343; Rua Voluntários da Pátria 446, Botafogo; ⊙ 7am-4pm Mon-Sat) The city's largest farmers' market sells plenty of flowers, veggies and fruits; there are also cafés and restaurants on hand for those looking for a bit more (p129).
- **Cobal de Leblon** (Map pp236-8; ☎ 2239 1549; Rua Gilberto Cardoso, Leblon; ⊙ 7am-4pm Mon-Sat) Smaller than Humaitá's market, the Cobal de Leblon makes a fine setting for stopping to smell the flowers – or the *maracujá* (passionfruit) – before settling down to a meal at one of the cafés there.
- **Copacabana feiras by day** Wednesday on Rua Domingos Ferreira, Thursdays on Rua Belford Roxo and Rua Ronald de Carvalho, Sundays on Rua Decio Vilares.
- **Ipanema feiras by day** Mondays on Rua Henrique Dumont, Tuesdays on Praça General Osório and Fridays on Praça NS da Paz.
- **Leblon feiras by day** Thursdays on Rua General Urquiza.

back serves heartier fare. The bookshop at the rear hosts an occasional poetry reading or record-release party.

LUZES DA CIDADE
Map pp232-3 · *Books & Music*
☎ 2226 4108; Rua Voluntarios da Pátria 35, Botafogo; ☼ 10am-10pm Mon-Fri, 2-10pm Sat & Sun

Inside the **Espaço Unibanco Cinema** (p141), this quaint bookstore attracts crowds on the weekends. Along with books geared toward the film arts, Luzes da Cidade stocks its shelves (and counter tops and floor space) with an odd assortment of books, including foreign-language volumes. It's a fine place to browse before a show at the cinema, hence its popularity.

RIO OFF-PRICE SHOPPING
Map pp232-3 · *Shopping Center*
☎ 2542 5693; Rua General Severiano 97, Botafogo; ☼ 10am-10pm Mon-Sat, 3-9pm Sun

Near Rio Sul Shopping, Rio Off-Price Shopping is something of a factory outlet center. It has many of the same stores as other malls – domestic and international designers – but prices are about 20% lower than other spots. It also has two cinemas and meal options (mostly fast food).

RIO SUL SHOPPING
Map pp232-3 · *Shopping Center*
☎ 2545 7200; www.riosul.com.br in Portuguese; Rua Lauro Müller 116, Botafogo; ☼ 10am-10pm Mon-Sat, 3-10pm Sun

The biggest shopping center you can reach without heading to Barra, Rio Sul has over 400 shops, featuring both the prominent and the obscure, cinemas, restaurants and – at least on weekends – overwhelming crowds.

FLAMENGO, LARANJEIRAS & COSME VELHO

BRUMADA Map pp232-3 · *Brazilian Handicrafts*
☎ 2558 2275; Rua das Laranjeiras 486, Laranjeiras; ☼ 10am-6pm Mon-Sat

Brumada sells handicrafts from all over Brazil – but particularly works from the Northeast. Wooden figurines, porcelain dolls, brightly hued tapestries, indigenous art and hand-woven baskets make up the bulk of what's on sale, but Brumada also has a handful of

Hippie Fair (opposite)

colonial furniture paintings and antiques. The many colorful carvings and ceramics – giraffes, horses, soldiers – make nice gifts for children.

JEITO BRASILEIRO
Map pp232-3   *Brazilian Handicrafts*
☎ 2205 7636; Rua Ererê 11A, Cosme Velho; ☺ 9am-6pm Mon-Fri, 9am-4pm Sat, 9am-1pm Sun
Next to the Corcovado train terminal in Cosme Velho, Jeito Brasileiro has a wide selection of

handicrafts from all over Brazil, including folk art made by members of the Camucim tribe.

MARACATU BRASIL
Map pp232-3   *Percussion Instruments*
☎ 2557 4754; www.maracatubrasil.com.br; Rua Ipiranga 49, Laranjeiras; ☺ 10am-6pm Mon-Sat
You can't miss the lime-green building that houses this small percussion store and workshop. Inside, you can buy *shakarees*, conga

Markets for the Masses

- **Av Atlântica Fair** (Map pp234-5; Av Atlântica near Rua Djalma Ulrich; ☺ 7pm-midnight) Paintings, drawings, jewelry, clothing and a fair bit of tourist junk make up this Copacabana market. It's located on the median along Av Atlântica.
- **Babilônia Feira Hype** (Map pp236-8; ☎ 2233 4238; www.babiloniahype.com.br; Jockey Club, Rua Jardim Botânico 971, Jardim Botânico; admission US$2; ☺ 2-10pm Sat) A younger crowd mills through the many clothing, sunglasses and jewelry stalls here on weekends. Often live bands and dance performances are staged here, and there are places to get your fortune read by *'místicos'* or receive a henna tattoo. Plenty of food stalls (mostly of the fried sausages and beer variety) litter the fairgrounds.
- **Feira de Música** (Map pp228-30; Rua Pedro Lessa; ☺ 9am-5pm Mon-Fri) On weekdays next to the Biblioteca Nacional, record and CD stalls line the small lane. You'll find American indie rock to vintage Brazilian funk, and most vendors will let you listen to any of their discs for sale – new or used.
- **Feira do Rio Antigo** (Map pp228-30; ☎ 3852 5516; Rua do Lavradio, Centro; ☺ 1st Sat of the month, 10am-6pm) Although the Rio Antiques Fair happens just once a month, don't miss it if you're in town. The colonial buildings become a living installation as the whole street (Rua do Lavradio) fills with antiques and music – samba and MPB bands – creating a fine ambience.
- **Feira Nordestina** (Map pp240-1; ☎ 3860 9976; Campo de São Cristóvão, São Cristóvão; Fri-Sun) For details see p88.
- **Hippie Fair** (Map pp236-8; Praça General Osório, Ipanema; ☺ 9am-5pm Sun) The Zona Sul's most famous market, the Hippie Fair (aka Feira de Arte de Ipanema) takes place once a month and has lots of artwork, jewelry, handicrafts, leather goods and the occasional piece of furniture for sale. A stall in the southeast corner of the plaza sells tasty Northeastern cuisine. Don't miss it.
- **Photography and Image Fair** (Map pp232-3; 2558 6350; Museu da Republica, Rua do Catete 153, Catete; ☺ 9am-5pm last Sun of month) Works from amateur and professional photographers are for sale at this once-monthly market in the verdant Parque do Catete. There's also a multimedia room where they host workshops, talks and slide projections.
- **Praça do Lido Market** (Map pp234-5; Praça do Lido, Copacabana; ☺ 8am-6pm Sat & Sun) Copacabana's response to Ipanema's widely popular Hippie Fair, this weekend affair features handicrafts and souvenirs, soccer jerseys, a few jewelry stands and, from time to time, a man selling amazing slices of chocolate cake.
- **Praça do Mercado Feira de Antiguidades** (Map pp228-30; Praça do Mercado; ☺ 9am-5pm Sat) This antique market next to the Niterói ferry terminal has a vast array of antique and not-so-antique finds – silverware, carpets, pocket watches, jewelry, typewriters, records, art deco and art nouveau items. You can find nearly anything out here, making it a browser's paradise.
- **Praça Santos Dumont Antique Fair** (Map pp236-8; Praça Santos Dumont, Gávea; ☺ 9am-5pm Sun) Small but substantial, Gávea's antique fair features jewelry, records, watches, dinnerware, books and other odds and ends.
- **Praça XV Handicrafts Fair** (Map pp228-30; Praça XV de Novembro, Centro; ☺ 8am-6pm Thu-Fri) This street fair near the Imperial Palace features craftsmen selling their works of leather, wood, porcelain, glass and silver. There are also stalls with regional Brazilian fare.
- **Shopping Cassino Atlântico Antiques Fair** (Map pp234-5; Av Atlântico 4240, Copacabana; ☺ 11am-6pm Sat) A bit more neutered than the others, Copacabana's antique fair consists of three floors of blown glass, sculpture, carpets, silverware and jewelry. Pieces are in much better condition here, which is clearly reflected in the price. A tearoom and live music help bring on the mood.
- **Stamp, coin and postcard collectors' market** (Map pp228-30; Rua de Passeio, Centro; ☺ 7am-1pm Sun; metro Cinelândia) In the stately gardens of the Passeio Publico, you can purchase some rare mementos of Rio.

and bongo drums, tambourines, and other Brazilian percussion instruments. Upstairs is a drum clinic, where you can study a number of styles with local musician-teachers. See p76 for more details.

PÉ DE BOI Map pp232-3 *Handicrafts*
☎ 2285 4395; Rua Ipiranga 55, Laranjeiras; ⏰ 9am-7pm Mon-Fri, 9am-1pm Sat
Traditional artisan handicrafts from Brazil feature prominently at Pé de Boi. Works in wood and ceramic as well as tapestries, sculptures and weavings showcase the talents of artists from Amazonia, Minas Gerais and the south. The shop also has works made by indigenous artists from further afield: Peru, Guatemala and Ecuador.

CATETE & GLORIA
MARIA FUMAÇA
Map pp232-3 *Books & Music*
☎ 2225 6711; Rua do Catete 164, Catete; ⏰ 2-8pm Mon, 10am-8pm Tue-Fri, 10am-6pm Sat
On the 2nd floor of one of Catete's charming and battered old buildings, Maria Fumaça is a classic bookshop with all the requisite trappings particular to used-book stores: the fat, lazy cat in the corner, the walls and walls of bookshelves stretching high to the ceiling, the erudite and disinterested owner with coffee and Joyce behind the counter, and of course an ample selection of books – and records (remember, this is Brazil).

CENTRO & CINELÂNDIA
ALFONSO NUNE'S ANTIQUARIO
Map pp228-30 *Antiques*
☎ 2232 2620; Rua do Lavradio 60, Centro; ⏰ 9am-7pm Mon-Fri, 9am-3pm
The old colonial edifice features an excellent selection of antiques – from tables and chairs to chandeliers and glassware. Discerning collectors will want to give the shop a good look over before proceeding to the other dozen or so antique stores lining this strip.

BAR DAS ARTES
Map pp228-30 *Books & Music*
☎ 2215 5795; Praça XV de Novembro 48, Centro; ⏰ 9am-8pm Mon-Fri, 9am-2pm Sat
Bossa nova plays overhead at this charming bookstore-music shop, which is also a **bistro**

(p119). In addition to new and used books (including a selection of foreign-language titles) Bar das Artes sells a handful of old prints and postcards. The music section is less extensive than the bookshop, and includes bossa, samba, *chorinho* as well as a number of pop bands.

CASA OLIVEIRA
Map pp228-30 *Musical Instruments*
☎ 2325 8109; Rua da Carioca 70, Centro; ⏰ 10am-6pm Mon-Fri
One of several excellent music shops on Rua da Carioca, Casa Oliveira sells a wide variety of musical instruments, including all the pieces that make up the rhythm section of Carnaval *baterias* (percussion sections). If *forró* is more your speed, you can also purchase a variety of mandolins as well as accordions and electric guitars.

EDITORA GEOGRÁFICA J PAULINI
Map pp228-30 *Maps*
☎ 2220 0181; Loja K, Rua Senador Dantas 75, Centro; ⏰ 10am-6pm Mon-Fri
This small shop on the way to the **bonde station** (p84) sells a decent selection of maps: national road maps as well as topographical, physical and nautical maps. They have a small selection of maps of other major Brazilian cities, in addition to Rio maps.

ESCH CAFÉ
Map pp228-30 *Cigars*
☎ 2507 5866; Rua Do Rosário 108, Centro; ⏰ noon until 10pm Mon-Fri
Centro's branch of the 'house of the Havana' is just as stocked with the fruit of the Cuban vine – or the leaf rather – as Leblon's. The end of the Carioca workday (from 5pm onward) is a lively time to stop by, and if it is not your scene you can always move on – with smokes in hand of course. Esch is also a bar; see p131.

H STERN Map pp228-30 *Jewelry*
☎ 2524 2300; Av Rio Branco 128, Centro; ⏰ 10am-6pm Mon-Fri
The jewelry giant's branch in Centro has an ample selection of their exquisite pieces, without the flash of Zona Sul locations. If gazing at all those diamonds puts you in a decadent mood, move it downstairs to **Eça** (p120) and sample some of the neighborhood's best cuisine.

Wild Rubber *Cassandra Loomis*

Amazon Life, Rio's most ecologically minded company, may lie some 3000km from the Amazon, but the forest plays a vital role in the company's products. Amazon Life's founders, Maria Beatriz Saldanha Tavares and João Augusto Fortes, were inspired by environmental activist and martyr Chico Mendes. Mendes brought attention to rubber tappers, who were losing their livelihood as the Amazon was cleared for farmland. Tavares and Fortes worked with local communities of rubber tappers, and soon Treetap, a wild rubber, was born. In addition to giving the local Indian communities an income, it has helped to preserve their lands, owing to the creation of extraction reserves. In the summer, the villages make Treetap, and in the winter they transport the product by canoe, then barge, to Rio. Treetap is now much in demand by environmentally responsible companies. Giant, the largest European bicycle company, ordered 10,000 bags made from Treetap; Hermès, the French fashion king, has used the wild rubber in the production of accessories. To see some of Amazon Life's products, order products online or visit their store **EcoMercado** (☎ 3878 2131; www.amazonlife.com; Rua General Almério de Moura 200, São Cristóvão).

LIVRARIA DA TRAVESSA
Map pp228-30 *Books & Music*
☎ 3231 8015; Travessa de Ouvidor 17, Centro;
⏲ 9am-8pm Mon-Fri, 10am-1pm Sat

Livraria da Travessa, hands down, wins Centro's most-charming-bookstore award. The location, tucked off the narrow alley Travessa do Ouvidor, accounts for a large part of it, then there's the knowledgeable sales staff, the **bistro** (p119), the light falling just so across the shelves, and the occasional readings and arts events. Nicely done. A second **Livraria da Travessa** (Map p228-30; No 44, Av Rio Branco) has a decent café overlooking the store.

LIVRARIA O ACADÊMICO DO RIO
Map pp228-30 *Books & Music*
☎ 2240 4061; Rua da Carioca 61, Centro; ⏲ 9am-7pm Mon-Fri, 9am-1pm Sat

Assuming he was Brazilian and an academic, your grandfather would love picking through the old books here. Some of the musty volumes piled haphazardly around the store are crumbling into dust. Other works are still salvageable, meaning their secrets are still obtainable. In contrast to rare and unusual Portuguese titles, most foreign-language titles are rather less academic, though selections change weekly. You can buy, sell and trade books here.

MERCADO MODERNO
Map pp228-30 *Home Furnishings & Antiques*
☎ 2508 6083; Rua do Lavradio 130, Centro; ⏲ 9am-6pm Mon-Sat

One of Rua do Lavradio's magical fusions of furniture and jazz, Mercado Moderno by day sells pod-shaped lounge chairs, modular sofas, vintage radios and sleek '60s accoutrements. By night – weekend night, we're talk-ing – the market transforms into a space for bossa-jazz (p134).

NOVA LIVRARIA LEONARDO DA VINCI
Map pp228-30 *Books*
☎ 2533 2237; Av Rio Branco 185, Centro; ⏲ 9am-7pm Mon-Fri & 9am-noon Sat

One of Rio's best foreign-language book collections, Da Vinci also has a wide range of art and photography books, as well as coffee-table books about Rio's history and architecture. It's one floor down – follow the spiral ramp down. A decent coffee shop lies next to the bookshop.

SUB & SUB
Map pp228-30 *Diving, Climbing & Hiking*
☎ 2509 1176; subsub.com.br; Sobreloja, Rua da Alfândega 98, Centro; ⏲ 10am-6pm Mon-Fri

Sub & Sub has an array of gear for outdoor adventure: climbing and mountaineering gear, diving and snorkeling equipment, camping equipment, hiking boots and backpacks. The knowledgeable sales staff can also recommend courses for those interested in learning a new craft. It's a bit hidden. Once you reach No 98, go in and take the stairs to the left; it's one flight up.

TABACARIA AFRICANA
Map pp228-30 *Tobacco & Cigars*
☎ 2509 5333; Largo do Paço 38, Centro; ⏲ 9am-5pm Mon-Fri

The sweet fragrance of pipe tobacco is embedded in the walls and furniture of this tiny shop facing the Praça XV. Regulars sit at the table in front slowly drawing on the pick of the day while the afternoon drifts by smokelike. In back, the glass jars contain a variety of flavors and aromas. Let the shopkeeper put a mix together for you, then join the gang up front.

UNIMAGEM Map pp228-30 *Photography*
☎ 2507 7745; Rua dos Andradas 29, Centro; ☺ 9am-6pm Mon-Fri, 9am-noon Sat; metro Cinelândia

The choice of professional photographers in the city, Unimagem has a good selection of new and used cameras (SLRs, TLRs, point-and-shoot) as well as all the accessories (tripods, film, paper). They also run a superb developing lab: black and white, color and slides. And they can provide one-hour developing service for both slide and color film.

SANTA TERESA & LAPA

BOLACHEIRO Map p231 *Music & Tattoos*
☎ 2507 9860; Rua Francisco Muratori 2A, Lapa; ☺ 10am-7pm Mon-Wed, 10am-10pm Thu & Fri, noon-10pm Sat & Sun

Only in Lapa will you encounter a place where you can pick through bins of old jazz records (or new electronic mixes) before stepping into the backroom to get a tattoo down your arm, inspired perhaps by that old Elza Soares record playing overhead. Bolacheiro

also has a decent selection of CDs, and the young helpful staff can make good recommendations – if samba-funk eludes you. Also, they'll let you listen to anything in the store. From time to time, the small store sponsors art openings and open turntable sessions (anyone with records can share their grooves), infusing the space with an improvisatory party atmosphere.

BRECHÓ ANTIGAMENTE
Map p231 *Thrift Shop*
☎ 2220 1878; Rua Almirante Alexandrino 428, Santa Teresa; ☺ 3-8pm Thu-Sun

One of Santa Teresa's better-stocked second-hand shops, Brechó Antigamente sells costume jewelry as well as clothes and attracts a wide mix of local residents. Brechós, incidentally, are secondhand stores, which come and go in this neighborhood.

BRECHÓ ARTE Map p231 *Thrift Shop*
☎ 2221 3205; Rua Monte Alegre, Santa Teresa; ☺ 10am-7pm Mon, 10am-9pm Tue-Sun

Brechó Arte features several racks of secondhand clothes as well as a few antique pieces – teapots, costume jewelry – for sale from time to time. Depending on your luck, you can come across some good finds here.

Santa Teresa (p83)

ÉDIPO REI

Map p231 *Books*

☎ 2508 6936; Rua Joaquim Silva 95, Lapa;
🕙 11:30am-7:30pm

Named after the tragically misguided hero Oedipus Rex, this small bookshop has a selection of dusty foreign-language titles in addition to old and unusual Brazilian works. A few records lie hidden somewhere among the tall shelves. The Russian owner also teaches classes, though her forte is the czar's tongue, not Portuguese.

FAVELA HYPE

Map p231 *Clothing & Home Furnishings*

☎ 3852 8504; www.favelahype.com; Rua Almirante Alexandrino 1458, Santa Teresa; 🕙 2-10pm Tue-Sun

Characteristic of Santa Teresa's unbridled creativity, Favela Hype is a gallery, a thrift shop and a café all rolled up into one rambling and very funky ensemble. Browse through fashions left over from the '50s, '60s and '70s – dresses and suits, hats and gloves – or take a peek at some of the vanguard fashions of local designers. Kitsch furnishings abound (some of it is for sale), and the gallery in the back hosts rotating exhibitions. In Boutique, the café in the store, serves up delicious sandwiches that pair nicely with the half a dozen *caipirinha* concoctions on hand. At the time of research, Favela Hype was set to begin hosting DJs for occasional parties. Stop in to see what's on.

LA VAREDA

Map p231 *Brazilian Handicrafts*

☎ 2222 1848; www.lavareda.hpg.com.br in Portuguese; Rua Almirante Alexandrino 428, Santa Teresa; 🕙 10am-9pm Tue-Sun, 1-9pm Mon

On the *bonde* line near Largo dos Guimarães, La Vareda stocks a colorful selection of Brazilian handicrafts as well as work from local artists and artisans. Pottery, furniture, paintings, handmade dolls and tapestries all cover the old store. You can also purchase stationery and prints highlighting historic Santa Teresa.

RASGANDO PANO

Map p231 *Clothing & Accessories*

☎ 2232 1389; Rua Santa Cristina 181A, Santa Teresa; 🕙 11am-8pm Tue-Sun

Down the hill from La Vareda, Rasgando Pano features a small selection of women's clothing and accessories, bags and pillows. Many items for sale are from India or show traces of Indian influences.

TRILHOS URBANOS

Map p231 *Brazilian Handicrafts*

☎ 2242 3632; Rua Almirante Alexandrino 402A, Santa Teresa; 🕙 10am-7pm Tue-Sat

Vying for attention near La Vareda, Trilhos Urbanos also stocks a small but interesting assortment of handicrafts. Works by local artists and artisans are also for sale – photographs, picture frames, paintings and works in metal.

BARRA DA TIJUCA & GREATER RIO

BARRA SHOPPING

Map p239 *Shopping Center*

☎ 3089 1000; www.barrashopping.com.br in Portuguese; Av das Américas 4666, Barra da Tijuca; 🕙 10am-10pm Mon-Sat, 3-10pm Sun

Rio's largest mall (and one of the largest in South America) is an easy place to shop away a few hours or days. Some 30 million shoppers pass through Barra's doors each year. Over 500 stores clutter the 4km-long stretch of stores, along with five movie screens, a children's parkland and a wealth of dining options.

RIO DESIGN CENTER

Map p239 *Shopping Center*

☎ 2461 9999; www.riodesign.com.br in Portuguese; Av das Américas 7770, Barra da Tijuca; 🕙 10am-10pm Mon-Fri, 10am-8pm (stores) 11am-midnight (restaurants) Sat, 3-10pm Sun

This architecturally rich center features a number of excellent home-furnishing stores selling designer lamps, vases, decorative pieces and furniture. It also has some of very good restaurants and a few art galleries.

SÃO CONRADO FASHION MALL

Map pp226-7 *Shopping Center*

☎ 3083 0300; Estrada da Gávea 899, São Conrado; 🕙 10am-10pm

Rio's most beautiful mall features all the big names – Armani, Versace, Luis Vuitton – and all of Brazil's most recognizable designers. It's located in the equally respectable neighborhood of São Conrado, near the Hotel Intercontinental.

SHOPPING DA GÁVEA

Map pp236-8 *Shopping Center*

☎ 2274 9896; Rua Marquês de São Vicente 52, Gávea; 🕙 10am-10pm Mon-Sat, 3-9pm Sun

Shopping da Gávea (modestly) touts itself as the preferred shopping center of artists and intellectuals. Although it is rather difficult to discern whether the shoppers here are painters, philosophers or gym coaches, Shopping da Gávea is a charming place – at least as far as *shoppings* go. Some 200 stores litter this mall. There are also four performance theaters and a number of decent restaurants, including the Italian **La Pasta Gialla**, which must be the bruschetta capital of Brazil with 28 different types.

VIA PARQUE SHOPPING
Map p239   *Shopping Center*
☎ 2421 9222; www.shoppingviaparque.com.br in Portuguese; Av Ayrton Senna 3000, Barra da Tijuca; ☽ 10am-10pm Mon-Sat, 3-10pm Sun

With 280 stores, six movie theaters and abundant restaurants, Via Parque is another option for visitors wanting to get to the heart of Rio's consumer culture. It is also home to one of the city's biggest concert arenas, **Claro Hall** (p137).

Sleeping

Sleeping

Rio's continued popularity as the Cidade Maravilhosa (Marvelous City) in the tropics means there is no shortage of accommodations. Until recently, most of these options were limited to boxy high-rises stacked with drearily furnished rooms and basic amenities. With the arrival of more and more visitors, however, hoteliers have begun reinvesting in the city, giving much needed face-lifts to old haunts, just as a wave of new hotels have opened. Although the options are sparser than in North American and European cities, Rio now boasts lavish beachfront high-rises, stylish boutique spots, art-deco hotels, a handful of hostels and even several bed-and-breakfast options.

Reservations are a good idea in Rio – you can save 30% just by booking in advance. Hotel rates rise during the summer months (December through February), particularly during New Year's Eve and Carnaval. Most mid-range hotels and up will only book in four-day blocks around these holidays.

Our mid-range accommodation rates start at US$40 per double with bathroom. Anything that costs less has been placed under Cheap Sleeps at the end of each section. Keep in mind that many hotels add a combined 15% service and tax charge. The cheaper places don't generally bother with this.

> ## Top Five Sleeps
> - Cama e Café (p177) Best B&B experience.
> - Copacabana Palace Hotel (p170) Best restaurant – Cipriani, inside the Palace.
> - Marina All Suites (p168) Best-looking guests and staff.
> - Rio Hostel (p177) Best penny-pincher.
> - Sofitel Rio Palace (p172) Best pools.

IPANEMA & LEBLON

Ocean views with access to some of Rio's loveliest beaches, restaurants and bars make Ipanema and Leblon a magnet among travelers seeking the best of Rio. Although many more hotels litter the beaches of Leme and Copacabana, there are abundant lodging options here from boutique hotels to serviced apartments with plenty of straightforward standards in between. Prices here are generally much higher than elsewhere, though it's still possible to find affordable – if rather modest – lodging.

ARPOADOR INN Map pp236-8 *Hotel*
☎ 2523 0060; www.riodejaneiroguide.com/hotel/arpoador_inn.htm; Rua Francisco Otaviano 177, Ipanema; s/d US$60/70
This six-floor hotel is the only one in Ipanema or Copacabana that doesn't have a busy street between it and the beach. The rooms have decent beds and renovated bathrooms, although the carpets are a bit worn. Rooms are a bit musty at times – not a problem if you booked a *luxo* (ocean-fronting room). Just throw the windows wide and let in the fresh sea breeze. A friendly staff, beach-facing bar-restaurant and excellent location near Ipanema make Arpoador an attractive choice.

CAESAR PARK Map pp236-8 *Hotel*
☎ 2525 2525; www.caesar-park.com; Av Vieira Souto 460, Ipanema; d from US$275
A classical pianist plays throughout the day in the lavish lobby of Caesar Park. One of Ipanema's finest hotels caters largely to business travelers, though the beachside location and excellent amenities attract a few well-heeled vacationers as well. Caesar Park features impeccable service, spectacular views, good beach security in front and modern, spacious rooms with artwork on the walls, flat-screen TVs and high-speed Internet connections. The restaurant **Galani** (p106) serves a legendary *feijoada* on Saturday.

EVEREST PARK Map pp236-8 *Hotel*
☎ 2525 2200; www.everest.com.br; Rua Maria Quitéria 19, Ipanema; d from US$95
Constructed in 1990, Everest Park is a polished Ipanema hotel. The multilingual staff

is friendly (and enthusiastic), and the rooms are comfortable and nicely maintained. A woodsy smell in the corridors brings a scent of the country to the place. The Everest is just a block from the beach in a fantastic neighborhood.

HOTEL SAN MARCO Map pp236-8　　Hotel
☎ 2540 5032; www.sanmarcohotel.net; Rua Visconde de Pirajá 524, Ipanema; d from US$54

Like the Vermont up the road, it's all about location if you stay at the San Marco. Rooms are a bit cramped, and the green bedspreads aren't winning any style awards. In its defense, the rooms are clean, the staff is friendly and the beach is quite close.

HOTEL VERMONT Map pp236-8　　Hotel
☎ 2522 0057; fax 2267 7046; Rua Visconde de Pirajá 254, Ipanema; d from US$62

One of the few nonluxury hotels in Ipanema, the Hotel Vermont offers guests no-frills accommodations in a high-rise a few blocks from the beach. The Vermont is clearly in need of renovation. The rooms are small and a bit worn. Still, the location can't be beat, and you'll be in the company of plenty of other travelers if you decide to stay here.

IPANEMA FLAT HOTEL RESIDÊNCIA
Map pp236-8　　Serviced Apartments
☎ 2523 1292; fax 2287 9844; Rua Gomes Carneiro 137, Ipanema; s/d US$50/65

The place is suffering from a bad case of style envy: cheaply furnished rooms are seriously short on it and just aching to get some. Still the simple apartments have kitchens, balconies (no view) and bland but clean bedrooms at prices you're not likely to find elsewhere in this neighborhood.

IPANEMA INN Map pp236-8　　Hotel
☎ 2523 6092; www.ipanema.com/hotel/ipanema _inn.htm; Rua Maria Quitéria 27, Ipanema; s/d from US$70/80

Ipanema Inn is a simple but lovely hotel. Rooms are pleasant with nice touches like woodblock prints on the walls and modern bathrooms with full tubs. Front-facing rooms (*superiores*) don't have ocean views, but if you lean far enough out the window, you get a glimpse of the glistening sea. Ipanema Inn has a friendly, multilingual staff. Several suites on the top floors can accommodate larger groups.

Leblon and Ipanema (p57)

IPANEMA PLAZA Map pp236-8　　Hotel
☎ 3687 2000; www.ipanemaplazahotel.com; Rua Farme de Amoedo 34, Ipanema; s/d US$215/250

One of Ipanema's newest additions, the 18-story Plaza features modern appointed rooms with tile floors, broad comfortable beds and spacious bathrooms (all with tubs). The views are stunning – whether from the room or the rooftop pool. In addition to friendly multilingual staff, the plaza has lots of amenities – Internet hookups in the room, two saunas, a fitness center and a stylish restaurant.

IPANEMA SWEET
Map pp236-8　　Serviced Apartments
☎ Rua Visconde de Pirajá 161, Ipanema; s/d US$80/110

Modern, furnished apartments with kitchen, lounge and balcony (no view) are a good value at this friendly Ipanema spot. The pool isn't as sparkling clear as one would like, but still makes a nice sunning spot for the mix of Brazilians and international visitors who stay at Ipanema Sweet – and consistently rate the place highly.

MAR IPANEMA Map pp236-8　　Hotel
☎ 3875 9190; www.maripanema.com.br; Rua Visconde de Pirajá 539, Ipanema; d from US$92

Mar Ipanema is a decent option for those seeking a nice place in Ipanema without spending a fortune. There are no ocean views and the corridors are dark, but the rooms are decent, with comfortable beds and modern furnishings.

MARINA ALL SUITES

Map pp236-8 *Boutique Hotel*

☎ 2540 5212; www.marinaallsuites.com.br; Av Delfim Moreira 696, Leblon; d from US$235

Marina All Suites offers style and comfort with lovely ocean views. The suites here are elegantly furnished with decent sound systems and a suitable environment to host your own small parties. That may be one of the reasons the All Suites is popular with Giselle Bündchen and Arnold Schwarzenegger among other well-known guests. The hotel's eight designer suites rank among Rio's best lodging. The rooftop pool, private lounge space for guests and small movie theater are all nice touches. On the 2nd floor, the **Bar D'Hotel** (p126) attracts a mix of the beauty crowd and modelizers.

MARINA PALACE Map pp236-8 *Hotel*

☎ 2540 5212; www.hotelmarina.com.br; Av Delfim Moreira 696, Leblon; d from US$140

Run by the same family that owns the Marina All Suites, the hotel here recently received a much-needed renovation. Rooms have contemporary furnishings, large-screen TVs and spacious bathrooms. The pleasant pool provides a tranquil spot to refresh yourself in the heat of the afternoon.

MONSIEUR LE BLOND

Map pp236-8 *Serviced Apartments*

☎ 2239 4598; www.redeprotel.com.br/Index4.htm in Portuguese; Rua Bartolomeu Mitre 325, Leblon; d from US$175

Monsieur Le Blond combines the service of a hotel with the convenience of an apartment. The colorful apartments are all comfortably furnished with small kitchens, combined living-dining areas and balconies – some with

---

The Universe According to Philippe Starck

In 2005 Rio will receive its highest profile hotel since the opening of the Copacabana Palace in 1923. The Rio Universe, designed by Philippe Starck, will open in Ipanema – on Av Vieira Souto, number 80, to be exact. Unlike other boutique hotels the mega-designer has worked on, this will receive Starck's total imprint from top to bottom. Starck chose Rio as the site for his work because of its energy, sensuality and beauty, a combination that he often tries to achieve in his own work.

---

fine views. The pool makes a fine place for sunbathing and mingling with the young mostly Brazilian clients.

RITZ PLAZA HOTEL

Map pp236-8 *Serviced Apartments*

☎ 2540 4940; Av Ataulfo de Paiva 1280, Leblon; d US$75, apt US$110

The lobby of the Ritz Plaza is a peaceful place. It's a suitable introduction to this elegant all-suites hotel along an excellent stretch of Leblon. The rooms all have kitchen units, balconies – some with partial ocean views – art on the walls, good lighting and spotless bedrooms. The one-bedroom apartments have a separate lounge/dining area. There's also a pool and a sauna, and a few stained-glass ceiling panels along some of the halls. The price for all this seems surprisingly low.

SHERATON Map pp236-8 *Hotel*

☎ 2274 1122; www.sheraton-rio.com; Av Niemeyer 121, Vidgal; d from US$220

The Sheraton is a true resort hotel, one of the few in Rio with large grounds. The small beach is nearly private and sports facilities are excellent, including tennis, lovely pools and a good health club. It has a tour desk, airline offices, a nonsmoking floor, a business center and two very good restaurants. The only drawback is that it's a bit far from the action.

SOL IPANEMA Map pp236-8 *Hotel*

☎ 2525 8484; www.solipanema.com.br; Av Vieira Souto 320, Ipanema; d from US$120

The 15-story Sol Ipanema has an enviable position overlooking the beach. The rooms recently received a much-needed renovation and now feature modern furnishings, sleek bathrooms and new carpeting. A pool on the top floor makes a nice place for a drink or a dip in the afternoon. Oceanfront rooms cost about 20% more and are worth a splurge if you can swing it.

VISCONTI

Map pp236-8 *Serviced Apartments*

☎ 2523 0400; www.promenade.com.br; Rua Prudente de Morais 1050, Ipanema; d from US$115

An all-suites hotel, the Visconti has stylish modern apartments (stuffed leather furniture, modular lamps) with small kitchens, dining-living rooms and bedrooms. It's on a lovely residential street a block from the beach. Your neighbors will mostly be Brazilians.

Rio's Love Motels

Living in such a crowded city, Cariocas sometimes have a terrible time snatching a few moments of privacy. For those living with their parents or sharing a tiny apartment with roommates, an empty stretch of beach, a park bench, a seat in the back of the café – all are fine spots to steal a few kisses, but for more…progressive action, Cariocas take things elsewhere – to the motel, aka the *love* motel.

Love motels aren't so much a Carioca oddity as they are a Brazilian institution. They are found in every part of the country, usually sprouting along the outskirts of cities and towns. Some are designed with lavish facades – decked out to resemble medieval castles, Roman temples or ancient pyramids – while others blend more discreetly into the surrounding landscape. Regardless of the exterior, the interior is far removed from the 'less is more' design philosophy. Mirrors cover the ceiling while heart-shaped, vibrating beds stretch beneath them. Rose-tinted mood lights, Jacuzzis, televisions loaded with porn channels, dual-headed showers and a menu on the bedside table featuring sex toys guests can order to the room – all these come standard in most love motels. Such places scream seediness in the west. In Brazil, however, they're not viewed as anything out of the ordinary. People need a place for their liaisons – they might as well have a laugh, and a bit of fun while they're at it. The motels are used by kids who want to get away from their parents, parents who want to get away from their kids and couples who want to get away from their spouses. They are an integral part of the nation's social fabric, and it's not uncommon for Cariocas to host parties in them.

Most motels rent by the hour, though some give discounted prices for four-hour blocks or offer lunchtime specials. In Rio many of them are out on the roads that lead to the city, such as Av Brasil in the Zona Norte and Av Niemeyer between Leblon and São Conrado. There are a few, however, scattered about Centro, Flamengo and Botafogo.

The quality of the motels varies, reflecting their popularity across social classes. The most lavish are three-story suites with a hot tub on the top floor beneath a skylight, a sauna and bathroom on the 2nd floor, and the garage underneath (allowing anonymity). They come standard with all the other mood-enhancement features mentioned earlier. For the best suites, expect to pay around US$100 for eight hours – more on weekends. Standard rooms cost quite a bit less, though Cariocas claim that an equally fine time can be had there.

For those interested in checking out this cultural institution, there are a number of motels in the Zona Sul: **Magic** (Map pp228-30; ☎ 2507 2037; Rua Santo Amaro 11, Glória), **Sinless** (Map pp236-8; ☎ 2512 9913; Av Niemeyer 214, Vidigal) and **Shalimar** (Map pp236-8; ☎ 3322 3392; Av Niemeyer 218, Vidigal), right next door are a few.

CHEAP SLEEPS

CASA 6 IPANEMA Map pp236-8   *Hostel*
☎ 2247 1384; www.casa6ipanema.com; Rua Barão da Torre 175, Ipanema; dm US$14, d US$36

Halfway between the beach and the lake, Casa 6 Ipanema is a converted home in one of Rio's loveliest neighborhoods. It's a small place with a familial air: just one double room and two six-bed dorms. The simple rooms get a lot of natural light and are well maintained, and the owner has a wealth of information about the neighborhood. Although it's a pleasant-enough spot, it's its location that draws most travelers here.

COPACABANA & LEME

Copacabana has the highest number of hotels of any neighborhood in the city. Av Atlântica from Leme to Forte de Copacabana is lined with them, while its backstreets offer accommodations as well. The quality and price varies considerably here – which suits the range of backpackers, tour groups, business travelers, families and horny teenagers that

all find their way here. During New Year's Eve, this is the best place to be. If you have a beach-facing view, you'll be able to see the fireworks from your window (which will be adequately reflected in your bill).

ACAPULCO Map pp234-5   *Hotel*
☎ 2275 0022; www.acapulcocopacabanahotel.com.br; Rua Gustavo Sampaio 854, Leme; s/d from US$45/55, ste US$75-145

Acapulco lies on a quiet street a block from the beach, making it a fine spot for those interested in spending all their time in the waves. Its 122 rooms are comfortable and clean, but could use an update. They also have a handful of suites for those seeking a bit more room.

APA HOTEL Map pp234-5   *Hotel*
☎ 2548 8112; www.apahotel.com.br; Rua República do Peru 305, Copacabana; s/d/tr US$45/50/62

The Apa would be one of Copacabana's most stylish hotels were the year 1973. Unfortunately, times have changed, but the anointed style of Apa's 52 rooms lives on. What the place lacks in aesthetics, however, is counterbalanced by decent prices and clean rooms.

ATLANTIS COPACABANA HOTEL

Map pp234-5 *Hotel*

☎ 2521 1142; atlantisreservas@uol.com.br; Rua Bulhões de Carvalho 61, Copacabana; s/d from US$55/65

On the border between Copacabana and Ipanema, Atlantis is an excellent location for exploring either neighborhood. The rooms here are short on style and cheaply furnished, but the price isn't bad and the staff is helpful. Rooms above the 9th floor have fine views. A modest pool and sauna are on the roof.

AUGUSTO'S COPACABANA

Map pp234-5 *Hotel*

☎ 2547 1800; www.augustoshotel.com.br; Rua Bolívar 119, Copacabana; s/d from US$65/75

Two blocks from the beach, Augusto's is a fairly recent addition to Copacabana (1998). Its modern, comfortable rooms attract a mix of Brazilian and foreign visitors and 'businessmen in affairs' (according to the brochure). A rooftop pool, Jacuzzi, sauna and fitness center are nice additions.

BIARRITZ Map pp234-5 *Hotel*

☎ 2522 3705; hoteisgandara@infolink.com.br; Rua Aires Saldanha 54, Copacabana; s/d US$40/50

You pay less for less at Biarritz. Rooms and elevators are designed for tiny, narrow people, and the bathrooms feature an unhappy marriage of pastels and linoleum. The price, however, is excellent for the area, and the rooms are well scrubbed by the staff. Biarritz is on a quiet street a block from the beach.

COPACABANA HOTEL RESIDÊNCIA

Map pp234-5 *Serviced Apartments*

☎ 2548 7212; www.copahotelresid.com.br; Rua Barata Ribeiro 222, Copacabana; s/d US$70/90

A few blocks from the beach, the Copacabana Hotel Residência is an excellent choice for those wishing for a bit more space. The 70 suites here all have small kitchen units, lounge rooms with good natural lighting and clean, well-maintained quarters. Although the rooms are all cheaply furnished, it's a good value for the money. (They also have a workout center, pool and bar in the building). They give bigger discounts the longer you stay, so plan accordingly.

COPACABANA PALACE

Map pp234-5 *Hotel*

☎ 2548 7070; www.copacabanapalace.com.br; Av Atlântica 1702, Copacabana; d from US$300

The city's most well-known hotel, the Palace has hosted heads of state, rock stars and prominent personalities in the past. The dazzling white facade dates from the 1920s, when it became a symbol of the city. Although its fate was uncertain as Copacabana fell into decline in the '70s and '80s, today it is again the premier hotel of Rio – following a massive face-lift. The Palace has spacious rooms with parquet floors and balconies, a lovely pool, excellent restaurants – the formal **Cipriani** (p113) and the Pergula – and service suitable for royalty (Princess Di stayed, as did Queen Elizabeth).

Copacabana Palace (above)

COPACABANA PRAIA HOTEL

Map pp234-5   *Hotel*

☎ 2522 5646; www.copacabanapraiahotel.com.br;
Rua Francisco Otaviano 30, Copacabana; d US$60

The 11-story Copacabana Praia provides a nice value for the money. All rooms have balconies and top floor ones have partial sea views. Its comfortable but compact rooms attract a mix of young travelers and Brazilians. The pool upstairs is small but makes a nice spot for a cocktail at sunset.

COPACABANA RIO HOTEL

Map pp234-5   *Hotel*

☎ 2267 9900; www.copacabanariohotel.com.br; Av
NS de Copacabana 1256, Copacabana; s/d US$50/60

A block from the beach, the Copacabana Rio offers basic rooms – some with balconies – and modern bathrooms. The rooms are a bit small, and some of the carpets here show some serious use, but the upstairs pool and bar area is nice.

DUCASSE RIO HOTEL

Map pp234-5   *Hotel*

☎ 2522 1191; www.hotelducasse.com.br in Portuguese; Rua Sá Ferreira 76, Copacabana; s/d US$45/55

In this price bracket, Ducasse is ahead of the rest. Its medium-sized rooms are simply furnished but bright and cozy. All rooms ending in 1, 2, 3 and 4 have balconies, which are just large enough to step onto and take a breath of ocean air. The rooftop sauna is nice, the pool so-so (with views of the favela Pavãozinho). English-speaking staff make it a homey spot.

HOTEL DEBRET Map pp234-5   *Hotel*

☎ 2522 0132; www.debret.com; Av Atlântica 3564,
Copacabana; d from US$65

The Debret is a traditional hotel in a converted apartment building. It has simple colonial-style furnishings and nice views from the top-floor restaurant. The ocean-fronting rooms are among the best you'll find at this price.

HOTEL SANTA CLARA

Map pp234-5   *Hotel*

☎ 2256 2650; www.hotelsantaclara.com.br; Rua
Décio Vilares 316, Copacabana; s/d US$35/42

Up the street from a neighborhood park lies the charming, three-story Hotel Santa Clara. The white-washed exterior and blue shutters face a peaceful street, making it a good choice for those looking for a more relaxed Copacabana experience. The upstairs rooms are best, with wood floors, a writing desk and a balcony that catches a nice breeze in the evenings.

HOTEL TOLEDO

Map pp234-5   *Hotel*

☎ 2257 1995; hoteltoledo@bol.com.br; Rua Domingos
Ferreira 71, Copacabana; minis/s/d US$30/45/55

A block from the beach, the Toledo offers good value for those who don't need beach-facing views. The rooms need a bit of modernizing, but they're clean and adequately furnished; the friendly staff here struggles with English. The Toledo also has some closet-sized singles (minis).

LE MERIDIEN OTHON PALACE

Map pp234-5   *Hotel*

☎ 3873 8888; www.meridien-br.com; Av Atlântica
1020, Leme; d from US$160

A decadent affair, Le Meridien has all the trappings of luxury (it's four stars, by the way): the crisply dressed staff, the elegant lobby, the excellent French restaurant overlooking the beach on the 37th floor. It's quite likely that your stay here will be a success. The rooms are comfortable and spacious but hardly inspiring. The view, however, is, so be sure to book the *de luxo* (ocean-fronting room).

LEME OTHON PALACE

Map pp234-5   *Hotel*

☎ 3873 5900; www.othon.com.br; Av Atlântica 656,
Leme; d from US$90

Looming over Leme Beach, the Othon Palace has all large, decent rooms with modern furnishings. Deluxe rooms cost only a fraction more than standard ones and have balconies with ocean views. At times the place betrays the characteristics of a bland, Copa high-rise hotel, but the helpful staff bring a humanizing element to it.

LUXOR COPACABANA

Map pp234-5   *Hotel*

☎ 2545 1070; www.luxorhoteis.com.br; Av Atlântica
2554, Copacabana; d from US$100, d with sea view
from US$150

Excellent service is a trademark at four-star Luxor Copacabana. Its 113 rooms are pleasantly furnished; the jacaranda wood finishings add an organic element to the earthy hues. Rooms in the standard category feel a bit small. Luxor also has a room with facilities for the disabled.

OLINDA OTHON CLASSIC

Map pp234-5   *Hotel*

☎ 2257 1890; www.othon.com.br; Av Atlântica 2230, Copacabana; d from US$85

The once-majestic Olinda Othon has an oversized marble lobby that recalls its prominence in the '50s. Although its grandeur has faded, it still has its charm. Rooms are spacious and comfortable, and many have ocean views (some also have balconies).

ORLA COPACABANA

Map pp234-5   *Boutique Hotel*

☎ 2525 2425; www.orlahotel.com.br; Av Atlântica 4122, Copacabana; s/d from US$95/120

The recently opened (2001) Orla Copacabana wins the style award – at least on this side of Arpoador. It has sleek lounge chairs, artfully lit flower bouquets and giant canvases lining the narrow lobby. Upstairs, the design falters a bit in lower-end rooms (standards) but still presents modern furnishings, excellent marble-fixtured bathrooms and decent views. At higher prices – particularly in the stylish suites – the simple but sleek design continues. The rooftop pool and patio are also gorgeous.

PARTHENON ARPOADOR

Map pp234-5   *Boutique Hotel*

☎ 3222 9600; parthenonarpoador@accorhotels.com.br; Rua Francisco Otaviano 61, Copacabana; suites from US$150

The all-suites Parthenon Arpoador opened in 2003, which makes it one of Rio's newest hotels. It's also one of its most stylish. Young good-looking staff lead guests to spotless suites. Each has sleek white leather sofas that open into beds, modern kitchenettes, TVs with a stereo and a DVD player, ambient lighting and comfortable bedrooms. All have verandas – though there's no view. The long, slim swimming pool is good for swimming laps, not for lounging. There's also a sauna and a workout room.

PESTANA RIO ATLÂNTICA

Map pp234-5   *Hotel*

☎ 2548 6332; www.pestanahotels.com.br; Av Atlântica 2964, Copacabana; d from US$220

The Pestana is one of Rio's best hotels, featuring spacious rooms with modern furnishings and all the amenities a pop star would expect (pool, small-screen theater, workout center, wet and dry saunas). You can get significant discounts by booking through a travel agent.

Top Five Hotel Bars

- **Copacabana Palace** (p170) Candles glowing on the tables at the **Poolside Bar** (p129), the tropical breeze, the night full of possibilities…
- **Marina All-Suites** (p168) At the **Bar D'Hotel** (p126) a super-stylish crowd gathers over tropical cocktails – with names like Urca and Ipanema – to the backdrop of waves crashing on Ipanema beach.
- **Rio Othon Palace** The 30th floor **Skylab Bar** (p129) makes a fine setting for *caipirinhas*, with the Cidade Maravilhosa unfolding beneath you.
- **Sheraton** (p168) Daring drink combinations, views of Ipanema and Leblon, and a mixed crowd, make it worth the trip to **Bar 121** (p125).
- **Sofitel** (p172) Sip scotch inside the wood-paneled **Horse's Neck Bar** (p129)… Or skip the scotch and step out on the terrace for stellar views of Copacabana Beach.

RESIDENCIAL APARTT

Map pp234-5   *Serviced Apartments*

☎ 2522 1722; www.apartt.com.br; Rua Francisco Otaviano 42, Copacabana; s/d US$60/75

Located in Arpoador between Copa and Ipanema Beaches, Residencial Apartt is an all-suites hotel with excellent prices. Apartt's 25 one-bedroom suites are complete with small kitchen units, a lounge room (with cable TV) and a bedroom. Furnishings here are dated – floral patterns, dingy yellows and greens dominate. Breakfast is included in the price (served until 1pm).

RIO ROISS HOTEL
Map pp234-5   *Hotel*

☎ 2521 1142; rioroiss@tropicalbr.com.br; Rua Aires Saldanha 48, Copacabana; s/d US$60/80

Like dozens of other hotels in Copacabana, Rio Roiss needs to modernize its look. Its rooms are decent enough – good beds and wood finishes, but you'll feel like you're stepping back in time at the Rio Roiss. Modern Rooms in the *luxo* category have partial sea views and are more spacious (though lacking in furniture to fill the space).

SOFITEL RIO PALACE
Map pp234-5   *Hotel*

☎ 2525 1232; www.accor-hotels.com; Av Atlântica 4240, Copacabana; d from US$180

Neck and neck with that *other* five-star hotel up the road (the Copacabana Palace), Sofitel does its best to dazzle visitors with its lavishness. The excellent service, large and comfortable rooms, exquisite restaurants, lovely pools and splendid views have earned Sofitel many fans – including Frank Sinatra, who once stayed and played here.

CHEAP SLEEPS

CHE LAGARTO Map pp234-5 _Hostel_

☎ 2256 2776; www.chelagarto.com; Rua Anita Garibaldi 87, Copacabana; dm/d US$14/30

A current favorite among young backpackers, Che Lagarto attracts a rowdy crowd that gathers around the pool table in the evening for cheap drinks and pickup games. The staff is particularly keen on arranging nights out for guests. It's a good place for meeting young partiers, but the quarters are very tight here.

COPACABANA PRAIA HOSTEL
Map pp234-5 _Hostel_

☎ 2547 5422; Rua Tenente Marones de Gusmão 85, Copacabana; dm/d/tr US$12/24/32

Overlooking a small park on a tranquil street, the Praia offers some of the cheapest beds in Copacabana. Although the staff at times doesn't take much interest in its guests, it remains popular with budget travelers.

HOTEL ANGRENSE Map pp234-5 _Hotel_

☎ 2548 0509; www.angrensehotel.com.br; Travessa Angrense 25, Copacabana; s/d US$28/42, without bath US$23/30

Next door to the Pousada Girassol (this page), the dark wood lobby of the Hotel Angrense vaguely resembles an old hunting lodge. It has several upstairs rooms with simple beds, windows that get nice light and basic bathrooms. The downstairs rooms are a bit grungier with shared bathrooms and dark rooms. The best features of Angrense are outside: the front patio makes a fine spot for a drink in the evening (you may need one if you stay here).

HOTEL COPA LINDA Map pp234-5 _Hotel_

☎ 2267 3399; 2nd fl, Av NS de Copacabana 956, Copacabana; s or d US$27

Couples traveling on a tight budget might consider the Copa Linda. The front room that opens onto the road is passable if a bit musty. The rooms in the back are dark and depressing.

POUSADA GIRASSOL pp234-5 _Hotel_

☎ 2256 6951; pousadagirassol@infolink.com.br; Travessa Angrense 25A, Copacabana; s/d/tr US$26/38/44

On a small lane off busy Av NS de Copacabana two small _pousadas_ lie side by side. Girassol is the better of the two with bright, cheerful rooms with ceiling fans, decent beds and fairly maintained bathrooms. The Girassol is nothing to get worked up over, but it's a good value for the neighborhood. The friendly staff speaks English.

RIO BACKPACKERS Map pp234-5 _Hostel_

☎ 2236 3803; www.riobackpackers.com.br; Travessa Santa Leocádia 38, Copacabana; dm US$14

Young backpackers flock to this popular spot in Copacabana. Guests have access to the pool table, lounge, kitchen and Internet. Many who pass through the doors here end up staying for much longer than they had planned – perhaps because of the hostel's relaxed vibe. The friendly owner can advise on how to spend a decadent night out, arrange Portuguese lessons or provide other traveler tips.

BOTAFOGO & URCA

Botafogo and Urca are among the least explored neighborhoods by foreign visitors. There aren't many accommodations in the area to draw them here, but there are abundant opportunities to experience authentic Rio – its tree-lined streets, old-school _botecos_ and hidden restaurants – if you do stay here.

O VELEIRO Map pp232-3 _B&B_

☎ 3473 3022; www.oveleiro.com; d US$50-80

Located in a lovely rustic house, O Veleiro is surrounded by remnants of Atlantic forest on all sides. It's a 20-minute walk up from Botafogo Beach on an old colonial cobblestone road, with a fine view of Cristo Redentor (p76). There's a pool, a backyard and a garden on site. The owners prefer not to include the address in guidebooks, so for more information, visit their website.

CHEAP SLEEPS
CARIOCA EASY HOSTEL
Map pp232-3 _Hostel_

☎ 2295 7805; www.cariocahostel.com.br; Rua Marechal Cantuária 168, Urca; dm US$15

This locally owned hostel gets excellent reviews from guests. A mix of Brazilian and

Botafogo (p65) and Cristo Redentor (p76)

international backpackers enjoy the tranquil location near Pão de Açúcar and the laidback vibe that flows through the space. The friendly English-speaking owner takes an interest in her guests and helps to arrange nights out to samba clubs, dance parties or whatever guests have in mind.

HI CHAVE RIO DE JANEIRO
Map pp232-3   *Hostel*

☎ 2286 0303; www.riohostel.com.br; Rua General Dionísio 63, Botafogo; dm US$12

The HI hostel in Botafogo was one of Rio's first hostels. It's still a successful endeavor, attracting a mix of Brazilians and international travelers here to drink up Rio's nightlife. The dorm accommodates 70, and it often gets crowded here (reservations are wise). Non HI card holders pay 50% more and can only stay 24 hours, but you can buy an HI card there for US$10.

FLAMENGO

Although decent beaches are far from Flamengo (Praia do Flamengo is near, but the water is too polluted for swimming), the neighborhood has its appeal. One of Rio's oldest neighborhoods attracts visitors who are seeking a more authentically Carioca experience – its neighborhood feel, traditional bars and youthful inhabitants adding to the charm. Flamengo's other big draw is its range of decent accommodations at much lower prices than those found in Copacabana or Ipanema.

HOTEL FLÓRIDA Map pp232-3   *Hotel*

☎ 2556 5242; www.windsorhoteis.com; Rua Ferreira Viana 81, Flamengo; d from US$72

One of Flamengo's best hotels, the Flórida has a variety of rooms available. At the low end, the space is small and the furnishings dated, but the mattresses are still new and the bathrooms are sleek and modern. At the other end of the checkered marble corridors are the *luxos* with huge beds, ample space and Jacuzzis in the bath. The pool on the roof has lovely views (including Pão de Açúcar), and there's a workout center and sauna on hand.

MENGO PALACE HOTEL
Map pp232-3   *Hotel*

☎ 2556 5343; mengohotel@infolink.com.br; Rua Corrêa Dutra 31, Flamengo; suites s/d US$45/55

Offering some of the more affordable suites in Rio, Mengo Palace is a clean, modern hotel with a forlorn air about it. The suites are small with pressed wood floors, carpeting on the walls and Jacuzzi bathtubs big enough for two. The beds are a little stiff but still do the trick. A few travelers find their way here, but the Mengo Palace draws most of its visitors from around Rio State.

CHEAP SLEEPS
HOTEL FERREIRA VIANA
Map pp232-3   *Hotel*

☎ 2205 7396; Rua Ferreira Viana 58, Flamengo; s with shared bathroom US$14, d with bath US$19-24

At these prices one would expect far less than the Ferreira Viana provides. There are a few nice rooms here with good light, bright tile floors, modern furnishings and plenty of space. Not all the rooms are decent, however, so take a look at a few of them before committing.

HOTEL PAYSANDU Map pp232-3   *Hotel*

☎ 2558 7270; wwwpaysanduhotel.com.br; Rua Paissandu 23, Flamengo; s/d with shared bathroom US$18/23, d with bath US$35-48

Occasionally classical music plays overhead in the lobby of the Paysandu. It's not a fancy place, but nice touches like these show that they're certainly trying. Rooms reflect much the same aesthetic: among the best selections, rooms feature high ceilings, balconies, good light and space to stretch out. The carpet is thin, but then so is the price tag.

HOTEL REGINA Map pp232-3 *Hotel*
☎ 2556 1647; www.hotelregina.com.br; Rua Ferreira Viana 29, Flamengo; s/d US$27/37

On a quiet street in Flamengo, the Hotel Regina offers decent rooms with recently renovated bathrooms. There are a few problems with the Regina: carpets are a bit worn, the furnishings are cheap and the floorboards creak when you walk across them. But you could do much worse in this neighborhood, and overall the Regina isn't bad.

CATETE & GLÓRIA

Budget hotels sprout like weeds from the crumbling buildings on either side of the Catete metro station. Although the exteriors of many of these hotels suggest that they're unpolished gems, once inside you realize that this is rarely the case. Many of these hotels need work – and lots of it. So if you don't mind roughing it, you'll be able to take advantage of the city's cheapest accommodations. Catete is already Rio's unofficial gringolândia, and if you're looking to hook up with other backpackers, this

area is a good start. Incidentally, both Catete and Glória have some excellent places to stay, and like Flamengo you'll pay much less than you would further south.

FLAMENGO PALACE Map pp232-3 *Hotel*
☎ 2557 7552; hotelflamengopalace.cjb.net; Praia do Flamengo 6, Flamengo; s/d from US$40/46

That look from 1975 – which is when the Flamengo Palace was built – never looked so good. Rooms are nothing special, it's true – basic beds with simple furnishings – but there are some interesting touches, like oval wooden-framed mirrors and daring combinations between the patterns on the curtains and the color of the carpeting. The staff is friendly, if a bit unused to seeing foreign guests; *luxo* rooms have excellent views of the bay but are noisier.

GLÓRIA Map pp228-30 *Hotel*
☎ 2555 7373; www.hotelgloriario.com.br; Rua do Russel 632, Glória; d from US$90

Once a grand 1920s beachfront hotel, Glória still retains the aura of its past splendor. Red carpets line the hallways with old paintings,

---

Long-Term Rentals

If you're planning to stay in Rio for longer than a few nights, you should consider renting an apartment. There are a number of agencies dedicated to tracking down short-term hires for foreigners, and it's a fairly straightforward affair. Usually, you pay a small deposit along with the price of the rental up front, sign away your life, and you're all set. Although most of the agencies are in Copacabana, they can help find flats in other areas of town if you want to get off the beaten path. As is the case for hotels, the price of apartment rentals rises considerably during Carnaval and New Year's – though there's almost always something available.

Apartur Imóveis (Map pp236-8; ☎ 2287 5757; Rua Visconde de Pirajá 371S/204, Ipanema) This Ipanema-based agency specializes in one- and two-bedroom apartments in the area and can also arrange vacation house rentals in other parts of the state.

Copacabana Holiday (Map pp234-5; ☎ 2542 1525; www.copacabanaholiday.com.br; Rua Barata Ribeiro 90A, Copacabana) This agency rents apartments for a minimum of three days starting at US$30 per night. The manager Cláudio speaks English and is very helpful.

Fantastic Rio (pp234-5; ☎ 2543 2667; www.fantasticrio.hpg.com.br; Apt 501, Av Atlântica 974, Leme) Multilingual Peter Corr of Fantastic Rio rents a range of apartments from modest one-bedrooms to spacious four-bedrooms with beach views.

Rio Apartment Services (☎ 2256 7920; www.rioapartmentservices.com) One of the larger agencies in town, it lists dozens of places for hire on its website. The agency also arranges airport transportation if you request.

Rio Flat Service (Map pp236-8; ☎ 2512 9922; Rua Guilherme 332, Leblon) This Leblon-based agency has a range of local listings.

Vanna Rocha (☎ 2548 5030; www.vannarioflats.com) Vanna maintains a website of apartment listings from Leblon, Ipanema and Copacabana. Her English is good, and she has competitive prices.

Yolanda Thiémard (Map pp234-5; ☎ 2267 0054; Av Prado Junior 165 C02, Copacabana) Yolanda has a small selection of apartments in Copacabana; her prices are among the best in the area. She speaks French and English.

Yvonne Reimann (Map pp234-5; ☎ 2267 0054; Apt 605, Av Atlântica 4066, Copacabana) Yvonne rents a range of apartments in the area – some with local phone service. She speaks French, German and English.

antique fixtures and a liberal use of brass spread evenly throughout the palatial hotel. Glória lost its glory when the tunnel to Copacabana was constructed. It later lost its beach when the landfill of 1965 was landscaped into the **Parque do Flamengo** (p75). None of that has stopped the Glória from maintaining its status as a fine hotel. If you plan to stay here, note that there are two parts to the hotel. The old part with the antique-filled rooms, fine verandas and sitting rooms naturally costs more. The new part was built around the late '80s and lacks the charm of the rest of the Glória.

HOTEL NOVO MUNDO Map pp232-3 *Hotel*
☎ 2265 2369; www.hotelnovomundo-rio.com.br; Praia do Flamengo 20, Flamengo; d from US$75

With its proximity to Centro, the Hotel Novo Mundo attracts a large percentage of business travelers. Its rooms range from small, well-maintained standards to large furnished suites with balconies overlooking the bay or the lush Catete gardens next door. Some things around the Novo Mundo could use a bit of modernizing, but overall it's a nicely run affair.

IMPERIAL HOTEL Map pp232-3 *Hotel*
☎ 2556 5212; www.imperialhotel.com.br; Rua do Catete 186, Catete; s/d from US$35/45

The Imperial Hotel is an excellent choice for Catete. The lovely white building has only three stories but goes back endlessly to reveal a new crop of recently renovated rooms and suites (the only difference between suites and the *luxos* are the Jacuzzi tubs – which for some unknown reason are quite popular in this part of the city.) The pool in back is nice, and most of the rooms are bright and well maintained.

CHEAP SLEEPS

HOTEL MONTERREY Map pp232-3 *Hotel*
☎ 2265 9899; Rua Arturo Bernardes 39, Catete; s with shared bath US$12, s/d with bath US$16/21

Short of sleeping in the metro station, you can't find much cheaper lodging than the Hotel Monterrey. Rooms here are basic: a small bed, a TV, a table, a fan and maybe a window, but the place is fairly clean, and the owner is a kind-hearted old soul. Watch the news with him in the lounge, and you'll learn plenty about the city. Breakfast arrives at your door every morning – a touch of luxury in an otherwise humble shelter.

HOTEL RIAZOR Map pp232-3 *Hotel*
☎ 2225 0121; hotelriazor1@hotmail.com; Rua do Catete 160, Catete; s/d/tr US$15/18/28

The lovely colonial facade of the Riazor hides basic quarters short on style. Rooms aren't bad for the price – sparkling wall paint and round beds are features in some. Others are simple, straightforward affairs: bed, bathroom, TV, air-conditioning, and a door by which to exit the room and explore the city. A good mix of travelers and Brazilians take advantage of Riazor's low prices.

HOTEL RIO CLARO Map pp232-3 *Hotel*
☎ 2558 5180; Rua do Catete 233, Catete; s/d/tw US$20/25/30

The bare bones Rio Claro is the best of the budgets hotels for those looking to sleep on the cheap. Clean well-maintained rooms and baths have white tile floors, air-conditioning and half-decent beds. Plenty of backpackers are around.

HOTEL TURÍSTICO Map pp228-30 *Hotel*
☎ 2557 7698; fax 2558 9388; Ladeira da Glória 30, Glória; s/d US$25/29

On a quiet street near the **Igreja da NS da Glória do Outeiro** (p78), the Turístico is a friendly spot that attracts a good mix of young Brazilian and international travelers. Its clean, well-maintained rooms with balconies are a good value, and the staff is much friendlier here than in most of the area's budget hotels.

CENTRO & CINELÂNDIA

Centro and Cinelândia cater mostly to Brazilian business travelers with small expense accounts. Aside from its proximity to excellent lunch spots, pedestrian shopping areas and a few noteworthy street Carnavals, the area doesn't offer many attractions. Centro gets deserted after 10pm during the week and remains pretty barren over the weekends, making it an unsafe area to linger. However, if it's business you're here for or just feel some indescribable urge to stay in Centro, there are some options.

CENTER HOTEL Map pp228-30 *Hotel*
☎ 2296 6677; www.centerhotel.com.br; Av Rio Branco 33, Centro; s/d from US$50/60

This 12-story hotel on busy Rio Branco is a good mid-range option for those wishing to stay in Centro. Rooms are clean and comfortable with nice touches in some – carved wood headboards, artwork on the walls. Higher floors have decent views of downtown.

GUANABARA PALACE Map pp228-30 *Hotel*
☎ 2216 1313; www.windsorhoteis.com; Av Presidente Vargas 392; d from US$110

Centro's nicest hotel has clean, modern rooms with hardwood furnishings and nice views of Baía de Guanabara. Some of the rooms feel cramped, although there's abundant space on the rooftop pool and bar – with spectacular views of the bay. There's also a small fitness center on site.

CHEAP SLEEPS
AMBASSADOR HOTEL Map pp228-30 *Hotel*
☎ 2299 2870; fax 2220 4783; Rua Senador Dantas 25, Centro; s/d US$24/28

This high-rise hotel has unintended style: a few art-deco fixtures and trim furniture with nice lines are scattered among rooms full of brown, angry curtains and clinical-looking beds. The carpets are worn, but the bathrooms are clean, and the price is, well, nice.

ITAJUBÁ HOTEL Map pp228-30 *Hotel*
☎ 2210 3163; itahotel@openlink.com.br; Rua Álvaro Alvim 23, Cinelândia; s/d/tr weekdays US$24/34/45, weekends US$18/22/34

If you're looking for monastic simplicity, Itajubá is the place for you. Rooms are sparse but clean, and the beds are neither good nor bad. The service here is decent, and each room has a TV, refrigerator and telephone.

SANTA TERESA
Although accommodations are still sparse in the Monmartre of the tropics, some of the more unusual accommodation options can be found just a short tram ride from Centro. Santa Teresa is not an area for those looking to spend their days on the beach. It does, however, attract a broad mix of travelers (some of whom later become expats), seeking the artistic heart of Rio. Vibrant restaurants and bars and its proximity to the samba clubs in Lapa add to Santa Teresa's appeal, though you'll want to take care when walking around here.

Airport Accommodations
At the international airport there are two hotels. The better of the two is the **Rio Luxor Aeroporto** (☎ 2468 8998; www.luxor-hotels.com.br; d US$120, day-use US$80). Situated on the 3rd floor of the airport, the 64 rooms here are comfortably furnished, with cable TV, modern bathrooms and 24-hour room service. There's also a bar in the hotel. The **Hotel Pousada Galeão** (☎ /fax 2398 3848; d from US$65) is on the 1st floor of international arrivals. Rooms are slightly smaller, but are comfortably furnished – lots of dark wood in the interior.

CAMA E CAFÉ Map p231 *B&B*
☎ 2221 7635; www.camaecafe.com; Rua Progresso 67, Santa Teresa; d from US$30

Run by three young Santa Teresans dedicated to rejuvenating the neighborhood, Cama e Café is a bed and breakfast network that links travelers with local residents. They have some 50 houses to choose from, and guests can select their accommodations by location, comfort level or shared interests – art, music, dogs – with their host(s). It's a brilliant way to experience one of the city's most charming neighborhoods. Accommodations range from modest to lavish, with a decent breakfast and sizable rooms with private bathrooms common to all. Cama e Café's website has listings.

CHEAP SLEEPS
HOTEL SANTA TERESA Map p231 *Hotel*
☎ 2508 9355; Rua Almirante Alexandrino 660, Santa Teresa; s/d/tr with bath US$17/27/44, s/d without bath US$12/18; bonde, bus 206, 214

The worn Hotel Santa Teresa has seen better days. Its murky swimming pool and grungy carpets need some work, and the rooms are spare. Still, there's something charming about the place. It has old banisters and wooden stairs, high ceilings and shutters opening onto the city. Whether this makes up for the flabby beds is the essential – and ultimately unanswerable – question.

RIO HOSTEL Map p231 *Hostel*
☎ 3852 0827; www.riohostel.com; Rua Joaquim Murtinho 361, Santa Teresa; dm/d US$13/32; bonde, bus 206, 214

The Rio Hostel provides travelers with a home away from home. The spacious lounge, backyard patio with pool, ping-pong room and kitchen for guests all add to the charm of one of Santa Teresa's hidden gems. The rooms are clean, and the lovely private room features stunning views when you throw open the shutters – book it if you can. The hostel overlooks downtown Rio and lies along the *bonde* line. It can be a bit tricky to find – if you reach Curvelo Square (the first *bonde* stop), you've gone too far. Disembark and walk 200 meters back down the hill.

BARRA DA TIJUCA & WEST OF RIO

A number of pleasant options lie west of Leblon. If you stay in Barra, you'll need a car to get around, but once there, you'll be able to enjoy some of Rio's most seductive beaches far from the tourist crowds.

ATLÂNTICO SUL Map p239　　　　　*Hotel*
☎ 2490 2050; www.atlanticosulhotel.com.br; Rua Professor Armando Ribeira 25, Recréio dos Bandeirantes; d from US$80

Overlooking the beach, the high-rise Atlântico Sul is at the far end of Barra Tijuca and the border of Recreio dos Bandeirantes. It has a fine pool, decent apartments and a lot of vacationing Brazilians. It's on the corner of Av Sernambetiba across from the beach.

CASA DEL MAR Map p239　　　　　*Hotel*
☎ 2253 1760; www.promenade.com.br; Av Sernambetiba 5740, Barra da Tijuca; d from US$160

This lovely all-suites hotel features modern furnishings spread between the living-dining

area and the bedroom. The location near the beach is excellent.

ENTREMARES Map p239　　　　　*Hotel*
☎ 2494 3887; www.entremares.com.br in Portuguese; Av Erico Verissimo 846, Barra da Tijuca; d from US$70

Entremares has pleasant, comfortable rooms that catch a nice ocean breeze. The Barra beach stretches out to the west (Entremares is among the first stops after the Gávea tunnel).

INTERCONTINENTAL Map pp226-7　　*Hotel*
☎ 3323 2200; Av Preifeito Mendes de Morais 222, São Conrado; d from US$250

The Intercontinental is the place to stay if you never want to leave the hotel. The restaurants are excellent, the pools are picturesque and the rooms are sumptuous – all have balconies. It's close to the São Conrado shopping mall, but apart from that there's not much you can walk to except the beach. The hotel runs a complimentary bus shuttle to Copacabana and Ipanema. The large grounds and abundant facilities make this ideal for kids.

PRAIA LINDA Map p239　　　　　*Hotel*
☎ 2494 2186; www.hotelpraialinda.com.br; Av Pepê, Barra da Tijuca; d from US$90

In an excellent location, facing the Praia do Pepê (Pepe Beach), the Praia Linda is the pick of the bunch if you're staying in Barra. The rooms are clean and comfortable, though the restaurant isn't – but the beach and the ocean views are the big draw here.

Excursions

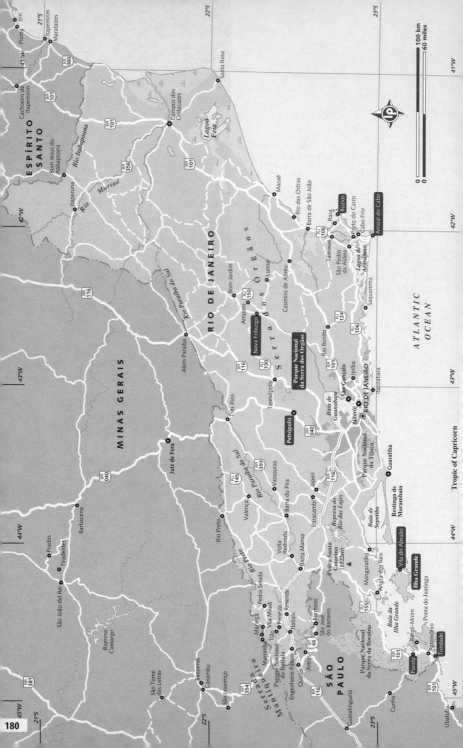

Excursions

The state of Rio de Janeiro, about the size of Switzerland, offers the traveler much more than just the Cidade Maravilhosa. Gorgeous beaches, forested islands, mountains and colonial settlements all lie within a few hours' drive from the city. Wherever you decide to go, the journey there is also likely to be a highlight – at least once you're out of the busy city center.

The city of Rio and the giant Baía de Guanabara, which has 131km of coast and 113 islands, divide the coast into two regions, the Costa Verde (to the west) and the Costa do Sol (to the east). Along the Costa Verde, where the mountains meet the sea, there are hundreds of islands and beaches waiting to be explored as well as lush forests complete with waterfalls, and panoramic views. East of the city lies the Costa do Sol, where the mountains begin to rise further inland. The littoral is filled with lagoons and swampland. Stretching away from the coast are plains that extend about 30km to the mountains.

North of Rio lies a wall of mountains covered in Atlantic rain forest, where temperatures are much cooler than in the city. Several charming towns in the area provide superb hiking and climbing opportunities.

ISLANDS

Two hours west of the city, just off the verdant Costa Verde, is one of the country's most beautiful islands. Ilha Grande (p184) has dozens of untouched beaches and lush, rain-forest-covered hills, which provide splendid hikes. The lack of cars on the island ensures a mellow, laid-back stay.

NATURE

Resplendent national parks set in the mountains offer abundant hiking and trekking options for those needing a dose of nature after a stay in the city. North of Rio, the fantastic peaks of the Parque Nacional da Serra dos Órgãos (p184) are cooled by crisp mountain air, offering a perfect escape from the tropical summer heat.

BEACHES

Búzios (p186) may no longer be the tiny fishing village it was back in the 1960s, but its beaches haven't changed much since then. Over a dozen lovely stretches of sand lie in the area, and by night, the bayside promenade offers plenty of diversions among the many outdoor restaurants and bars. Beautiful beaches also lie near Paraty (p182), while Arraial do Cabo (p188) and surfer-favorite Saquarema (p188) draw their share of visitors.

TOWNS

Amid a cool mountainous climate, Petrópolis (p189), with its canals, landscaped parks and city squares, has a European air. It's also a good place to soak up some history in its palaces and museums. Or head west to Paraty (p182), a perfectly preserved colonial town, whose colorful buildings and cobbled streets hide some of the state's culinary gems.

DRIVES

The Costa Verde (Green Coast) provides the setting for one of the country's most spectacular drives. The panoramic road hugs the ocean as it winds its way past lush peaks, beaches and colonial settlements.

PARATY

☎ 24

'...If there were paradise on earth, it wouldn't be very far from here!' Explorer Amerigo Vespucci was dumbfounded when he first laid eyes on the steep, forested mountains going right down into the sea, the jumbled coastline with hundreds of islands and jutting peninsulas, and the clear, calm waters of the Baía da Ilha Grande lapping at the shore. All of this forms the backdrop to one of Brazil's most enchanting settlements, the 17th-century village of Paraty.

Transportation

Distance from Rio 261km
Direction West
Travel Time 4 hours
Car From the Zona Sul, head north on Av D Infante Henrique, which follows the curve of the bay as it goes north to Centro and eventually links up with Av Presidente Kubitschek. Look for signs to merge onto Av Brasil; this turns into BR 101, which leads all the way out to Paraty.
Bus Buses depart eight times daily from Rio between 5am and 9pm (US$8) from Novo Rio bus station.

Paraty is a colonial relic. Richly hued buildings with tile roofs seem all the more striking against the mountains in the distance, while dozens of restaurants and music-filled cafés infuse the old town with a vibrant energy. On weekends, the plazas come to life – particularly Praça da Matriz. There is no doubt that Paraty is very much a tourist town. Its colonial beauty and an abundance of handsome beaches nearby ensure no shortage of visitors, but in spite of this Paraty is a delight.

Beautiful old homes and churches are evidence of Paraty's 18th-century prosperity. Three main churches were used to separate the races. The Igreja Nossa Senhora do Rosário e São Benedito dos Homens Pretos (1725; opposite) was built by and for slaves. Renovated in 1857, the church has gilded wooden altars dedicated to Our Lady of the Rosary, St Benedict and St John.

Igreja Santa Rita dos Pardos Libertos (1722; opposite) was the church for freed mulattos. It has a tiny museum of sacred art, and some fine woodwork on the doorways and altars.

The Capela de Nossa Senhora das Dores (1800; opposite) was the church for the colonial white elite, and it was renovated in 1901. Its cemetery is fashioned after the catacombs in Rome.

Matriz Nossa Senhora dos Remédios (1787; opposite) was built on the site of two 17th-century churches. Inside you can see art from past and contemporary local artists. According to legend, the church was financed by a pirate treasure hidden on Praia da Trindade.

Forte Defensor Perpétuo (opposite) was built in 1703 to defend gold being exported from Minas Gerais from pirates. It was rebuilt in 1822, the year of Brazil's independence, and was named after Emperor Dom Pedro I.

Paraty has 65 islands and 300 beaches in its vicinity. The first beach you'll reach walking north of town is Praia do Pontal. It's just on the other side of the canal, but it tends to get a little murky at times. Praia do Forte, a quick walk north from there, is cleaner and relatively secluded. It attracts a young, mixed crowd. Another 2km north is Praia do Jabaquara, a big spacious beach with great views, shallow waters and a small restaurant overlooking the sand.

For visits to the less accessible beaches, schooner tours depart daily, making stops at several beaches; book through Paraty Tours (opposite). An alternative is to hire one of the small motorboats at the port. Skippers and local boatmen know excellent beaches in the region and would be happy to take you if the price is right (plan on US$15 per hour).

Colonial architecture, Paraty (this page)

Sights & Information

Capela de Nossa Senhora das Dores (Rua da Capela & Rua Fresca)

Centro de Informações Turísticas (☎ 3371 1266 ext 218; Av Roberto Silveira; ⊙ 9am-9pm) It distributes good maps of the area (as does Paraty Tours, next door) and maintains updated information on hotels and restaurants in the area.

Travel Tip

Paraty is renowned for its *cachaça* (cane liquor). To see a selection, and perhaps try a sample, visit **Empório da Cachaça** (☎ 3371 6329; Rua Dr. Samuel Costa 22) or **Toca da Cachaça** (☎ 3371 1310; Rua da Matriz 9).

Forte Defensor Perpétuo (⊙ 9am-noon & 1.30-5pm Wed-Sun) The fort is located on the Morro da Vila Velha, the hill just past Praia do Pontal, a 20-minute walk north of town. The fort also houses an arts center.

Igreja Nossa Senhora do Rosário e São Benedito (Rua Dr Samuel Costa; admission free; ⊙ 9am-noon Tue)

Igreja Santa Rita dos Pardos Libertos (Praça Santa Rita; museum US$1; ⊙ 9am-noon & 1-6pm Wed-Sun) A small museum of sacred art is housed within the church.

Matriz Nossa Senhora dos Remédios (Rua da Matriz; admission free; ⊙ 9am-noon Mon, Wed & Fri, 9am-3pm Sun)

Paraty Tours (☎ 3371 1327; www.paratytours.com.br; Av Roberto Silveira 11; ⊙ 9am-8pm) Located just before you reach the colonial part of town, Paraty Tours is a good source of information and offers a range of tours, including ones for kayaking, biking, horseback-riding and diving. Its schooner tours are its biggest sellers; these five-hour cruises cost US$9 and depart daily at 10am, 11am and noon. Paraty Tours also rents bicycles for US$1.75 per hour or US$7 per day.

Teatro Espaço (☎ 3371 1575; Rua Dona Geralda 327) For years the Teatro Espaço has been garnering praise for its famous puppet theater. Even if you can't speak Portuguese, the lifelike puppets and beautifully executed work make for a fine show.

Eating

Academia de Cozinha (☎ 3371 6468; Rua Dona Geralda 288; all-included dinner US$35) A mix of theater and haute cuisine, the Academia de Cozinha stages cooking shows – in Portuguese and English. Guests learn about the regional cuisines, watch chef Yara Castro Roberts in action, then enjoy the fruits of her labor. The price of dinner includes cocktails, wine, desserts and a wide variety of fare.

Casa do Fogo (☎ 3371 6359; Rua do Comércio 58) Offers a handful of tables on the street out front and live jazz coming from inside most nights. It's the chef who's the real attraction – and lends the House of Fire its name for his flamboyant use of flame in the kitchen. The small menu features tangy seafood dishes.

Miracolo (☎ 3371 1045; Praça da Matriz 80) Run by an Italian expat, this small ice-cream parlor and snack spot serves creamy gelato in a range of flavors. The outdoor tables at the front are a meeting spot on Friday and Saturday nights.

Paraty 33 (☎ 3371 7311; Rua da Lapa 357) A cozy spot with an eclectic menu, and live music most nights. On weekends, an occasional dance party takes over the ambient-rich space.

Refúgio (☎ 3371 2447; Loja 4, Rua Fresca, Praça do Porto) Refugio's candlelit interior and scenic location near the docks may make you feel like you're stepping into a *telenovela* (soap opera), but don't let that deter you from experiencing the restaurant's delicious seafood specialties.

Paraty's Festivals

Among the biggest events in the region is Paraty's **Festa do Divino Espírito Santo**, which features all sorts of merry-making revolving around the *fólios*, musical groups that go door to door singing and joking. The colorful festival begins nine days before Pentecostal Sunday (the seventh Sunday after Easter).

Festas Juninas are held throughout June, when the town becomes the stage for music, street parties and folk dancing such as the *xiba* (a circle clog dance) and the *ciranda* (a *xiba* with guitar accompaniment). The final festival is on June 29 with a maritime procession to **Ilha do Araújo**, one of the islands near Paraty.

From Friday to Sunday on the third weekend in August, Paraty hosts its popular **Festa da Pinga** (*pinga* is another name for *cachaça*, a spirit made from sugar cane). Many local distilleries are on hand to dazzle (or at least intoxicate) visitors with their rare spirits.

The **Festa de NS dos Remédios** is celebrated on September 8, with street processions and religious events.

The city also attracts a crowd to its **Carnaval**, which is held the weekend before Ash Wednesday (the partying runs from Friday night through Tuesday), and is becoming known for revelers covering themselves in mud and dancing through the streets.

Sleeping

Estalagem Colonial (☎ 3371 1626; Rua da Matriz 9;
d from US$40) One of the finest colonial hotels in Paraty,
with a range of rooms – from spacious, antique-filled
chambers to a top-floor room with magnificent views.

Hotel Solar dos Gerânios (☎ /fax 3371 1550; Praça da
Matriz 2; s/d US$20/25) Overlooking the Praça da Matriz, this
old hotel features wood and ceramic sculptures, rustic heavy
furniture and *azulejos* (Portuguese tiles). Some rooms are
better than others, so check a few first before committing.

Pousada do Ouro (☎ 3371 1378; www.pousadaouro
.com.br; Rua da Praia 145; d from US$60) Another excel-
lent spot with pool, billiards, sauna and lovely rooms in a
colonial setting. Mick Jagger and Tom Cruise have stayed
here.

Pousada Pardeiro (☎ 3371 1370; www.pousada
pardieiro.com.br; Rua do Comércio 74; d from US$110)
A tranquil garden setting with pool, good service and
nicely appointed rooms are features of this elegant
pousada.

Detour

Paraty's resplendent natural setting makes for some fine (and highly recommended) exploring. Its excellent beaches lie
within a 30-minute drive and a one-hour boat ride, and most are surrounded by green mountains with deep blue seas
lapping at the shore. Two of the best beaches are **Praia de Paraty-Mirim**, 27km east of Paraty, where there are a few
barracas on the beach and signs advertising houses for rent, and **Praia da Trindade**, with calm seas that reflect the lush
vegetation surrounding it. If you'd prefer to hike into the forest, visit a waterfall and take a dip in a natural swimming
hole, there's the nearby **Parque Nacional da Serra da Bocaina**. This national park has a lot of rich plant and animal life
(of the latter are several types of monkeys, anteaters, otters and sloths) but, sadly, with the park's limted infrastructure
it's hard to see much of this. For a short visit, head west out of Paraty along the Paraty–Cunha road, which winds its way
uphill. Stop at the Cachoeira (waterfall) do Tobogã (look for signs; it's right off the Paraty–Cunha road about 15km) for
a short hike to the waterfall, where you can go for a swim.

On your way back from the waterfall to Paraty, stop at the lovely **Vila Verde** (☎ 3371 7808; Km 7, Estrada Paraty
Cunha; mains US$6-10; ⏱ 11am-6pm Tue-Sun low season, 11am daily until last customer high season), which serves
homemade pastas, risottos and smoked salmon as well as good desserts and coffee. The restaurant is beautifully landscaped – a small brook trickles through the property, surrounded by lots of greenery.

ILHA GRANDE

☎ 24

Ilha Grande (Big Island) has dazzled visitors for centuries. On the southern coast of Rio
de Janeiro, Brazil's third largest island offers tropical scenery and gorgeous beaches among
the island's sheltered bays, brooks and waterfalls. Its hillsides are covered in lush forests,
an important piece of the rapidly disappearing Mata Atlântica ecosystem.

Vila do Abraão is the principal village on Ilha Grande, and the launchpad for many adventures around the island. From here, you can take any number of schooner tours to gorgeous
beaches such as **Lopes Mendes** (which often tops charts listing the world's most beautiful
beaches), **Saco do Céu**, **Lagoa Azul** or **Lagoa Verde**. The schooner companies (opposite) offer tours
to Lopes Mendes at least once per day, and organize regular trips to other beaches.

There are numerous hikes you can do from Vila do Abraão. The hike to **Pico do Papagaio**
(982m) gives you the chance to see the island's rich ecosystem (and perhaps some wildlife)
and, from its summit, take in the splendid views. Another hike takes you over the top of the
island; you can cool off in Dois Rios at the end. For these trips, hire a guide (opposite); it's
easy to get lost in the thick forest. One trip you can do on your own is the short walk to **Praia
Preta**. This trail runs north from town and leads to the ruins of a prison.

In addition to hiking, kayaking is also a good way to experience the island. Early in the
morning when the seas are calm is the best time to go out. Most Cariocas, however, are content to simply lounge away the afternoon on one of the island's many beaches. On summer
weekends, the island can get crowded, though during the week (and any time in the winter)
Ilha Grande nearly always remains quite peaceful.

To get to the island, you'll have to catch a ferry from either Mangaratiba or Angra dos Reis.
No cars are allowed on Ilha Grande. Maps of the island and Vila do Abraão are available at
the ferry dock. Be sure to change money before coming to Ilha Grande.

Sights & Activities

Papyk Turismo (☎ 9791 7471; Praia do Abraão) One of the many companies offering schooner cruises to beaches around the island. During summer weekends, these boats can get packed, so check them out before you commit to anything.

Sudoeste SW Turismo (☎ 3361 5516; www.sudoeste sw.com.br; Rua da Praia 647) Next door to O Pescador hotel, Sudoeste has excellent Portuguese/English-speaking guides available for hikes around the island. You can also rent one of its kayaks or arrange private boat tours.

Eating

Kathe's Coffee House (Rua Santana; ⏰ 4-11pm) Cappuccinos, cakes and sweets are served in this pleasant café. If it's raining it sometimes opens earlier in the day (chess board available).

Minha Deusa (Rua da Igreja 7) Next to the church, this simple eatery serves excellent *caldo de camarão* (shrimp soup) and *moqueca* (seafood stew cooked in coconut milk).

Restaurante AleCrim (Rua da Praia 34) Next door to Pousada Casablanca, AleCrim is a small, pleasant spot, serving excellent dishes.

Sleeping

Ilha Azul (☎ 3361 5091; Rua da Igreja; d from US$30) Straight up from the dock is the decent Ilha Azul. Its upstairs rooms are the best, with plenty of light. A pool and hot tub are popular features.

O Pescador (☎ 3361 5114; opescadordailha@uol.com.br; Praia do Abraão; d from US$40 low season, US$55 high season) Cozily furnished rooms and one of the island's best

Ilha Grande (opposite)

restaurants (don't miss the tasty *casquinha de seri* – a crabmeat appetizer mixed with manioc flour) make an excellent combination at this charming spot overlooking the beach. The friendly owners speak English.

Pousada Casablanca (☎ 9962 0990; Rua da Praia 34; d from US$30) Just off the main beach path, Casablanca has clean, modern rooms, some with small balconies.

Pousada Portal dos Borbas (☎ 3361 5085; Rua das Flores 4; d from US$38) Rooms open onto a fine courtyard garden at this friendly, laid-back spot.

Transportation

Distance from Rio 150km
Direction West
Travel Time Two hours to Mangaratiba or 2½ to Angra and then a 45-minute ferry ride.
Car From the Zona Sul, head north on Av D Infante Henrique, which follows the curve of the bay as it goes north to Centro and eventually links up with Av Presidente Kubitschek. Look for signs to merge onto Av Brasil. This turns into BR 101, which leads all the way out to Mangaratiba or Angra. Both places offer long-term parking near the dock for around US$5 per day.
Ferry Once you reach either Mangaratiba or Angra, you'll need to catch the ferry to Vila do Abraão. Boats from Mangaratiba depart at 8am and return at 5.30pm daily. From Angra, boats depart at 3.30pm Monday to Friday and 1.30pm Saturday and Sunday; they return to Angra at 10am daily. One way, a ferry ride costs US$2 Monday to Friday and US$4.50 Saturday and Sunday. Ferry schedules fluctuate, so it's wise to confirm times with your hotel when you make a ferry reservation.
Bus Buses depart every half hour from the main Novo Rio bus station between 5am and 10pm to either Mangaratiba (US$4.50) or Angra (US$6). Make sure you verify ferry connections to avoid getting stuck overnight in Angra or Mangaratiba.

Natives, Pirates & Prisons *Rodolfo Klautau*

The name Ilha Grande (Big Island) is the Portuguese translation of *Ipaum Guaçu*, the name given by the Tunpinambá Indians in their native language, Tupi. The island's name was first recorded by Hans Staden, a young German adventurer who was shipwrecked on the island in 1550. He was held prisoner by the Tunpinambá Indians for nine months, during which he avoided being roasted and eaten by the tribe, one of their customs when dealing with enemies. Most of the hiking trails that are still used today were opened by this Indian tribe.

During the 16th, 17th and 18th centuries the island was a shelter for pirates and smugglers, who found a safe haven for their ships in the island's bays, especially at Enseada das Estrelas, where they used to anchor for a few days to refill their ships with water and firewood. At **Praia do Morcego**, in Baía de Ilha Grande, we find **A Casa do Morcego** (Bat House), one of the oldest brick houses in Brazil. The house was apparently built in 1629 by Juan Lorenzo, a pirate who decided to settle on the island after marrying one of the locals. Legend has it that the prow of Lorenzo's ship displayed the gold statue of a bat, which explains the origin of the name of the beach, the house and the islet in front of it. Today, A Casa do Morcego is privately owned and is impeccably restored and preserved, though unfortunately it's off limits for visitors.

The building of **Lazareto** in 1886 at Abrãao Bay marked the beginning of Ilha Grande's history as a prison. Lazareto was built as a quarantine hospital for immigrants with contagious diseases, but as early as 1893 it received both prisoners and the infirm, until it was closed in 1913. It was reopened years later to receive prisoners of the Constitutionalist Revolution of 1932. The writer Orígenes Lessa served time in the prison and wrote a book describing his suffering behind bars. Another distinguished prisoner, the great Graciliano Ramos, also penned a famous book during incarceration, *Memórias do Cárcere*, which was later turned into a Brazilian film.

During the 1940s Lazareto hospital also received war prisoners but in 1963 under Carlos Lacerda, governor of Rio de Janeiro, it was closed and demolished. The only remaining ruins are the prison cells (located by the side of the Praia Preta brook) and the aqueduct (a construction measuring 125m that provided Lazareto hospital with one million liters of clean water per hour).

Following the closure of Lazareto hospital, the prisoners were transferred to a prison in Dois Rios, on the south side of Ilha Grande. It was originally built to receive common prisoners, but later became a maximum security prison. The most famous escape from Dois Rios prison took place in 1985, when the drug dealer José Carlos Encina was airlifted to freedom in a helicopter stolen by an accomplice. Not a single shot was fired as the guards thought that the helicopter was delivering the prison warden.

In 1994, under the government of Leonel Brizola, the prison of Dois Rios was demolished and its land and buildings donated to the Universidade do Estado do Rio de Janeiro. The State University of Rio de Janeiro has set up a Center for Environmental Studies and Sustainable Development on this site.

Ironically, the fact that Ilha Grande was a prison for 100 years contributed to its preservation. It never fell prey to the real estate speculation, which spread along the coast between Rio de Janeiro and São Paulo throughout the 1970s. Since 1994 tourism has been Ilha Grande's main income as visitors from all over the world discover this fantastic island.

BÚZIOS
☎ 22

Armação de Búzios, known simply as Búzios, is a lovely beach resort on a peninsula surrounded by about 20 beaches jutting into the Atlantic. It was a simple fishing village until the early 1960s, when it was 'discovered' by Brigitte Bardot and her Brazilian boyfriend. Today, Búzios offers much more than just its spectacular natural setting. The village has boutiques, elegant restaurants, open-air bars and lavishly decorated B&Bs. Many foreign-owned (especially Argentinean) *pousadas* and restaurants have sprouted along the peninsula's shores, and a mix of international travelers adds to the jumble of languages you'll hear on the streets.

The village itself has two main streets running through it. The **Rua das Pedras**, which hugs the shoreline, is lined with *pousadas*, bars and restaurants overlooking the water. The large stones lining the narrow road add to its charm – but be careful after a few *caipirinhas* (*cachaça* cocktails). Rua das Pedras turns into Orla Bardot as it heads north. **Rua Turibe Farias**, just behind Rua das Pedras, has a number of boutiques, ice-cream parlors and a pleasant

Travel Tip

A good Portuguese- and English-language website with information on the region – nightlife, beaches, maps and tours – is www.buziosonline.com.br.

square (**Praça Santos Dumont**), which becomes a gathering spot for Búzios' youth at night.

The beaches are the daytime attraction in Búzios, and there are quite a few to choose from. To get a taste of the offerings, take a schooner tour on the *Queen Lory* (p188), or rent a buggy and explore the area on your own. In general, the southern beaches are trickier to get to, but they're prettier and have better surf. The northern beaches are closer to the towns and more sheltered. Just before entering the peninsula you'll see a **tourist information office** (p188); there's also one in the center of town (p188). Stop into either office and pick up one of their maps, which show all of the beaches around the area.

One of the most popular beaches is **Geribá**. It has a long stretch of sand and good surf (and surfers), with an abundance of restaurants and bars. It's the place to go if you want to be on a social beach. A bit calmer and less-developed is the small **Ferradurinha** (Little Horseshoe), which lies just east of Geribá. Continuing counterclockwise is the beach of **Ferradura**. It, too, is horseshoe-shaped but much wider; it's popular with windsurfers. Next are **Lagoinha**, a rocky beach with rough water, and **Praia da Foca** and **Praia do Forno**, both of which have colder water than the other beaches. **Praia Olho de Boi** (Bull's Eye) has the unique distinction of being named after Brazil's first postage stamp. It's a pocket-sized beach reached by a little trail from the long, clean beach of **Praia Brava**, which lies to the west.

João Fernandinho and **João Fernandes** are both good locations for snorkeling, as are the topless beaches of **Azedinha** and **Azeda**. **Praia dos Ossos**, **Praia da Armação**, **Praia do Caboclo** and **Praia dos Amores** are pretty to look at, but are not ideal for lounging around, as they can be crowded with boats offshore, which won't leave you much privacy. **Praia da Tartaruga**, on the other hand, is quiet and pretty. **Praia do Gaucho** and **Manguinhos** are town beaches further along the coastal strip.

Transportation

Distance from Rio 176km
Direction East
Travel Time 2½ hours
Car From the Zona Sul, head north to the Rio–Niterói bridge (toll US$1). After passing the toll, take RJ 101 in the direction of Rio Bonita. After reaching Rio Bonito, take BR 124 (Via Lagos Hwy; toll US$2 to US$3) west. Stay on this highway until it ends, then continue east another 7km until you reach an Ipiranga gas station at the entrance of São Pedro da Aldeia. Take a left at the gas station and then a right onto BR 106 in the direction of Macaé/Búzios. After another 14km you will reach the Até que Enfim gas station. Turn right and stay on this road until reaching Búzios. For those who'd rather take the slower, scenic route a coastal road runs from Itacoatiara out to Cabo Frio then north.
Bus From Novo Rio bus station, **Viação 1001** (☎ 2516 1001) has buses departing seven times daily. The trip takes 3½ hours (US$6). Alternatively, take an hourly bus to Cabo Frio and transfer to Búzios.

João Fernandes Beach (above)

Detour

Along the way from Rio to Búzios there are a number of scenic beaches, surfing spots and fishing villages.

Follow the directions for getting to Búzios (ie take the Rio–Niterói bridge, and turn off at Rio Bonito). Turn onto RJ 124 at Rio Bonito (the Via Lagos Hwy), and continue for 23km until you reach the turnoff for Saquarema. This small community lies about 100km east of Rio de Janeiro, with long stretches of open beach, bordered by lagoons and mountains. The town still has a somnolent air to it, though on weekends it attracts a large surfer crowd thanks to the waves of up to 3m. A number of beaches lie near town, including the popular **Barra Nova** and **Praia da Vila**. About 3km north of Saquarema is **Praia Itaúna**, a good spot that hosts an annual surfing contest during the first two weeks of October.

From Saquarema continue east along the coastal road for another 60km and you'll reach **Arraial do Cabo**, a moderate-sized village with beaches that compare to the finest in Búzios. Unlike Búzios, however, Arraial is a sleepy, somewhat blue-collar town. Discovered a few centuries ago by Amerigo Vespucci, Praia dos Anjos has beautiful turquoise water, but a little too much boat traffic for safe swimming. It also has a **Museum of Oceanography** (Praia dos Anjos; 🕑 9am-noon & 1-4.30pm Tue-Sun). Aside from Praia dos Anjos, the most popular beaches in Arraial do Cabo are **Praia do Forno**, **Praia Brava** and **Praia Grande**.

The **Gruta Azul** (Blue Cavern) on the southwestern side of Ilha de Cabo Frio is another beautiful spot. Be alert to the tides: the entrance to the underwater cavern isn't always open. There are lots of dive operators, including **Arraial Sub** (☎ 2622 1945) and **PL Divers** (☎ 2622 2633).

Ten kilometers north of Arraial do Cabo lies **Cabo Frio**, which sits between the Canal do Itajuru on one side and the ocean on the other. It's a bit overdeveloped for tourism, but there is some lovely landscape nearby. East of town, along a scenic road, is the Praia do Forte with bleached white sand and a backdrop of low scrub, cacti and grasses. At the northern end of Praia do Forte is a stone fortress, **Forte São Mateus** (🕑 10am-4pm Tue-Sun), which was built in 1616 and served as a stronghold against pirates.

The **sand dunes** around Cabo Frio are one of the region's most interesting features. The dunes facing the excellent surfing spot of **Praia do Peró** lie 6km north of town in the direction of Búzios. Praia do Pero is near Ogivas and after **Praia Brava** and **Praia das Conchas**. The **Pontal dunes** of Praia do Forte stretch from the Forte São Mateus to Miranda Hill, while the **Dama Branca** (White Lady) sand dunes are on the road to Arraial do Cabo. The dunes can be dangerous due to robberies, so talk to locals before heading out.

In addition to Búzios, there are two other settlements on the peninsula – **Ossos** and **Manguinhos** – and one further north on the mainland, called **Rasa**. Ossos, at the northernmost tip of the peninsula, is the oldest and most attractive. It has a lovely harbor and yacht club, a few hotels and bars, and a tourist stand. Manguinhos, at the isthmus, is the most commercial; it even has a 24-hour medical clinic. Northwest along the coast is Rasa and the island of Rasa, where Brazil's political dignitaries and CEOs come to relax. Owing to its charm and popularity with Cariocas, prices here go up quite a bit on holidays (especially New Year's Eve and Carnaval).

Sights & Information

Armação Bikes (☎ 9213 4597; Manoel De Carvalho 229, Búzios) This is a good spot to rent bikes; it charges around US$10 per day.

Bike Tour (☎ 2623 6365; Rua das Pedras 266, Búzios) Bike rental is available here for around US$10 per day.

Búzios Trolley (☎ 2623 2763; www.buziostrolley.com.br; Orla Bardot 550; tickets US$15) This open-sided bus travels around to 12 of the beaches on the peninsula. The two-hour tours depart daily at 9am, noon and 3pm.

Cine Bardot (Travessa dos Pescadores) Right next door to Vila do Mar hotel, this 111-seat theater shows a range of Brazilian and foreign films.

GusCar (☎ 2623 8225; www.guscar.com.br; Estrada da Usina 444) GusCar rents buggies and cars for around US$50 per day. It also offers boat tours to nearby beaches.

Kite Surfing (☎ 9241 9393; www.kitenews.com.br; Praia Rasa, Rasa) If you want to learn kite surfing (which is like windsurfing, but you hold onto a parachute-like kite overhead rather than a sail), this school offers classes, with English-language instruction available.

Queen Lory (☎ 2623 1179; Rua João Fernandes 89, Ossos) This schooner makes daily trips out to Ilha Feia, Tartaruga and João Fernandinho. The 2½-hour trip costs US$15, while the five-hour trip costs US$22. Both are good value, especially since *caipirinhas*, soft drinks, fruit salad and snorkeling gear are included in the price. To make a reservation, book direct with Queen Lory Tours or ask at your *pousada*. All tours depart from the Pier do Centro in Búzios at 9.30am, 12.30pm and 3pm.

Secretaria de Turismo (☎ 2623 2099; Praça Santos Dumont, Búzios; 🕑 9am-9pm) This tourist information office is one block up from the Rua das Pedras. Another branch (☎ toll-free 0800 249 999; 🕑 24hr) is at the entrance to

Búzios. From any newsstand pick up a copy of *Guia Verão Búzios* (US$3), which has information in English and Portuguese, including a list of places to stay (but no prices).

True Blue (☎ 2623 2173; Rua das Pedras, Búzios) Leads diving excursions around the peninsula, with regular trips out to Ilha Âncora, 10km off the coast.

Eating & Drinking

Boom (☎ 2623 6254; Rua Manuel Turíbio de Farias 110) A good per-kilo place offering a delicious lunch buffet and pleasant ambience.

Café Concerto (☎ 2623 4300; Rua das Pedras 156) This indoor/outdoor bar has music shows and DJs on the weekends.

Chez Michou Crêperie (☎ 2623 2169; Rua das Pedras 90; crepes US$3-5) This lively outdoor spot serves tasty dinner and savory and sweet crepes. Delicious piña coladas are also served.

Cigalon (☎ 2623 2261; Rua das Pedras 265; mains US$7-11) Decadent French cuisine is served here, with lovely beachside views.

Pátio Havana (☎ 2623 2169; Rua das Pedras 101; mains US$8-12) A combination of jazz bar, restaurant, tobacco shop and wine cellar, the Pátio Havana makes a good place to hang out in the evening. Live music shows —Música Popular Brasileiro (MPB), DJs and jazz — happen throughout the summer here.

Sawasdee (☎ 2623 4644; Orla Bardot 422; mains US$7-10) One of the newest restaurants in Búzios features dazzling Thai cuisine which showcases the fresh seafood from the area. The *kaipilychias* (lychee *caipirinhas*) are quite tasty.

Sorvetes Mil Frutas (☎ 2623 6436; Rua das Pedras 59) With dozens of ice-cream flavors on offer, Mil Frutas is a lovely spot to refresh yourself.

Takatakata (Rua das Pedras 256; ☽ usually from 6pm) This lively bar is a popular place for sampling one of the fiery concoctions of expat owner Kijzer Van Derhoff.

Sleeping

Brigitta's Guesthouse (☎ 2623 6157; www .buziosonline.com.br/brigitta/pousada.htm in Portuguese; Rua das Pedras 131; d from US$60) Overlooking the water, this charming guesthouse has the feel of a B&B. The owners are friendly and there is an excellent restaurant.

Casa da Pedra (☎ 2623 1499; Travessa Lúcio A Quintanilha 57; s/d US$25/35) A Tudor-style *pousada* with clean, modern rooms and a patio in front.

Casas Brancas (☎ 2623 1458; www.casasbrancas.com.br; Morro do Humaitá 10; d from US$150) Set on a hill overlooking the bay, the Mediterranean-style Casas Brancas has bay views, spacious rooms (some with balconies and living rooms), a swimming pool (also with excellent views) and a lovely patio.

La Mandrágora (☎ 2623 1348; www.buzios online.com.br/mandragora; Praça La Mandrágora; d from US$90) Offering accommodations in either lavishly decorated rooms or cozy bungalows, this respected *pousada* has attractive extras: a Jacuzzi bar, a lovely pool and patio, a workout center and a tennis court.

Pousada Mainá (☎ 2623 1636; www .pousadamaina.com.br in Portuguese; Rua João Fernandes 77; d from US$35) Mainá has simple but pleasant rooms facing onto a small pool, with patio bar. It's a friendly, popular place, with a mix of foreigners and locals.

Pousada Santa Fe (☎ 2623 6404; Praça Santos Dumont 300; d from US$24 Mon-Fri, US$34 Sat & Sun) This charming mission-style *pousada* has lovely rooms with stone floors and organic touches throughout; some rooms have balconies overlooking the plaza.

Vila do Mar (☎ 2623 1466; www.buziosonline.com.br /viladomar in Portuguese; Travessa do Pescadores 88; d from US$25) A fine *pousada*, with a variety of rooms; the best have breezy views over the bay. There is a swimming pool below and a comfortable lounge area with wood furnishings.

PETRÓPOLIS

☎ 24

Just 68km north of Rio, Petrópolis has the air of a European mountain retreat. Horse-drawn carriages still clatter through the streets, and the city's small bridges and canals, manicured parks and old-fashioned lampposts add to its charm. The city makes a fine place for strolls, visiting the museums and taking in the fine landscaping.

Emperor Dom Pedro I first came across the lovely setting on a journey from Rio to Minas Gerais. It was just farmland in the 1830s, but Dom Pedro liked it so much that he decided to buy some land here. Although he abdicated the throne and returned to Portugal, the land passed on to his son, Dom Pedro II, who was also an admirer of the area. He built a summer retreat here, and it soon became popular with the whole court. A palace was erected in the 1840s. Later, mansions and a looming cathedral were added to the landscape, and Petrópolis soon earned the nickname the 'Imperial City.'

In the late 19th century, the city became a center for intellectuals and artists. Santos Dumont was one of Petrópolis' most famous residents at that time. The inventor, architect and writer is considered the 'father of Brazilian aviation' for his early flights; he is also considered the inventor of the wristwatch, and he designed his own house. You can take a tour of this small, fascinating home – which is now the **Museu Casa de Santos Dumont** (below) – and have some fine views of the mountains at the same time. Other great men who contributed to the artistic climate of 19th-century Petrópolis include composer Rui Barbosa and the Austrian writer Stefan Zweig.

Transportation

Distance from Rio 68km
Direction North
Travel Time 1½ hours
Car Linha Vermelha Hwy. After passing signs for the international airport, be on the lookout for BR 040; you'll merge onto this highway (also called Rodovia Washington Luís) and follow the signs to Petrópolis.
Bus A **Viação 1001** (☎ 2516 1001) bus departs every 20 minutes between 5.15am and 7pm (US$4) from Novo Rio bus station. For the best views be sure to leave well before sundown. Buses arrive on Praça Juiz Machado Jr, not far from the Centro Historico.

In the 1940s, the city developed a reputation for its large, elegant casino, known as the **Palácio Quitandinha** (opposite). A large international crowd, including Frank Sinatra, came and went from the palace, and it was once the largest casino in South America.

Today, Petrópolis is no longer a hotbed of intellectual activity, and gambling is illegal. However, as well as being the home of the pretender to the throne, the grandson of Princesa Isabel, Dom Pedro de Orleans e Bragança, the city is – more importantly – establishing quite a culinary reputation, as some of Rio's best chefs open small, château-like restaurants in the area. You'll need a car to visit these places as they are located outside of the city center.

In the daytime, however, historic Petrópolis is easily explored on foot. The **Museu Imperial** (below) is one of the city's gems. The Neoclassical palace served as the home away from home for Dom Pedro II and his wife, Dona Teresa, when the humidity (and mosquitoes) in Rio became unbearable. North of the palace-museum is the **Catedral São Pedro de Alcântara** (below), which houses the tombs of Dom Pedro II, Dona Teresa and their daughter Princesa Isabel. Although the ruler was sent into exile following a coup d'etat, his love of Brazil eventually brought him back – albeit long after he was dead. From the steps of the cathedral, you'll have fine views of the region, with the spires set against the mountains.

The **Casa do Barão de Mauá** (below) is north of the cathedral. The Neoclassical mansion was the baron Mauá's former residence and is open for visits on weekends and holidays. It also houses a tourist information office open daily. If you turn left from here, you'll reach the **Palácio de Cristal** (opposite). The palace was built for Princesa Isabel in France and brought to the country in 1884. It was used back then – and is still used today – as a greenhouse. It is also the setting for cultural events and exhibitions (eg orchid shows) throughout the year. The **Centro de Cultura Raul de Leoni** (below) also has gallery exhibitions as well as a theater and cinema. For shopping, several streets are worth strolling: **Rua 16 de Março** and **Rua Teresa.**

Petrópolis is only 60km from Rio and, due to its crisp, calm nights and ample supply of cottages and B&Bs, makes a fine overnight trip.

Travel Tip

Avoid visiting Petrópolis on Monday, as that's when most of its museums are closed.

Sights & Information

Carriage Rides (Rua da Imperatriz; 🕒 8am-5pm Tue-Sun) In front of the Museu Imperial, you can hire a carriage for a *passeio* (tour) about town.

Casa do Barão de Mauá (☎ 2246 9300; Praça da Confluência 3; admission free; 🕒 9am-6pm Sat, 9am-5pm Sun & holidays)

Catedral São Pedro de Alcântara (☎ 2242 4300; Rua São Pedro de Alcântara 60; admission free; 🕒 8am-noon & 2-6pm Tue-Sun)

Centro de Cultura Raul de Leoni (☎ 2247 3747; Praça Visconde de Mauá 305; 🕒 exhibitions 1-8pm Mon-Sat)

HSBC (Rua do Imperador 884; 🕒 10am-5pm Mon-Fri) It has an ATM.

Museu Casa de Santos Dumont (☎ 2247 3158; Rua do Encanto 22; admission US$1; 🕒 9.30am-5pm Tue-Sun)

Museu Imperial (☎ 2237 8000; Rua da Imperatriz 220; admission US$2; 🕒 11am-5.30pm Tue-Sun) This museum has exhibits from the imperial collection, including a 1.7kg crown covered with 639 diamonds and 77 pearls.

Detour

The lush greenery of the mountains makes a lovely setting for a scenic drive, but if you'd like to see it from the inside, head to **Parque Nacional Da Serra Dos Órgãos** (admission US$2; main entrance ☼ 8am-5pm). The national park has extensive trails through Mata Atlântica rain forest and has a variety of rich plant and animal life, including hummingbirds, wild cats, deer, monkeys, agoutis and the tiny flea toad (at just 10mm long). The park is also well known for its oddly shaped peaks – many of which can be seen from other parts of the region. **Dedo de Deus** (God's Finger), **Cabeça de Peixe** (Fish Head) and **Verruga do Frade** (Friar's Wart) are among the more imaginative names bestowed on the mountains.

Unfortunately, most of the trails are unmarked and off the extents of available maps. Those interested in hiking, or climbing one of the peaks, should inquire at **Rios Brasileiros Rafting** (below) in Petrópolis.

Those who just want a short hike (and a picnic) can take the 3.5km walking trail, visiting the waterfalls, natural swimming pools, tended lawns and gardens. There are also campsites (per person US$4) as well as a **lodge** (per person US$15, incl breakfast & evening soup). There are two entrances to the park, both on BR 116. The one closer to Teresópolis offers more facilities.

Another village in the mountains is **Nova Friburgo**, in an area, which, like Petrópolis, offers good hotels and restaurants, as well as many lovely natural attractions: woods, waterfalls, trails, sunny mountain mornings and cool evenings. Do be aware that it gets chilly and rainy during the winter months, from June to August.

A romantic setting for dinner is **Hotel Auberge Suisse** (☎ 2541 1270; Rua 10 de Outubro, Amparo; mains US$9-14; cabins d from US$40), where you can also pass the night in one of its chalets. The restaurant serves trout as well as traditional Swiss cuisine, including raclettes and fondues. To reach the hotel, head northeast out of Nova Friburgo on RJ 150. After 14km you'll reach the town of Amparo, where you'll see signs to the hotel.

The area around Nova Friburgo first settled by families from the Swiss canton of Friburg. During the Napoleonic wars, Dom João encouraged immigration to Brazil. At the time, people were starving in Switzerland, so in 1818 around 300 families packed up and headed for Brazil. The passage overseas was grueling and many families died en route. Those who survived settled in the mountains and established the small village of Nova Friburgo in the New World.

A **tourist information office** (☎ 2523 8000; Praça Dr Demervel B Moreira; ☼ 8am-8pm) is in the center of town. In addition to maps, it has a complete list of hotels in the area. Most of the sights are a few kilometers out of town. Scout out the surrounding area from **Morro da Cruz** (1800m), which is accessible by **chairlift** (☼ 9am-6pm Sat-Sun & holidays); the chairlift station is in the center at Praça Teleférico. Alternatively, there's **Pico da Caledônia** (2310m), offering fantastic views and launching sites for hang-gliders. It's a 6km uphill hike, but the view is worth it.

From Nova Friburgo you can hike to **Pedra do Cão Sentado**, explore the **Furnas do Catete** rock formations or visit the mountain towns of **Bom Jardim** (23km northeast on BR 116) or **Lumiar** (25km east of the turnoff at **Muri**, which is 9km south of Nova Friburgo). In Lumiar hippies, cheap pensions, waterfalls, walking trails and white-water canoe trips abound. Another fine spot is the **Jardim do Nêgo** (admission US$2.50), which is 13km northwest of Nova Friburgo between Campo do Coelho and Conquista on RJ 130. The *jardim* contains a fantastic sculpture garden with huge moss-covered sculptures of human and animal forms.

On weekends, the palace hosts a **sound-and-light show** (tickets US$8; ☼ 8pm Thu-Fri, 8pm & 9.15pm Sat), which relates the history of the imperial family. Shows are staged in the gardens facing the museum.

Palácio de Cristal (☎ 2247 3721; Rua Alfredo Pachá; admission free ☼ 9am-5.30pm Tue-Sun) On Saturday evenings at 6pm, the palace periodically hosts live concerts featuring MPB, *chorinho* (a type of folk music), classical music and samba bands.

Palácio Quitandinha (☎ 2237 1012; Av Joaquim Rolla 2, Quitandinha; admission US$1.50; ☼ 9am-5.30pm Tue-Sun) This palace and former casino is the only one not within walking distance from the historic center. It lies in the northeast of the historic center, best reached by a US$2 taxi ride.

Rios Brasileiros Rafting (☎ 2243 4372; www.rbrafting.com .br; Room 104, Rua Silva Jardim 514) Rios organizes rafting, rappelling and hiking adventures around the area. Portuguese- and English-speaking guides are available.

Tourist Information Office (☎ 2246 9377; Praça dos Expedicionários; ☼ 9am-5pm) It has brochures, maps and information on places to stay. There's also a good information office at the obelisk on the way into town from Rio.

Trekking Petrópolis (☎ 2235 7607; www.rioserra.com.br /trekking) Organises hikes into the nearby Parque Nacional Da Serra Dos Órgãos.

Eating

Casa de Chá (☎ 2237 8000; Av Imperatriz 220; mains US$5-9; ☼ noon-7pm Tue-Sun) Within the Museu Imperial complex, this charming bistro and teahouse serves excellent light dishes as well as more substantial offerings such as filet mignon and roast duck.

Chimarron Churrascaria (☎ 2237 3779; Av Ayrton Senna; all-you-can-eat US$10) Decked out like an old lodge – with lots of wood – the Chimarron is a good

European-inspired architecture, Petrópolis (p189)

churrascaria (traditional barbecue restaurant) popular with Brazilian families. It's a bit out of the way, so you'll need to have a car or hire a taxi to get here. Its fine setting is next to the Palácio Quitandinha, overlooking a small lake.

Chocolates Katz (☎ 2245 1818; Rua do Imperador 912) This lovely coffee shop and patisserie makes a fine stop for a cappuccino and chocolate torte.

Luigi (☎ 2246 0279; Praça Rui Barbosa 185; mains US$5-10; ☼ 11am-midnight Mon-Sat) A charming Italian restaurant set in an old house with high ceilings, creaky floors and candlelit ambience. It packs in the crowds on Friday and Saturday nights, with its live music.

Travel Tip

If you have a car, check out the restaurants along the 'culinary highway', Estrada União Indústria, on the way to Itaipava. About 20km from Petrópolis there are dozens of excellent spots in lush natural settings.

Majórica Churrascaria (☎ 2242 2498; Rua do Imperador 754; mains US$7-10; ☼ noon-10pm Tue-Sun) This *churrascaria*, within a short distance of the Museu Imperial, has excellent cuts of meat – served à la carte.

Parrô do Valentim (☎ 2222 1281; Estrada União Indústria 10289, Itaipava; mains US$8-13; ☼ 11:30am-10pm Tue-Thu & Sun, 11:30am-midnight Fri & Sat) Serves elegant Portuguese cuisine, including excellent lamb dishes, barbecued sardines and decadent desserts.

Radio Bar & Jazz – Boite (☎ 2222 2027; Estrada União Indústria 9314, Itaipava) Features live music on weekends in a stylish lounge space.

Sleeping

Casablanca (☎ 2242 6662; www.casablancahotel.com.br; Rua do Imperatriz 286; d from US$48) Housed in an old mansion near the Museu Imperial, the Casablanca has a range of rooms: the best feature high ceilings, old shutters, long bathrooms with tubs, and antique furnishings.

Hotel Colonial Inn (☎ 2243 1590; www.colonialinn.com.br in Portuguese; Rua Monsenhor Bacelar 125; d from US$46) Rooms here feature a mix of antique and art-nouveau furnishings, and there's a friendly, homelike feel. It's located just down the street from the Museu Casa de Santos Dumont.

Pousada Parador Santarem (☎ 2222 9933; Estrada Júlio Cápua, Vale do Cuibá; chalets from US$150) Surrounded by forest, with hiking trails, and several lakes amid the scenery, this *pousada* makes for a verdant getaway. Other features include palatially decorated rooms (canopy beds being a common feature), live music in the restaurant each Saturday night, a private theater, the list goes on…

Pousada Tankamana (☎ 2222 9181; www.tankamana.com.br in Portuguese; Estrada Júlio Cápua, Vale do Cuibá; chalets from US$150) 16 chalets surrounded by 900,000 sq meters of stunning forest, mountains and streams. There is a pool, sauna, outdoor bar, games room (with pool table) and heliport. Guests can make excursions on horseback or hike into the mountains. The **restaurant** (mains US$8-14) is also tops. Farm-raised trout is the specialty (US$10-13), with plenty of other tasty selections. It lies outside Petrópolis.

Directory

Directory

TRANSPORTATION

AIR

Most international flights pass through São Paolo before arriving in Rio at the Aeroporto Internacional Antonio Carlos Jobim (commonly called Galeão) on Ilha do Governador. **Varig** (www.varig.com) is Brazil's biggest international carrier, with flights to many destinations.

Airlines

Most of the major airlines have main offices in Centro (metro stop Cinelândia). You can also visit their ticket counters in the Aeroporto Santos Dumont.

American Airlines (Map pp234-5; ☎ 0300 789 7778; www.aa.com; Av Atlântica 1702, Copacabana)

British Airways/Qantas (☎ 0300 789 6140; www.ba.com, www.qantas.com.au; Terminal 1, International Airport)

Continental (Map pp228-30; ☎ 2531 1850; www.continental.com; Rua da Assembléia 10, No 3711, Centro)

United Airlines (Map pp228-30; ☎ 0800 162323 toll-free; www.ual.com; 5th fl, Av Presidente Antônio Carlos 51, Centro); **Copacabana** (Map pp234-5; ☎ 2545 6575; Hotel Mariott, Av Atlântica 2600)

Varig (Map pp228-30; ☎ 2510 6650; www.varig.com; Av Rio Branco 277, Centro; **Copacabana** (Map pp234-5; ☎ 2541 6343; Rua Rodolfo Dantas 16A); **Ipanema** (Map pp236-8; ☎ 2523 0040; Rua Visconde de Pirajá 351)

VASP (Map pp228-30; ☎ 3814 8081; www.vasp.com.br in Portuguese; Rua Santa Luzia 735, Centro); **Ipanema** (Map pp236-8; ☎ 3814 8098; Rua Visconde de Pirajá 444)

Airport

Rio's Galeão international airport (Map pp226-7) is 15km north of the city center on Ilha do Governador. Santos Dumont airport, used by some domestic flights, is by the bay in the city center, 1km east of Cinelândia metro station.

Real Auto Bus (☎ 0800 240 850 toll-free) operates safe air-conditioned buses from the international airport (outside the arrivals floor of terminal 1 or the ground floor of terminal 2) to Novo Rio bus station, Av Rio Branco (Centro), Santos Dumont airport, southward through Glória, Flamengo and Botafogo and along the beaches of Copacabana, Ipanema and Leblon to Barra da Tijuca (and vice-versa). The buses run every 20 to 30 minutes, 5:20am to 12:10am, and will stop wherever you ask. Fares are around US$2.25. You can transfer to the metro at Carioca station.

Heading to the airports, you can get the Real bus in front of the major hotels along the main beaches, but you have to look alive and flag them down.

Standard or *comun* taxis from the international airport are generally safe, though there are occasional robberies reported. Radio taxis are safer, but more expensive. You pay a set fare for them at the airport. A yellow-and-blue common taxi should cost around US$25 to Ipanema if the meter is working. A radio taxi costs about US$35.

DEPARTURE TAX

The international departure tax from Brazil is US$36. This may be included in the price of your ticket, but if it's not, you have to pay it in cash (either in US dollars or *reais*) at the airport before departure.

BICYCLE

Although traffic can be intimidating on Rio's roads, the city has many miles of bike paths along the beach, around Lagoa and along Parque do Flamengo. You can rent bikes from a stand along the west side of Lagoa Rodrigo de Freitas for US$6 per hour. A few places to rent bikes include the following:

Ciclovia (Map pp234-5; ☎ 2275 5299; Av Prado Junior 330, Copacabana) A small selection, but good prices at US$10 per day.

Consuelo (Map pp234-5; ☎ 2513 0159, 8811 5552; Av Atlântica near Posto 4, Copacabana) In addition to having pickup service on Copacabana Beach, they also deliver to all hotels in the Zona Sul.

Special Bike (Map pp236-8; ☎ 2521 2686; www.specialbike.com.br; Rua Visconde de Pirajá 135B, Ipanema; ☺ 9am-7pm Mon-Fri, 9am-2pm Sat) US$5 per hour; US$15 per day.

Zaga Bike (Map pp234-5; ☎ 2235 1859; Rua Barata Ribeiro 834A, Copacabana) Featuring a good selection of new and used bikes for sale and rent.

BOAT
Ferries

Rio has several islands in the bay that you can visit by ferry; another way to see the city is by taking the commuter ferry to Niterói. See p89 for more information on the following trips.

ILHA DE PAQUETÁ
☎ 2533 6661 (ferries), ☎ 2533 7524 (hydrofoils)

The regular ferry takes an hour and costs US$0.50. The more comfortable hydrofoil takes only 25 minutes and costs US$5. Ferry service goes from 5:30am to 11pm, leaving every two to three hours. During the week, the hydrofoil leaves at 10am, noon, 2pm and 4pm and returns at 7:40am and 11:40am and 12:30pm, 2:30pm and 4:30pm. On weekends, it leaves Rio every hour on the hour from 8am to 4:30pm and returns hourly from 8:30am to 5:30pm.

ILHA FISCAL Map pp228-30
☎ 3870 6992; US$3; 1pm, 2:30pm & 4pm Thu-Sun except on the 2nd weekend of each month

Boats depart from the Espaço Cultural da Marinha (Map pp228-30) three times a day from Thursday to Sunday and include a guided tour of the **Palácio da Ilha Fiscal** (p89). It's a short ride (15 minutes).

NITERÓI Map pp226-7
Niterói's principal attraction is the **Museu do Arte Contemporânea** (p90), but many visitors board the ferry just for the fine views of downtown, and the surrounding landscape. The ferry costs US$0.75 and leaves every 20 minutes from Praça XV de Novembro in Centro (Map pp228-30). Faster and more comfortable catamarans run every 15 minutes from 7am to 4pm and cost US$2.

BUS

Buses connect Rio with cities and towns all over the country. Most arrive and depart from the loud **Novo Rio Rodoviária** (Map pp240-1; ☎ 2291 5151; www.novorio.com.br in Portuguese; Av Francisco Bicalho 1, São Cristóvão), which lies about five minutes by bus north of the city center. The people at the Riotur desk on the bus station's ground floor can provide information on transportation and lodging.

The other Rio bus station is the **Menezes Cortes Rodoviária** (Map pp228-30; ☎ 224 7577; Rua São José 35, Centro), which handles services to the Zona Sul and some destinations in Rio de Janeiro state, such as Petrópolis and Teresópolis. You can catch buses to these two destinations from Novo Rio as well.

If you arrive in Rio by bus, it's a good idea to take a taxi to your hotel, or at least to the general area you want to stay. Traveling on local buses with all your belongings is a little risky. A small booth near the Riotur desk organizes the yellow cabs out front. Excellent buses leave every 15 minutes or so for São Paulo (six hours). Most other major destinations are serviced by very comfortable *leito* (executive) buses leaving late at night.

It's a good idea to buy a ticket a couple of days in advance if you can, especially if you want to travel on a weekend or during a Brazilian holiday period. Many travel agents in the city sell bus tickets. If you're in Centro, try **Dantur Passagens** (Map pp228-30; downstairs store 134, Av Rio Branco 156, Centro; ☯ 10am-5pm Mon-Fri).

You can find out all the latest information about bus travel from Rio on www.novorio .com.br. Even though it's in Portuguese, it's pretty easy to navigate. Just click on the *Horários e Preços* (Hours and Prices) button and plug in your destination city.

CAR
Driving & Parking

In the city itself, driving can be a frustrating experience even if you know your way around. Traffic snarls and parking problems will not make for an enjoyable holiday. If the bus and metro aren't your style, there are plenty of taxis. However, if you do drive in the city, it's good to know a couple of things: Cariocas don't always stop at red lights at night, because of the small risk of robberies at deserted intersections. Late at night, cars slow at red lights and proceed if no one is around. Another thing to know is that if you park the car on the street, it's common to pay the *flanelinha* (parking attendant) a few *reais* for looking after it. Some of them work for the city; others are 'freelance,' but regardless it's a common practice throughout Brazil.

Rental

Renting a car is relatively cheap, but gasoline is expensive. If you can share the expense with friends, it's a great way to explore some of the remote beaches, mountain towns and national parks near Rio. Getting a car is fairly simple as long as you have a driver's license, a credit card and a passport. To rent a car you must be at least 25 years old. Ideally, you should have an international driver's permit, which you'll need to pick up from your home country. In reality, rental car companies accept any driver's license – it's the cops who will want to see an international driver's permit.

Prices vary between US$40 and US$80 a day, but they go down a bit in the low season. There is a bit of competition between the major agencies, so it's worth shopping around. If you are quoted prices on the phone, make sure they include insurance, which is compulsory.

Car rental agencies can be found at either airport or scattered along Av Princesa Isabel in Copacabana. At the international airport, **Hertz** (☎ 3398 4377), **Localiza** (☎ 3398 5445) and **Unidas** (☎ 3398 3452) provide rentals. In Copacabana among the many are **Hertz** (Map pp234-5; ☎ 2275 7440; Av Princesa Isabel 500), **Localiza** (Map pp234-5; ☎ 2275 3340; Av Princesa Isabel 150) and **Actual** (Map pp234-5; ☎ 2541 3444; Av Princesa Isabel 181).

METRO

Rio's **subway system** (Map p242) is an excellent, cheap way to get around. It's open from 5am to midnight Monday through Saturday and 7am to 11pm on Sundays and holidays. During Carnaval the metro operates nonstop from Friday morning until Tuesday at midnight. Both air-conditioned lines are clean, fast and safe. The main line from Siqueira Campos in Copacabana to Saens Peña has 17 stops. The first 14 – from Copacabana to Estácio – are common to both lines. The lines split at Estácio: the main line continues west toward the neighborhood of Andarai, making stops at Alfonso Pena, São Francisco Xavier and Saens Peña, while the secondary line goes north to São Cristóvão, Maracanã and beyond. The main stops in Centro are Cinelândia and Carioca. More stations are planned in the coming years, and eventually Ipanema (Praça General Osorio) will be linked to the system.

You can buy one-way, roundtrip or 10-ride tickets. A basic single costs US$0.75, and there's no discount for roundtrip or multiple-ride tickets. Free subway maps are available at most ticket booths.

MINIVAN

In the last decade, minivans (Cariocas call them *vans)* have become an alternative form of transportation in Rio. Technically they are illegal but no one seems to mind. They're much quicker than buses and run along Av Rio Branco to the Zona Sul as far as Barra da Tijuca. On the return trip, they run along the coast almost all the way into the center. They run frequently, and the flat fee is US$2. They are probably not a good idea if you have luggage.

TAXI

Rio's yellow-and-blue taxis are prevalent throughout the city. They're fairly inexpensive and provide a good way to zip around. Unfortunately, they aren't completely safe and hassle-free. A few rare cases have been reported of people being assaulted and robbed by taxi drivers. A much more common problem is fare inflation. Many of the taxi drivers who hang around the hotels are sharks, so it's worth walking a block or so to avoid them.

Make sure the meter works. If it doesn't, ask to be let out of the cab. Meters have a flag that switches the tariff; this should be in the number-one position (80% fare), except on Sunday, holidays, between 9pm and 6am, when driving outside the Zona Sul and during December.

The flat rate is US$1, plus around US$0.50 per km. **Radio-taxis** (☎ 2560 2022) are 30% more expensive than others, but safer.

Most people don't tip taxi drivers, but it's common to round the fare up.

A few radio taxis include **Centraltáxi** (☎ 2593 2598), **Coopatáxi** (☎ 3899 4343), **JB** (☎ 2501 3026) and **Transcoopass** (☎ 2560 4888).

TRAIN

The suburban train station, **Estação Dom Pedro II** (Central do Brasil; Map pp240-1; ☎ 2296 1244; Praça Cristiano Ottoni, Av Presidente Vargas, Centro). To get there, take the metro to Central station and head upstairs. This is the station featured in the Academy Award–nominated film *Central do Brasil (Central Station).*

TRAM

Rio was once serviced by a multitude of trams with routes throughout the city. The only one still running is the Santa Teresa tram, known locally as the *bondinho*. It's still the best way to get to this neighborhood from downtown.

The **bonde station** (Map pp228-30; Rua Lélio Gama 65) in Centro is best reached traveling up via Rua Senador Dantas and taking a left on Rua Lélio Gama. At the top of the small hill, you'll find the station. *Bondes* depart every 30 minutes. The two routes currently open have been in operation since the 19th century. Both travel over the **Arcos do Lapa** (p86) and up Rua Joaquim Murtinho before reaching **Largo do Guimarães** (Map p231; Rua Almirante Alexandrino) in the heart of Boho Santa Teresa. From there, one line (Paula Matos) takes a northwestern route, terminating at Largo das Neves. The longer route (Dois Irmãos) continues from Largo do Guimarães uphill and southward before terminating near the water reservoir at Dois Irmãos.

Although a policeman often accompanies the tram, the favelas down the hillsides still make this a high-crime area. Go by all means, but don't bring any valuables. See p84 for more details.

PRACTICALITIES

ACCOMMODATIONS

Accommodations listings in the Sleeping chapter (p165) are organized by neighborhood, with mid-range and top-end places arranged alphabetically, and 'Cheap Sleeps' listed last. In Rio, the average double room with bathroom costs about US$75, with seasonal variations (highest in summer – from December to February). During New Year's Eve and Carnaval, most hotels charge about double what they normally do, and most will only book a minimum of four days. Generally, we've quoted standard rates, which are usually higher than the specials and discounted rates many hotels will give. Booking online can save you quite a bit. Two good websites that allow you to peruse listings and make reservations online are www.ipanema.com and www.riodejaneiro.com.

BUSINESS

Be prepared for business negotiations to take longer than you may be accustomed to at home. Cariocas will want to get to know you before getting down to serious business. Meetings can go on for a long time.

Red tape is notorious in Brazil and can be very frustrating. All you can do is find out the regulations and comply with them, no matter how long it takes. If it gets to be too much, you may be tempted to hire a *despachante* to help. *Despachantes* are experts at cutting through red tape. They can get things done in a couple of days that would take you a couple of weeks. It's probably not appropriate here to provide a list of

despachantes, but your business contacts should be able to put you in touch with one through their network of functional friends.

It pays to make appointments well in advance and confirm them at least once by phone. While Cariocas are known for their tardiness on social occasions, they may not like being kept waiting by a foreigner. Make sure you allow for traffic delays when going to appointments, especially if it's raining.

Business cards are used extensively. It's a good idea to have the information in Portuguese on one side and English on the other.

Hours

Office hours in Rio are from 9am to 6pm, Monday to Friday. Most shops and government services (such as the post offices) are open from 9am to 6pm Monday to Friday, and from 9am to 1pm on Saturday.

Because many Cariocas have little free time during the week, Saturday mornings are often spent shopping. Shops are usually open weekdays from 9am to 7pm and on Saturday from 9am to 1pm. Stores in the large shopping malls are open from 10am to 10pm Monday through Saturday and on Sundays from 3pm to 10pm.

Banks, always in their own little world, generally open from 9am or 10am to 3pm or 4pm Monday to Friday. Currency exchange places often open an hour after that, when the daily dollar rates become available.

Centers

Before you arrive in Brazil, check out the web pages of **Brazilian-American Chamber of Commerce** (www.brazilcham.com) and **American Chamber of Commerce in Brazil** (www.amcham.com.br). Both provide comprehensive information about the various industry sectors and have good links to other business-related sites. Once in Rio, business travelers will find the **Rio Convention & Visitors Bureau** (p260) most helpful.

The larger hotels have business centers for all your networking needs. For mobile phone rental, see p206. To rent temporary office space in Rio, try one of the following:

Business & Legal Center (☎ 3804 7600; www.blcrio .com.br; 5th fl, Av Presidente Wilson 231, Centro)

Business Quality (☎ 3231 9000; www.bq.com.br in Portuguese; 4th fl, Rua São José 40, Centro)

Tempos Modernos (☎ 2508 8389; www.tmoffice.com.br in Portuguese; sobreloja, Travessa do Ouvidor 50, Centro)

CHILDREN

Brazilians are very family oriented, and many hotels let children stay free, although the age limit varies. Baby-sitters are readily available and most restaurants have high chairs.

Lonely Planet's *Travel with Children*, by Cathy Lanigan and Maureen Wheeler, gives a lot of good tips and advice on traveling with kids in the tropics.

See p81 for more details on sights and activities for children.

CLIMATE

Rio lies only a few dozen kilometers north of the Tropic of Capricorn, so it has a classic tropical climate. In summer (December to March), Rio is hot and humid; temperatures in the high 30s (Celsius) are common, and days sometimes reach the low 40s. Frequent, short rains cool things off a bit, but the summer humidity makes things uncomfortable for people from cooler climates. The rest of the year Rio is cooler, with temperatures generally in the mid 20s, sometimes rising to the low 30s.

CONSULATES

Many foreign countries have consulates or embassies in Rio. For those not listed here, you'll find consulates listed in the back of Riotur's bimonthly Rio Guide.

Argentina (Map pp232-3; ☎ 2553 1646; sobreloja 201, Praia de Botafogo 228, Botafogo)

Australia (Map pp228-30; ☎ 3824 4624; 23rd fl, Av Presidente Wilson 231, Centro)

Canada (Map pp234-5; ☎ 2543 3004; 5th fl, Av Atlântica 1130, Copacabana)

France (Map pp228-30; ☎ 2210 1272; 6th fl, Av Presidente Antônio Carlos 58, Centro)

UK (Map pp232-3; ☎ 2555 9600; britconrio@openlink.com. br; 2nd fl, Praia do Flamengo 284, Flamengo)

USA (Map pp228-30; ☎ 2220 0439; Av Presidente Wilson 147, Centro)

COURSES

Rio makes a fine setting for soaking up an exhilarating dose of the tropics; but if you'd like to take center stage, there's a wealth of opportunities for visitors from diving to surfing to honing one's volleyball game on the sands. See the Sports, Health & Fitness chapter (p143) for more information on the courses listed below.

Dance Classes
CASA DE DANÇA CARLINHOS DE JESUS Map pp232-3
☎ 2541 6186; www.carlinhosdejesus.com.br; Rua Álvaro Ramos 11, Botafogo

Carlinhos and his instructors give classes daily – mostly from about 7pm to 10pm. Samba, *forró*, salsa and hip-hop are among the popular offerings.

CENTRO CULTURAL CARIOCA
Map pp228-30
☎ 2252 6468; www.centroculturalcarioca.com in Portuguese; Rua Sete de Setembro, Centro; ☯ 11am-8pm Mon-Fri

Samba and other styles are popular at this cultural center. Most classes meet twice a week and cost from US$25 to US$35 for a six-week course. Their large dance hall hosts parties on Fridays, when they bring samba bands to perform. Sundays are often dedicated to tango. Check their website for more information, or just stop in.

ESTUDANTINA CAFÉ Map pp228-30
☎ 2242 5062; www.estudantina.com.br; Praça Tiradentes 79, Centro

A broad mix of skilled and unskilled meet for Tuesday- and Friday-night classes at this cultural center and samba club. For information on parties here, see p134.

NÚCLEO DE DANÇA Map pp228-30
☎ 2221 1011; Rua da Carioca 14, Centro

A large upstairs spot on the edge of Lapa, Núcleo de Dança gives classes on *forró*, tango, salsa and samba. Most are held during the day – around noon – so stop in to see what's on.

SOCIAL DANCE Map pp228-30
☎ 2220 6020; Rua do Ouvidor 12, Centro

Specializing in tango, Social Dance offers beginner and intermediate classes twice a week. Classes run from 6pm to 8pm Tuesday and Thursday, and cost US$20 a month. On Friday nights they often throw open dance parties for students and guests.

Diving

CALYPSO Map pp228-30

☎ 2542 8718, 9939 5997; www.calypsobrasil.com.br in Portuguese; no 502, Rua México 111, Centro

Calypso offers courses (up to Dive Master) in waters near Rio. They also offer excellent excursions to Arraial do Cabo and Angra dos Reis, once they get you up to speed.

DIVE POINT Map pp236-8

☎ 2239 5105; www.divepoint.com.br in Portuguese; Shop 4, Av Ataulfo de Paiva 1174, Leblon

This company offers a variety of dive courses and dive tours around Rio's main beaches and the Cagarras Islands, as well as Rio State's premier dive spots in Angra dos Reis and Buzios.

Drumming

MARACATU BRASIL Map pp232-3

☎ 2557 4754; www.maracatubrasil.com.br; 2nd fl, Rua Ipiranga 49, Laranjeiras; ☷ 10am-6pm Mon-Sat

Maracatu offers courses in a number of different drumming styles: *zabumba*, *pandeiro*, symphonic percussion and others. Private lessons are US$30 per hour or sign up for group classes (US$20 to US$60 a month). See also p159.

Hang Gliding

ASSOCIAÇÃO BRASILEIRO DE VÔO LIVRE

☎ 3322 0266; www.abvl.com.br in Portuguese; Av Prefeito Mendes de Morais, São Conrado

If you've had a taste of hang gliding, and you think you've found your calling, the Associação de Vôo Livre (Brazilian Association of Hang Gliding) also offers classes.

TANDEM FLY

☎ 2422 6371, 2422 0941; www.riotandemfly.com.br

Although they're more commonly recruited for tandem flights, the outfit here also gives lessons for those wanting to learn how to fly solo. They have three levels, each consisting of 10 classes to reach the next level.

Language Courses

FEEDBACK IPANEMA Map pp236-8

☎ 2522 0598; www.cursofeedback.com.brin Portuguese; Rua Farme de Amoedo 35, Ipanema

Feedback offers group and private courses at their schools throughout the city (they also have locations in Copacabana, Botafogo and Centro). Private classes run US$17 per hour. Classes for two cost US$11 an hour per person.

INSTITUTO BRASIL-ESTADOS UNIDOS Map pp234-5

☎ 2548 8430; www.ibeu.org.br; 5thfl, Av NS de Copacabana 690, Copacabana

IBEU is one of the older, more respected language institutions in the city. They have four different levels of classes from beginner through to advanced. Classes typically meet two hours a day Monday through Thursday for four weeks. The cost for a four-week course held three times a week is about US$500. For information stop by or visit their website. They have a decent English library in the same building.

Surfing

ESCOLINHA DE SURF BARRA DA TIJUCA Map p231

☎ 3209 0302; Av Sernambetiba, 1st kiosk after Post 5, Praia da Barra da Tijuca

This surfing school is run by a Brazilian ex-champion and former professional surfer. Young surfers aged five and up are supervised by a team of lifeguards. It's open every day.

ESCOLINHA DE SURF PAULO DOLABELLA Map pp236-8

☎ 2490 4077, 2259 2320; Ipanema Beach in front of Rua Maria Quitéria

Ask around for champion surfer Paulo Dolabella. He's earned excellent reviews in the past, and Arpoador is a good place to learn. Lessons typically run US$7 per hour, or sign up for a month for US$40.

Volleyball

ESCOLINHA DE VÔLEI Map pp236-8

☎ 9702 5794; www.voleinapraia.com.br in Portuguese; near Garcia D'Ávila on Ipanema Beach

Those interested in improving their game – or just meeting some Cariocas – should pay a visit to Pelé. Pelé, who speaks English, has been giving one-hour volleyball classes for 10 years. Try in the morning between 8am and 11am or in the afternoon between 5pm and 7pm. He charges around US$17 for the month and you can come as often as you like. Look for his large Brazilian flag on the beach near Garcia D'Ávila. Pelé's students are a mix of Carioca and expats, who then meet for games after honing the fundamentals.

CUSTOMS

Travelers entering Brazil are allowed to bring in one radio, tape player, typewriter, video and still camera. Personal computers are allowed. Goods worth up to US$500 are permitted duty-free.

At Rio airport, customs use the random check system. After collecting your luggage, you pass a post with two buttons; you push the appropriate button regarding whether you have anything to declare. A green light allows you to proceed straight through; a red light means you've been selected for a baggage search. They are usually fairly lenient with foreigners, preferring to check the baggage of Brazilians returning to Brazil with lots of overseas purchases.

DISABLED TRAVELERS

Rio is probably the most accessible city in Brazil for disabled travelers to get around, but that doesn't mean it's always easy. It's convenient to hire cars with driver-guides, but for only one person the expense is quite high compared to the average bus tour. If there are several people to share the cost, it's definitely worth it.

The metro system has electronic wheelchair lifts, but it's difficult to know whether they're actually functional.

The streets and sidewalks along the main beaches have curb cuts and are wheelchair accessible but most other areas do not have cuts. Many restaurants have entrance steps.

Most of the newer hotels have accessible rooms, and some cable television is close-captioned.

Organizations

The **Centro de Vida Independente** (Map pp236-8; ☎ 2512 1088; fax 2239 6547; Rua Marquês de São Vincente 225, Gávea) can provide advice for the disabled about travel in Brazil.

Those in the USA might like to contact the **Society for Accessible Travel & Hospitality** (SATH; ☎ 212 447 7284; www.sath.org). SATH's website is a good resource for disabled travelers. Another excellent website to check is www.access-able.com.

ELECTRICITY

In Rio de Janeiro, the current is almost exclusively 110 or 120 volts, 60 cycles, AC. Many hotels also have 220. The most common power points have two sockets, and most will take both round and flat prongs. If you're packing a laptop – or any electronic device – be sure to take along a surge protector.

Electrical current is not standardized in Brazil, so if you're traveling around the country it's a good idea to carry an adapter. Check the voltage before you plug in.

EMERGENCY

If you have the misfortune of being robbed, you should report it to the **Tourist Police** (Map pp236-8; ☎ 3399 7170; Rua Afrânio de Melo Franco 159, Leblon; 🕙 24hr). No big investigation is going to occur, but you will get a police form to give to your insurance company.

To call emergency telephone numbers in Rio you don't need a phone card. Useful numbers include the following:

Ambulance	☎ 192
Fire	☎ 193
Police	☎ 190

GAY & LESBIAN TRAVELERS

Rio is the gay capital of Latin America. There is no law against homosexuality in Brazil. During Carnaval, thousands of expatriate Brazilian and gringo gays fly in for the festivities. Transvestites steal the show at all Carnaval balls, especially the gay ones. Outside Carnaval, the gay scene is active, but less visible than in cities like San Francisco and Sydney.

You may hear or read the abbreviation GLS, particularly in the Entertainment section of newspapers and magazines. It stands for Gays, Lesbians and Sympathizers, and basically indicates that anyone with an open mind is welcome. In general, the scene is much more integrated than elsewhere; and the majority of parties involve a pretty mixed crowd.

The **Rio gay guide** (www.riogayguide.com) is an excellent website full of information for gay and lesbian tourists in Rio, including sections on 'Bars and Cruisy Areas,' 'Rio Gay Carnival' and 'Rio for Beginners.' It's available in German, English and Portuguese versions. Another informative site with lots of good links is www.pridelinks.com/Regional/Brazil.

HOLIDAYS

On public holidays banks, offices, post offices and most stores close. Public holidays include the following:

New Year's Day January 1

Epiphany January 6

Carnaval February or March

Good Friday & Easter March or April

Tiradentes Day April 21

Labor Day May 1

Corpus Christi May or June

Independence Day September 7

Our Lady of Aparecida Day October 12

All Souls' Day November 2

Proclamation Day November 15

Christmas Day December 25

School break coincides with Rio's summer, which runs from mid-December to mid-February. During this time, the city gets overrun with both Brazilian vacationers and travelers from abroad. Another break occurs in July, which is another crowded time to be in the city.

INSURANCE

A travel insurance policy to cover theft, loss and medical problems is a good idea. The policies handled by STA Travel and other student travel organizations are usually a good value. Some policies offer lower and higher medical expense options; the higher ones are chiefly for countries, such as the USA, that have extremely high medical costs. There is a wide variety of policies available, so check the fine print.

Some policies specifically exclude 'dangerous activities,' which can include scuba diving, motorcycling and even hiking. Note that a locally acquired motorcycle license is not valid under some policies.

You may prefer a policy that pays doctors or hospitals directly rather than you having to pay on the spot and claim later. If you have to claim later, make sure you keep all documentation.

Some policies ask you to call back (reverse charges) to a center in your home country for immediate assessment of your problem.

Check that the policy covers ambulances or an emergency flight home.

INTERNET ACCESS

Most top-end hotels and a few mid-range ones have the technology to allow you to plug in your laptop and access the Internet from your room. Download the details of your ISP's access numbers before you leave home. The major Internet providers in Brazil are **Universo Online** (www.uol.com.br in Portuguese) and **Brazil Online** (www.bol.com.br in Portuguese).

Internet cafés are prevalent throughout Rio, with Copacabana having the highest concentration of them. Most places charge between US$2 and US$4 an hour.

Central Fone – Centro (Map pp228-30; basement level, Av Rio Branco 156, Centro; 9am-9pm Mon-Fri, 10am-4pm Sat)

Central Fone – Ipanema (Map pp236-8; loja B, Rua Vinícius de Moraes 129, Ipanema; 9:30am-8pm Mon-Fri, 11am-6pm Sat & Sun)

Cyber Café (Map pp228-30; Av Rio Branco 43, Centro; 9am-7pm Mon-Fri)

Cyber Café Fundição Progresso (Map pp228-30; Rua dos Arcos 24, Lapa)

El Turf Cyber Bar (Map pp232-3; Shop D91, Rio Sul Shopping Mall, Botafogo; 10am-10pm Mon-Sat)

Fone Rio (Map pp234-5; Rua Constante Ramos 22, Copacabana; 9am-midnight)

Letras e Expressões (Map pp236-8; Rua Visconde de Pirajá 276, Ipanema; 8am-midnight)

Letras e Expressões (Map pp236-8; Av Ataulfo de Paiva 1292, Leblon; 24hr)

Locutório (Av NS Copacabana 1171, Copacabana; 8am-2am)

Museu da República (Map pp232-3; 153 Rua da Catete, Catete; 9am-10pm Mon-Fri, 9am-9pm Sat & Sun) The entrance is in back of the museum through the Parque do Catete.

Tele Rede (Map pp234-5; Av NS de Copacabana 209A, Copacabana; 8am-2am)

LEGAL MATTERS

You are required by law to carry some form of identification. For travelers, this usually means a passport, but a certified copy of the ID page will usually be acceptable.

The police in Rio are very poorly paid, with the honest ones needing to hold down two or three other jobs to make ends meet. As for the others, corruption and bribery are not uncommon.

Marijuana and cocaine are plentiful in Rio, and both are very illegal. The military regime had a distinct aversion to drugs and enacted stiff penalties, which are still enforced. Nevertheless, marijuana and cocaine are widely used and, as with many things in Brazil, everyone except the authorities has a tolerant attitude toward them.

Be very careful with drugs. If you're coming from one of the Andean countries and have been chewing coca leaves, be especially careful to clean out your pack before arriving in Rio – Brazil is a staging post for a large amount of cocaine smuggled out of Bolivia and Peru.

An allegation of drug trafficking or possession provides the police with the perfect excuse to extract a fair amount of money from you – and Brazilian prisons are brutal places.

MAPS

Lonely Planet produces an excellent city map for Rio de Janeiro. Within Brazil, the maps used by most Brazilian and foreign travelers are produced by Quatro Rodas, which also publishes the essential *Guia Brasil,* a travel guide in Portuguese that is updated annually. The Rio city maps provided in *Guia Brasil* help with orientation. The guides are readily available at newsstands.

Riotur (p206) also provides a useful map of the city with detailed street layout. It's available free from their information booths.

For topographic maps, visit **Editora Geográfica Paulini** (Map pp228-30; ☎ 2220 0181; shops J & K, Rua Senador Dantas 75, Centro).

MEDICAL SERVICES

Some private medical facilities in Rio de Janeiro are on a par with US hospitals. The UK and US consulates have lists of English-speaking physicians.

Brazilian blood banks don't always screen carefully. Hepatitis B is rampant, so if you should require a blood transfusion, do as the Brazilians do: have your friends blood-typed and choose your blood donor in advance. If you need an injection, ask to have the syringe unwrapped in front of you, or use your own.

Pharmacies stock all kinds of drugs and sell them much more cheaply than in the West. However, when buying drugs anywhere in South America, be sure to check expiration dates and storage conditions. Some drugs available there may no longer be recommended, or may even be banned, in other countries. Common names of pre-scription medicines in South America are likely to be different from the ones you're used to, so

ask a pharmacist before taking anything you're not sure about.

Some pharmacists – such as ones in the Drogaleve pharmacy chain – will give injections (with or without prescriptions). If you're concerned about hygiene, always purchase fresh needles.

Clinics

Galdino Campos Cárdio Copa (Map pp234-5; ☎ 2548 9966; Av NS de Copacabana 492, Copacabana; ☿ 24hr) has English- and French-speaking staff.

Hospitals

Hospital Ipanema (Map pp236-8; ☎ 3111 2300; Rua Antônio Parreiras 67, Ipanema)

Miguel Couto (Map pp236-8; ☎ 2274 2121; Av Bartolomeu Mitre 1108, Gávea)

MONEY

Since 1994 the monetary unit of Brazil has been the *real* (R$; pronounced hay-*ow*); the plural is *reais* (pronounced hay-*ice*). The *real* is made up of 100 *centavos*.

Now comes the fun part. There are two types of one-, five-, 10-, 25- and 50-centavo coins in circulation – the old aluminum ones and the newer ones that differ from one another in size and color. There's a one-*real* note, as well as both old and new one-*real* coins.

Notes are different colors, so there's no mistaking them. In addition to the green one-*real* note, there's a bluish-purple five, a red 10 (and a new plastic 10), a brown 50 and a blue 100.

ATMs

ATMs for most card networks can be found throughout the city, with more and more springing up all the time. Banco do Brasil, Bradesco, Citibank and HSBC are the best banks to try when using a debit or credit card. Look for the sticker with your card's network (Visa, MasterCard, Cirrus or Plus), as usually there's only one ATM in a branch that accepts outside cards. Even though many ATMs advertise 24-hour service, these 24 hours usually fall between 6am and 10pm. On holidays, the ATM access ends at 3pm.

You can find ATM machines in the following locations:

Banco do Brasil (3rd fl, Antônio Carlos Jobim International Airport); **Centro** (Map pp228-30; Rua Senador Dantas 105); **Copacabana** (Map pp234-5; Av NS de Copacabana 1292)

Banco 24 Horas (Map pp228-30; outside Carioca metro stop, near Av Rio Branco, Centro)

Citibank (Map pp228-30; Rua da Assembléia 100, Centro); **Ipanema** (Map pp236-8; Rua Visconde de Pirajá 459A)

HSBC (Map pp228-30; Av Rio Branco 108, Centro)

Changing Money

Good places to exchange money include the following:

Banco do Brasil (Map pp228-30; 2nd fl, Rua Senador Dantas 105, Centro); **Copacabana** (Map pp234-5; Av NS de Copacabana 594); **Antônio Carlos Jobim International Airport** (3rd fl, Terminal 1)

Banerj (Map pp228-30; Av Nilo Peçanha 175, Centro) Traveler's checks only.

BankBoston (Map pp228-30; Av Rio Branco 110, Centro) Amex traveler's checks only.

Citibank (Map pp228-30; Rua da Assembléia 100, Centro); **Ipanema** (Rua Visconde de Pirajá 459A)

Easier than dealing with banks is going to *casas de câmbio* (money exchanges, usually shortened to *câmbios*). Recommended *câmbios* include **Casa Aliança** (Map pp228-30; Rua Miguel Couto 35C, Centro; 🕙 9am-5:30pm) and **Casa Universal** (Map pp234-5; Av NS de Copacabana 371, Copacabana). A number of other *câmbios* can be found in the following areas: in the center of the city on either side of Av Rio Branco and a couple of blocks north of the intersection with Av Presidente Vargas (Map pp228-30). Be very cautious carrying money around town and don't take much to the beach.

In Copacabana (Map pp234-5), there is a cluster of money-exchange places behind the Copacabana Palace Hotel, near the intersection of Av NS de Copacabana and Rua Fernando Mendes. Ipanema has several money exchanges scattered around along Rua Visconde da Pirajá just west of Praça NS de Paz.

US dollars are the preferred foreign currency, and the dollar has gradually been gaining strength against the *real*. It's hard to see this trend changing in the short term, especially as the government has now stopped interfering with the exchange rate.

Anyone can buy or sell US dollars at Rio's *câmbios*, though they take their percentage of course. US dollars are easier to exchange and are worth a bit more than other currencies. Have some US dollars in cash to use when the banks are closed.

It's also a good idea to have an emergency stash of US dollars stored separately from your other money, in case your traveler's checks or credit cards are stolen.

There are currently three types of exchange rate operating in Brazil: *comercial, turismo* and *paralelo*.

The commercial and tourist rates are normally a bit lower than the parallel rate. Full parallel rates are available only at borders and at official money exchanges in Rio and São Paulo. If you're changing money at hotels or travel agencies, you'll have to settle on exchanging cash for a couple of points lower than the full parallel rate quoted for that day.

Exchange rates are written up every day on the front page and in the business section of the major daily papers, *O Globo, Jornal do Brasil* and the *Folha de São Paulo,* and are announced on the evening TV news.

Credit Cards

Visa is the most widely accepted credit card in Rio; MasterCard, American Express and Diners Club are also accepted by many hotels, restaurants and shops.

Credit card fraud is rife in Rio, so be very careful. Keep your credit card in sight at all times.

To report lost or stolen credit cards, ring the following emergency numbers:

American Express	☎ 0800 785050
Diners Club	☎ 0800 784444
MasterCard/Credicard	☎ 0800 784411
Visa	☎ 0800 784556

NEWSPAPERS & MAGAZINES

Brazil's media industry is concentrated in the hands of a few organizations. The companies that own the two major TV stations, O Globo and Manchete, also control several of the nation's leading newspapers and magazines. Both companies are based in Rio.

Portuguese-Language Press

The *Jornal do Brasil* and *O Globo* are Rio's main daily papers. Both have entertainment listings. *O Povo* is a popular daily with lots of gory photographs.

The country's best-selling weekly magazine is *Veja*. In Rio, it comes with the *Veja Rio* insert, which details the weekly entertainment options (it comes out on Sunday). It's a colorful well-done magazine, and it's not difficult reading if you're learning Portuguese. *Isto É* has the best political and economic analysis, and reproduces international articles from the British *Economist,* but it's not light reading. It also provides good coverage of current events. *Balcão* is a weekly paper with Rio's only classified advertisements, a good source for buying anything. *O Nacional* is a weekly paper that has some excellent critical columnists.

Environmental and ecological issues (both national and international) are covered in the glossy monthly magazine *Terra.* It seems genuine about environmental concerns, and runs some great photos. *Placar* is the weekly soccer magazine and a must for fans.

The gay and lesbian press in Rio and Brazil is represented by *O Grito* and by the glossy *G Magazine* – both available from most newsstands.

Foreign-Language Press

In Rio you will find three daily newspapers in English: the *Miami Herald, USA Today* and the *International Herald Tribune.* They are usually on the newsstands by noon.

Time and *Newsweek* magazines are available throughout Brazil. What else is there to be said about these icons? Their coverage is weakest where the *Miami Herald* is strongest: Latin America and sports. The *Economist* is sold in Rio and São Paulo and costs about US$6.

In Rio imported newspapers and magazines are available at some newsstands, but these are quite expensive. Newsstands on Av Rio Branco in Centro have the best selections of foreign newspapers and magazines. In Copacabana the newsstand close to Le Meridien has a wide selection of English, French and German newspapers and magazines. In Ipanema, the newsstand in front of the Praça NS de Paz has French and English newspapers and magazines. Several of the bookstores in Ipanema and Leblon offer excellent selections of foreign-language publications. See Shopping (p151) for details.

PHARMACIES

There are scores of pharmacies in town, a number of which stay open 24 hours. In Copacabana try **Drogaria Pacheco** (Map pp234-5; Av NS de Copacabana 115 & 534; 24hr) or **Farmácia do Leme** (Map pp234-5; Av Prado Júnior 231). In Leblon try **Farmácia Piauí** (Map pp236-8; ☎ 2274 8448; Av Ataulfo de Paiva 1283; 24hr).

POST

Postal services are decent in Brazil, and most mail seems to get through. Airmail letters to the USA and Europe usually arrive in a week or two. For Australia and Asia, allow three weeks.

There are yellow mailboxes on the street, but it's more secure to go to a post office. Most post offices *(correios)* are open 8am to 6pm Monday to Friday, and until noon on Saturday. The branch at the international airport is open 24 hours a day.

Other branches include Praia de Botafogo 324 in Botafogo, Rua Prudente de Morais 147 in Ipanema (Map pp236-8) and Av NS de Copacabana 540 in Copacabana (Map pp234-5).

Any mail addressed to Posta Restante, Rio de Janeiro, Brazil, ends up at the post office at Rua Primeiro de Março 64, in Centro (Map pp228-30). They hold mail for 30 days and are reasonably efficient. A reliable alternative for American Express customers is to have mail sent to the **American Express office** (Map p234-5; ☎ 2548 7056; loja 1, Av Atlântica 1702, Copacabana).

RADIO

FM radio stations are plentiful in Rio, and by law at least a third of the music they play must be Brazilian. For the latest Brazilian and foreign hits, try tuning into Jovem Pan (94.9), 98 (98.1), RPC (100.5), Transamérica (101.3) and Cidade (102.9). For jazz, tune into Globo (92.5) or MEC (98.9).

For authentic Brazilian *pagode* (a relaxed and rhythmic form of samba, first popularized in Rio in the 1970s) and pop, switch to Roquette (94.1), O Dia (90.3), JB (99.7), Tropical (104.5) or Universidade (107.9).

SAFETY

Rio gets a lot of bad international press about violence, the high crime rate and *balas perdidas* (stray bullets) – but don't let this stop you from coming. Travelers to Rio have as much chance of getting mugged as in any other big city, so the same precautions apply here. If you travel sensibly when visiting the city, you will probably suffer nothing worse than a few bad hangovers. All the same, theft is not uncommon, and you should do what you can to minimize the risks of getting robbed.

Buses are well-known targets for thieves. Avoid taking them after dark, and keep an eye out while you're on them. Take taxis at night to avoid walking along empty streets and beaches. That holds especially true for Centro, which becomes deserted in the evening and on weekends, and is better explored during the week.

Copacabana and Ipanema Beaches are safer than others, owing to a police presence there, but don't get complacent. Don't take anything of value to the beach, and always stay alert – especially during holidays when the sands get fearfully crowded. Late at night, don't walk on the beach – stay on the sidewalk – and if you're in Copacabana, it's better to keep to the hotel side of Av Atlântica rather than the beach side.

Get in the habit of carrying only the money you'll need for the day, so you don't have to flash a wad when you pay for things. Cameras and backpacks also attract a lot of attention. Consider using disposable cameras while you're in town; plastic shopping bags also nicely disguise whatever you're carrying. Maracanã football stadium is worth a visit, but take only spending money for the day and avoid the crowded sections. Don't wander into the favelas at any time, unless you have a knowledgeable guide.

Beaches are the most common places for robbery. A common beach scam is for one thief to approach you from one side and ask you for a light or the time. While you're distracted, the thief's partner grabs your gear from the other side.

If you have the misfortune of being robbed, hand over the goods. Thieves in the city are only too willing to use their weapons if given provocation.

TELEPHONE

Rio is not known for its efficient telephone service, and it hasn't improved much after privatization. Lines cross and fail with irritating frequency. The only solution is to keep trying.

Brazilian public phones are nicknamed *orelhões*, which means 'floppy ears.' They take phone cards *(cartão telefônico)*, which are available from newsstands and street vendors. The cheapest cards are US$1 for 20 units and they go up to US$4.50 for 90-unit cards. All calls in Brazil, including local ones, are timed. Generally, one unit is enough for a brief local call. The phone will display how many units your card has left. Unless you're very lucky, you will probably have to try at least two or three phones before you find one that works.

Wait for a dial tone and then insert your phone card and dial your number. For information, call ☎ 102. The Portuguese-speaking operator can usually transfer you to an English-speaking operator.

To phone Rio from outside of Brazil, dial your international access code, then 55 (Brazil's country code), 21 (Rio's area code) and the number.

Long-Distance & International Calls

International calls aren't cheap in Brazil. You'll pay less if you have an international calling card. Embratel phone cards are available from newsstands (sold in denominations of US$10, $15, and $35). These have a bar on the back that you scratch off to reveal a code to enter along with the number you are calling. (Instructions are printed on the cards in English and Portuguese.) You can make calls through pay phones. Rates generally run about US$0.50 a minute for calls to the USA, US$0.75 to Europe and about twice that to Asia and Australia.

Another way of making long-distance calls is through phone offices. Many Internet cafés in Copacabana also have private phone booths for making calls. Rates, which fluctuate quite a bit, run US$1 to the USA, US$1.25 to Europe and much more to Australia and Asia. In Copacabana, try **Telenet** (Map pp234-5; Rua Domingos Ferreira 59, Copacabana; ☺ 9am-10pm Mon-Sat, 11am-9pm Sun) or **Tele Rede** (Map pp234-5; Av NS de Copacabana 209, Copacabana; ☺ 8am-2am). In the center of town, **Central Fone** (basement level, Av Rio Branco 156, Centro; ☺ 9am-9pm Mon-Fri, 10am-4pm Sat). In Ipanema **Central Fone – Ipanema** (Map pp236-8; loja B, Rua Vinícius de Moraes 129, Ipanema; ☺ 9:30am-8pm Mon-Fri, 11am-6pm Sat & Sun) also offers Internet and international phone calls, as does **Locutório** (Map pp234-5; Av NS Copacabana 1171, Copacabana; ☺ 8am-2am).

To make a call to other parts of Brazil, you need to select the telephone company you want to use. To do this, you must insert a two-digit number between the 0 and the area code of the place you're calling. For example, to call Búzios from Rio, you need to dial ☎ 0 + xx + 22 (0 + phone company code + Búzios city code) + the seven- or eight-digit number. Embratel (code 21) and Intelig (code 23) are

Brazil's biggest carriers – and the only ones that permit you to call abroad from Brazil.

Unfortunately, you cannot make collect calls from telephone offices. Public phones and those in hotels are your best bet. For calling collect within Brazil from any phone, dial ☎ 90 + phone company code + area code + phone number. A recorded message (in Portuguese) will ask you to say your name and where you're calling from, after the beep.

Mobile Phones

Mobile telephones are very common in Rio. Locals call them *celular*, which is also the nickname given to hip flasks of liquor.

Cell phones have eight-digit numbers, which usually begin with '9.' You can rent one from one of the following places for around US$7 a day plus call charges:

CONNECTCOM
☎ 2275 8461; www.connectcomrj.com.br
Offers pick-up and drop-off service to your hotel.

FAST CELL Map pp234-5
☎ 2548 1008; www.fastcell.com.br; no 919, Rua Santa Clara 50, Copacabana
Provides excellent service. English-speaking staff will pick up and deliver to your hotel. You can also email them before your trip and they can set you up with a number before you arrive.

HERTZ
☎ 0800 701 7300; www.hertz.com.br
In addition to automobiles, Hertz also rents cell phones. Call or go online to make a reservation (drop-off service available).

TELEVISION

The most popular local programs are the *novelas* (soap operas), which are followed religiously by many Brazilians. They're on at various times between 7pm and 9pm, and are a good way to practice your Portuguese.

O Globo and Manchete, the two principal national networks, both have national news shows. Cable TV is now common in most hotels mid-range and up. ESPN, CNN, RAI (Radio Televisione Italia) and MTV are all available. Brazilian MTV is worth tuning in to, as it has plenty of local content.

TIME

Brazil has four official time zones. Rio, in the southeastern region, is three hours behind GMT. When it's noon in Rio, it's 11am in New York, 8am in Los Angeles, 3pm in London and 10pm the next day in Sydney. Daylight saving time runs from February to October.

TIPPING

Most service workers get tipped 10%, and as the people in these services make the minimum wage – which is not enough to live on – you can be sure they need the money. In restaurants the service charge is usually included in the bill and is mandatory; when it is not included in the bill, it's customary to leave a 10% tip. If a waiter is friendly and helpful, you can give more.

There are many other places where tipping is not customary but is a welcome gesture. The people at local juice stands, bars, coffee corners, and street and beach vendors are all tipped on occasion. Parking assistants receive no wages and are dependent on tips, usually the equivalent of US$1. Gas-station attendants, shoe shiners and barbers are also frequently tipped. Taxi drivers are not usually tipped, but it is common to round the fare up.

TOURIST INFORMATION

Riotur is the very useful Rio city tourism agency. They operate a tourist information hot line called **Alô Rio** (☎ 0800 707 1808, 2542 8080) from 9am to 6pm. The receptionists speak English and are very helpful. Riotur's useful multilingual website, at **www.rio.rj.gov.br /riotur**, is also a good source of information.

All of the Riotur offices distribute maps and the excellent (and updated) bimonthly *Rio Guide*, listing the major events of the season. The **Centro branch** (Map pp228-30; 9th fl, Rua Assembléia 10; 🕙9am-6pm Mon-Fri; metro Carioca) is the best. English-speaking staff are always on hand, and they'll call around for you to find a hotel if you show up without a reservation.

There is have another branch in **Copacabana** (Map pp234-5; ☎ 2541 7522; Av Princesa Isabel 183; 🕙9am-6pm Mon-Fri). Riotur also has information booths with brochures and maps at the **Novo Rio bus station** (Map pp240-1; Av Francisco Bicalho 1, São Cristóvão; 🕙 8am-8pm), **Maracanã** (Map pp240-1; Rua Professor Eurico Rabelo, São Cristóvão; 🕙 9am-6pm) and the **Antônio Carlos Jobim international airport** (🕒 6am-11pm).

Another good source of information is the Praia de Botafogo (☎ 2511 2592; www.riocon ventionbureau.com.br; Rua Visconde de Pirajá 547, Ipanema).

Many hotels have free copies of *Rio this Month*, which provides a useful guide in Portuguese and English to the main attractions.

TRAVEL AGENCIES

AMERICAN EXPRESS Map pp234-5

☎ 2548 2148; Av Atlântica 1702, Copacabana; 🕒 9am-5:30pm Mon-Fri

This agency does a pretty good job of getting and holding onto mail and can also book flights for you.

ANDES SOL Map pp234-5

☎ 2275 4370; Av NS de Copacabana 209, Copacabana

A good multilingual agency, offering city and regional tours. They can also find discounted lodging in Rio.

CASA ALIANÇA Map pp228-30

☎ 2224 4617; casaalianca@casaalianca.com.br; Rua Miguel Couto 35C, Centro; 🕒 9am-5:30pm

Runs a fine outfit and exchange office, with information on local and regional tours to suit every budget.

LE BON VOYAGE Map pp236-8

☎ 2287 4403; lebonvoyage@hotmail.com; Rua Visconde de Pirajá 82, Ipanema

Particularly noted for its affordable excursions to Búzios and the Costa Verde, this travel agency also offers the convenience of an on-site exchange office.

VISAS

Brazil has a reciprocal visa system, so if your home country requires Brazilian nationals to secure a visa, then you will need one to enter Brazil. American, Canadian, Australian and New Zealand citizens need visas, but UK and French citizens do not. Check your status with the Brazilian embassy or consulate in your home country.

Tourist visas are issued by Brazilian diplomatic offices. They are valid for arrival in Brazil for a 90-day stay. They are renewable in Brazil for an additional 90 days. In most embassies and consulates, visas can be processed within 24 hours. You will need to present one passport photograph, a round-trip or onward ticket (or a photocopy of it), and a valid passport. If you decide to return to Brazil, your visa is valid for five years.

The fee for visas is also reciprocal. It's usually between US$40 and US$60, though for US citizens visas cost US$100 (those who find this excessive should write their local congressional representative and ask why the US charges Brazilians so much to enter the states).

Applicants under 18 years of age must also submit a notarized letter of authorization from a parent or legal guardian.

Business travelers may need a business visa. It's also valid for 90 days and has the same requirements as a tourist visa. You'll also need a letter on your company letterhead addressed to the Brazilian embassy or consulate, stating your business in Brazil, your arrival and departure dates and your contacts. The letter from your employer must also assume full financial and moral(!) responsibility for you during your stay.

Tourist Card

When you enter Brazil, you will be asked to fill out a tourist card, which has two parts. Immigration officials will keep one part, and the other one will be attached to your passport. When you leave the country, this will be detached from your passport by immigration officials.

Make sure you don't lose your part of the tourist card, or your departure could be delayed until officials have checked your story.

For added security, make a photocopy of your section of the tourist card and keep this in a safe place, separate from your passport.

WOMEN TRAVELERS

In Rio foreign women traveling alone will scarcely be given a sideways glance. Although machismo is an undeniable element in the Brazilian social structure, it is less overt here than in Spanish-speaking Latin America. Flirtation – often exaggerated – is a prominent element in Brazilian male-female relations. It goes both ways and is nearly always regarded as amusingly innocent banter. You should be able to stop unwelcome attention merely by expressing displeasure.

WORK

Brazil has high unemployment, and visitors who enter the country as tourists are not legally allowed to take jobs. It's not unusual for foreigners to find English-teaching work in language schools. The pay isn't great (if you hustle you can make around US$700 a month), but you can still live on it. For this kind of work it's always helpful to speak some Portuguese, although some schools insist that only English be spoken in class. Private language tutoring may pay a little more, but you'll have to do some legwork to get students.

To find this type of work, log on to a Brazilian web server like zaz, terra or uol and search for English academies. You should also ask around at the English schools.

Language

Language

It's true – anyone can speak another language. Don't worry if you haven't studied languages before or that you studied a language at school for years and can't remember any of it. It doesn't even matter if you failed English grammar. After all, that's never affected your ability to speak English! And this is the key to picking up a language in another country. You just need to start speaking.

Learn a few key phrases before you go. Write them on pieces of paper and stick them on the fridge, by the bed or even on the computer – anywhere that you'll see them often.

Locals appreciate travelers trying their language no matter how muddled you may think you sound. So don't just stand there, say something! If you want to learn more Portuguese than we've included here, pick up a copy of Lonely Planet's comprehensive but user-friendly *Brazilian Portuguese Phrasebook*.

PRONUNCIATION

A characteristic of Brazilian Portuguese is the use of nasal vowels. Nasalisation is represented by n or m after a vowel, or by a tilde over it (eg ã). Nasal vowels are pronounced as if you're trying to force the sound out your nose rather than your mouth, creating a similar sound to when you hold your nose. Similar sounds exist in English words like 'sing,' where the 'ing' is nasalised.

SOCIAL
Meeting People

Hello.
Olá.
Hi.
Oi.
Goodbye.
Tchau.
Please.
Por favor.
Thank you (very much).
(Muito) obrigado/obrigada.
Yes/No.
Sim/Não.
Do you speak (English)?
Você fala (inglês)?
Do you understand?
Você entende?
I understand.
Eu entendo.
I don't understand.
Eu não entendo.
Excuse me.
Com licença.

Could you please ...?
Você poderia por favor ...?
repeat that	repetir istos
speak more slowly	falar mais devagar
write it down	escrever num papel

Going Out

What's on ...?
O que está acontecendo ...?
locally	aqui perto
this weekend	neste final de semana
today	hoje
tonight	á noite

Where can I find ...?
Onde posso encontrar ...?
clubs	um lugar para dançar
gay venues	lugares gays
places to eat	lugares para comer
pubs	um bar

Is there a local entertainment guide?
Existe algum guia de entretenimento dessa área?

PRACTICAL
Question Words

Who?	Quem?
What?	(o) que?
When?	Quando?
Where?	Onde?
How?	Como é que?
Why?	Por que?
Which?	Qual/Quais? (sg/pl)

Numbers & Amounts

0	zero
1	um
2	dois
3	três
4	quatro
5	cinco
6	seis
7	sete
8	oito
9	nove
10	dez
11	onze
12	doze
13	treze
14	quatorze
15	quinze
16	dezesseis
17	dezesete
18	dezoito
19	dezenove
20	vinte
21	vinte e um
22	vinte e dois
30	trinta
40	quarenta
50	cinquenta
60	sessenta
70	setenta
80	oitenta
90	noventa
100	cem
200	duzentos
1000	mil

Days

Monday	segunda-feira
Tuesday	terça-feira
Wednesday	quarta-feira
Thursday	quinta-feira
Friday	sexta-feira
Saturday	sábado
Sunday	domingo

Banking

Where can I ...?
Onde posso ...?
I'd like to ...
Gostaria de ...

cash a cheque	descontar um cheque
change money	trocar dinheiro
change travellers cheques	trocar traveller cheques

Where's ...?
Onde tem ...?

an automatic teller machine	um caixa automático
a foreign exchange office	uma loja de câmbio

Post

Where is the post office?
Onde fica o correio?

I want to send a ...
Quero enviar ...

fax	um fax
letter	uma carta
parcel	uma encomenda
postcard	um cartão-postal

I want to buy ...
Quero comprar ...

an aerogram	um aerograma
an envelope	um envelope
stamps	selos

Phones & Mobiles

I want to make ...
Quero ...

a call (to ...)	telefonar (para ...)
a reverse-charge/ collect call	fazer uma chamada a cobrar

I'd like a/an ...
Eu gostaria de ...

adaptor plug	comprar um adaptador
battery for my phone	comprar uma bateria para o meu telephone
mobile/cell phone for hire	alugar um cellular
phone card	comprar um cartão telefônico
prepaid mobile/ cell phone	comprar um cellular pré-pago
SIM card for your network	comprar um cartão SIM para sua rede

Internet

Where's the local Internet cafe?
Onde tem um internet café na redondeza?

I'd like to ...
Gostaria de ...

check my email	checar meu e-mail
get online	ter acesso à internet

Transportation

When's the ... (bus)?
Quando sai o ... (ônibus)?

Language

first primeiro
last último
next próximo

What time does it leave?
Que horas sai?
What time does it get to (Paraty)?
Que horas chega em (Paraty)?

Which ... goes to (Niterói)?
Qual o ... que vai para (Niterói)?
boat barco
bus ônibus
plane avião
train trem

Is this taxi free?
Este táxi está livre?
Please put the meter on.
Por favor ligue o taxímetro.
How much is it to ...?
Quanto custa até ...?
Please take me to (this address).
Me leve para (este endereço) por favor.

FOOD
breakfast café da manhã
lunch almoço
dinner jantar
snack lanche
eat comer
drink beber

Can you recommend a ...
Você pode recomendar um ...?
bar/pub bar
café café
restaurant restaurante

Is service/cover charge included in the bill?
O serviço está incluído na conta?

For more detailed information on food and dining out, see the Eating chapter, p101.

EMERGENCIES
Help!
Socorro!
It's an emergency.
É uma emergência.
Could you please help?
Você pode ajudar, por favor?
Call a doctor/an ambulance!
Chame um médico/uma ambulância!
Call the police!
Chame a polícia!
Where's the police station?
Onde é a delegacia de polícia?

HEALTH
Where's the nearest ...?
Onde fica ... mais perto?
(night) chemist a farmácia (noturna)
dentist o dentista
doctor o médico
hospital o hospital
medical centre a clínica médica

I'm ill.
Estou doente.
I need a doctor (who speaks English).
Eu preciso de um médico (que fale inglês).

Symptoms
I have (a) ...
Tenho ...
diarrhoea diarréia
fever febre
nausea náusea
pain dor
sore throat dor de garganta

Glossary
See p103 for a more extensive list of food terms, and p29 for more Carnaval terms.

agouti – small rodent; looks like a large guinea pig
albergues de juventude – youth hostels
apartamento – hotel room
a quilo – per kilo
areia – sand
avião – aeroplane

bacana – cool, excellent
baía – bay
baile – dance, ball

baixo – popular area with lots of restaurants and bars
banca de jornal – newspaper
banda – a procession of drummers and singers during Carnaval; followed by anyone who wants to dance through the streets
banheiro público – public toilet
barraca – food stall
batida – strong mixed drink made of *cachaça*, sugar and assorted fruit juices
beija-flor – hummingbird
berimbau – stringed instrument used to accompany *capoeira*
biblioteca – library

bicicleta – bicycle
bilhete – ticket
blocos – see *bandas*
bonde – tram
boteco – small, open-air bar
botequim – bar with table service
caboclo – person of mixed European and Brazilian Indian descent
cabo verdes – straight-haired black person
cachaça – potent cane spirit
cadeira – undercover stadium seats
câmbios – exchange house
capoeira – Afro-Brazilian martial art cum folk dance
capela – chapel
cara – guy, dude (used in slang to denote male or female)
Carioca – native of Rio
carro – car
carros allegoricos – decorated Carnaval floats
cartão telefônico – phonecard
cerveja – beer
cervejaria – pub
chocante – cool, excellent
chope – draft beer
chorinho or **choro** – romantic, intimate samba
churrascaria – traditional barbecue restaurant
ciclóvia – bike path
código – area code
comprimídos – tablets (pills)
convento – convent
couvert – appetiser

desconto – discount

embalagem – doggie bag
emergentes – the nouveaux riches; Brazilian yuppies
época baixa – low season
escola de samba – samba school
estação do metro – metro (subway) station
estrada – road

falou – OK, agreed
farmácia – pharmacy (chemist)
favela – shanty town
fazenda – ranch or large farm
feira – open-air market
festa – party
fio dental – literally 'dental floss'; a tiny bikini
forró – popular dance music
frescão – air-conditioned bus
frescobol – paddle game played on the beach with two wooden bats and a rubber ball
futebol – football (soccer)
futevolei – volleyball played with feet only

gafieira – dance club
gata – attractive young woman
gato – cat (literally); also an attractive young man

gente – 'people' or 'we'
grampo – bolt

igreja – church
ilha – island

jardim – garden
jeitinho – a way around something
jogo do bicho – numbers game

lanchonete – a cross between a deli and a café
livraria – book shop

malandros – con men
mirante – lookout
mochila – backpack
moreno – dark-skinned white person
mosteiro – monastery
mulato – light-skinned black person
museu – museum

novela – soap opera

orelhôes – public telephones
orixás – Afro-Brazilian deities

pagode – relaxed and rhythmic form of samba; first popularized in Rio in the 1970s
parque – park
ponte – bridge
ponto de onibus – bus stop
posto – lifeguard station
posto telefônico – telephone office
pousada – guesthouse
praça – square
praia – beach
prancha – surfboard
prato feito – fixed plate of the day; often abbreviated to pf
promoção – sale/special
Prorrogação da Vista – visa extension
protetor solar – sunblock

queda – a fall

real – Brazil's unit of currency since 1994
refrigerante – soft drink
remédio – medicine
rio – river
rodoviária – bus terminal
rua – street

salva vida – lifesaver
sobreloja – above the store; first floor up
suco – juice bar
sunga – Speedo-type swimsuit used by Carioca men
supermercado – supermarket

tanga – tiny bikinis commonly used by Carioca women
tchauzinho – goodbye
toalha – towel

Zona Norte – Northern Zone
Zona Sul – Southern Zone

Behind the Scenes

THE LONELY PLANET STORY

The story begins with a classic travel adventure: Tony and Maureen Wheeler's 1972 journey across Europe and Asia to Australia. There was no useful information about the overland trail then, so Tony and Maureen published the first Lonely Planet guidebook to meet a growing need.

From a kitchen table, Lonely Planet has grown to become the largest independent travel publisher in the world, with offices in Melbourne (Australia), Oakland (USA), London (UK) and Paris (France).

Today Lonely Planet guidebooks cover the globe. There is an ever-growing list of books and information in a variety of media. Some things haven't changed. The main aim is still to make it possible for adventurous travelers to get out there – to explore and better understand the world.

At Lonely Planet we believe travelers can make a positive contribution to the countries they visit – if they respect their host communities and spend their money wisely.

THIS BOOK

This 4th edition of *Rio de Janeiro* was written by Regis St. Louis, with contributions by Rodolfo Klautau, Cassandra Loomis, Carmen Michael, Tom Phillips and Marcos Silviano do Prado. Andrew Draffen wrote all previous editions of the book, with contributions from Heather Schlegel on the 3rd edition.

Commissioning Editor Wendy Smith
Coordinating Editor Simon Williamson
Coordinating Cartographer Andrew Smith
Coordinating Layout Designer Sonya Brooke
Assisting Editors & Proofreaders Holly Alexander, Carly Hall, Kristin Odijk, Linda Suttie, Elizabeth Swan & Kate Evans
Assisting Cartographers James Ellis, Anthony Phelan & Amanda Sierp
Assisting Layout Designers Jacqui Saunders, Tamsin Wilson, Sally Darmody & Nicholas Stebbing
Cover Designer Wendy Wright
Series Designer Nic Lehman
Series Design Concept Nic Lehman & Andrew Weatherill
Managing Cartographers Alison Lyall & Laurie Mikkelsen
Managing Editors Kerryn Burgess & Danielle North
Layout Manager Adriana Mammarella
Mapping Development Paul Piaia
Project Managers Huw Fowles & Andrew Weatherill
Language Content Coordinator Quentin Frayne
Regional Publishing Manager David Zingarelli
Series Publishing Manager Gabrielle Green

Cover photographs Woman in lavish costume at Carnaval, John Maier Jr/Lonely Planet Images (top); Surfers on Grumari beach, south of Rio de Janeiro, Judy Bellah/Lonely Planet Images (bottom); Window and door of house in Jardim Botânico, John Pennock/Lonely Planet Images (back).

Internal photographs by Ricardo Gomez/Lonely Planet Images and John Maier Jr/Lonely Planet Images except for the following: p74 (#1), p182 Tom Cockrem/Lonely Planet Images; p2 (#1), p2 (#2), p74 (#2), p185 John Maier Jr/Lonely Planet Images; p74 (#4), p187 John Pennock/Lonely Planet Images; p192 Leonardo Pinheiro/Lonely Planet Images. All images are the copyright of the photographers unless otherwise indicated. Many of the images in this guide are available for licensing from Lonely Planet Images: www.lonelyplanetimages.com.

THANKS
REGIS ST. LOUIS

This book is dedicated to the memory of my dear friend, Chris Wolk. *Muito obrigado* (many thanks) to Beatriz for her extensive tips on all things Carioca, Carina for her many introductions and showing me around the city, Alissa and Akemi for fashion tips and cunning insight into Rio's best restaurants, Damian for his cooking skills, Rodolfo and friends for showing off Ilha Grande, Carmen and Fabio for introducing me to Lapa's best *gafieiras* (dancehalls). Thanks also to Yolanda, Fernanda, João, Juliana, Claudio, Hans and Molly, all of whom helped to elucidate the admirable Carioca philosophy. In the US *abraços* (hugs) to Mom, France, J and Cassandra for their invaluable support throughout the project.

OUR READERS

Many thanks to the travelers who used the last edition and wrote to us with helpful hints, useful advice and interesting anecdotes. Your names follow:

Manoel da Silveira Netto, Cédric Argolit, Jörg Ausfelt, Roman Baedorf, Fernando Zubikoa Bainales, Carol Binder, Michael Brandenburgsky, John Breski, Adam Canter, Nick Carney, Henry Carson, Nicola Cauchy, Bjorn HB Clasen, Carol Conte, Ron Coolen, Ninna Dalgaard, Candida D'Arcy, Joseph Deleonardo, Luisa Doplicher, Kristof Downer, Gene Dunaway, Paula Elias, Gabrielle Fennessy, Pernille & Kennet Foh, Damian Francabandiera, Margaret Gallery, Manoel Giffoni da Silveira Netto, John Gillis, Paul W Gioffi, Asger Grarup, Giorgio Grazzini, Tim Harcourt, Paul Harker, Paul Harris, Michael Hartmann, Jon

Hepworth, Alex Hijmans, Debby & Jim Hogan, Per Holmkvist, Alex Howarth, David M Hunt, Jeremy Ireland, Caitlin Johnson, Sara Jones, Yorgos Kechagioglou, Andrea Kinauer, Lucie Kinkorova, Justine Kirby, Paul Kondratko, Jan Kvet, Johannes Lahti, Gregor Laing, Paul Lambert, Richard Lee-Hart, Adeline Levine, Sam Levitt, Dirk Luebbers, Volker Maiworm, Zukiso Makalima, George Malliaros, Fernando Marins, Georgina Mason, Nara Mattoso, Michael T Maus, Kelly McCarthy, Michael Miano, Carlos Millan, Yannick Neron, Manoel Netto, Gitte Nielsen, Ken Noble, Daniel Norton, Pedro Novak, Jose Olimpio, Aleksandra Oziemska, Aristea Parissi, Denise Pendexter, Brad Petersen, MA Pitcher, Leacy Pryor, Branden Rippey, Walace Rodrigues, Wally Rogelstad, Dan Ruff, Ben Rule, Lawrence Ryz, Christine Sadler, Al Sandine, Peter Sapper, Urmimala Sarkar, Klaus-Dieter Schmatz, Jerad Schomer, Bill Seidel, Jacob Seligmann, Sharlene Shah, Pete Siegfried, Michael Simek, Alastair Simpson, Peter Smolka, Tom Sobhani, David Sowell, JS Spijker, RL Spolton, Andre Starobin, Louis H Stone, Faith Symon, Roman Tatarsky, Thomas Teltser, Frank Thianer, Niels Thommesen, Theo Tjes, Debra Townsend, Johan Veneman, Zeeger Vink, Fernanda Vitalino, Connie Voeten, Thomas Vogt, Frank von Reeken, Colin Walker, Peter Weis, Rachel Worzencraft, Andrew Young, Aritz Zubikoa.

SEND US YOUR FEEDBACK

We love to hear from travelers – your comments keep us on our toes and help make our books better. Our well-traveled team reads every word on what you loved or loathed about this book. Although we cannot reply individually to postal submissions, we always guarantee that your feedback goes straight to the appropriate authors, in time for the next edition. Each person who sends us information is thanked in the next edition – and the most useful submissions are rewarded with a free book.

To send us your updates – and find out about LP events, newsletters and travel news – visit our award-winning website: www.lonelyplanet.com. Note: we may edit, reproduce and incorporate your comments in Lonely Planet products such as guidebooks, websites and digital products, so let us know if you don't want your comments reproduced or your name acknowledged. For a copy of our privacy policy, visit www.lonelyplanet.com/privacy.

Notes

Index

See also separate indexes for Eating (p223), Shopping (p224) and Sleeping (p224).

Index

000 map pages
000 photographs

Index

000 map pages
000 photographs

Index

MAP LEGEND

ROUTES

Tollway	One-Way Street
Freeway	Unsealed Road
Primary Road	Mall/Steps
Secondary Road	Tunnel
Tertiary Road	Walking Tour
Lane	Walking Tour Detour
Track	Walking Path

TRANSPORT

Ferry	Rail
Metro	Tram
Bus Route	

HYDROGRAPHY

River, Creek	Mangrove
Intermittent River	Water
Swamp	

BOUNDARIES

State, Provincial	Marine Park

AREA FEATURES

Airport	Cemetery, Christian
Area of Interest	Cemetery, Other
Beach, Desert	Land
Building, Featured	Park
Building, Information	Sports
Building, Other	Urban
Building, Transport	

POPULATION

CAPITAL (NATIONAL)	CAPITAL (STATE)
Large City	Medium City
Small City	Town, Village

SYMBOLS

Sights/Activities	Entertainment	
Beach	Entertainment	Embassy/Consulate
Monument	**Shopping**	Hospital, Medical
Museum, Gallery	Shopping	Information
Picnic Area	**Sleeping**	Internet Facilities
Point of Interest	Sleeping	Parking Area
Ruin	**Transport**	Petrol Station
Snorkeling	Airport, Airfield	Police Station
Zoo, Bird Sanctuary	Bus Station	Post Office, GPO
Eating	Cycling, Bicycle Path	Telephone
Eating	General Transport	Toilets
Drinking	Taxi Rank	**Geographic**
Drinking	**Information**	Lookout
Café	Bank, ATM	Mountain, Volcano

Map Section

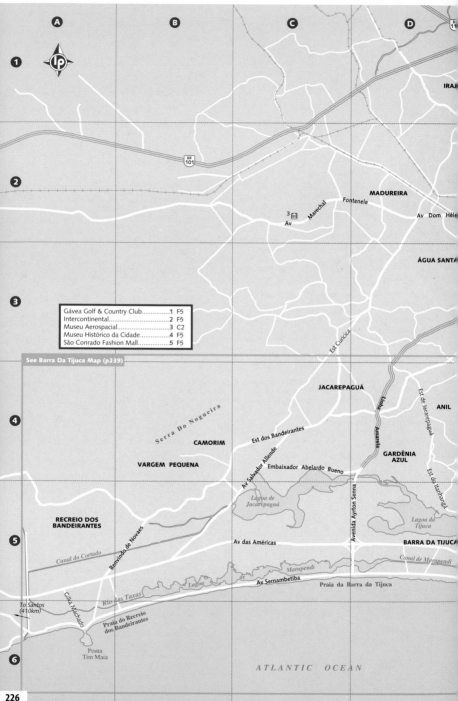

A **B** **C** **D**

1

2

MADUREIRA

Fontenele

Av Dom Hêle

³ 🏛
Av Marechal

ÁGUA SANTA

3

Gávea Golf & Country Club	1	F5
Intercontinental	2	F5
Museu Aerospacial	3	C2
Museu Histórico da Cidade	4	F5
São Conrado Fashion Mall	5	F5

See Barra Da Tijuca Map (p239)

JACAREPAGUÁ

Serra Do Nogueira

ANIL

4

CAMORIM

Est dos Bandeirantes

GARDÊNIA
AZUL

VARGEM PEQUENA

Embaixador Abelardo Bueno

Av Salvador Allende

Lagoa de
Jacarepaguá

Lagoa da
Tijuca

RECREIO DOS
BANDEIRANTES

Benvindo de Novaes

Avenida Ayrton Senna

5

Av das Américas

BARRA DA TIJUCA

Canal do Cortado

Canal de Marapendi

To Santos
(410km)

Cilha Machado

Rio das Taxas

Lagoa de Marapendi

Av Sernambetiba

Praia da Barra da Tijuca

Praia do Recreio
dos Bandeirantes

6

Ponta
Tim Maia

ATLANTIC OCEAN

BR
101

IRAJ

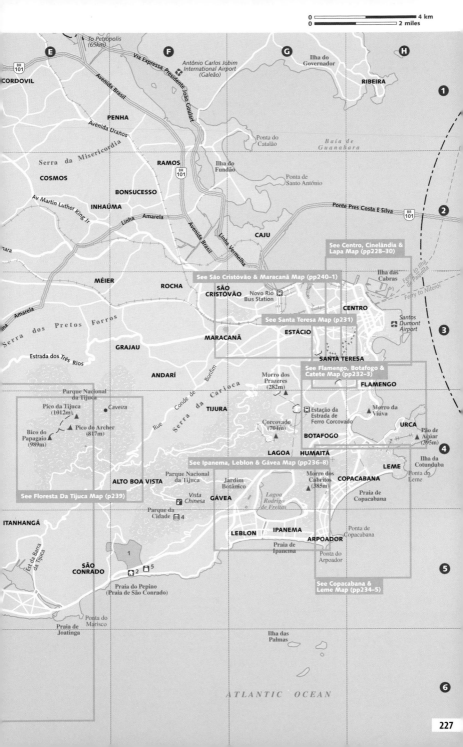

0 | 4 km
0 | 2 miles

E | **F** | **G** | **H**

BR 101

To Petrópolis (65km)

Antônio Carlos Jobim International Airport (Galeão)

Ilha do Governador

CORDOVIL

Via Expressa Presidente João Goulart

Avenida Brasil

RIBEIRA

1

PENHA

Avenida Urano

Ponta do Catalão

Baía de Guanabara

Serra da Misericórdia

RAMOS

BR 101

Ilha do Fundão

Ponta de Santo Antônio

COSMOS

BONSUCESSO

Av Martin Luther King Jr

INHAÚMA

Linha Amarela

Avenida Brasil

Linha Vermelha

Ponte Pres Costa E Silva

BR 101

2

CAJU

MÉIER

Ilha das Cabras

Ferry to Ilha de Paquetá

See Centro, Cinelândia & Lapa Map (pp228–30)

ROCHA

See São Cristóvão & Maracanã Map (pp240–1)

SÃO CRISTÓVÃO

Novo Rio Bus Station

CENTRO

Ferry to Niterói

Linha Amarela

Serra dos Pretos Forros

GRAJAÚ

MARACANÃ

See Santa Teresa Map (p231)

ESTÁCIO

Santos Dumont Airport

3

Estrada dos Três Rios

ANDARÍ

Rue Conde de Bonfim

Serra da Carioca

SANTA TERESA

See Flamengo, Botafogo & Catete Map (pp232–3)

Parque Nacional da Tijuca

Morro dos Prazeres (282m)

FLAMENGO

Pico da Tijuca (1012m)

Caveira

TIJURA

Corcovado (704m)

Estação da Estrada de Ferro Corcovado

Morro da Viúva

Bico do Papagaio (989m)

Pico do Archer (817m)

BOTAFOGO

URCA

Pão de Açúcar (395m)

4

LAGOA

HUMAITÁ

See Ipanema, Leblon & Gávea Map (pp236–8)

Ilha da Cotunduba

Ponta do Leme

ALTO BOA VISTA

Parque Nacional da Tijuca

Jardim Botânico

Morro dos Cabritos (385m)

LEME

COPACABANA

See Floresta Da Tijuca Map (p239)

Vista Chinesa

GÁVEA

Lagoa Rodrigo de Freitas

Praia de Copacabana

ITANHANGÁ

Parque da Cidade

LEBLON

IPANEMA

ARPOADOR

Ponta de Copacabana

Est da Barra da Tijuca

Praia de Ipanema

Ponta do Arpoador

5

1

SÃO CONRADO

2   5

See Copacabana & Leme Map (pp234–5)

Praia do Pepino (Praia de São Conrado)

Ponta do Marisco

Praia de Joatinga

Ilha das Palmas

6

ATLANTIC OCEAN

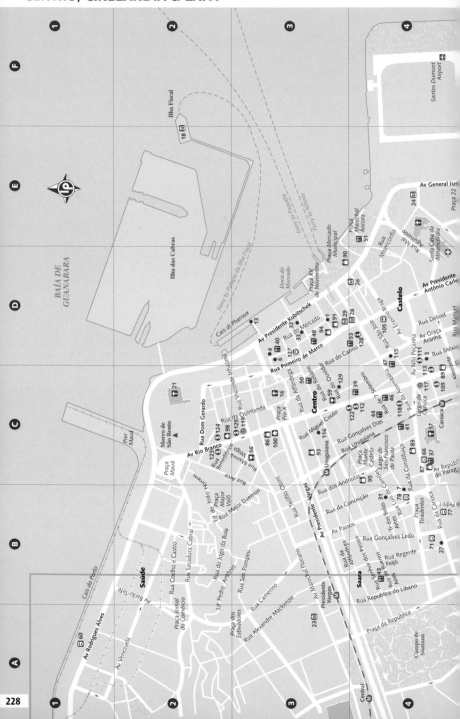

Rua do Russel

Praia do Flamengo

Enseada da Glória

Marina de Glória
19

Parque do Flamengo

20

See Flamengo, Botafogo & Catete Map (pp232–3)

Av F Roosevelt
Av Churchill
121
Av F Roosevelt
106 45
114 108
130
126 107
84
Cinelândia
2 34
10
Av Rio Branco
22
Praça Itália
Av Beira Mar
Av Presidente Wilson
Praça Floriano
R Pedro Lessa
R de Santa...
R Araújo Porto...
Passeio Gandhi
Praça Mahatma
Gandhi
Praça
Deodoro
Rua Tardel Jercolis
Av Infante Dom Henrique

Rua do Russel
99
Glória
52
15
101
Glória
103
42
See Santa Teresa Map (p231)

Av Beira Mar
Av Infante Dom Henrique

Praça
Paris
Av Augusto Severo
Rua da Glória

Av Rio Branco
25
72
92
67
73
97
102
Passeio Público
Largo da
Lapa
Rua da Lapa
36
Rua Joaquim Silva
Rua Teixeira de Freitas
Lapa
58
57
61
65
96 12
13
Rua Tavel
131
Rua Candido Mendes
Rua Santo Amaro
Rua Benjamim Constant
Rua Santa
Cristina
Rua Santa
Cristina
Ld de Santa Teresa
Rua Dias de Barros
Rua Hermenegildo de Barros

Av 13 de Maio
Av Almirante
Alvim
79
Cinelândia
120
110
Rua Senador Dantas
Rua Evaristo
da Veiga
Arcos da Lapa
104
30
5
14
80
35
49
75
88
64
68
69
82
Rua do Riachuelo
Rua Silvio Romero
Rua dos Arcos
Rua Joaquim
Murtinho
Rua Teresópolis
Rua Bernardino dos Santos
Fátima
Santa
Teresa

Rua Viscondo
Rio Branco
85
81
Av Gomes Freire
Rua dos Invalidos
Rua do Lavradio
Rua do Senado
Rua da Relação
Av Mem de Sá
Rua Ubaldino Amaral
Rua Carlos Sampaio
Rua do Rezende
Rua André Cavalcanti
Rua Triunfo
Rua Aprazível

See São Cristóvão & Maracanã Map (pp240–1)

0 ————————————— 500 m
0 ————————————— 0.3 miles

229

CENTRO, CINELÂNDIA & LAPA (pp228–9)

SANTA TERESA

0 — 500 m
0 — 0.3 miles

SIGHTS & ACTIVITIES (pp51–92)
Casa de Benjamin Constant........1 B3
Centro Cultural Laurinda Santos
  Lobo..2 B3
Museu Chácara do Céu................3 C2
Museu do Bonde..........................4 C3
Parque das Ruínas.................(see 3)

EATING (pp101–22)
Aprazível.....................................5 B4
Bar do Mineiro............................6 B3
Mike's Haus................................7 A4
Nega Teresa.................................8 A4
Porta Quente...............................9 C3
Sansushi....................................10 C3
Sobrenatural..............................11 C3

DRINKING (pp125–31)
Bar do Gomes............................12 B3
Café Neves.................................13 B2
Goia Beira..................................14 B2
Simplesmente............................15 B3

SHOPPING (pp151–64)
Breché Rasgando Pano...............16 C3
Brechó Antigamente...................17 C3
Brechó Arte................................18 B3
Favela Hype.........................(see 8)
La Vareda..................................19 C3
Trilhos Urbanos..........................20 C3

SLEEPING (pp165–78)
Cama e Café...............................21 B2
Hotel Santa Teresa.....................22 B3
Rio Hostel..................................23 D2

TRANSPORT (pp194–6)
Largo das Neves..........................24 C3
Largo do Guimarães....................25 C3

231

FLAMENGO, BOTAFOGO & CATETE

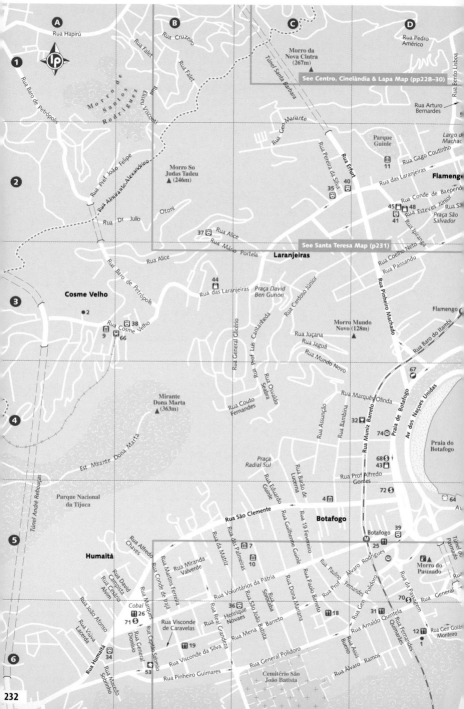

Rua Hapirú

Ⓐ

Rua Cruzeiro

Ⓑ

Rua Falet

Rua Falet

Ⓒ

Morro da
Nova Cintra
(267m)

Túnel Santa Bárbara

See Centro, Cinelândia & Lapa Map (pp228–30)

Ⓓ

Rua Pedro
Américo

Rua Brento Lisboa

Rua Arturo
Bernardes

1

Rua Baro de Petrópolis

Eliseu Visconti

Morro de
Santos
Rodriguez

Rua Gen Mariante

Parque
Guinle

Largo do
Machad

Rua Gago Coutinho

11

2

Rua Pref João Felipe

Rua Almiránte Alexandrino

Morro So
Judas Tadeu
▲ (246m)

Otori

Rua Pereira da Silva

Rua Erfurt

40

35

Rua das Laranjeiras

Rua Conde de Baepend

Flameng

45 48

Rua Esteves Júnior

Rua Sã

Rua Iparang

Praça São
Salvador

41

Rua Dr Julio

Rua Alice

37 Rua Alice

Rua Mário Portela

Laranjeiras

See Santa Teresa Map (p231)

3

Rua Alice

Rua Baro de Petrópolis

Cosme Velho

● 2

38

Rua Cosme Velho

9 66

44

Rua das Laranjeiras

Praça David
Ben Gurion

Rua General Glicério

Rua Prof Luis Cantanhebda

Rua Cardoso Júnior

Morro Mundo
Novo (128m)
▲

Rua Juçana

Rua Jaguá

Rua Mundo Novo

Rua Coelho Neto

Rua Paissandu

Rua Pinheiro Machado

Flamengo

Rua Baro do Itambi

67

4

Túnel André Rebouças

Mirante
Dona Marta
▲ (363m)

Est Mirante Dona Marta

Rua Couto
Fernandes

Rua Osvaldo
Sedura

Rua Assunção

Rua Bambina

Rua Marquês Olinda

Rua Muniz Barreto

Praia de Botafogo

Av dos Nações Unidas

32

74

Praia do
Botafogo

Praça
Radial Sul

Rua Eduardo
Guinle

Rua Barão de
Lucerna

Rua Prof Alfredo
Gomes

68

43

72

4

64

5

Parque Nacional
da Tijuca

Humaitá

Rua Alfredo
Chaves

Rua São Clemente

Rua da Matriz

Rua das Palmeiras

Botafogo

39

Botafogo

M

25

Ⓕ ▲

Morro do
Pasmado

Rua

Túnel do
Pasmado

7

10

Rua Miranda
Valverde

Rua Martins Ferreira

Rua Conde de Irajá

Rua Voluntários da Pátria

Rua 19 Fevereiro

Rua Guilherme Guinle

Rua Paulino

Rua Paulo Barreto

Rua Álvaro Rodrigues

Rua Prof Fernandes

Rua Gen Polidoro

Rua da Passagem

Rua General

70

6

Rua Humaitá

Rua David
Campista

Rua Cestrio
Alvim

Rua João Afonso

Rua Viúva
Lacerda

Rua Macedo
Sobrinho

Rua Marquês

Rua Capitão Salomão

Rua General
Dionísio

Cobal

26

71

Rua Visconde
de Caravelas

34

53

Rua Pinheiro Guimares

19

Rua Visconde da Silva

36

Rua Henrique
Novaes

Rua Real Grandeza

Rua São João Batista

Rua Mena Barreto

Rua Sorocaba

Rua Dona Mariana

18

Cemitério São
João Batista

Rua General Polidoro

31

Rua Arnaldo Quintela

Rua Assis
Bueno

Rua Fernandes
Guimarães

12

1

Rua Gen Goiás
Monteiro

Rua Álvaro Ramos

SIGHTS & ACTIVITIES	(pp51–92)
Arte-Sesc Cultural Center	(see 29)
Artindia	(see 7)
Casa de Dança Carlinhos de Jesus	1 D6
Largo do Boticário	2 A3
Museu Carmen Miranda	3 E4
Museu Casa de Rui Barbosa	4 C5
Museu da República	5 E1
Museu de Ciência da Terra	6 F6
Museu do Índio	7 C5
Museu Folclórico Edson Carneiro	8 C5
Museu Internacional de Arte Naïf do Brasil	9 A3
Museu Villa-Lobos	10 C5
Palácio da Laranjeiras	11 D2
Palácio do Catete	(see 5)

EATING	(pp101–22)
Adega do Valentim	12 D6
Alho e Óleo	13 E2
Amazónia	14 E1
Bar Urca	15 G4
Belmonte	16 E2
Bistro Jardins	17 E1
Bom Dia Maria	18 C6
Carême Bistro	19 B6
Catete Grill	20 E1
Churrascaria Majórica	21 E2
Estação República	22 E1
Garota da Urca	23 G4
Lamas	24 E2
Livraria Prefácio	25 D5
Pax	(see 43)
Pizza Park	26 B6
Porção Rio's	27 F3
Praia Vermelha	28 F6
Senac Bistro	29 E1
Tacacá do Norte	30 E2
Yorubá	31 D6
Zin	(see 43)

DRINKING	(pp125–31)
Big Ben	32 D4
Nautillus	33 E1

ENTERTAINMENT	(pp123–42)
Ballroom	34 A6
Beat Acelerado	35 C2
Casa da Matriz	36 C6
Casa Rosa	37 B2
Cinemark Botafogo	(see 43)
Clan Café	38 B3
Espaço Museu da República	(see 5)
Espaço Unibanco de Cinema	39 D5
Hideaway	40 C2
Rio Sul	(see 50)
Severyna	41 D2
São Luiz	42 E2

SHOPPING	(pp151–64)
Botafogo Praia Shopping	43 D4
Brumada	44 B3
Jeito Brasileiro	(see 66)
Luzes da Cidade	(see 39)
Maracatu Brasil	45 D2
Maria Fumaça	46 E1
Photography & Image Fair	47 E1
Pé de Boi	48 D2
Rio Off Price Shopping	49 E5
Rio Sul Shopping	50 E6

SLEEPING	(pp165–78)
Carioca Easy Hostel	51 F5
Flamengo Palace	52 E1
HI Chave do Rio de Janeiro	53 B6
Hotel Ferreira Viana	54 E1
Hotel Flórida	55 E1
Hotel Monterrey	56 D1
Hotel Novo Mundo	57 E1
Hotel Paysandu	58 E2
Hotel Regina	59 E1
Hotel Riazor	60 E1
Hotel Rio Claro	61 E1
Imperial Hotel	62 E1
Mengo Palace Hotel	63 E1

TRANSPORT	(pp194–6)
Botafogo Boat Dock	64 D5
Buses to Centro or Zona Sul	65 F5
Corcovado Train Station	66 B3

INFORMATION	
Argentinian Embassy	67 D4
Banco do Brasil	68 D4
Banco do Brasil	69 E1
Bradesco ATM	70 D5
Bradesco ATM	71 B6
Bradesco ATM	72 D5
British Embassy	73 E2
El Turf Cyber Bar	(see 50)
Internet Access	(see 5)
Post Office	74 D4

OTHER	
Canecão	75 E6

233

ATLANTIC OCEAN

Leme

Copacabana

See Ipanema, Leblon
& Gávea Map (pp236–8)

235

Parque Lage

A **B** **C** **D**

1

Rua Visc Itaúna
Rua Inglês de Souza
Rua Lopes Quintas
Rua Peri
Rua Faro
Rua Oliveira Rocha

Rua Fernando Magalhes
Rua Zara
Rua von Martius
Rua Coronado
Jardim Botánico
51
68
Av Lineu de Paula Machado
Av Borges de Medeiros
111
70

Rua Pachaco Leão
Rua Saturnino de Brito

2
Jardim Botánico
Rua Gen Garzon
Ilha Piraquê

Rua Jardim Botánico
Parque dos Patins

Av Borges de Medeiros
3
91
38
Rua Major Rubens Vaz
74
113 Praça Santos Dumont
83
Parque Brigadeiro Faria Lima
Rua dos Oitis
32
16
Joquei Clube
80
115 Rua Marquês de São Vicente
Hipódromo da Gávea
Gávea
Rua Artur Araripe
Av Bartolomeu Mitre
Av Rodrigo Otávio

145
150
Rua Mário Ribeiro
Clube de Regatas Flamengo
Ilha dos Caiçaras
4
10
Av Padre Leonel Franca
Praça NS Auxiliadora
Rua Adalberto Ferreira
49
Rua Gilberto Cardoso
Av Afrânio de Melo Franco
Largo da Memórial
Cobal de Leblon
Praça Milton Campos
To Parque da Cidade (5km);
Instituto Moreira Salles (4km)
Rua Cap Cesar de Andrade
60
55
Rua Itiquira
85
Rua Conde de Bernadotte
6
152
11
Rua Humberto de Campos
Jardim de Álah
Rua Codajás
73
Rua Humberto de Campos
132
63
Leblon
133
Praça Espanha
5
66
22
59
140
114
35
34
95
58
36
28
43
Praça Almirante Saldanha Gama
96
Rua Dias Ferreira
54
141
13
69
87
77
86 102
14
26
84
Praça Antero Quental
Av Gen San Martin
19
48
104
2
134
Av Ataúlfo de Paiva
53
61
30
44
131
Av Delfim Moreira
Rua Paul Redfern
78
29
Rua General Venâncio Flores
Av Visconde de Albuquerque
Rua General Artigas
Rua General Urquiza
Rua João Lira
Rua José Linhares
Rua Cupertino Durão
Rua Carlos Góis
Rua Almirante Guilhem
Rua Henrique Dumont
Av Epitácio Pessoa
Av Borges de Medeiros
71
110
97
67
12
Rua Aparana
Praia de Leblon
Posto 11
6
Rua Aristides Espínola
Posto 12
Morro dois Irmãos
89
155
A T L A N T I C
To Sinless (100m);
Shalimar (100m)
135
Praia do Vidigal
Av Niemeyer

0   500 m
0   0.3 miles

E

Av Alexandre Ferreira
42
47 Rua Maria Angélica
Rua Frei Leandro
15

F

Lagoa

Rua da Fonte da Saudade

Parque Tom Jobim

Av Epitácio Pessoa

Lagoa Rodrigo de Freitas

Av Epitácio Pessoa

Parque da Catacumba
39
9
5

Parque do Cantaglo

Av Henrique Dodsworth

G

Morro da Saudade (245m)▲

Morro dos Cabritos (385m)▲

Morro do Cantagalo (202m)▲

Morro do Pavão▲

H

Rua Euclides da Rocha
Rua Siqueira Campos

1

Rua Maestro Francisco Braga
Rua Santa Clara

2

Copacabana

Túnel Major Vaz

Rua Constante Ramos
Rua Pompeu Loureiro
Rua Barata Ribeiro
Rua Barão de Ipanema
Rua Bolívar

3

Rua Xavier da Silveira
Rua Miguel Lemos
Av Nossa Senhora de Copacabana

4

Rua Saint Roman

See Copacabana & Leme Map (pp234-5)

Av Epitácio Pessoa
Rua Aníbal de Mendonça
Rua Garcia D'Ávila
82
64
Rua Alberto de Campos
Rua Barão de Jaguaripe
Rua Nascimento da Silva
Rua Redentor
27
40 25
33
123
8 41 100
108
29 112 109
139
Rua Barão da Torre
106
90
94
93
Praça Nossa Senhora de Paz
142
116 18 144
105 143 144
99
50
72
57
98
137
118 **Ipanema**
Rua Prudente de Morais
126
122
120
Av Viera Souto
Posto 10
Praia de Ipanema
4
Rua Maria Quitéria
Rua Joana Angélica
88
136
Posto 9
52
46
121
124
146
31 11 45
65
103
127
81
Rua Vinícus de Moraes
Rua Farme de Amoedo
62
117
154
128
24
Rua Teixeira de Melo
56
138
Praça General Osório
151
20 79
149
37
147
148 125
92
Rua Antônio Parreiras
101 75
21
17
Praça General Osório
1
Rua Gomes Carneiro
Rua Raihha Elizabeth
Rua Bulhões de Carvalho
Rua Conselheiro Lafaiete
Rua Francisco Sá
Rua Júlio de Castilhos
Rua Raul Pompéia

5

Rua Joaquim Nabuco
Rua Francisco Otaviano
Praia do Arpoador
119
Parque Garota de Ipanema

Arpoador

Praça do Arpoador
Praia do Diabo

6

OCEAN

Ponta do Arpoador

237

FLORESTA DA TIJUCA

0 — 1 km
0 — 0.5 miles

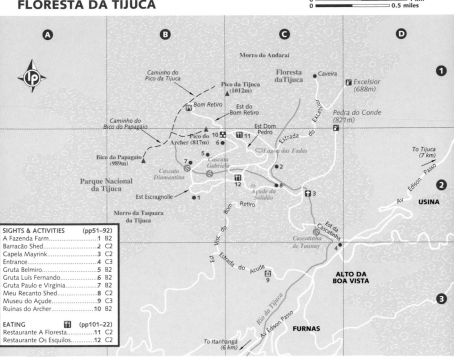

Morro do Andaraí

Caminho do Pico da Tijuca

Pico da Tijuca ▲ (1012m)

Floresta da Tijuca

Caveira

⚑ Excelsior (688m)

Bom Retiro

Est do Bom Retiro

Est Dom Pedro

Pedra do Conde (821m)

Caminho do Bico do Papagaio

Pico do Archer (817m) 10 6

11

To Tijuca (7 km)

Lagoa das Fadas

Bico do Papagaio (989m) ▲

7 5

Cascata Gabriela

2

Av Edison Passo

USINA

Parque Nacional da Tijuca

Cascata Diamantina

12

Açude da Solidão

8

3

Est Escragnolle

1

Retiro

Morro da Taquara da Tijuca

Est da Cascatinha

4

Cascatinha de Taunay

ALTO DA BOA VISTA

9

Rio da Tijuca

Av Edison Passo

FURNAS

To Itanhangá (6 km)

SIGHTS & ACTIVITIES (pp51–92)
A Fazenda Farm	1	B2
Barracão Shed	2	C2
Capela Mayrink	3	C2
Entrance	4	C3
Gruta Belmiro	5	B2
Gruta Luís Fernando	6	B2
Gruta Paulo e Virginia	7	B2
Meu Recanto Shed	8	C2
Museu do Açude	9	C3
Ruínas do Archer	10	B2

EATING (pp101–22)
Restaurante A Floresta	11	C2
Restaurante Os Esquilos	12	C2

BARRA DA TIJUCA

0 — 2 km
0 — 1 mile

SLEEPING (pp165–78)
Atlântico Sul	17	A2
Casa del Mar	18	C2
Entremares	19	D2
Praia Linda	20	D2

TRANSPORT (pp194–6)
Jacarepaguá Airport	21	C2
Urban Bus Terminal	22	C2

INFORMATION
Entrance to Parque do Marapendi	23 A2

JACAREPAGUÁ

Curicica

CAMORIM

Est dos Bandeirantes

ANIL

Parque Nacional da Tijuca

GARDÊNIA AZUL

Est de Jacarepaguá

10

Embaixador Abelardo Bueno

See Floresta Da Tijuca Map (p239)

Est do Itanhangá

Lagoa de Jacarepaguá

21

13

11

Lagoa da Tijuca

ITANHANGÁ

12

RECREIO DOS BANDEIRANTES

Est dos Bandeirantes

Av Salvador Allende

Av das Américas

16

14

15

6

Est da Barra da Tijuca

To Praia do Pepino (2km)

Av Ayrton Senna

2

22

BARRA DA TIJUCA

4

Rio das Taxas

Canal do Cortado

Lagoa de Marapendi

Canal de Marapendi

18

5

3

19

20

ATLANTIC OCEAN

23

17

Av Sernambetiba

Praia da Barra da Tijuca

9

7

Praia de Joatinga

To Museu Casa do Pontal

Praia do Recreio dos Bandeirantes

Praia do Pontal de Sernambetiba

To Prainha; Praia do Grumari; Praia de Guaratiba; Bira; Tia Palmira; Sítio Burle Marx

SIGHTS & ACTIVITIES (pp51–92)
Autódromo Nelson Piquet	1	B1
Bosque da Barra	2	C2
Cafe do Gol	3	D2
Downtown Entertainment Complex	4	D2
Golden Green Golf Course	5	D2
Itanhangá Golf Club	6	D2
Nuth Lounge	7	D2
Parque Ecológico Municipal Chico Mendes	8	A2
Rio Ibiza Connection	9	D2
Riocentro Convention Center	10	B1
Terra Encantada	11	C2

EATING (pp101–22)
Barreado	12	A2

ENTERTAINMENT (pp123–42)
Claro Hall	13	C2
New York City Center	14	C2

SHOPPING (pp151–64)
Barra Shopping	15	C2
Rio Design Center	16	B2
Via Parque Shopping	(see 13)	

SÃO CRISTÓVÃO & MARACANÃ

SIGHTS & ACTIVITIES	(pp51–92)
Campo de Santana	1 H3
Fiera Nordestina	2 C1
Jardim Zoológico	3 A3
Museu do Primeiro Reinado	4 C2
Museu Nacional	5 B3
Sambódromo	6 G4

TRANSPORT	(pp194–6)
Dom Pedro II Train Station	7 G2
Lagas das Neves	8 G5
Novo Rio Bus Station	9 D1

OTHER	
Maracanã Stadium	10 A4

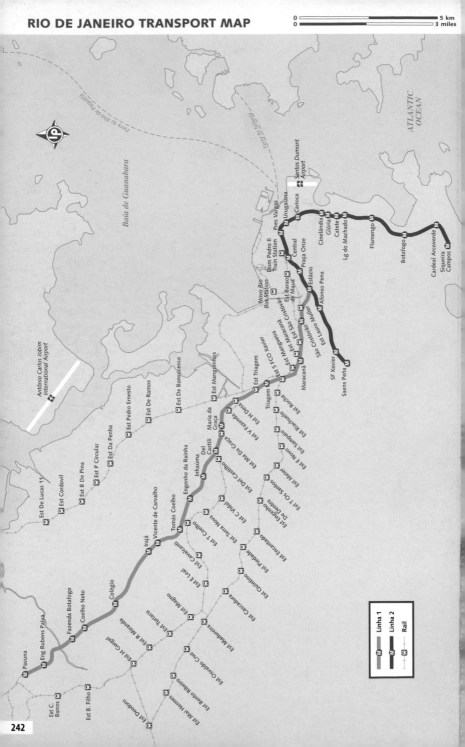

RIO DE JANEIRO TRANSPORT MAP

0 ▬▬▬▬▬ 5 km
0 ▬▬▬▬▬ 3 miles

ATLANTIC OCEAN

Baía de Guanabara

Ferry to Illia de Paquetá

Ferry to Niterói

ANTÔNIO CARLOS JOBIM International Airport

Santos Dumont Airport

Novo Rio Bus Station

Dom Pedro II Train Station

Linha 1 stations:
Pres Vargas
Uruguaiana
Carioca
Cinelândia
Glória
Catete
Lg do Machado
Flamengo
Botafogo
Cardeal Arcoverde
Siqueira Campos

Central
Praça Onze
Estácio
Afonso Pena
São Cristóvão
Est Lauro Müller
SF Xavier
Saens Peña

Est Barão de Mauá

Est Maracanã
Est São Cristóvão
Maracanã
Est São Cristóvão

Est S FCO Xavier
Est Mangueira
Est Triagem
Triagem
Est Rocha
Est Riachuelo
Est Sampaio
Est Maracanã

Est Mangueira

Est Mangrinhos
Est V Fazenda
Est H Dissa
Maria da Graça
Est E Novo
Est Meier
Est T Os Santos
Est Engenho De Dentro
Est Ma Da Graça
Est Del Castillo
Del Castillo
Inhaúma
Engenho da Rainha
Tomás Coelho
Vicente de Carvalho
Irajá
Colégio
Coelho Neto
Fazenda Botafogo
Eng Rubens Paiva
Pavuna

Est Triagem
Est H Dissa

Est Ramos
Est De Ramos
Est Pedro Ernesto
Est Da Penha
Est P Circular
Est B De Pina
Est Cordovil
Est De Lucas 11

Est Del Castillo
Est Vidal
Est Terra Nova
Est Piedade
Est Encantado
Est Quintino
Est Cascadura
Est Madureira
Est Osvaldo Cruz
Est Bento Ribeiro
Est Mar Hermes
Est Deodoro

Est T Coelho
Est Cavalcanti
Est E Leal
Est Magno
Est Turiacu
Est R Miranda
Est H Cugel

Est C. Barros
Est B. Filho

Legend:
Ⓜ Linha 1
Ⓜ Linha 2
Ⓡ Rail

242